The Rosary, the Republic,
and the Right

Dedication
For my mother

The Rosary, the Republic, and the Right

Spain and the Vatican Hierarchy,
1931–1939

KARL J. TRYBUS

Brighton • Chicago • Toronto

Copyright © Karl J. Trybus, 2014.

The right of Karl J. Trybus to be identified as Author of this work has been asserted in accordance with the Copyright, Designs and Patents Act 1988.

2 4 6 8 10 9 7 5 3 1

First published 2014, in Great Britain by
SUSSEX ACADEMIC PRESS
PO Box 139
Eastbourne BN24 9BP

SUSSEX ACADEMIC PRESS
Independent Publishers Group
814 N. Franklin Street, Chicago, IL 60610

and in Canada by
SUSSEX ACADEMIC PRESS (CANADA)
24 Ranee Avenue, Toronto, Ontario, M6A 1M6

All rights reserved. Except for the quotation of short passages for the purposes of criticism and review, no part of this publication may be reproduced, stored in a retrieval system, or transmitted, in any form or by any means, electronic, mechanical, photocopying, recording or otherwise, without the prior permission of the publisher.

British Library Cataloguing in Publication Data
A CIP catalogue record for this book is available from the British Library.

Library of Congress Cataloging-in-Publication Data
Trybus, Karl J.
 The rosary, the republic, and the right : Spain and the Vatican hierarchy, 1931–1939 / Karl J. Trybus.
  pages cm
 Includes bibliographical references and index.
 ISBN 978-1-84519-614-1 (hbk : alk. paper)
  1. Catholic Church—Foreign relations—Spain—20th century. 2. Spain—Foreign relations—Catholic Church—20th century. 3. Catholic Church—Spain—History—20th century. 4. Spain—Politics and government—1931–1939. I. Title.
 BX1585.T79 2014
 327.460456'34—dc23

2014017868

Typeset & designed by Sussex Academic Press, Brighton & Eastbourne.
Printed by TJ International, Padstow, Cornwall.
Printed on acid-free paper.

Contents

Acknowledgements vii
List of Abbreviations and Acronyms ix

Introduction 1

I A Troubled Past and a Tense Introduction: The Second Republic is Born 10

II From Caution to Contention: The Republican Constitution and Catholic Confrontation 25

III Republican Reorganizations: Elections of 1933 and 1936 50

IV The Uprising Begins, the Republic Reacts, and the Vatican Protests 80

V Humanitarian Concerns Increase as the War Continues 99

VI Foreign Requests for Vatican Intervention: The Hope of a Spiritual Authority? 119

VII How to Save the Basque: Vatican Mediation Meets Rebel Opinions 149

VIII Bombing and Civilians: Rebel Rejection of Mediation 168

Conclusion 186

Notes 193
Bibliography 246
Index 258

Acknowledgements

This book represents a long adventure scattered with highs and lows. In the end, however, many people who cared about this project and me allowed this work to be finished. I thank them all.

I must acknowledge the archives that allowed me to complete my project. I wish to thank the Centro Documental de la Memoria Histórica in Salamanca, Spain. I visited this archive in 2005 and 2009, and it was a wonderful experience. I remember requesting numerous boxes of information, photocopies and microfilm rolls. The archivists helped me more than they could have imagined! I would like to thank the Director in 2009, María José Turrión García, for taking the time to meet with me and discuss my project—even though it was at such an early stage. I also owe a great deal to the Archivio Segreto Vaticano at the Holy See. By opening the files of Pope Pius XI, the ASV has allowed scholars from around the world to understand more clearly the actions and attitudes of the Vatican. I must thank the archivists for their timely copies and well-organized materials. My research from the ASV would not be possible, however, without the help of Dr. Alessandro Visani. Dr. Visani was my guide and expert for Vatican materials. He was able to assist me whenever I needed help. Without Alessandro Visani, this project could not have been completed, and I owe him a severe debt.

I need to thank the two professional organizations that assisted me throughout my graduate and early professional career by allowing me the opportunity to present at their conferences. First, I thank the Association for Spanish and Portuguese History (ASPHS) for their welcoming annual meetings and scholarly professionalism. For all those who sat on panels with me or who were in the audience, thank-you. I wish to give special thanks to former ASPSH Secretary General Dr. Daniel Crews for his constant help. I also want to recognize Dr. Wayne Bowen and Dr. Shannon Fleming for their positive outlook and support for new scholars. Second, I wish to thank the American Catholic Historical Association for its conferences and scholarship. I would specifically like to thank Dr. Charles Gallagher and Dr. Robert Ventresca for their helpful feedback.

Two journals in the field of Spanish history published portions of this book as peer-reviewed articles, and I wish to acknowledge them. First, I thank the *Bulletin for Spanish and Portuguese Historical Studies* for publishing my work "For the Republic or the Church: The Vatican's Reactions to the Development of Spain's Second Republic in 1931" in its December 2011 edition, volume 36. Sections of this article may be found in Chapters 1 and 2 of this book. Also, I would like to thank the *International Journal of Iberian Studies* for publishing "The Sad and Painful News from Spain: Vatican Relations with the Second Spanish Republic at the Start of the Spanish Civil War, 1936" in its January 2012 edition, volume 24. Chapter 4 contains sections of that article. I wish to thank both journals for assisting a new scholar and also for granting permission for these articles to be reproduced, with changes, for this book.

This project began during my time as a graduate student at the University of Connecticut, and there are important individuals that I must recognize for their support. I must begin with the Office of International Affairs at UConn—and I must give special thanks to Dr. Elizabeth Mahan and Ludmilla Burns. Without their support, nothing could have ever been finished. In the UConn History Department, I wish to thank Drs. Shirley Roe, Christopher Clark, Lawrence Langer, Brendan Kane, and Charles Lansing. Each of you assisted me with special academic concerns (or trials and tribulations) over the course of my studies. I must thank the two most important people in the History Department: the fabulously retired Dee Gosline made sure I was remembered and the late Nancy Mottes Comarella was the person I could share stories with no matter the time. Without Dee and Nancy, nothing could have been accomplished.

No discussion of this project would be complete without thanking my three advisors who sat on my dissertation committee and worked with me to finish this project. I wish to thank Dr. Frank Coppa for his invaluable knowledge of Vatican diplomacy and politics. His research gave me a strong background in the topic and his support showed me that my work did matter and would pay dividends. I also wish to thank Dr. Joel Blatt for his help on this project. He worked tirelessly to help me structure a strong work and to make sure that I always looked at both sides of every historical debate. I owe the largest amount of gratitude to my primary advisor, Dr. Gustavo Nanclares. Gustavo was willing to work on my project when many were not. Through the countless numbers of meeting, emails, and phone calls I learned how to build confidence in my own work and I learned how to fight for what I believe. If it wasn't for Gustavo's guidance, I would have never earned my doctorate. Gustavo is the epitome of a scholar and a mentor, and I thank him.

I must thank my institution, Limestone College, for its support. After working so many years to become a historian, it was a great feeling to earn a job at small liberal arts school. As much as I love my research, I really love being in the classroom, and Limestone College has allowed me to succeed in both. I would like to thank my students, colleagues, History Department, and Administration for their continued support.

Many friends have guided me along the way—both personal and professional. I need to thank Justin Morgatto, Alison Porpora Lassiter, Bevin Goodniss, Shan-Estelle Brown, Giuseppina Russo, Michael Peluso, Nancy Wright, Erin Gardner, and Catherine Page. You each know how you've helped. If you don't know how you've helped, take a guess. There are also a large number of others to thank, and I hope you know I am in your gratitude.

The last group I must thank is my family. To my grandparents, Karl and Genevieve: I am forever indebted to you for your interest in my education even when one was not possible for you. To my grandfather James: though we never had the chance to meet, I thank you for your sacrifices. To my grandmother, Alexandria: you always prayed and rooted for me to succeed—and I hope I have. To my father, Karl: you did not have a chance to see me finish my doctorate, but I think you'd have been proud in the fact that I not only finished, but I fought and did what was right. To my mother, Margaret: thank you. You always understood the amount of stress I was under and you always tried to make it better, even from far away. Even when you had problems, you would always focus on keeping me strong so I could finish and follow my dreams. You've become an expert on the interactions of Vatican diplomacy and Spain during the 1930s—I bet that was never the goal, but it happened! All I can do is write a few words of thanks, but know they are so near to my heart.

Abbreviations and Acronyms

AES	Affari Ecclesiastici Straordinari (Extraordinary Ecclesiastical Affairs of the Vatican).
ASV	Archivio Segreto Vaticano (Vatican Secret Archives).
CEDA	Confederación Española de Derechas Autónomas (Spanish Confederation of Autonomous Rights, Right-Wing Parties).
CNT	Confederación Nacional del Trabajo (National Confederation of Labor).
FAI	Federación Anarquista Ibérica (Anarchist Federation of Iberia)
FE y de las JONS	Falange Española de las Juntas Ofensiva Nacional Sindicalista (Spanish Phalanx of the Assemblies of the National Syndicalist Offensive).
JAP	Juventud de Acción Popular (Youth of Popular Action, CEDA Youth Group).
JOC	Jeunesse Ouvrière Chrétienne (Young Christian Workers).
PCE	Partido Comunista de España (Communist Party of Spain).
PNV	Partido Nacionalista Vasco (Basque Nationalist Party).
POUM	Partido Obrero de Unificación Marxista (Worker Party of Marxist Unification).
PP	Partido Popular (Popular Party).
PSOE	Partido Socialista Obrero Español (Spanish Socialist Worker Party).
UGT	Unión General de Trabajadores (General Union of Workers).

Introduction

In November 2010, Pope Benedict XVI visited Spain to celebrate mass at Santiago de Compostela and consecrate Antoni Gaudí's Sagrada Familia Basilica in Barcelona. During his trip to Spain, Benedict XVI commented on the role of religion stating, "The clash between faith and modernity is happening again, and it is very strong today."[1] The Holy See saw faults with the successes of the Socialists' secularization campaigns for the Spanish state—including the termination of religious education in public schools, the legalization of abortion on-demand, and the legalization of gay marriage. The Pope called for a "meeting between faith and secularism and not a confrontation" and warned of "the birth of a strong and aggressive anti-clericalism" which was similar to that in Spain during the 1930s.[2] The 1930s were a difficult and frequently violent period in Spanish history, and references made to these events can often create controversial and conflicting stories of the past. For this conservative pope, it was necessary to summon the grievous memories of a violent past when he saw the Church under possible attack.

The interactions between the Vatican and Spain shifted following the 2011 election of a conservative Spanish government and the 2012 appointment of the seemingly liberal Pope Francis I. The conservative *Partido Popular* (PP) made no cuts to clerical salaries and it removed Socialist "civic education classes." The Archbishop of Madrid, Antonio María Rouco, pushed for Prime Minister Mariano Rajoy to act more decisively to return a conservative religious nature to Spain, yet Pope Francis I made no public comments about these issues whist meeting the Spanish leader.[3] Not every pope or every Vatican hierarchy member saw the world the same, and therefore, the Vatican's response to global concerns shifted depending on its leadership and international tensions. Similarly, the political ideology of a secular government would obviously affect the relationship between the Church and State. These differentiations support the suggestion that the Church and secular states had constant disagreements and misunderstandings over the centuries, especially when the role of the Catholic Church is the central issue and the reaction of the Vatican towards a political actor is not static, but is related to a variety of ingredients existing at a particular time and a particular place.

This book investigates the multiple relationships developed between the Holy See and various Spanish governments from 1931–1939. The Second Spanish Republic (1931–1936) and Pius XI's Vatican had an often contentious relationship, as Spain's political left wanted to secularize the state and remove many traditional privileges of the Catholic Church had over Spanish society during this period. The Vatican used its diplomatic corps in Spain to try to persuade the Second Republic to suspend its plans for secularization and defend the Catholic Church's traditional role and guarantee its safety, but for many on the left the Church represented an unjust social monopoly that needed to be dismantled. At specific times, leftist mobs attacked Church property and murdered clerics—increasingly souring the relationship between the Republic and the Holy See. When the political left controlled the government (1931–1933 and 1936), Vatican representatives constantly worked to influence or to undermine political decisions, but to no avail. When the center-right governed (1933–1936), the Vatican presumed it had a new ally, even when the government used military force against a violent leftist rebellion in 1934. Clearly, the Vatican did not approve of leftist politicians and their secularization campaign, but the Holy See was willing to support a center-right Republican government that promised protection for Church property and safety, and possibly to restore its previous privileges in Spain.

This book explores numerous examples of Vatican-Republican communications that highlight the contentious relationship between the two states, particularly concerning the role of Catholicism in Spain. This project investigates a vast network of correspondences sent from Papal Nuncios and the Spanish Governments to the Holy See as Vatican representatives in Spain held numerous meetings with the Republican government to discuss the role of the Catholic Church. Often, the Republic was unwilling to accept Vatican criticism, and Vatican influence could not change the government's actions. This research will also explore portions of a global network of communications concerning the Second Republic, highlighting the ever-increasing international concerns about this new Spanish government.

My project also scrutinizes the interactions between the Holy See and the two Spanish belligerents—Republicans and Rebels—during the Civil War (1936–1939).[4] The Rebels claimed their uprising against the Republic was a true crusade to liberate Spain from a perceived communist and atheist threat, which had destroyed traditional Spanish society. The Republic hoped the Holy See would acknowledge the legitimacy of a democratically elected government, but previous tensions could not be overcome. While the Insurgency claimed to support a religious crusade, their leadership remained often cold and unwilling to listen to Vatican opinions. When the Vatican suggested cessations in hostilities or possible negotiations, the Insurgents demanded the Vatican remain silent.

Problems surrounding the role of Republican Catholics, Rebel atrocities, violence against clergy and churches, civilian deaths, negotiations, and foreign involvement each created serious complications for the Holy See when considering how to act concerning the Civil War. If the Vatican became too vocal and openly supported one belligerent over another, violence directed at the Church could have increased substantially as retribution for its decision. The Vatican appeared to want the bloodshed in Spain to end, but it was unwilling to make the Catholic Church a larger target for retaliations by either side.

This project is possible due to the recent opening of the Secret Vatican Archives (ASV) concerning the Papacy of Pius XI (1922–1939).[5] Materials from the Foreign Ecclesiastical Affairs division offer internal Vatican statements, as well as communications from foreign governments and private organizations with Catholic representatives from around the world. Materials from the ASV include notes from Cardinal Eugenio Pacelli, Madrid Nuncio Federico Tedeschini, the Republican Government, the Burgos Government, and others. While the ASV has opened its files on Pius XI, this project does acknowledge the possibility that some important materials might not be currently accessible, for one reason or another. Even with this caveat, the ASV is the central focus for this project and provides an important font of knowledge for studying Vatican-Spanish interactions in the 1930s.

The combination of these new sources with previous studies creates a more complete picture of the Vatican's actions. Historians have shown that the Spanish Catholic Church and Spanish liberals had a contentious relationship from the 19th century onward, and this combative relationship exploded during the period of the early Second Republic.[6] The Second Republic wanted to create an egalitarian and secular state, but Spain had a powerful conservative segment, and it would not take kindly to these serious changes. The *Spanish* Catholic hierarchy was a vocal opponent of Republican changes—and it also faced violence on numerous occasions. Historians have outlined the Spanish Catholic hierarchy's support for the Rebel "Uprising" because the Rebels supposedly developed the façade of a crusade to save Spain from secularism.[7] Most Spanish clergy hoped the Rebels would win, but they also realized they could not control all their behaviors. Overall, the majority of the Spanish Catholic hierarchy distrusted the Republic, and most Republican leaders distrusted the Catholic Church.

Recently, historians have been able to scrutinize the relationship between Pope Pius XI and his Secretary of State, Cardinal Eugenio Pacelli, to understand better their differences on diplomatic questions. Frank Coppa has highlighted the diverse views of these two men suggesting Pope Pius XI was a supporter of "confrontation" with foreign states when governments contradicted the teachings of Catholicism, whereas Secretary of State Pacelli favored "conciliation" with foreign powers. The Cardinal, who was the protégé of former Secretary of State Pietro Gasparri, supported diplomatic actions influenced by impartiality that would not harm the Catholic Church within other states.[8] Pacelli adopted the diplomatic opinion that the Pope "could condemn principles in conflict with the faith, but as universal father he must remain impartial and not favor one side or state against another."[9] Pacelli, therefore, believed the Holy See should remain neutral and impartial in political crises, unless all sides agreed upon Vatican involvement. The divide between Pius XI and Pacelli can be shown in the interpretation of Article 24 of the Lateran Accords between the Vatican and Fascist Italy, which states, "the Holy See declares that it desires to remain and will remain outside of any temporal rivalries between other States and the international congresses called to settle such matters, unless the contending parties make a mutual appeal to its mission of peace; it reserves to itself in any case the right to exercise its moral and spiritual power."[10] Cardinal Pacelli appeared to support the idea that the Holy See "will remain outside of any temporal rivalries between other States," in the hopes of protecting the Catholic Church from political competitions that could become dangerous. Pius XI, however, seemed to back the concept that the Holy See also had "the right to exercise its moral and spiritual power," especially during times of humanitarian crisis or when the Church was being attacked by secular governments. Pacelli believed the Holy See needed to remain impartial, while Pius XI wanted to confront evils. This conflict between the two men is highlighted during the period of the Second Spanish Republic and Spanish Civil War. Both the Pope and his Secretary of State were aware of the violence and ideological conflict occurring in Spain, yet they took different approaches. Cardinal Pacelli often remained pragmatic, as he realized the violence was ideologically driven and capable of producing serious problems for the Church in the future. The Pope saw the "moral" problems occurring in Spain, and wanted to comment, but Pacelli's fear the Rebels could strike against the Church after the War ended must have tempered the Holy See's actions.

With these Vatican sources and previous historical studies, it is now possible for this project to ask new questions. While it might appear as "common knowledge" that because the Spanish Catholic hierarchy openly opposed the Republic the Vatican must have worked to undermine the new government, new ASV sources allow this project to explore communications within the Vatican hierarchy to pinpoint how the Holy See interacted with the Republican government. This book will show that while the Vatican hierarchy did not like the political attitude of the Republic, the Holy See constantly used its diplomatic corps to maintain open communications with the government. While the Vatican did not always make its opinions public, it certainly had no fears of private communications with the Republic about a variety of topics—including complaints about Republican behaviors. Exploring these previously unavailable communications gives new insight into how the Vatican understood this new government and how it wanted the Republic to act. Republican sympathizers also suggest that because the Spanish Catholic hierarchy supported the Rebel cause, the Holy See must have done everything possible to alienate and to oppose the Republic during the Civil War. By exploring ASV sources, this work presents the complicated relationship between the Holy See and both belligerents as the Vatican suggested armistices, prisoner exchanges, and cessations, but the Insurgents rejected Vatican involvement. My work will show that the connection between the Holy See and Rebel forces was not monolithic—in fact, the Rebels often forcefully suggested the Vatican remain uninvolved in the conflict. The ASV sources used in this project also address concerns such as: foreign calls for mediation, private calls for mediation, Vatican complaints over aerial bombardments, and concerns over the Basque. In the end, this project offers a clear conversation of Vatican-Spanish concerns in the 1930s that fits well with previous literature while establishing future avenues of study.

Contemporary literature concerning the Second Republic and Civil War remains divided as scholars develop distinct interpretations regarding the political nature of 1930s Spain. Historians Stanley Payne and Paul Preston have two distinct opinions on 1930s Spain, and each has written numerous works and spawned many followers on this topic. Paul Preston views the creation of the Second Republic as a legitimate declaration that attempted to save Spain from the backwardness of tradition and create a secular state for all Spaniards, suggesting the Second Republic was a bastion of liberty and the government's actions were consistently justified.[11] Regarding the Civil War, Preston suggests the Insurgents bore the sole responsibility for the conflict, and Rebel repression was substantially greater than anything the Republic could muster. For Stanley Payne, the Second Spanish Republic's declaration offered hope for the country as Spain's underclasses could gain equal access before the law and *all* citizens would have equal rights.[12] Payne contends that as the Republic progressed leftists quickly radicalized and passed legislation and constitutional reforms meant to protect their values while punishing conservative and traditional elements in society for their previous social crimes. As Payne's works identify, leftists in the Second Republic believed the government was exclusively theirs, and any attempt of conservatism to gain political power was a direct attack against Republicanism. While Preston asserts that the Rebels were primarily responsible for the Civil War, Payne explains that the Second Republic intentionally antagonized the right and exclusively targeted symbols of conservatism in order to destroy their footprint in Spain. The Civil War, therefore, was the fault of both sides, and both used violence.

The role of the Catholic Church in Spain has inspired its own historical study interested in clarifying the role of religion in the country. William Callahan and Frances Lannon each explored the Spanish Catholic Church and these historians acknowledge the extremely important and influential role played by the Catholic Church in Spain, and they agree that Monarchy, Conservatism, Traditionalism, and the Church were interconnected throughout Spain's Early Modern and Modern histories.[13] Because the Catholic Church was associated with the monarchy and conservatism, liberals and republicans believed the Church was a tool of repression used on the Spanish people. When the Second Republic was declared, these historians suggest the Republic specifically targeted the Spanish Catholic Church due to its historical position. Importantly, though, each suggests that while the Spanish Catholic Church condemned the Republic and supported the Rebel cause, the Church could neither control the Rebels' actions nor define the Franquista doctrine. The Spanish Catholic Church may have supported the Rebels, but the Insurgency acted independently of Church influence. Conservative historians José Sánchez and Gonzalo Redondo view the Civil War as a culminating battle between secularism and religiosity, blaming the Republic for its weaknesses yet, even with this opinioned view, these works offers invaluable statistics for religious victimhood at various conflict points in the 1930s.[14] Hilari Raguer and Vicente Cárcel Ortí, both clergymen, have established their own opinions on the role of the Catholic Church in Spain's conflicts.[15] For conservative Cárcel Ortí, the Catholic Church was not responsible for the Civil War and tried to act as a calming force. The more liberal Hilari Raguer suggests the Spanish Catholic Church became overly involved in Spanish politics, and its antagonism does take some responsibility. While these views are not completely contradictory, they highlight the nuance needed when studying the role of the Catholic Church in Spain. Even though these scholars may not all arrive at the exact same conclusion about the Spanish Catholic Church and Civil War, they each demonstrate that the Catholic Church was a primary interest for both Rebels and Republicans, and the Catholic Church worried a great deal about 1930s Spain and its possible future.

The final historical debate affecting this research involves the role of Vatican diplomacy in European society during the 1930s. Pope Pius XI released encyclicals about political ideology, but a debate exists about if more could have been done to prevent radical views from taking root. Pius XI's Secretary of State, Eugenio Pacelli, would become Pope Pius XII in 1939, and lead the Church during the Second World War and Holocaust.[16] Actions of Pius XI and Pacelli have been scrutinized and some have suggested the Church did not do enough to help ease suffering during WWII. Historians like Susan Zuccotti, John Cornwall, and Carol Rittner created firestorms when they suggested the Holy See did not do enough to oppose the Holocaust, and the Church worked with fascists.[17] In response to these works, the Vatican released certain documents from Pius XII and the period of Pius XI. Historians like Lucia Ceci, Hubert Wolf, Emma Fattorini, Alessandro Duce, and Frank Coppa have each used ASV sources to explore the role of the Holy See in international diplomacy, with a focus on fascism.[18] According to these historians, and with the help of previously unavailable documents, Pope Pius XI was clearly against all radical political ideologies that worked to undermine the authority of the Church over spiritual concerns. These historians suggest Pope Pius XI wanted to speak out against these radical ideologies, even against Fascist ideologies, but Secretary of State Pacelli believed this was a dangerous idea. Pacelli did not support these ideologies, but he understood that increased public communications from the Holy See about fascism could create very powerful enemies that would work to destroy the Catholic Church in Italy and Germany. A clear example of Pacelli's fears can be found when he did not release Pius XI's final encyclical, the *Humani Generis Unitas*, following the Cardinal's ascension to Pope. The new Pope Pius XII believed this encyclical, which spoke out against anti-Semitism and racism, would irreparably harm the condition of the Church in Germany and Italy, and this needed to be prevented. Pius XII did not support the actions of Nazi racist policies, but his interest in conciliation pushed him to avoid endangering the Church's tenuous position.[19] In this period of increasingly aggressive ideological dysfunction in Europe, the Catholic Church needed to be very careful about the opinions it expressed publicly.

This project is divided into eight chapters that explore the more serious moments of the Spanish Second Republic and Civil War. Chapter I, "A Troubled Past and a Tense Introduction," offers a historiographical background of the political and clerical tensions in Spain and explores the declaration of the Second Republic in April 1931. Chapter II, "From Caution to Confrontation," investigates the often anticlerical political changes introduced by the Second Republic and the Holy See's reactions to the new laws and violence and defense of clericalism. Also explored are the implications of the Papal encyclical *Dilectissima Nobis* and its effect on Vatican-Spanish relations. Chapter III, "Republican Reorganization," explores the elections of November 1933, the subsequent Radical Government, and the Popular Front electoral victory of 1936. The emphasis here is on the increasing political polarization in Spain and shows Church concerns about possible class-based revolution as the state became less stable and faced violence from Left and Right. Chapter IV, "The Uprising Begins, The Republic Reacts, and the Vatican Protests," analyzes the first months of the Spanish Civil War as the Insurgents won numerous victories, yet the Holy See worried about uncontrolled violence against Catholics and Catholic institutions. Chapter V, "Humanitarian Concerns Increase as the War Continues," discusses the continued violence perpetrated by the Rebel forces throughout Spain, with focus directed towards the northern Basque Country. As the Civil War spilled into 1937, the Vatican grew very nervous the devout Basque might have suffered too greatly. Chapter VI, "Foreign Requests for Vatican Intervention," investigates international calls for Vatican mediation in the Civil War. Foreign governments and organizations asked the Holy See to intervene in the conflict and act as a broker for peace. Each attempt, though, was hampered by the Vatican's avoidance of involvement with initiatives from other countries and by the Rebels rejecting any outcome other than a complete military victory. Chapter VII, "How to Save the Basque," outlines the projects undertaken by the Vatican hopefully to save the Basque from a devastating war and the threat of possible Rebel retaliation. Chapter VIII, "Bombings and Civilians," analyzes the final months of the Civil War as a Rebel victory seemed guaranteed. The Republicans and their supporters hoped the Holy See could negotiate some end to the Civil War, yet the Vatican found the Insurgents were unwilling to accept anything but a complete victory. The Vatican could not influence the military decisions or strategies of the Rebels as the Civil War reached its end.

With a topic as contentious as the Second Spanish Republic, Civil War, and Vatican diplomacy I believe it is vital to also state what this work is not attempting to do. My work neither intends to answer the question of the Second Republic's legitimacy nor does it work to judge the fairness of its legislation. This project is concerned with the Vatican's *reaction* to these Spanish changes—correct or not. For this work, the Vatican is the main actor, and its opinions—justifiable or otherwise—are being highlighted. Secondly, I am not working to defend or condemn the Civil War. My work is focused on the Vatican's *perceptions* and *opinions* about the conflict, not working to prosecute the War. I am also neither working to condemn nor to defend the actions taken by the Holy See and Catholic Church during this era. I wish to create a sustainable narrative based on archival materials to project clearly Vatican opinions. As an American citizen without Spanish blood, my interest in this topic has remained purely academic and has never tried to manipulate the political. I have worked to strip away any possible misinterpretations of personal ideological beliefs in this work, but I realize that when documenting a narrative of belief, conflict, spirituality, ideology, and interpretation of facts readers may project their own political opinions onto the sources documented. I must also admit that the possible existence of other Secret Vatican Archival materials may one day influence future studies of the

Vatican diplomatic method during the 1930s, but a balanced representation of materials has been obtained to draw conclusions in this work.

As with any major revolution or civil war, numerous atrocities and forms of repression occurred during this period in Spain—and these are clearly horrible consequences. Republican leaders believed they were doing the best for a new Spain, but their unwillingness to allow *all* Spaniards to participate in democracy and their acceptance of brutal repression hurt their message. The Rebels fought against what they considered violent and dangerous ideologies, but their uprising unleashed a violent and bloody Civil War in which Franco's forces committed many atrocities as they attempted to rid Spain of the ideas of their opponents. Finally, the Holy See could have been more public and spoken out louder against the violence of the Civil War, but the Holy See frequently thought of its best interest first. Overall, both the Republic and the Church saw themselves as victims and they were both victimized by forces interested in their destruction. Most importantly, though, it appears as if the Rebel forces manipulated this conflict and the primary actors to their own advantage. When the War ended, it was neither the Republic nor the Church that were militarily victorious, but it was the forces of Francisco Franco that would continue to dominate the social and political practices for decades to come.

I

A Troubled Past and a Tense Introduction

The Second Republic is Born

The declaration of the Second Republic in April 1931 initiated a period of uncertainty for the relationship between Spain and the Holy See. The Vatican and its representatives nervously awaited the developments in the new government. Spain had been a symbol for Catholicism for centuries, but the establishment of this new Republic opened the door for secular changes to the state. Conversely, Spanish liberals braced themselves for possible attacks from conservatives and their Church-backed allies who would fight to restore Catholic privileges and prevent a modernization of the state. The Vatican did not interfere directly with this early Spanish political process, but relied upon its representatives in Spain to express its concerns regarding the new state policies towards the traditional privileges of the Catholic Church in Spanish society.

The growing political divide of 1930s Europe pressured the Holy See to sign numerous Concordats with a variety of states to protect the ability of Catholics to practice their faith freely, but these agreements often required the Vatican to reduce its political influence. The Lateran Accords of 1929 between Fascist Italy and the Holy See, which created a physical Vatican state, included a condition that the Holy See must remain uninvolved in conflicts unless all sides agreed upon Catholic mediation. During the administration of Pope Pius XI, the Holy See made numerous Concordats with states either friendly to the Holy See, like Austria, Poland, and Romania, or with states that posed possible threats to Catholicism, like Italy (Lateran Accords of 1929) and Nazi Germany (Reichskonkordat in 1933). These Concordats did not mean that the Holy See was in complete agreement with the policies of the state, but they tried to carve out a safe-zone for Catholic practices.[1]

The Vatican had become constrained by various political ideologies on the continent that intended to weaken religious influence in numerous states. At the same time, the clerical/anticlerical divide in Spain had continued to grow following the Restoration of the Bourbon

Monarchy in 1814.[2] Following the declaration of the Second Republic in April 1931, liberal political elements hoped to create a separation between the Church and the State and to reduce the powerful influence of the Catholic Church on the state, but conservatives responded by defending Catholicism's historical tradition in Spain. The political back-and-forth between clericals and anticlericals became in many ways predictable and institutionalized, and it should, therefore, not come as a surprise that the Second Spanish Republic hoped to change the direction of Spain away from its conservative past.[3] While the Holy See obtained a great deal of information about the political goals of the Republic from its leaders, Papal Nuncios, and Catholic leaders, the Holy See consistently relied upon its diplomatic channels to express its concerns to the Republic rather than make public statements.[4] Catholic representatives presented Vatican opinions to the Republic hoping to change the government's views, but even subtle attempts by the Vatican to express its opinions were met with resistance from many Republicans who had pushed for the secularization of the state. The Second Republic developed a clear plan to reduce the power and influence of the Catholic Church in Spain. Indeed, some Republicans believed the Catholic Church had previously consolidated too much power in Spanish society, and they viewed Vatican opinions as meddling in national affairs. In the end, the first period of the Republican Government saw a clear increase in Church concerns about Spain, but it also witnessed the growing weakness of Vatican diplomatic actions, even within historically Catholic states.

This chapter explores the Vatican's diplomacy with the Second Spanish Republic in the first weeks by searching the communication networks between the Holy See and its representatives. By exploring these communications, this chapter argues that initially the interactions between the Second Republic and Holy See were cordial, but once the Vatican realized the Second Republic would not maintain Catholic privileges in Spain, this relationship deteriorated. Both the Second Republic and the Holy See believed their world-views and opinions were more accurate and were in the best-interest for the Spanish people (or their power base), but neither side wanted to compromise. This lack of mutual understanding between the two powers prevented future cooperation. There exists a large historiography about the declaration, politics, social change, religious conflict, and other elements of the Second Spanish Republic that allow historians to explore the 1930s in Spain.[5] This work, however, is a study of the communications between the Vatican hierarchy and its representatives in Spain to explore the relationship between the two states. First, this chapter will highlight some of the most important religious conflicts that occurred in Spanish politics following the Restoration of King Ferdinand VII in 1813–14 until the end of the Miguel Primo de Rivera dictatorship of 1930. It is noteworthy how one of the most perceived Catholic states in Europe had struggled for many decades over the role of the Church in politics. The second section will closely examine the Vatican's concerns about the early days of the Republic. While the Republic's declaration drew several celebrations, numerous organizations across the political spectrum—from anarchists to monarchists—tried to undermine the future state apparatus. The Vatican hierarchy instructed its representatives to send numerous reports to the Holy See to explain the activities of the new government yet the Holy See worried about which political group would seize control and how they would interact with the Catholic Church. Would moderate Republicans control Spain, or would anticlerical Radical Socialists, Socialists, and/or Communists create an environment hostile to Catholicism? The Second Republic had a right to develop its new political system without foreign intervention, but the Catholic Church also had an obligation to defend its property and priests.

Brief Review of the Spanish Clerical–Anticlerical Divide

The anticlerical actions of the Second Republic did not occur in a historical vacuum. The struggle between groups that supported a powerful and central role for the Catholic Church in the Spanish Government versus those who demanded a liberalization of the Spanish State had begun decades earlier. During the Napoleonic invasion, Spanish liberals met in Cádiz and established the state's first parliament in 1810. Following the victory over the French, the Spanish crown reestablished absolutist control under the leadership of King Ferdinand VII. When Ferdinand's absolutist rule was threatened during the constitutional period of the Trienio Liberal (1820–3), the Spanish king called upon the Holy Alliance of Russia, Prussia, and Austria in 1822 to help him reestablish his complete control and prevent political liberalization. France's conservative King Louis XVIII offered his army, *The Hundred Thousand Sons of Saint Louis*, to restore Ferdinand's authority. After absolutism's military victory, Ferdinand continued to rule until his death in 1833, but he faced a serious problem in relation to his family's dynastic rule: the king sired only a daughter, Isabel. Ferdinand changed the rules of succession to the Spanish crown, and three year-old Isabel took the throne with the guidance of her regent-mother, Maria Cristina. Isabel's ascension to the throne, however, opened a new conflict between Spanish liberals and conservatives. Conservatives wanted Ferdinand's brother, Carlos, to lead Spain, so Isabel needed to establish alliances with Spanish liberals to justify her rule. This new alliance with nineteenth-century Spanish liberals initiated new conflicts between clericals and anticlericals. Spanish liberalism experienced its own unique growth, like all liberal movements. As William J. Callahan explains, "Liberals agreed on the necessity of imposing constitutional restraints on royal power but disagreed on the exact political configuration of their new order. The more conservative and prosperous landowners, merchants, and lawyers eventually formed the Moderate party, which favored a strong executive power and a narrow electoral franchise." He continues, "Conflict between the opposing camps of liberalism dominated the country's political history from the mid-1830s to the revolution of 1868."[6] At certain moments during Isabel's rule, violent mobs attacked symbols of the Catholic Church in 1834 and 1835, even seriously injuring monks.[7] In order to help the Spanish economic crisis, Isabel's government—at the behest of Ministers to the Regent Juan Álvarez Mendizábal and Pascual Madoz— "confiscated and sold 83% of religious community property, 40% of diocesan clergy land, and 75% of ecclesiastical property," in a process known as *desamortización*.[8] The sale of Church land was not meant to destroy the Catholic Church in Spain—far from it—but Spanish conservatives (especially clerical supporters) viewed these sales as signs that liberalism and anticlericalism had infiltrated the government, and the monarchy needed to reconfirm its support for Catholicism.[9]

Even though Isabel's government initiated the expropriation of Church property, Spain and the Vatican of Pope Pius IX agreed upon a Concordat in 1851 to safeguard the rights of the Church and establish a clerical budget to be paid by the government in a Catholic Spanish state. The clerical budget represented compensation for the loss of Church lands during *desamortización*. Pope Pius IX, who had been battling the political unification of Italy, was leading a general campaign in the Catholic world to defend the rights of the Church against liberalism and nationalism. As Frank Coppa explains, "Pius's principal aim was to strengthen Catholic ideology and safeguard the integrity of the pontifical magistracy which he believed to be threatened by the revisionist, liberal, and heretical currents that had become diffused in Europe from 1830 onward."[10] In order to secure the role of the Catholic Church and reduce the threats of liberalism that had swept through Spain and the rest of Europe, the Pope initiated and secured Concordats with European states like Austria, Portugal, and Russia. In return, the Vatican promised to support—or at least not to challenge—governments in these states.[11] For some European liberals, this tacit Vatican support for conservatism was a serious threat against liberalism everywhere. By obtaining these agreements with foreign governments, the Pope hoped to guarantee protection and influence for Catholicism and to avoid the continued deterioration of relationships between the Vatican and liberalizing governments. The relationship between the Vatican and each foreign state was unique and based upon specific historical and social situations.

Therefore, it is not possible to say that all states dealt with the Vatican in the same manner, or can one say the Vatican had identical requests from all states.

The Concordat of 1851 established the diplomatic framework between Spain and the Holy See until the declaration of the Second Republic in 1931. Both liberal Spain and the Vatican made concessions in order to gain security. As William Callahan explains "Pope Pius IX (1846–1878) accepted the sale of Church property carried out until that time, confirmed the traditional patronage rights of the Spanish Crown over episcopal appointments, and endorsed the principle of diocesan and parish reorganization," while Spain "accepted responsibility for supporting the diocesan clergy, reorganized the rights of bishops to act independently in the exercise of their pastoral functions, and consented to a limited reestablishment of the male religious orders in an ambiguous clause soon to arouse controversy."[12] For Spanish liberals, the Concordat represented a logical agreement made in order to secure an amicable relationship between the Spanish state and the Catholic Church, as well as establish the Vatican's acceptance of Isabel II as the rightful monarch. Pro-clerical elements in Spain, however, were concerned about vagueness in the Concordat. The agreement was meant to establish Catholicism as the official religion in Spain, which would be pleasing to some clericals, yet other Church supporters worried that the Spanish government would be either unable or unwilling to deliver on its promise to make Catholicism the only religion in Spain. Callahan continues, "Although the Moderates were willing to placate the Church, within limits, as one of the many interest groups supporting the regime, they had no intention of restoring the enormous privileges once enjoyed by the institution."[13] So on one hand, the Concordat of 1851 established the groundwork for a positive relationship between the Catholic Church and the Spanish state; on the other hand, pro-clerical Spaniards assumed the government was not committed to protecting the elevated position of the Church against the increasing onslaught of liberalism.

Ecclesiastical leaders used the troubles of Isabel's reign to push for greater authority, especially in education. As a result of the queen's growing political difficulties, the Spanish Progressive Party organized an overthrow of the monarchy in 1868, and Isabel abdicated from exile in 1870. The Prime Minister's death in 1868, the unpopularity of the queen, a severe economic crisis, military pressures, animosity from supporters of King Ferdinand's brother Carlos (Carlists), and urban anger all combined to lead to the queen's removal.[14] The Progressives imported a new king, Amadeo de Savoy, but he soon faced a serious divide among the liberal parties and he too abdicated. In response, Spanish liberals declared a Spanish Republic in 1873. This short-lived experiment with Republicanism did not have an easy path as internal confusion and squabbles in the Republican elite doomed any serious organization. However, the First Republic did attempt to create a separation between the Catholic Church and the state as its draft Constitution promised to separate the two entities, but also promised to continue paying nuns' salaries, guaranteed Church property rights, and honored contracts for government-funded improvements on ecclesiastical properties. As William Callahan explains, this plan for Church-State separation was much less dramatic than the plans of the Second Republic.[15] In the end, the First Republic was unable to establish this separation due to the resignation of its President and a following military coup d'état by Madrid's captain-general in January 1874, which killed the First Republic, and initiated the Restoration of Alfonso XII. Supporters of increased liberalization in the government hoped that the First Republic would succeed in secularization, but its failure signaled a return to the monarchy and possible pro-clerical success.

Antonio Cánovas del Castillo led the political Restoration of King Alfonso XII, in which he attempted to create stability in Spain by developing a new constitution containing an article concerning the Spanish religious question. Article 11 declared Roman Catholicism to be the official state religion, but it also allowed the private practice of other Christian denominations. Article 11 was supposed to be a compromise—one that reaffirmed the connection between the state and the Catholic Church, but also took some steps towards Christian religious freedom.[16] The compromise, however, was not appreciated by all. Anticlericals criticized the establishment of a state religion, and clericals did not want to allow other denominations to practice in the country. Cánovas and Alfonso XII wanted the Constitution to support the revival of Catholicism, but it did not work evenly throughout the country.

Some southern landless peasants and certain Barcelona factory workers had turned to Spain's unique version of anarchism instead of Catholicism to speak on their behalves. Spanish anarchism preferred local authority over the power of the state or other large institutions, like the Catholic Church. In certain cases, these anarchists struck out against symbols of conservatism and the Church to express their anger.[17] The clerical/anticlerical divide continued to grow, leading to violent attacks against the Church. In 1909, *Tragic Week* rocked Barcelona as "an orgy of violence against ecclesiastical personnel and buildings, because the Church was seen as a class enemy."[18] In response to this class-based violence against the Church, clericals worked to solidify their political power through their organization, the National Catholic Association of Propagandists. It was at this time that the influence of the Catholic Church in Spain became a serious political focus for all politicians in the country, especially clericals and anticlericals.[19]

Anarchism and Socialism began to influence working-class Spanish society by the latter half of the nineteenth century by taking advantage of economic and social factors in the country.[20] Anarchism first became popular in Andalucía among the landless poor. Historically, the question of access to land was a major concern in southern Spain, as the tradition of the *latifundio* prevented the majority of farm workers from purchasing land. Some poor believed anarchism and its occasional outbreaks of violence could change these economic and social disparities, but the traditional elite maintained their authority. By the 1890s, anarchism began to affect Catalan cities like Barcelona, resulting in violence and unrest, with the assassination of Cánovas in 1897 being the most serious attack. Following the Spanish-American War in 1898, Spain lost its last major overseas territories, and Cataluña lost its most important trading partners, leading to serious economic decline and social upheaval in the region. Mostly concerned about the growing economic instability in Spain, the Socialist union, *Unión General de Trabajadores* (General Union of Workers or UGT), grew from fifteen thousand members in 1900 to over eighty thousand by 1911.[21] Neither the anarchists nor the socialists posed a major threat to the traditional elite in Spain, "But their development signaled a fundamental change in the organization of the working class that boded ill for a regime that had failed to come to grips with the social problems produced by economic dislocation."[22] As the economic and social conditions in Spain deteriorated, anarchist and socialist movements' influence grew and continued to pressure the state.

In 1923, Miguel Primo de Rivera seized power through a bloodless military coup d'état. He promised to act alongside King Alfonso XIII to restore order and prestige to the Spanish state. While religious harmony was not the central focus for the Primo de Rivera dictatorship, the dictator saw benefits in co-opting Catholic identity as an ideological tool to unify Spain and strengthen his authority. Frances Lannon explains that Primo de Rivera initiated "a dictatorship under the king, utterly committed to the Church's view of a national Catholic culture that eschewed political and ideological pluralism. Unfortunately for the Church, the dictatorship did not last very long."[23] During this period, the dictatorship tried to establish a divide between "Spain" and "anti-Spain." In true Spain, Catholicism was the central religion, and foreign cultural influences weakened the state.[24] While Primo de Rivera used Catholicism as a unifying factor for the state, it may have not been everything the Church wanted. True, Spanish schools again taught Catechism, but not for sincere reasons. While supporters of Primo de Rivera regarded the Catholic Church as a means to unify the nation,[25] for the Catholic Church religious homogeneity was more important than nationalism. For Primo de Rivera, the nation trumped religion, but the Church wanted the dictatorship to acknowledge religion's supremacy.[26] Yet even though the Church did not get all it wanted from the dictatorship, Primo de Rivera's pro-clerical attitudes influenced Republicans who wanted to rid Spain of the monarchy and its allies. Believing he could no longer succeed in his position, Primo de Rivera stepped down from office in March 1930. Following his departure, the Spanish monarchy stumbled towards the elections of April 1931, and its subsequent overthrow.

THE REPUBLIC BEGINS

On 12 April 1931, Spanish municipalities elected local councils in Spanish towns and cities for the first time since the end of the Miguel Primo de Rivera dictatorship. Originally, the Post-Primo de Rivera government scheduled these elections as the first in a series, eventually leading to nation-wide balloting for a new national government. The results inspired a new political atmosphere, as Republican supporters viewed their victories in certain urban centers as a sign that the Monarchy had lost popular support. Candidates from Monarchist parties obtained 22,150 seats on town councils, yet a third of these candidates had no opposition on the ballots. While the results in rural areas went overwhelmingly to supporters of the Monarchy, the situation differed in large cities and provincial capitals. The conservative historian Gonzalo Redondo reports Republican supporters won 5,875 seats, a large majority in major urban centers.[27] Even though Republicans and their supporters did not win a majority of towns in Spain, they used the momentum of victories in major cities to move towards the creation of a republic, yet they needed to move quickly because Republican and leftist parties still remained in their nascent stages and had to act for power consolidation.[28]

Less than forty-eight hours after the municipal elections, supporters of a republic declared a new national government in Eibar, Guipuzcoa, followed by a series of declarations of support for the new Republic in major Spanish cities.[29] The Spanish King, Alfonso XIII, left the country—and most monarchists did not fight to preserve the crown's authority.[30] Well-informed about the actions of the Catholic Bourbon King and his family, the Vatican acknowledged through a short communiqué from Vatican Cardinal Secretary of State Pacelli to the Nuncio in Spain that the monarch and his family had safely arrived in France.[31] Overall, the creation of the Republic occurred without major incident, with little or no bloodshed on the first day.[32] Twentieth-century liberals viewed the Second Republic as a positive step for democracy in 1930s Europe, but the powerful ideological battles raging on the continent would soon affect the Spanish state. For Spain, this violence led to the Civil War of 1936–1939.

When the Second Republic was declared on 14 April, the Vatican quickly learned of the changing political environment in Spain from its

Papal Nuncio in Madrid, Federico Tedeschini,[33] other religious leaders, and through the Republic's communications with Church representatives. According to José M. Sánchez, Tedeschini was neither a supporter of Spain's intransigent Traditionalists nor moderate Alfonsists, he connected most with the liberal Catholic reformers as he was a "firm believer in moderate social reform, Tedeschini was also aware of the gravity of religious problems in socially underdeveloped countries."[34] The Nuncio's belief in moderate social reform allowed him to see the possible benefits of republicanism in Spain, but his beliefs put him at odds with conservative religious leaders like Cardinal Primate of Toledo, Pedro Segura y Sáenz. As the Republic began to establish its legal framework, Tedeschini's personal beliefs in reform modified as he believed the government had radicalized. The Republic soon viewed protests by organizations, such as the Catholic Church, as sedition. The Republic, however, represented a new and challenging entity for the Holy See because it appeared unclear how the Second Republic would be structured and how it would react to the Catholic Church.

One of the first communications between the Provisional Republican Government and the Vatican hierarchy stationed in Spain occurred on 17 April 1931. The newly appointed Minister of the State, Alejandro Lerroux of the centrist Radical Party, sent an official letter to Tedeschini to describe the changes occurring in Spain over the previous days.[35] According to Tedeschini, Lerroux had abandoned his formerly anticlerical views and became a political moderate.[36] The Nuncio explained to the Holy See the spontaneous departure of the monarch.[37] According to Lerroux, Alfonso XIII had voluntarily left Spain and the new Republic had obtained control over national sovereignty. Lerroux further suggested that the Catholic Church should quickly acknowledge the legitimacy of the new government, which would help the Republic to stabilize and garner international support.[38]

Thus, Lerroux's first communication with the Nuncio avoided confrontation, and made a respectful request for Vatican assistance. Lerroux, who represented the Spanish political middle and worked for compromise among the various political parties in the government, had extended a hand to the Church in the hope that cooperation between the two would stabilize the Republic. Lerroux's willingness to work in the political middle made enemies on both political extremes, but as Nigel Townson explain, the "centrist pragmatism" of the Radicals was key to the Republic's development.[39] Lerroux, of course, was not the only member of the Spanish Provisional Government, and the Spanish Catholic hierarchy began to grow concerned about more radical Leftist representatives gaining positions and influence in the new government.[40] The Catholic Church did have political influence in Spain, and it hoped less-radical elements—like President of the Republic Niceto

Alcalá Zamora or Lerroux—could direct the Republic and renew the relationship between the two states.

The Second Republic hoped to obtain "Recognition" from the Holy See for the new government. Papal Nuncio Tedeschini wrote to Vatican Secretary of State Pacelli on 26 April 1931 to discuss the issue of recognition and report on the developments that had occurred over the first weeks of the Republic. Tedeschini explained that the Minister of State Lerroux had requested the Vatican openly recognize the Second Republic, and in doing so, the Catholic Church would be able to support the Republic's attempts to maintain peace and order within the state.[41] The Second Republic saw the benefits of Vatican support to maintain order in the new regime. After all, Vatican recognition would help the government prove its legitimacy to observant Spanish Catholics. Tedeschini, however, would not suggest the Holy See fully recognize the Republican Government until Madrid made specific promises to the Catholic Church. The Nuncio continued by expressing concerns over a lack of proposed legislation to protect the freedom of religion—actually the lack of protection for Catholicism's privileged position.[42] The Republic courted the Vatican for support and recognition, but the new government had not offered the Catholic Church the guarantees needed, which made it difficult for the Holy See to give its complete support for the Republic. After a short period, however, the Holy See and the Spanish Catholic Church agreed that the recognition of the Second Spanish Republic was in their best interests. Recognition would allow the Vatican to initiate a formal diplomatic channel with the new government in hopes of preserving Catholic privileges in Spain.

The Republic gained Vatican recognition on 9 May 1931, yet the increased influence of radical leftists within the Republican leadership made Tedeschini nervous.[43] The 18 April 1931 letter from Nuncio Tedeschini to Secretary of State Pacelli contained a report about the composition of the Republican government and Tedeschini's concerns regarding its Leftist inclusion: "The composition of the new Government is a mixture of Republicans and Socialists."[44] Members of Republican and Socialist political parties—including Catholic Republican Parties—had previously agreed upon the "Pact of San Sebastian" on 17 August 1930, promising to unite to obtain political goals in Spain.[45] The Republic's provisional government brought together a variety of individuals ranging from moderates to Radical Socialists—making a complete understanding of the Republican ideology uncertain.[46] The mixture of socialists and other liberal parties gave supporters of the Republic larger numbers, but it also did not result in a smooth transition. As Manuel Álvarez Tardío explains, the wide spectrum of Republican supporters meant that unanimous agreements on the actions of the Republic could rarely be made. As an example, the elections for the Constitutional Convention in

June resulted in fragmented leftist control. Radical Socialists, Socialists, Republican Action, Independent Republicans, Esquerra Republicana of Cataluña, and others acted as the majority coalition. Conservative Republicans and the Radical Party of Lerroux did not always agree with the majority coalition. Each of these parties had specific goals for Spain, so it can be easily understood why the Vatican representatives were so wary about the future of Spain—who would become the dominant power in the state still remained unclear.[47] The Papal Nuncio thought it possible to work with President Niceto Alcalá Zamora; he had been a Minister for the Crown before becoming a Republican, and even more importantly, he was a political moderate and a Catholic,[48] but the Nuncio had expressed concerns about many others. Tedeschini concluded the government was not completely "anticlerical," but he alluded to strong atheist and Masonic influences, though he did not list specific names.[49] Even with this uncertainty, Gonzalo Redondo explains, and evidence from the Secret Vatican Archives shows that the Holy See was not completely "anti-republican" or hostile to the Republican cause at the government's inception, but it would have preferred a regime that protected Catholic privilege.[50]

For Tedeschini, it appeared as if the uncertain composition of the new Republic posed the main concern for the Vatican and its diplomatic attitudes on Spain. The Nuncio believed the new government could either follow a moderate republican structure, or it could be commandeered by radical leftist elements. For the Nuncio, though, either outcome signaled the new Republic would be different from the monarchies of the past, specifically for the fact that it would most likely choose to follow a secular structure.[51] Moderate Republicans had distinct differences with Radical Socialists in how far their secularizing process would go. The Vatican had growing fears of Leftist parties, especially communists, because they had become increasingly influential through the support of the Soviet Union and its Communist International. Tedeschini seemed to be uncertain as to which groups would take the lead in the government: "It is difficult, not to say impossible, that these diverse forces will be able to go a long way together."[52] Less than a week after the declaration of the Republic, the Papal Nuncio explained his apprehensions about the more radical elements of the political Left becoming active in the government, even if he was still unclear what roles they would play. Even as the threats of atheism and secularism remained possible in the Republic, the Vatican hierarchy took a wait-and-see attitude. The Holy See's approach protected it from anticlerical hostility in Spain, but it also showed that the Vatican still believed moderates could lead the state.

The structure of the Republican government was an important matter, but so was the territorial integrity of the state. From the moment the

Republic was announced, various regions demanded their autonomy. Certain areas in Spain, particularly Cataluña and País Vasco, had historical and cultural differences from dominant Castilla, and the Republic's declaration gave these regions an opportunity to push for greater self-determination.[53] With the monarch now gone, and confusion existing in Madrid, this was the best time to make these declarations. The most vocal came on 14 April as the leader of the Catalan Estat Català and Esquerra confederation, Francesc Macià, declared a "Catalan State" that would work towards the creation of a new "Confederation of Iberian Peoples."[54] This news was significant for the composition of the Republic as well as for the diplomatic channels of the Holy See. Tedeschini reported to the Vatican his anxieties about this new "Catalan Republic," which men like Macià and Barcelona mayor Lluis Companys supported. Tedeschini feared this government would be left-wing and more secular than the Church would prefer.[55] Tedeschini also reported the possible spread of regionalism in País Vasco, Valencia, and Galicia.[56] Regionalism, like the formation of the new Republic, proved to be a concern for the future of the relationship of the Church with its followers because each region's political consolidation could affect the level of Catholic influence. Regions with greater anticlerical views, like Cataluña, could further reduce Catholicism's influence in the state. The Vatican's fear of regionalism reinforced the suggestion that the Church did miss the centralized authority of a monarch or the power of Dictator Miguel Primo de Rivera—even though he used Catholicism more for his own purposes rather than creating a true Catholic revival.

Communications between the Spanish Minister of State Lerroux and Papal Nuncio Tedeschini remained cordial and positive as long as each side had something to offer the other. Communiqués from Vatican Secretary of State Pacelli to Lerroux show the Vatican was willing to assist the new Republic. A 24 April 1931 letter from Tedeschini explained that Vatican Secretary of State Pacelli "Has ordered me to communicate with Your Excellency that the Holy See is prepared to back the Provisional Government in the work of conserving order, in the confidence that the Government will also respect on its part the rights of the Church and of the Catholics in a Nation in which all people profess the Catholic Religion."[57] On 25 April, Lerroux responded to Tedeschini's letter, suggesting the Republic was happy to continue working with the Holy See. Lerroux explained that the Republican Government deeply wanted to maintain the historical relationship between "both Powers" in the hopes that the connection would lay the groundwork for continued Vatican support.[58] If the Catholic Church maintained its role in society and if the Republic secured order, then it appeared that both sides could cooperate. The optimistic repartee between the two lasted only weeks as the Republican Constitutional Convention—opened in July—began to diminish the role of Catholicism within the state.

The Holy See became increasingly concerned with the growing anti-clerical street-violence directed towards priests, monks, churches, and monasteries, even while the communications between the Provisional Government of the Second Republic and the Holy See progressed in the normal course of political formality.[59] This violence initiated a series of telegrams between the Holy See and its Nuncio in Spain to determine what actions should be taken. On 10 May 1931, the *Círculo Monárquico*—an organization of Monarchists opposed to the Republic—met for the first time since the declaration of the Republic in Madrid.[60] This first meeting of the *Círculo* did not end peacefully, as Republican militias attacked and burned its building, leading to several deaths. The burning of the *Círculo Monárquico* and the violence surrounding that day were the basis for an 11 May 1931 note from Tedeschini to Pacelli.[61] In it, the Nuncio reported a *"Situazione Grave"* [Grave Situation] in Madrid due to the sacking of the *Círculo Monárquico*, the attack on the Monarchist *ABC* newspaper, and a reported *"Chiesa Gesuiti incendiata"* [burned Jesuit Church].[62] For the Vatican hierarchy, the increase in violence against the Church and its supporters showed that the Republic seemed either unable or unwilling to protect the safety of the clergy and their property.[63] In reality, it was most likely the former—as the Republic needed to guarantee its partnerships during this confusing time, even with the more radical elements. But for the hierarchy, it appeared to be an unwillingness to act to protect the Church.

Extreme leftists increased their attacks against symbols of the *Ancièn Régime* in Spain, particularly Church property. On 15 May 1931, only five days after the violence at the *Círculo Monárquico* and *ABC* incidents in Madrid, Tedeschini wrote to the Holy See to inform the Vatican of the new carnage: "One cannot say certainly that the Government has provoked the incendiary movement, but it is easy to demonstrate that it has done nothing to stop it."[64] Tedeschini and the Spanish Catholic Church began to identify problems within the promises of the Republic: "The Government's pretext is that it was not able to defend all the numerous convents that exist in Madrid: but it would be very easy to respond that it could defend at least one."[65] The violence in Madrid and other Spanish cities against the Church and its property was a serious concern for the Holy See and Tedeschini speculated that certain members of the government, particularly those sympathetic to communism or anarchism, took advantage of the lack of government intervention as an excuse to destroy the physical influence of Catholicism in Spain.[66] Centrist Republican Minister of the Interior, Miguel Maura, resigned his post in protest to the state's "passivity" towards these attacks, but he later returned to the government—but the damage between the Church and

State had already occurred.[67] The Spanish Catholic Church offered a protest to the Spanish Republic to ask for greater help in protecting its property and for the payment of reparations for damages, but the Second Republic denied these claims.

The memories of the May 1931 events did not disappear from Tedeschini's thoughts in 1932 as he wrote Pacelli to request support for a protest marking the one-year anniversary of the original violence. Tedeschini's letter explained that a formal complaint from the Papal Nuncio in Madrid could act as a peaceful, yet forceful, reminder to the Republic of the destruction of Catholic Churches and religious organizations that had occurred in May 1931.[68] The Catholic Church in Spain was not about to forget the violence from a year earlier, nor was it willing to overlook the denial of reparations it requested. Most importantly, the Church believed that spring 1931 was a disastrous season—full of violence directed against Catholicism in Spain—and Vatican representatives should continue their reminders to the Republican leadership. The Church held the state responsible for the lack of protection. The Vatican hierarchy allowed the Papal Nuncio in Spain to release his personal letter of protest to the Spanish Government speaking for the Holy See directly. In his letter of 11 May 1932, Tedeschini wrote that the Holy See reiterated its "peaceful and determined protest" to the Republican Government to obtain reparations that had been requested due to the events of the previous year in the hopes of returning justice to the "noble and Catholic Spanish Nation."[69] During the Civil War, the Holy See referenced the attacks of the Republican period to pressure the government for protection from violent militias. The early plan for Vatican diplomacy appeared to be strongly worded yet respectful letters to remind the Republic of the Church's vulnerable position in Spain.

Concluding Thoughts

At the Republic's inception, the Holy See viewed the new government with caution and speculation, just like many Spaniards. The Church feared that these secularists in Spain wanted to push the country too far to the left and abolish Catholic privileges, but many Republicans rightfully feared that the Church would persuade its conservative allies to undermine the government's ability to lead. Therefore, both sides needed to reach an initial understanding of each worldview, but they appeared either incapable or unwilling to do so. The early communications between the Papal Nuncio in Madrid and the Holy See contained sympathy for men like Lerroux and Alcalá Zamora, but apprehension about the influence of the political Left in the new Spanish government grew. The Holy See did not react conclusively towards this new regime, but appeared to take a wait-and-see attitude. However, it does appear that serious miscommunications began to occur. Previous clerical/anti-clerical tensions must have been on the minds of the Church and the Republican leadership as these fears were reinvigorated as the Republic tried to take shape. The Republican Government viewed violence against the Church as random and uncontrollable mobs that could not be stopped. For the Church, because many of the mobs had Republican sympathies, the government was at least tacitly condoning, or even leading, these actions. This attitude, however, would be tested as the Provisional Government faced its next major concern—the creation of a Spanish Constitution.

II

From Caution to Contention
The Republican Constitution and Catholic Confrontation

In the summer of 1931 the Provisional Government and its Constitutional Convention met to draft the primary political and legal document for the new Republic. From this document all new Spanish Republican laws would be derived and therefore, its creation would be the touchstone as long as the government survived. The Papal Nuncio in Madrid informed the Vatican about the convention's actions, and he expressed the Church's concerns to the Provisional Government, particularly regarding the "anticlerical" Article 26 of the new Constitution. After that, the Vatican feared that an anticlerical constitution would permanently reduce the privileges of the Church. Even though the Republican coalition may not have set out to undermine the Catholic Church in Spanish society completely, the Holy See viewed much of this document as completely antagonistic.

This chapter next explores two types of legislation passed by the Republic that affected the privileges of the Catholic Church in Spain and will provide evidence for the growing divide between the Vatican and the Second Republic. First, the Holy See feared governmental interference with practices previously monopolized by the Catholic Church, such as the secularization of marriage and the take-over of cemeteries. The Second Republic understood these actions as being the next logical step towards a secular society, which would reject historical religious privileges and domination, but the Vatican interpreted these actions as nothing more than insensitive attacks against Catholic doctrine. Second, this chapter will explore the 1933 *Ley de Confesiones y Congregaciones Religiosas* (Law of Confessions and Religious Congregations) and the Papal response of the encyclical *Dilectissima Nobis*. The 1933 Law of Confessions was the first to elicit an official Papal response regarding the perceived attack against the Catholic Church in Spain, but the varied reactions to the encyclical may have forced the Holy See to return to silence for fears that the Republicans would view the Vatican as a seditious foreign actor.

Vatican archival evidence shows that the Holy See rarely took public steps to express its concerns about Republican Spain; instead the Holy See relied heavily upon its representatives with first-hand experience within the state, hoping to distance itself from political turmoil and maintain its religious authority. The Vatican hierarchy instructed its representatives to obtain political information and work to defuse anticlerical attitudes in Spain. Even though the Vatican was concerned about the shifting political environment in Spain, the uncertain composition of the Republican leadership made it difficult for the Holy See to take many concrete steps to voice its complaints. Most importantly, however both the Republic and the Church appeared unwilling to compromise or change their worldviews. The Vatican appeared to believe its strongly worded messages would shift the Republic's behaviors, but after centuries of traditional domination, many on the left were completely unwilling to allow any vestiges of conservatism to return.

THE CONSTITUTION OF 1931: PROVISIONS AND PRAYERS

Two and a half months after the declaration of the Republic, the Provisional Government held parliamentary elections on 28 June 1931. Supporters of the Republican structure, particularly the Socialists, won an overwhelming majority of seats.[1] The Left created a Republican Coalition that promised to move Spain away from the "failed" policies of the past and create a new constitution to shift Spain into the future.[2] The Spanish Constitutional Convention convened in Madrid on 14 July, Bastille Day, which must have been a symbolic date for the political left. The creation of this constitution included serious discussion regarding the role of traditional elements of Spain, particularly the Church. The Constitution was finalized and signed in December 1931. The path to the elections of 28 June and the Constitutional Convention was of particular importance for the Catholic Church because anticlerical language and actions had increased. The Constitutional debate represented the greatest concern for the Catholic Church because all future Spanish laws would be derived from this document. The Vatican feared the government could use constitutional articles to attack Catholic privileges in Spain. The Republic, however, understood the creation of this constitution as an attempt to create a modern democratic system from the ruins of a traditionalist state.

The election of 28 June was important for the state because the victorious party would have control over the writing of the new Constitution. As Luis Arranz Notario suggest, the Republican electoral system, which gave overwhelming representation to parties receiving 40% of the vote, helped to polarize the electoral process and campaigns.[3] On 20 June Papal

Nuncio Tedeschini wrote of the chaos leading to the vote, "Since last night, alarms restarted in convents and religious houses and uncertainty and panic reign because of maneuvers by syndicalists and communist unionists who are trying to prevent the election for the Cortes this 28th."[4] Violence surrounding the upcoming election was a major anxiety for the Holy See because fear could prevent "good Catholics" from voting. According to the memo, some workers' unions and communists had seized the period before the election to threaten their political enemies, but as Gabriel Jackson concludes, political disarray on the Right lost the election for conservatives—unfortunately for the Church, its allies were not ready for the fight.[5]

Tedeschini's concern about violence in the weeks before the election colored the Holy See's views of the Provisional Government. On 1 June 1931, the Office of Extraordinary Ecclesiastical Affairs (AES) of the Holy See compiled a report on "Religious Affairs in Spain." This report will be explored over the next few pages; in it the Holy See drew concrete conclusions about how the Second Republic acted towards the Spanish Catholic Church: "The provisional Government, composed almost entirely of sectarians, continues its advance against the rights of the Church without stopping in its path."[6] The report stated the goal of the government was to attack and reduce the influence of the Church in Spain. The report continued with a critical review of the proposed theme of freedom of religion relating to education: "The decree of Religious Freedom in education speaks of *commitments from the Government*? With whom?? How far do these comments go?"[7] The Church report suggested the Republic was systematically reducing religious influence in Spain and did not think it received the respect deserved. The report asserted the Church worked for peace and was respectful towards any state and any form of government, as long as its privileges were being protected.[8] The Church, though, believed the Provisional Government was not respecting its rights in Spain and Catholics became more concerned with the future path. The conflict between the Church and the State came to a head during the official process of drafting the state's Constitution, but still no Papal communications were directed to the government.

This Office of Extraordinary Ecclesiastical Affairs report contained a warning for the Catholic hierarchy in Spain about Church and personal documents. Because information coming from Spain had frequently commented on the deteriorating conditions for the clergy, the report included warnings for the production and dissemination of religious materials in the country: "The pastoral documents, in these circumstances, should be published with extreme caution due to the grave dangers of their interpretations."[9] While the Vatican Archives speak in generalities, it can be assumed that this note referred to the pastorals of men like Cardinal Pedro Segura y Sáenz, who had saluted the fallen

Spanish monarch and pushed for Catholics to initiate a new government based on Catholic principles—angering the Republic.[10] José M. Sánchez suggests that since the declaration of the Third French Republic in 1870, the Holy See tried to soften its opinions about republican governments in order to protect it from further violence, but he also believes that this fear of violent reprisals from republicans influenced the Holy See, and the Spanish Catholic hierarchy, to appear willing to work with the Second Spanish Republic.[11] Cardinal Segura, the Archbishop of Toledo, however, was unwilling to placate republicanism and this language produced an angry response from Madrid—expelling him from Spain in July. This pastoral may have been seen as a catalyst for the attacks against religious sites on 10 and 11 May. Most interestingly, Sánchez concludes that the Holy See and the Nuncio would have been happy with Segura's expulsion from Spain in the hopes it would improve Church-State relations, particularly as the constitutional debates appeared on the horizon.[12] The Holy See had not instructed its clergy to *stop* pastoral letters, even those critical of the Republic, but it did warn its religious leaders to be careful with their documents—the Vatican wanted to avoid conflict and was willing to allow controversial Church figures to be removed.

Even with these warnings, the Office of Extraordinary Ecclesiastical Affairs did not think that good Catholics in Spain needed to abandon their participation in the Constitutional Convention. The 1 June AES report called for good Catholics, whether they were "*monarchiche o repubblicane*," to run for office in the Spanish Parliament.[13] The Vatican assumed that no matter the political persuasion of a candidate, if he were a good Catholic he would try to protect the Church. This attitude of possible cooperation with a secular government shared similarities with the 1890s French *Ralliement*, in which French Catholics attempted to work with the Third Republic "in order to influence it in a conservative way," however, like the *Ralliement*, Spanish clericals appeared unable to affect major changes in the state.[14] The problem for the Holy See was the overwhelming Leftist and Socialist victories in the elections prevented "good Catholics" from gaining positions in the Convention. Yet even though the Vatican had grave concerns about the formulation of the Republic, it advised the Catholic hierarchy to persuade parishioners to run in the elections. The Holy See requested that its followers work in the political system of the Republic—like during the Third French Republic. José Sánchez and Hilari Raguer explain that during the Papacy of Leo XIII (1878–1903), the Pope released his encyclicals *Quod apostolici muneris* (1878), *Immortale Dei* (1885), and *Au milieu des solicitudes* (1892), which encouraged Catholics to accept a republican form of government and participate in the political realm as long as the government protected Church rights.[15] The Church may have not liked the possible composition of the Republic, but it is important to note that the Vatican still proposed that its supporters work in the confines of the rules to foster Catholic interests.[16] A 2 June 1931 letter from Madrid to the Holy See also supports the idea that the Catholic Church saw itself as working within the legal framework of the government and that the Church was not supporting any particular political groups. As Nigel Townson suggests, the Catholic Church might have found a unique avenue in the "ambivalent attitude" of the Radicals as "On one hand, the party, in keeping with republican tradition, upheld the separation of church and state, the freedom of worship, and the restrictions on the activities of the religious communities. On the other hand, the Radical leader was repeatedly to stress that reform of the church should not amount to 'revenge'."[17] The letter stated that the supporters of the Church were "a defensive force of Catholic interest" yet Catholics did not necessarily have to support one form of government over another.[18]

While the Constitutional Convention was meeting, Papal Nuncio Tedeschini and others in the Spanish Catholic hierarchy sent numerous communications to the Vatican to keep them posted on developments. While the representatives discussed much in the Convention, they focused on those articles dealing with the role of the Catholic Church in Spain. The first major dilemma for the Nuncio, Article 3, declared that Spain would be a state without an official religion. In a 7 July 1931 letter, Tedeschini expressed his concerns about this controversial issue:

"A State religion does not exist. The Catholic Church will be considered as a corporation of public right. Other religious organizations will be similarly considered upon request, if by their constitutions and number of members they offer guarantees of sustenance."

Let us examine by parts this article published in an absolute and almost bitter form.

"A State religion does not exist." What does one mean by that? Logically examined this proposition is universal and negative and resolves itself into something else: the religion of the state does not exist. From this one can deduce that no state has or should have a religion, which is to say that the State is atheistic: an error condemned by the Church and by reason itself. The state, like man, depends on God in its existence and in its government and should recognize this dependency and render it the religious due professed by the only true religion.

According to the authors of this plan, the Spanish nation does not have religion and declares itself atheist: henceforth it expels God from its chest and commits a true social deicide.[19]

The Nuncio viewed the Convention's plan to secularize the state as a direct attack against the connection between the state and religion.

Tedeschini equated the legal framework to the existence of God and the supremacy of the Catholic Church. By removing Catholicism's influence, Tedeschini believed only errors would follow. The Church did not view "freedom of religion" (meaning the state did not have an official religion) as "freedom for religion" (the Catholic Church's special and traditional position in the state was removed). Tedeschini wrote, "The article states that freedom of conscience is guaranteed. This is false because as far as this arrangement is guaranteed, it is freedom to err by the irreligious."[20] Tedeschini, therefore, did not appear willing to accept the idea of the separation of Church and State in Spain. Tedeschini would work with a republican government, but that republic could not remove the Church from the political arena. Some in the Second Republic wanted to end Church influence and privilege completely, and Tedeschini could not accept this. It was becoming increasingly clear that the Vatican hierarchy and the leadership of the Second Republic had two distinct views about the future of Spain. The perceived attacks of the Republic against the Church were enough to sound greater alarm-bells for the Papal Nuncio in Madrid. While the Vatican knew of provisions such as this, it did not respond publicly to these concerns, instead it relied on its Spanish hierarchy to present its own protests. Cardinal Secretary of State Pacelli thanked Tedeschini on 11 August for reporting on religion's deteriorating condition in Spain, but he gave no major directive as to how the Spanish Catholic hierarchy should go about dealing with the scenario.[21] Even though the Spanish hierarchy was concerned about the changes in Spain, the Vatican hierarchy did not offer concrete plans of action for the Spanish Church to deal with these problems.

Some Catholic Press presented opinions about the conditions in Spain and tended to associate any actions on the left with communism and an increase of Bolshevik ideology. As Socialists gained more influence in the government, Catholic periodicals began to worry about the possible increase of Soviet interference, particularly in an era when it appeared that communism was on the offensive. For many on the political right, any party of the left with class-consciousness concerns equated to Bolshevism; Socialism and Bolshevism were not separate for the Catholic periodicals when they discussed Spain. The semi-official Vatican periodical *La Civiltà Cattolica* made its concerns about the Republic clear on 10 July 1931, when it published that the increased Bolshevik interference within Spain that was geared at trying to undermine the role of the Church.[22] The fear was that the Soviet Union would use its connections through its Communist International to make Spain even more hostile to the Catholic Church by establishing a purely atheistic state. Three months later, while Article 26 of the Constitution was being discussed and after the passage of the Law of the Defense of the Republic, *La Civiltà Cattolica* continued its warnings about the Republic on 31 October "The question that is now debated in Spain, is not a simple manifestation of hostility against this or that Religious Order; it is a real declaration of war against the Catholic Church and against everything that it represents; open war, official, with attention that has this inspiration from a satanic government, to bring more surely the blow and render it to irreparable ruin."[23] *La Civiltà Cattolica* believed the Republic acted not only against the Religious Orders, but had struck out against any and all Catholic practices in Spain.

La Civiltà Cattolica was not the only publication that feared the possible influence of Bolshevism in the Republic. The more liberal *L'Esprit International*, in its unsigned article "Le Changement de Régime en Espagne" (The Regime Change in Spain), mentioned its concerns about the possible growing closeness of Soviet Communism and the Republic.[24] The article explained that by reducing Catholic influence in Spain, Soviet Bolshevism would attempt to fill the void. While the Holy See had not directly spoken out against the Republic, media sympathetic to the Catholic Church began to warn about the new direction of the Republic, especially when the threat of communism and Bolshevism seemed to appear. In reality, socialism—more than Bolshevism—gained a foothold in Spain, but political ideologies that could reduce religious influence were all seen as enemies of the Church—even if their clear political intentions had not been made obvious.

While the separation or removal of the Catholic Church from the Spanish State represented a major shift in the Spanish legal codes, Article 26 of the Spanish Constitution created the most heated debate in the Convention and for the Catholic Church. At its opening, the law declared "All religious confessions will be considered associations governed by a special law. The state, the regions, provinces and municipalities will not maintain, favor or support economically any church, religious association or institution," which stripped the Church of it financial backing granted under the monarchy, and going as far as creating "A special law [that] will regulate the total elimination of the clerical budget within a maximum of two years."[25] In a direct attack against the Jesuits, the law stated "All religious orders will be dissolved who impose, in addition to the three canonical vows, another special vow of obedience and authority different from the authority of the state. Their goods will be nationalized and devoted to charity and education."[26] Those religious orders that would survive this law faced six "principles" meant to restrain their power: (1) any orders that "may constitute a danger to the security of the state" could be dissolved, (2) these orders must file a registration at the Ministry of Justice, (3) "Prohibition of acquiring or maintaining, either in their own name or in those of separate parties, any property beyond what can be proved to be necessary to maintain their members and direct fulfillment of their specific activities," (4) "Prohibition of the right to participate in industry, commerce or education," (5) new taxation, and (6) "The obligation to make an annual report to the state on the involvement of their assets in relation to the goals of the association." Finally, the law clearly stated "The property of religious orders is legally subject to nationalization."[27] This article designed sweeping changes to Spain's relationship with the Church. No longer would religious orders educate children, something controversial in a state where the public education system remained not fully developed.[28] Large public assemblies, particularly those of Catholics, were prevented under the guise of "public health."[29] Most importantly, this provision promised to dissolve any religious orders that had allegiances to a power other than the Spanish State—such as the Society of Jesus.[30] Even though delegates from the political Left had a large majority in the Convention, some Republican supporters disapproved of this provision, leading to the President of the Government, Alcalá Zamora, resigning his post in protest. The debates in the Convention showed that not all Spaniards and not all Republicans favored the provision, but the Church regarded its mere suggestion as a blatant attack against Catholicism.

As Fernando de Meer Lecha Marzo explains, the anticlerical actions of the Convention resulted from fear of Spain's past.[31] Radical Socialists and Socialists saw Catholic ideology as incompatible with modern Republican ideals. Therefore, the Constitution needed to prevent the Church from dominating Spanish society, and Article 26 became logical.[32] De Meer and others interpreted Article 26 as an intentional Republican plan to handcuff the authority of the Church, resulting in greater social and cultural conflict. Frances Lannon explains that while certain Church entities—like its educational system—had become unpopular, the manner chosen to reduce Catholic influence was not beneficial as "it was counter-effective in its mobilization of a mass Catholic opposition; it was inept in its method and timing. But the fear and determination that inspired it were neither misplaced nor exaggerated. The Church was a danger to the democratic and modernizing republic well before the republic tried, futilely, to disarm it."[33] As with previous attempts to secularize, clericals pushed back. The creation of the Republican Constitution, and particularly the debate surrounding Article 26, sparked the most serious debate about the role of religion in Republican Spain.

While the Vatican hierarchy did not lead the specific protests against the Spanish Constitution of 1931, it knew it had allies in Spain to act on its behalf. Historically, Catholics—both through the clergy and the laity—met any attempt to reform the role of the Church with resistance. Conservatives had reacted to 19th century attempts to reduce Catholicism's role in the state, and it should have come as no surprise that more vocal protests should come during the Second Republic.

William Callahan explains that attacking Church privilege was always met with responses like "The expansion of the religious orders, the proliferation and modernization of Catholic associations, particularly in the field of social Catholicism, and the identification of ecclesiastical interests with those of an educated, wealthy bourgeoisie provided the Church with a more resilient foundation for resistance than that available to the clergy struggling against nineteenth-century liberalism."[34] The Vatican had numerous vocal allies in Spain that could fight the battles for the Holy See. So the Vatican hierarchy did not need to lead all the protests against the Republic, but relied on active organizational participation in Spain. Radical Socialists and Socialists might have believed the only way to completely modernize the state would be to extinguish all Catholic influence, but this would have been nearly impossible, and the Republican leadership must have known resistance would come in one form or another. This fight over religious influence was the next logical step.

While the debates leading towards the passage of Article 26 were occurring in the Constitutional Convention, Catholic leaders and the Papal Nuncio expressed their anxieties about the possible legislation to the Holy See. Tedeschini's 16 September letter came days after a meeting with the Justice Minister Álvaro de Albornoz Liminiana failed to persuade the Republic not to adopt "anticlerical" articles in the Constitution. Tedeschini wrote, "Preservation of Religious Congregations is a grave battle. But [the Church] will defend preservation in totality, but be warned that if specific Jesuits' questions are raised the probability of [survival] is ninety per cent negative."[35] While the debates over Article 26 raised numerous issues, including the education of children and the ability of the Church to have businesses, the fate of the Jesuits in Spain posed the most daunting issue for the Vatican because the Republic directly targeted the group. The next day, Secretary of State Pacelli responded, requesting his Nuncio in Spain take public action against this possible article by working with Spanish Catholic Action, but he did not lead the protest.[36] The Holy See's lack of public commentary highlights the fact that it did not want to broaden the conflict in the media, but to keep it within the normal paths of formal diplomacy. If the Holy See had spoken out, Radical Socialists might have used those words as evidence for the necessity of this provision.

The Vatican requested the Papal Nuncio become more active in his protests against Article 26. In an 11 October letter to Pacelli, Tedeschini wrote of his meeting with Lerroux regarding the possible passage of the article and he reported that even though some of the Provisional Government, like Lerroux, did not favor it, the Church could not foster enough votes to stop it.[37] Yet even though the Church's ability to prevent the passage of Article 26 diminished each day, the Vatican would not give up on the Jesuits. On 12 October, Pacelli wrote to Tedeschini in the name of Pope Pius XI, stating that the Holy See was unwilling to sacrifice any religious order in Spain, especially the Jesuits. He urged the Nuncio to persuade Spanish Bishops to take up the cause of religious societies in Spain by directing their followers to speak out against antireligious aspects of the proposed Spanish Constitution.[38] The Vatican, in response to Article 26, accepted a grassroots plan to protest the passage of this possible law, particularly in defense of its religious orders. However, this attempted protest did not pay off for the Church. Tedeschini reported to the Vatican on 13 October that the grave situation had gotten worse as "Socialist and Radical Socialists in yesterday's meeting had decisively voted together for the article to dissolve religious orders and confiscate property."[39] According to Tedeschini, after days of heated debate and exchanges, the leadership of the Socialists was to blame for the passage of the Article. Tedeschini's reaction that the Socialists were to blame for the passage of Article 26 was correct, but it was not as simple as that. As Manuel Álvarez Tardío explains, not all Socialists agreed upon how radical the Article should be, and days of debate followed.[40] In the end, Radical Socialists did not get the full authority to dismantle all religious orders, like they had wanted. On the other hand, Conservative Republicans were not able to prevent the Article from passing. President Alcalá-Zamora believed that the success of the Republican revolution was something for all Spaniards to enjoy, and constitutional provisions like Article 26 were unnecessary. Manuel Azaña viewed the discussion of Article 26 as purely political and not an infringement into religious rights, separating himself from the concerns of Alcalá-Zamora. In the end, Álvarez Tardío explains that the more-or-less passive attitude of the centrist parties allowed Article 26 to pass. Therefore, while the socialists did help Article 26 succeed, the socialists did not manage to get all they wanted out of the provision.[41] With the final approval of the Constitution in December 1931 came the exit of the center Radical Party, as they felt abandoned by the Republican parties for the sake of the Socialists.[42]

At its inception, the future of the Second Republic was uncertain. As noted, the Vatican had received reports from its Papal Nuncio on the confusing situation during the first weeks of the Republic, but the communications became more distressed once the Republic began to draft its Constitution. The hope in men like Lerroux and Alcalá Zamora began to deteriorate after the Vatican better understood their supporters were outnumbered in the government and parliament. The Vatican representatives, under the directives of Pope Pius XI and the Cardinal Secretary of State, protested the language of Article 26. As the evidence has shown, though, the Vatican's directives for its Spanish hierarchy were not enough to prevent the passage of certain provisions, including the approval of Article 26. The formal diplomacy, on which the Vatican had relied, did not garner results for the Holy See. Even though the Vatican did not win this battle, it relied on its diplomatic representatives because they appeared to be the only possible avenue for the Church to express its concerns. The attitude of the Vatican was that formal diplomatic channels would prevent the Holy See from being targeted as an outside power attempting to control the Republican Government and preventing the need for Article 26. Of course, this Article represented a major dilemma for the Holy See. For if speaking out was sedition, and silence was weakness, it was difficult to determine what the Holy See should have done to protect Catholicism in Spain. Most seriously, with the ratification of the Republican Constitution, the groundwork for future legislation hostile towards the Church had been established. The Constitution would allow the Republican Government to reduce other Catholic privileges in Spain during the first period of the Second Republic.

OTHER LAWS: FRUIT OF THE POISONOUS TREE?

Following the approval of the Republican Constitution, new laws could be passed to further reduce the power and influence of perceived religious enemies of the Republic. First, this section will explore the Republican Government's actions to reduce Church monopolies over marriage and cemeteries. For the Republic, these new laws allowed individuals who did not accept Catholic doctrine to have equal access to important sociocultural practices. For the Catholic Church, on the other hand, these laws delegitimized marriages, families and religious practices as control was removed from religious doctrine. Second, this section will explore sweeping Republican legislation meant to reduce the influence of perceived enemies to the Republic. The Government believed it necessary to reduce anti-republicanism to protect its sovereignty by targeting various groups—especially the Catholic Church. The Church regarded these laws as direct attacks against Catholic leaders. Overall, these controversial laws had their roots in the Republican Constitution passed months earlier.

The Republican Constitution not only seized Church property, confiscated money and art, attempted to dissolve Religious Orders, and prevented religious education in the public schools; the Republic also passed laws that secularized certain practices hitherto monopolized by the Catholic Church. Beginning in November 1931, the Spanish Cortes debated, and later passed laws allowing for civil marriage, divorce, civil funerals, and nationalized cemeteries. Whereas the creation of the Republican Constitution laid the groundwork for anticlerical legislation, the first part of this section will look specifically at Spanish laws designed to remove Catholic monopoly and privilege over cultural practices. The Vatican hierarchy in Spain was concerned with these legal changes even though the majority of Spaniards did not choose to follow the secular practices. Overall, the Catholic Church rejected the Republic's attempts to end these monopolies and declared in private that Republican actions had become outright attacks against Catholic doctrine.

One of the central Catholic advocates against civil marriage and divorce in Spain was the Cardinal of Seville, Eustaquio Ilundaín. After the 2 February 1932 legalization of divorce in Spain, Ilundaín sent a note via the Papal Nuncio to the Holy See in April 1932, stating that religious law and secular law do not agree in the case of divorce and asked what Catholics in Spain should do.[43] In May 1932, Ilundaín also inquired what to tell Catholic lawyers asked to work in divorce cases. "I have answered them that I hope the Holy See will give us pertinent instructions to these subjects."[44] In a response from 3 June 1932, the Vatican Office of Sacraments confirmed that only the church could permit "Conjugal Separation," meaning that state civil divorce cannot be acknowledged.[45] The response continued that the legalization of divorce in Spain was "*un'odiosa disparità*" with the treatment of Catholics.[46] The Church worried about the legalization of divorce in Spain because it seemed as if the government specifically attacked spiritual practices, and it suggested that while Catholics needed to be respectful of national laws, they should not condone the practice in any way.[47] The Republic, however, regarded this law as giving women greater social freedoms. The logic from both sides contained validity, but each group could not understand (or would not acknowledge) the counterargument.

The battle shifted from the ending of marriages to their start as the Catholic Church also condemned the legalization of civil marriage as an attack against the practice of the Holy Sacraments in Spain. According to the Catholic Church, only Church marriages were legitimate.[48] On 31 July 1932, Papal Nuncio Tedeschini expressed his unease to Pacelli and asked for advice on civil marriage. The Church understood the addition of civil marriage to the Spanish Civil Code as a clear attack against Catholic sacraments,[49] and as a strike against Catholic families.[50] After Franco's 1936 Uprising, the Nationalists co-opted the rationale of the defense of family values—particularly religious practices—as a supposed core element for the war.[51]

The Sacrament of the Last Rights and religious burial also became a prime anxiety for Catholics. Just as the Republican government had legalized divorce and civil marriage, it changed rules concerning the burial of the dead. The legalization of cremation became the first issue relating to the deceased that angered the Catholic Church, and on 10 January 1932, Papal Nuncio Tedeschini wrote to the Vatican:

> While the most serious problems of National life hang over this unfortunate Nation, and they await in vain their resolution, the Republican Government has had another outlandish idea against the Church and has hastened to convert it into a decree, giving with this another satisfaction to the sectarians and to the Masons. The new burden deals with a particular issue that, among other things, not only worries Spain, but also was not passed through the antechamber of the brain. I am referring to <u>cremation</u>, which was made legal by a Decree signed by the Catholic President of the Republic, Mr. Alcalá-Zamora, and from the Government Minister, Mr. Santiago Casares Quiroga.[52]

The issue became a grave concern for the Papal Nuncio because cremation was not acceptable in Catholic doctrine and threatened the integrity of Catholic practices. Tedeschini identifies this piece of legislation as an "outlandish idea against the Church." Cremation, therefore, attacked not only the practices of the Church, but the core principles of Catholic doctrine. The Nuncio referenced President Alcalá Zamora, who had resigned as the Head of the Provisional Government in protest against the passage of the controversial Article 26 of the Constitution, but was later elected President of the Republic after the passage of the Constitution, a job that he reluctantly took since he represented a possible political middle ground for the country.[53] Previous communications between the Papal Nuncio and the Holy See had described Alcalá Zamora as a good Catholic with realistic goals for Spain; however, with the passage of this law, the Nuncio questioned Alcalá Zamora's adherence to Catholicism as he signed this piece of legislation. In the eyes of the Vatican hierarchy, former allies had now abandoned the Catholic Church and the Republic would now enter a period of continued radicalization.

Tedeschini continued by explaining the wider use of cremation within Spain as it would be practiced on unclaimed bodies in Spanish morgues. Therefore, individuals who died without a family to claim their remains, or those with non-Catholic kin, would be cremated rather than buried. Tedeschini criticized the act of cremating the corpse of an unclaimed individual as an abuse against faith as well as the community. He concluded, "It is evident also to the disposed that the will of atheist kin could cremate the cadaver of a good Christian."[54] Tedeschini alluded that the state had accepted cremation as a viable practice and left behind a culture of life for a "*culto dei morti.*" The burning of bodies would prevent the possible resurrection of the body and soul, which attacked Catholic doctrine and beliefs.[55] Even though the Secret Vatican Archival materials did not contain a formal response, Tedeschini's discussion of cremation helps to explain the severity of this issue for Catholics.

The Republic's changes for corpses did not end with cremation, as the state also debated control over cemeteries. On 30 January 1932, the Republic passed a law to secularize *all* Spanish cemeteries—transferring control to municipalities—and to offer secular and state funerals for those who chose them.[56] Nuncio Tedeschini expressed concern because all cemeteries within Spain would no longer be owned and controlled by the Church,[57] and the Church could no longer protect the bodies of the deceased in sacred ground, stating "The Cortes, when it deals with the Church, does not feel another mission than of oppression to it in everything and through everything, refusing to examine whatever reason and every frustrated attempt of reasoning on the part of the Catholics." Cemetery control was an analogy for the entire Church/State debate as "These inclinations shake the thinking of those who know the discussions on the plan of law concerning the relationship between the Church and the State."[58] Tedeschini viewed the Republican actions as discrediting the opinions and needs of Catholics and producing legislation harmful to the Church. The secularization of cemeteries, in the view of the Holy See, was yet another *direct* and *open* attack against the Church's beliefs, practices, and property. Whether or not the Republic meant to reduce directly the power and structure of the Church is not the key element; what was important were the perceptions of the Holy See and its hierarchy. Interestingly, though, the Republic did not *force* individuals to have secular funerals and *allowed* Catholic burials to continue. In fact, allowing people a choice to be buried respectfully, even if they were not Catholic, represented a positive step for the Republic.

The Spanish Catholic hierarchy and the Vatican hierarchy were not alone in their concerns about the possibility of being "forced" into a secular funeral. On 10 May 1932, Tedeschini sent a letter to Pacelli to show a form of "protest" by some Spaniards who wanted to guarantee a Catholic burial. They asserted that those worried about the secularization of cemeteries and cremation could carry a set of cards in their pockets declaring their desire to be buried in a Catholic cemetery and receive Catholic rites before burial. These cards would guarantee proper burial, but could also be a personal protest against the secularization of cemeteries. The instructions to the card read "Catholics at least 20 years of age: if you want to be buried in a Catholic cemetery, you should immediately sign three declarations like the one presented. One should be worn always with you in the wallet or purse; another, delivered to your parish, where it will be archived; and another, to be put in the headboard of you bed or in a place known by the family."[59] The individual would then sign a card that stated:

> I [first and last names] declare to be an Apostolic Roman Catholic and want to die, like I have lived, in the bosom of the Catholic Church. I REQUEST to my family members, friends, and good people who love

me, have the charity to advise me when I come to the point of death, and procure me a Catholic priest who will administer to me the holy sacraments which henceforth I desire and ask for. I DECREE bluntly that my body is given an ecclesiastical burial in sacred ground, with all the ceremonies, rites, and benedictions of the Catholic Church; and that above my grave, blessed by a Catholic priest, be placed a Holy Cross.[60]

The existence of these cards highlights that not all Spaniards approved of the government's secularization plans and those who feared the Republic's interference with funerals had created a system to protect their bodies after death. Tedeschini happily informed the Vatican that even though this legislation was created to reduce Church control, the Republic rarely succeeded in influencing Spanish funeral and burial practices. In December 1932, Tedeschini reported the number of civil funerals paled in comparison to those practiced under the auspices of the Catholic faith, as out of the 963 funerals conducted in Madrid in October, only twelve had been "Civil Funerals."[61] William Callahan also supports the conclusion that no large number of Spaniards followed this secular funeral, but what was important was that the Republic had been able to spread its secularizing campaign to small villages throughout Spain for the first time as each community needed to offer this secular option.[62] While the Catholic Church continued to express its disdain for the Republic's efforts to secularize funerals and burials into 1933, the vast majority of Spaniards continued to choose a Catholic funeral and a burial conducted by the Church, showing Catholicism still maintained spiritual leverage.[63]

The Catholic Church and Holy See continued to watch the secularization of Church cemeteries for years to come. In 1938, two years into the Civil War, General Franco ordered the return of cemeteries to the control of the Catholic Church throughout the country. The Papal Nuncio in 1938, Gaetano Cicognani, expressed pleasure in Franco's change to the Spanish legal code as "the government of General Franco continues in his work of rebuilding a Catholic and patriotic state; and the provision mentioned was greeted with warm approval by the Spanish people, who he had always had for their cemeteries, brightened by the hope of life eternal, an intimate and special care."[64] This Papal Nuncio's emphasis on Franco's attempt to move Spain back to a "Catholic and Patriotic" state revealed Cicognani's positive view of Franco and his allies. On 31 December 1938, the Holy See responded to Cicognani, "The Holy Father, completely concerned about this issue, has received knowledge of this law with the liveliest paternal interest and is pleased at the same time with this new proof of filial devotion to the Church given by General Franco."[65] The Church's approval of General Franco's action is important for future discussions of the Holy See's reactions towards the Insurgents during the Civil War, but the evidence does not support the Holy Father's agreement with all Rebel actions.[66]

The Republic attempted to pass other laws to reduce political dissent and strengthen governmental control. The *Ley de Defensa de la República* [Law of Defense of the Republic] elicited a negative response from Church representatives. After the October 1931 resignation of Alcalá Zamora as Head of the Government, Manuel Azaña replaced him. Ideologically to the left of Alcalá Zamora, Azaña attempted to push the government to secularize and liberalize at a faster rate (too quickly for conservatives). To do so, Azaña intended to reduce the cultural and political influences of the monarchy and the Church. Stanley Payne writes, "To Azaña, as to the left in general, the Republic was not so much a form or set of institutions—constitutional democracy and the rules of the game—as it was a specific reform project in church and state, education and government policy."[67] Azaña was also more critical of the Catholic Church. October 1931's Law of Defense of the Republic had been Azaña's first piece of legislation, intended to prevent individuals or organizations hostile to the Republic from overtly expressing their discontent or condemning its legislation. The law identified eleven types of crimes:

> (1) incitement to resist or disobey the law; (2) incitement to military indiscipline or conflict between the armed forces and the government; (3) diffusion of news or rumors designed to disturb the peace or the economy; (4) acts of violence against persons or property, the incitement thereto; (5) any deed or statement calculated to cast discredit on the government and its institutions; (6) apology for the monarchy or its leaders, and use of emblems or insignia associated therewith; (7) illegal possession of firearms or explosives; (8) any form of suspension of employment or labor, without just cause; (9) all strikes not announced eight days in advance (unless modified by subsequent legislation), all strikes unrelated to working conditions, and all strikes in which strikers refused to submit to arbitration; (10)unjust price increases; and (11) lack of zeal or negligence by public employees.[68]

The Azaña government justified this legislation as necessary to protect the Republic and defend certain freedoms, while withholding those rights from others. Opponents of the Republic saw this legislation as a direct attack against individual rights and as a censorship law. The Republic used provisions one through six to close almost any unsupportive organizations or arrest certain individuals who differed with Azaña's Republican Government. The law also intended to prevent numerous organizations, including but not limited to the Catholic Church, from speaking out against Republican ideology and actions. Open protest by the Church could be considered a crime, further reducing religious influence in the state. Those found guilty of the law "might be subject to arrest for an indefinite period, internal exile, or a fine as much as 10,000 pesetas," placing "civil rights in jeopardy" and could prohibit any organizations—including religious—from meeting, appealing a conviction was almost impossible.[69]

The Law of Defense of the Republic was the partial subject of a 12 March 1932 letter from the Spanish Catholic Hierarchy to Secretary of State Pacelli. The Spanish Catholic Hierarchy believed that the state passed the Law solely to remove the Church's rights to complain about the expulsion of the Jesuits and the removal of the Catholic Church from its role in education. The law helped to silence protests against the Republic and required anti-Republican demonstrations to act covertly. The letter characterized the law as "draconian" and "used exclusively against Catholics,"[70] which prevented all peaceful meetings of Catholics, censored the pro-clerical periodical *El Debate*, and prevented the publication of obituaries for certain priests because the Government wanted to prevent large groups of Catholics organizing at the funerals in case the events turned political. In the eyes of the Church, Republican laws were not designed to protect the Republic, but had been designed to destroy the social fabric of the Catholic Church in Spain. The Vatican believed basic religious activities, such as funerals, frightened the Republic because large numbers of pious Catholics would be massed in one location. Whether or not the *Ley de Defensa de la República* focused solely on the Church is not the main concern, but the fact that certain Spanish Catholics identified the law as being primarily antireligious gives a greater insight into the growing list of Catholic fears about the Republican administration.[71] Laws like the *Ley de Defensa de la República* highlight the Republic's narrow interpretation of certain rights and liberties. The Catholic Church could identify laws like the *Ley de Defensa* to garner sympathy from its supporters inside and outside of Spain, even though other groups had also been targeted.

The Law of Defense of the Republic was explained as legislation necessary to "protect" the Republic from its enemies, but the government also drafted additional laws to reduce the influence of the Catholic Church. In October 1932, the Spanish Parliament began to debate the *Ley de Confesiones y Congregaciones Religiosas* [Law of Confessions and Religious Congregations], controversial because it would place major limits on Catholic actions in Spain.[72] While the intended goals of the legislation may have not been as truly vindictive as previously thought, the fact that the Church interpreted this legislation as an open and direct attack against its ability to practice the faith freely is the main concern for this project. The law aimed to remove religious clergy from the educational field, prohibit the majority of Spanish Catholic charities, and nationalize all Church property (even though the Church could still use religious buildings for spiritual reasons).[73] Manuel Azaña signed the law into effect on 2 June 1933, eliciting the first vocal and direct response from the Holy See.

Before Parliament debated the law in October 1932, Papal Nuncio Tedeschini attempted to influence its outcome by meeting on various occasions with the Spanish Justice Minister Álvaro de Albornoz Liminiana. In a letter dated 9 April 1932, Tedeschini wrote of his meeting with the Justice Minister where he raised concerns about the possible Law of Confessions and Religious Congregations. Tedeschini expressed his apprehensions about the possible implementation of such a law, but his letter provides little information about how the Republic responded.[74] In another letter Tedeschini characterized a meeting as cordial as he expressed his concerns, but added that the state had made few concrete promises "The Minister listened with respect, and I stated it again with delicateness. He even listened with respect to the diatribe with which I ended my reasoning: you had written, I said, a worthless page and that it should be corrected; you had abused our patience, and abused the knowledge of conscience, because you know that the Church not only does not use violence, but considers patience and sacrifice a virtue."[75] The Papal Nuncio demanded more proof from the Spanish government that they were not going to attack the Church. Of particular interest, Tedeschini openly noted that the Church did not use violence and its practices were based on sacrifice. The Nuncio portrayed the Church as virtuous in its demands, believing it was acting in the best interest of all Catholics in Spain. While he questioned Republican political motivation, Tedeschini asserted the "purity" of the Church's motives; the Church professed clearly that it was the victim of the Republic's new legal aims. Yet even though Tedeschini had become more forceful in his conversations with the Republican leadership, he did not threaten any particular retaliation by the Holy See against Republican Spain. The Republican government and liberals, however, had witnessed the centuries of Church manipulation of the Spanish crown, and a possible destruction of Church privileges could prevent this from happening again.

The October debate of the Law of Confessions inspired a new series of letters from Tedeschini to the Holy See about changing conditions in Spain. On 15 October 1932, Tedeschini declared the "sad" news of Azaña's announcement of parliamentary debate on this law; and it provided an interesting review of the Church's condition over the past year as well as his increased apprehensions.[76] According to the Nuncio, the Republic unleashed its "true evil" against the Spanish Church. The Republic's Constitution, the dissolution of the Society of Jesus, and finally the debate surrounding the Law of Confessions and Religious Congregations had each attacked the structure of the Catholic Church.

Protests, religious debates, and formal meetings had been unable to persuade the Republic to abandon its campaign to weaken the place of religion in Spanish society.[77] In Tedeschini's view, the previous year in Spain had been disastrous for the Church, but with the debate of the Law of Confessions and Religious Congregations, the situation had become even worse. This law was the final straw for the Church, and Tedeschini argued, "I want to issue an especially more forceful protest about the forthcoming law of the Confessions and Religious Congregations."[78]

It was not only Tedeschini who expressed anger against the Second Republic's attacks on the Church's rights. Parent groups in Spain also expressed concern about the effects that the Law of Religious Confessions and Congregations would have on the lives of children in schools. In December 1932, an archetypical conservative parents' organization, the *Reunión de Padres Provinciales de España* [Meeting of Provincial Parents of Spain], protested the actions of the Republican educational system, calling the situation of Spanish schools "poor and full of pessimism."[79] A report denounced the destruction of the moral influence of the Catholic Church in its mission to educate Spain's children as well as the perceived influence of communism within the state and schools, alleged the Republican schools had been receiving "Soviet Instructions" on how to create class warfare in the schools.[80] This parenting organization, which obviously supported the Catholic Church, believed that the lack of Catholic education in Spanish schools and society would destroy Spain's foundations. Just like the Catholic Press in 1931, this parenting group believed the state allowed communists to replace the Church in schools, thereby corrupting children, especially those in working-class families.[81] They believed Catholic education was the only way to prevent working-class families from being infected by communism.

After months of debate, President Azaña signed The *Ley de Confesiones y Congregaciones Religiosas* on 2 June 1933. The next day, Pope Pius XI released the encyclical *Dilectissima Nobis*, clearly revealing that the Pope had been working on this encyclical for some time before the law was signed. An internal memo dated "1932" from the Sacra Congregazione degli Affari Ecclesiastici Straordinari (Holy Congregation of the Foreign Ecclesiastical Affairs) reads:

> An encyclical on the religious condition of Spain (a) would be very ample because it would remind many of the very grave violation of the laws of the Church and of the mind: (b) it would seem rather delayed after so much injustice accomplished by the new government of Spain: (c) given the solemnity of the document, is more likely due to a feeling of persecution.
>
> In another way, it seems to be able to affirm the necessity that the Holy See makes its voice public. It could perhaps take occasion from

the new law on the religious congregations to elevate a public form of protest.

By noting that in the new law there is, more or less, content very grave and wrong and the very enormous pretenses of the State already established in the Constitution.

(1) Article 1 remembers the Constitution and the freedom of belief,

(2) Article 2 remembers the separation of the State from the Church,

(3) The law is inspired by the concept of total supremacy of the State over the Church: the State makes available the items and the sacred persons without limitation: it will state the public ownership of churches, episcopates, seminaries, monasteries, works of art,

(4) It prohibits the religious from teaching, assuming the protection of the treacherous.

Scheme for the encyclical.

Beginning: Speak of regret, of the afflicted manner of Spain, exhortation to prayers.

Pretrial: The Church is not the enemy of any form of government. Rather the same Church is the better help for conserving order and peace. Depolarization of the violence committed against the items and holy persons and of the constitutional disposition averse to God and to the religion.

In particular deploring:

(a) the separation of the Church from the State and the shape that the separation wants to give,

(b) the suppression of the benefits deserved to the clergy by law,

(c) the suppression of the Society of Jesus with a motivation that offends the same vicar of Christ,

(d) the limitations made on the religious orders, especially with the prohibition of teaching,

(e) the disposition against the holiness of marriage.

It concludes by urging people to use legitimate means to change the constitution, to remain agreed, to boost Catholic Action, to persevere in prayers.[82]

This memo reveals the diplomatic concerns of the Holy See regarding Spain. First, the Pope and the Holy See did not wait until the law had been signed, but paid close attention to "anticlerical" action in the Republic and prepared to offer a quick response. The memo also expressed the concerns of the Holy See not only regarding the Law of Confessions and Religious Congregations but the government of the Republic itself. It was, however, the formulation of the Law of Confessions and Religious Congregations that sparked this response. The memo contained complaints about previous issues, such as the separation of Church and State, the creation of secular marriage, and the expulsion of the Jesuits.

But the Holy See did not formally respond to these issues *until* this law appeared ready to be passed. Most importantly, though, the Holy See had decided to make its first public and formal protest to the entire Catholic world after nearly two years of perceived attacks by the Republic.

In its introduction, the encyclical states that Catholics had not failed in their defense of the Church, but this note needs "to point out often to the present Government of Spain how false was the way they followed."[83] The encyclical, therefore, was not a total condemnation of the Spanish Republic, but a commentary on the poor choices of the government in relationship to the Catholic Church. The primary Spanish law that was mentioned as a problem was the Law of Confessions and Religious Congregations, which was described as "a new and grave offense not only to Religion and the Church, but also to those declared principles of civil liberty on which the new Spanish regime declares itself based."[84] The Pope questioned the Republic's willingness to protect collective rights, not only individual rights. In order to justify his claims, the Pope asserted that the Holy See and Catholic Church had worked with the Republic to "maintain order and social tranquility" by recognizing the legitimacy of the government.[85] Therefore, the Republic needed to respect Church rights in Spain. The encyclical goes on to discuss the disrespect shown by secularizing schools, expelling the Jesuits, legalizing divorce, and allowing for civil burials. One of the more rousing comments in the encyclical reads "The more the enemies of the Church seek to alienate people from the Vicar of Christ, the more affectionately the latter, through the providential disposition of God, Who knows how to bring good out of evil, draw closer to Him, proclaiming that from Him alone is radiated that light which illuminates the way darkened by so many perturbations..."[86] For the devout Catholic, this statement can be interpreted as encouragement for their beliefs and Papal support for their struggle against secularism. Anticlericals, however, interpreted this statement as a threat against the safety of the Republic. If interpreted as a threat, how would the Holy See try to make it come true? The Pope wrote, "We have sent to heaven fervent prayers asking God to pardon the offenses against Him. He, Who may fully illumine the minds, rectify the wills, and turn the hearts of the rulers to better advice."[87] The Holy See prayed for change—which was completely understandable. However, by stating that the Republican leaders needed "better advice," the Pope challenged the political sagacity of the Republic. He did not call for earthly revolution, but for spiritual understanding. So even though this appeared benign, Republicans could still claim that praying to change the minds of the Republican leadership was praying for the end of the Republic. Who should give the Republican leadership advice on governing Spain? The Holy See? Staunch Republicans could accuse the Holy See of trying to interfere in state affairs, making the Catholic Church a greater threat to the government. The Pope called for moderation in the Republic's actions towards the Church, but individual interpretations of the message varied.

Pope Pius XI made the *Dilectissima Nobis* public on 3 June 1933. The Spanish Republic, according to Papal Nuncio Tedeschini, had heard the complaints and concerns of the Holy See through his own words via personal meetings with Spanish leaders, but now the Catholic Church informed the Catholic world of the "problems" in Spain. Religious leaders in Spain, like Tedeschini and Monsignor Giuseppe Pizzardo, had the opportunity to review the Spanish draft of the *Dilectissima Nobis* and commented on the "beautiful and important words" that it contained.[88] Once Tedeschini announced to the Holy See that the Law of Confessions and Religious Congregations was about to be signed, Pacelli released a communication to Tedeschini on 2 June that an Italian newspaper had published evidence that the law had been signed in Spain, and the encyclical would be included in *L'Osservatore Romano* the very next day.[89] The Holy See made its first public and worldwide condemnation of the actions of the new Spanish Government with mixed results.

The Holy See followed closely the responses to its first encyclical concerning Spain. According to Tedeschini, in the days after its release in Spain, the faithful responded positively, as many Spaniards liked the formal Vatican response.[90] Tedeschini noted that positive news had come in from Madrid, San Sebastian, and other locations throughout the country. Not everyone though responded favorably. Radical Socialist Member of Parliament, Ruiz del Río e Vargas called the Pope's actions a "seditious protests of the Holy See and the Spanish Episcopate, with the coercion and threats of the organs of the press of the extreme right and the propaganda of the reactionary parties, supporting actions of rebellion and disobedience in connection with the Law of Confessions and Religious Congregations."[91] Ruiz del Rio e Vargas's claim that the Holy See and Catholic Church actively worked to undermine the Republic might have led to further anger against the Church in radical and Leftist circles. In the same letter, Tedeschini noted that the use of the word "seditious" was based on a "phobia" of the Church that still existed within the Republican Government.[92] The Spanish Catholic periodical *Cruz y Raya*, which had a more liberal view of the world than *La Civiltà Cattolica* or *L'Osservatore Romano*, contained an unsigned editorial critical of the Law of Confessions and Religious Congregations after the publication of the encyclical. Even with its more liberal stance, the periodical agreed that the actions of the Spanish Republic, through Article 26 of the Constitution and the Law of Confessions and Religious Congregations, had become too hostile towards the Church and it initiated "New aggressions to liberty."[93]

The dividing lines between those supporting the more radical views of the Second Republic and those supporting the Holy See had been increasingly defined, potentially affecting the future relationship between the two entities. Ultimately, the passage of the Law of Confessions and Religious Congregations, along with the Papal response of the *Dilectissima Nobis*, can be seen as galvanizing forces for the political left and right. The faithful had finally received what they wanted, a message from the Pope regarding Spanish Catholic privilege. Radical Socialists, however, perceived this encyclical as proof the Holy See was trying to undermine Republican modernization and secularization.

The Pope's encyclical did not just create reaction in Spain, but it reached a worldwide audience. On 9 July 1933, Bishop John McNicholas of Cincinnati wrote the Holy See to express the concerns of Cincinnati Bishop Noll, who had suggested that American Catholics make it a point to support the Pope and his encyclical. Noll wanted to send a cable to the Spanish President Manuel Azaña or the American ambassador H. Freeman Matthews in Spain to announce the protest of "2,000,000 Catholics" against the actions of the Republic towards the Catholic Church.[94] McNicholas asked if the Holy See would send some reply as to what actions could or should be taken, but he expected that the Holy Father would not be sending a direct message.[95] The 14 July response from the office of the Vatican Secretary of State read "His Holiness highly appreciates the attitudes of the Hierarchy of America with regard to the persecution in Spain, which causes His Holiness so much sorrow and anxiety, but in the existing circumstances the Holy See does not deem the action suggested advisable: while fully appreciating the spirit which prompts it."[96] The encyclical appeared to have done its job as it had awakened an interest about the concerns in Spain, both for Spaniards and others, but the Holy See would not take another formal and public action against the Republic. The Holy See clearly wanted to avoid further confrontations with the Republican Government because it could continue to strain the relationship between Republicans and Catholics. The protest had been made, but more action was not requested from outsiders. The Holy See's concerns in Spain had moved from the back page to the front page for Catholics in the world. At the same time, once words like "seditious" were used against the Catholic Church, the Holy See may have considered further commentary to be dangerous—as it would affect the future relationship between the Catholic Church and the Republican Government.

FINAL THOUGHTS ON THE REPUBLIC'S NEW LAWS

The founding of the Second Spanish Republic brought forth numerous possibilities. While the rest of Europe had begun to succumb to radical political extremes, it seemed that Spain might follow a path of calm and liberal democracy. The Republic, though, brought both hope and confusion. Debates about the legitimacy of the Republic's declaration haunted the Provisional Government. The Russian Provisional Government of 1917 remained aloof and indecisive, resulting in the Soviet overthrow; maybe the Spanish had learned a lesson about consolidating authority? The Republic learned to act quickly and forcefully to protect itself. The Second Republic drafted a constitution meant to guarantee rights that had not existed under the monarchy, but in order to do so it would have to weaken the pillars of the monarchy, such as the Church. Indeed, the Republic had not intended to destroy completely the Catholic Church, which Frances Lannon and William J. Callahan acknowledge would be next to impossible, but the secular Republic had hoped to "constrain" it. After all, any attempt to affect the status of Catholicism in Spain, however, was never going to be simple, and some form of reactionary response should have been expected.

The tense relationship between the Holy See and the first government of the Second Republic can be summed up with a discussion of the Holy See's desires to confirm the Concordat signed in 1851. The 1851 Concordat signed between the Holy See and Queen Isabel II's government deemed Roman Catholicism as the only legal religion in Spain, granted the Church control over the educational system and powerful influence over the press. Months later, the Concordat was strengthened by additions to the Spanish legal codes to prevent the spread of Protestantism in the state. The Republic responded that the Concordat had been signed with a monarchical government, and therefore, was not valid once the national sovereignty changed hands—something the Holy See had previously acknowledged.[97] Pacelli answered that the Holy Father wanted Tedeschini to remind the Republic that another agreement had been signed between the two states in 1921.[98] The Holy See referenced the Concordat of 1851 on 30 June 1932 as a reason why the Republic must not sign laws reducing the rights of Catholics.[99] During the debate over the Law of Confessions and Religious Congregations, Tedeschini suggested a new Concordat with the Republic to protect the Church's rights, but the First Government of the Second Republic never agreed to work on such a document.[100] The Holy See believed that it had a special and historical position within Spain and that it deserved a special level of respect. However, the Republic did not acknowledge the Church's historical position in Spain and rejected previous agreements.

What the Republic saw as reasonable pieces of legislation, the Papal Nuncio and the Spanish Catholic Hierarchy saw as direct attacks against the Catholic Church's sovereignty and power in Spain. Aware of the actions of the Republic, the Holy See viewed many of these laws as problematic, and at first relied on meetings between the Papal Nuncio and the

Republican Ministers as a means to introduce its apprehensions. Made aware of these concerns, the Republic did not agree with the Church's attitude. The Holy See remained officially silent on the political matters of Spain, but constant legal changes in Spain posed difficult for the Vatican. Not only was the Constitution a problem, but so too was the Law of the Defense of the Republic, the changing of the legal codes for marriage and burial, and finally, the Law of Confessions and Religious Congregations. The Second Republic may not have considered its legislation divisive, but these issues ultimately led the Holy See to respond with the encyclical *Dilectissima Nobis* in June 1933.[101]

For the Republic, the main problem was Spain's nineteenth-century tradition of clerical and anticlerical political disputes, which almost forced the Government to act in a brash manner when trying to subdue religio-political animosities. The Republic and the Vatican had two separate world-views regarding politics and Catholic privilege. With the publication of that encyclical, the Second Republic and the world became publicly and formally aware of the Pope's concerns. Although the Vatican did not push for more aggressive actions from its supporters, the lines had been drawn. Unlike previous decades, when stern reactions from the Holy See or the Spanish Catholic clergy had persuaded Spanish Governments to soften their liberalization policies regarding religious authority, the Second Republic refused to succumb to such pressures. The Republic was not afraid to call the Vatican "seditious"—even though Catholicism had influenced Spanish politics for centuries. The Holy See could either speak out as an "enemy of the Republic," or suffer silently as the new regime stripped its privileges even further. It found neither option completely acceptable. Was allowing non-Catholics safe burial inside maintained cemeteries reasonable? Yes, but was it also reasonable to take ownership of cemeteries away from the Church? That question is much more difficult to answer. The Republican leadership, especially men like Manuel Azaña, was not afraid to challenge the Catholic Church, even if it meant creating strong enemies. As a result, decisive Republican actions resulted in Catholic anxiety. Consequently, as the Second Republic edged closer to civil war in the following years, the divide between the Holy See and the Leftists in the Second Republic became more and more visible. Was the Second Republic concerned that it could never regain any favor from the Holy See, or was the Holy See trying to become clearer about its views in an ideologically divisive era? These questions may not be answerable in a finite manner, but they express the underlying concerns of the two sides and may help to explore the relationship between these two entities during the Civil War.

III

Republican Reorganizations

Elections of 1933 and 1939

The Vatican hierarchy's opinion of the Second Spanish Republic shifted following national elections in 1933 and 1936. The Church appeared more sympathetic to the politics and actions of the Spanish right—or even middle—over the Spanish left during these electoral cycles. The hierarchy worried Manual Azaña's Republican Government failed to protect the Catholic Church, and the hierarchy welcomed the creation of a rightist coalition that could defeat the left. Following the 1933 elections, the Catholic hierarchy supported Alejandro Lerroux's centrist Radical Government (and its conservative allies), and the Church seemed to care about the Republic's survival. The Vatican hierarchy openly feared the development of the leftist Popular Front, and the Church worked to undermine the coalition's chances in 1936, but to no avail. The Catholic hierarchy in Spain believed the political right shared its values, but the Church understood the left as a continuation of political and physical threats against it. The Holy See would view the centrist Radical Party as a political archetype for the rest of Europe—a pro-Catholic and anti-pagan regime, yet the Church viewed the Popular Front of 1936 as the antithesis of the Republic they hoped to see.

The Holy See clearly understood that Spain's political instability would lead to a violent uprising, and soon events like the 1934 Asturias Revolution and 1936 military "*Alzamiento*" exposed the Republic's chaotic existence. In November 1933, the Spanish electorate voted for a new national government. From the declaration of the Second Republic in April 1931 until these elections, a secular and left-leaning government ruled Spain and initiated constitutional acts and legislative actions under the premise of creating an egalitarian state with rights for all citizens. As discussed in Chapter 2, while Manuel Azaña's government believed its actions were justified and beneficial, conservative Spaniards found the state's actions too secular and too radical. The Constitutional Convention of June 1931 and the Azaña government focused on secularizing the state and removing the historical privileges once enjoyed by the Catholic hierarchy. For conservatives, these acts were dangerous and needed to be stopped and reversed—a government of the right could change the Church's fortunes. The Vatican hierarchy regarded this first government as disastrous and its sole intent seemed to be to destroy Catholicism in Spain.

This chapter investigates the Vatican hierarchy's reactions to the 1933 centrist Radical and 1936 Popular Front Governments. First, this research explores the Vatican hierarchy's responses to the defeat of the political left and the legislative agreement allowing Alejandro Lerroux and his centrist Radical Party to rule the Second Republic from 1933–36. The *Confederación Española de Derechas Autónomas* (Spanish Confederation of Autonomous Rights, CEDA) of José María Gil Robles won the elections, but leftist threats against the state combined with the right's political inexperience prevented them from obtaining power. The Vatican welcomed the defeat of the Socialists, Radical Socialists, and Communists, and placed hope in Lerroux to stabilize the state and restore Catholic privileges. Lerroux's government, however, was unable to make serious changes or return civility to the Spanish political process and numerous problems followed: Socialists pressured for governmental inclusion, Lerroux's decision to remove Socialists and replace them with conservative members of CEDA, political corruption, and the growing revolutionary sentiment in working class regions like Asturias coupled with regionalist violence in Cataluña and País Vasco all threatened the government's stability. These challenges to Lerroux's coalition weakened the center's authority and the Vatican grew more concerned about the future of Spain.

This chapter will next investigate the period surrounding the 1936 elections. The political influence of the center had eroded, and the right and left grew more radical in their demands. The Catholic Church feared the new Popular Front coalition—a unification of all parties of the political left, including communists and socialists, created to defeat the growing rise of fascism in all European countries. The Vatican worried the Popular Front would succumb to communist influence, and the Church would again be attacked. Following the Popular Front victory in February 1936, Spain descended further into chaos and political violence. In 1936, 1108 strikes occurred in Spain, with the vast majority coming after April. CEDA politician and staunch conservative, José María Gil Robles, publicly claimed that from 15 February-15 June, 269 people were assassinated, 1287 were injured in political violence, 160 churches were destroyed, and 251 churches were damaged.[1] On 2 July, leftists attacked a Falange bar in Madrid, killing two. The following day, rightists attacked the working-class neighborhood of Casa del Pueblo, also killing two. Police found the bodies of two Falange allies the next day. Socialist and assault guard commander José del Castillo was assassinated on 12 July, and the government ordered the arrest of José Calvo Sotelo—the rightist leader of the political opposition, who was murdered on the night of 13 July, making him the highest-ranking political official killed during the Second Republic. The murder of a major political figure was a serious attack on the Republic's ability to function.[2] This section will explore the Vatican hierarchy's concerns about the Popular Front victory as well as the growing threat of a civil war. The Vatican and its representatives understood the political stalemates and political violence of the Second Republic as a sign of impending collapse, but they were uncertain which side—the right or the left—would overthrow the government.

A Review of Spain's Political Conditions

The Provisional and First Republican Governments redefined Spain as a secular state for the first time in modern history. To obtain this goal, the government initiated a series of legislative actions—based on the newly approved 1931 Constitution—directed at reducing the public and political influence of traditional elements in the state, particularly the Catholic Church.[3] Leftist Republicans viewed these actions as necessary to provide greater rights to their countrymen by reducing the dominance of large landowners, the military, monarchists, and the Church. Conservative Spaniards, however, viewed these changes as unacceptable, and inferred that communism and Bolshevism interfered with Republican politics. As shown in the previous chapter, Papal Representatives in Spain viewed the Republic's actions as direct assaults against the Spanish Catholic Church's ability to practice freely and maintain authority over social behaviors, even though many new laws were targeted at opening the Spanish electoral system for greater involvement. The growing pressures from the Republic, especially regarding the Law of Confessions and Religious Congregations, inspired Pope Pius XI to release the encyclical, *Dilectissima Nobis*, in June 1933. The Vatican hierarchy hoped the encyclical would inspire the Republic to moderate, but this was not the case.

Even though this left-leaning government succeeded in establishing a liberal and secular state through its Constitution, in-fighting and political disagreements by the left about Spain's future weakened its alliance. Schisms in the leftist coalition began as early as the summer of 1932. By the 23 April 1933 municipal elections, the left coalition only won 5,048 seats of the approximately 19,000 available. Rightist parties won about the same number of seats, and center Republicans—not in the ruling coalition—won over 6,000. In the summer of 1933, the Socialist Party began to move away from some of the radical principles of the Radical Socialists. The last major problem for the coalition was a three-way split of the Radical Socialist party, which led to serious in-fighting and the inevitable end to the ruling coalition's stability.[4] As the left reeled from internal turmoil, the political right consolidated. Many right-leaning political organizations—conservatives, monarchists, land-owners, Agrarians, military, and Catholic organizations—came together in the hopes of defeating the left. The most successful movement was CEDA, founded in February 1933. According to Stanley Payne, the language of Catholicism had a major influence in CEDA, persuading large numbers of women to join the movement—approximately forty-five percent of the group's membership.[5] While CEDA did not explicitly define many of its goals, the coalition supported the idea of a corporatist Catholic Republic in Spain. CEDA did not officially call for the termination of the Republic, but the organization believed Catholic influence should replace radical revolutionary politics and workers' unions in order to restore civility and tradition in Spain.[6] CEDA saw Catholicism's influence as both historical and beneficial for the Spanish state and the coalition opposed secularizing of the Republic.[7] CEDA was the first mass conservative coalition in Spain, allowing the unified Right to participate in the Republican political structure.[8]

The dismantling of the leftist coalition and the growth of CEDA initiated a new political atmosphere in Spain. In the November 1933 Cortes elections, the CEDA coalition and its allies won the most votes, followed by the centrist Radical Party, while parties of the left suffered the greatest losses.[9] The majority of the Spanish electorate had moved away from the political left to parties of the center and center-right. The failures of the political left to mobilize and cooperate along with CEDA's ability to capture Catholic middle-class and northern voters who wanted to slow radicalization in Spain created a Cedista victory.[10] Manuel Álvarez Tardío suggests CEDA understood that Catholics needed to participate in the Republican political system, but CEDA did not have a clear plan as to what they stood for or how they would govern.[11] The Revolutionary left, Socialists, and Left Republicans combined for only 99 Cortes seats, the Radicals earned 176 seats, and the Moderate and Extreme Right combines for 198 seats.[12] The political left feared that a CEDA Government would attempt to undo the changes made in the first period. Radical leftists considered the Republic as their creation, and they swore violent action if the right obtained power. Álvarez Tardío suggests the losers needed to admit and understand that they actually lost.[13] The President of the Republic, Niceto Alcalá Zamora, persuaded CEDA to allow Lerroux to form a new government, trying to save the Republic from leftist calls for overthrow.[14] The hope was Lerroux would be a political compromise and the Radical Party attempted to form a government that would stabilize the state by acting in the political middle.[15] The Radicals hoped to incorporate Catholics into the Republican governmental structure, which would help to legitimize this form of government for more Spaniards.[16] The Radicals promised to uphold the successful advancements of the Republic, while trying to correct any "abuses" that had occurred during its first period. CEDA and conservatives did gain from the political compromise with Lerroux as the new government ignored the *Ley de Confesiones y Congregaciones Religiosas*, again allowing members of the clergy to educate Spanish children while the state undertook the construction of more public schools (a possible compromise for both extremes).[17] The new government tried to improve the relationship with the Vatican by discussing the possibilities of a new Concordat, agreeing to pay the salaries of priests, and allowing Holy Week to be celebrated publicly in Sevilla.[18] The Radical Government of Lerroux hoped to create a middle ground between the two political extremes in Spain, but the political atmosphere continued to grow extremely toxic as compromises lessened.[19]

Even though the political left had not won the election of 1933, it did not mean their ideological beliefs simply disappeared from Spanish society. Some leftists, especially Radical Socialist, Communist, and Anarchist political organizations and unions increased their activities in Spanish factories, agricultural regions, and on the streets over the months following June 1933. Nigel Townson explains that the political left could not trust this new Republican government of the middle as "Central to the socialists' rejection of the Republic and of the republicans was the conviction that the Radical Party was a 'reactionary' force that would dismantle the reformist achievements of the first biennium."[20] As unemployment increased,[21] violence and protests against the government grew. Numerous forces worked to undermine the centrist government. According to Paul Preston's 1975 study, CEDA had decided to work within the Republican political structure in order to destroy the Republican system. Preston asserts that CEDA forced the Radical Government to bow to conservative pressures. The leader of CEDA, José María Gil Robles, convinced President Alejandro Lerroux to remove three liberal Republicans from their Ministry posts in March 1934— Diego Martínez Barrio (Interior), Antonio Lara (Finance), and Pareja Yébenes (Education).[22] Due to a restructuring of the government, Gil Robles convinced Lerroux to add three *Cedistas* to the list of Ministers— José Oriol Anguera de Sojo (Labor), Rafael Aizpún (Justice), and Manuel Giménez Fernández (Agriculture).[23] The Ministers of Labor and Agriculture greatly influenced peasants' and workers' concerns, and they worked to undermine previously passed legislation for land reform and wage increases. These three posts were very important to the political left and its relationship with the working classes, and they had now been handed to the right. For Preston, CEDA had initiated a "Trojan Horse" plan to infiltrate the government and take apart the Republican structure from the inside.

While CEDA had plans to dismantle Republican stability, they were not the only group that worked to weaken the state. In reality, CEDA and its allies had legitimately won the elections of November 1933. Manuel Álvarez Tardío suggests that CEDA was never a serious threat to overthrow the government as it seemed to understand that the monarchy was never going to be restored, the electoral process was useful, the corporativist system presented was ambiguous, and their organization contained a wide spectrum of views that presented internal issues.[24] Leading to the elections, however, Radical Socialist leaders and communists, like Socialist Francisco Largo Caballero, initiated a campaign to prevent a conservative victory. His speeches often contained warnings of a fascist take-over in Spain and called for violence against *Cedistas*. These actions agitated workers' unions and the poor by delegitimizing the political right.[25] Following CEDA's victory, Largo Caballero spoke of a new fight against the government *and* the Republic. Once radical leftist parties saw the possibility that their legislation could be undermined, some decided to act forcefully.[26] Largo Caballero believed the Republic had allowed the "enemy" to gain power and had undermined the state.[27] He made comparisons to the Russian Revolution of 1917—hoping to create an atmosphere of more radical revolution and extremism. Largo Caballero and his supporters spread this message of revolution throughout Spain during the summer and fall of 1934, radicalizing the left. When Lerroux added the three *Cedistas* to Minister Posts in October 1934, radical leftists viewed this as a sign the government should be overthrown. CEDA deserved *some* representatives in the government—if not the right to govern completely, but they had agreed to relinquish power. Both the extreme political right and extreme political left undermined the authority and stability of the Republic, and both sides bear responsibility for its overthrow.

The leftist anger against the government and its ministerial changes manifested in a period known as "Red October" or the "Revolution of Asturias."[28] The socialist workers' union UGT (*Unión General de Trabajadores* or General Union of Workers) joined with the anarchist union CNT (*Confederación Nacional del Trabajo* or National Confederation of Labor) in a series of planned major national strikes against the government. Initially, the left planned for a full revolution throughout Spain to overthrow the government,[29] but the events remained most active in Asturias. On 4–5 October 1934, union members and their supporters led revolts in the mining region of Asturias, forcibly occupying towns with their militias and targeting Church property and clergy as supporters of conservatism. William Callahan asserts that the action "differed from earlier anticlerical outbursts by identifying the Church not only as a secondary ally of conservative interests but also as a primary symbol of opposition to economic and social change, one that took concrete form in every town or village possessed of a parish church or other religious and educational institutions."[30] At that point, the national government needed to call in the army to put down the uprising. In the following weeks, the army managed to subdue the revolts, but not without hundreds of fatalities. Estimates suggest 1,200 rebels died along with 450 members of the police and army.[31] For months to follow, stories of this violence resonated in Spain. The state also quashed revolutionary activity that affected regions with high levels of autonomous sentiments like Cataluña and País Vasco. CEDA leader, José María Gil Robles, demanded serious force be used to put down this rebellion, and conservatives demanded the Army of Africa,[32] which was Spain's most violent military section, be used.[33] For Paul Preston, the use of the Army of Africa was a sign the political right wanted to use the military to destroy the left, and Francisco Franco was the perfect candidate to lead such an action.[34] Supporters of the left viewed the military's and government's actions as unacceptable, and the right identified these actions as proof of the threat of communism/anarchism and as a reason to delegitimize the left. As Gabriel Jackson explains, the period of the Asturian Revolution and its aftermath represented a breaking point for the Republic, as political organizations of the right and left, fanaticism, and violence laid the groundwork for the Civil War.[35] Whereas José M. Sánchez identified modern Spain's historical divide between clericals and anticlericals as the main cause for the Spanish Civil War, Jackson points to the Revolution in Asturias and its aftermath as the evidence that a major conflict was the only possible outcome.[36] Both historians, however, agree that the Spanish political divide grew insurmountable with war as the only logical outcome. After this revolution in Asturias and subsequent military action, the left and right became polarized and crystallized.

Politically speaking, the Radical Government of Lerroux accomplished few changes to the Spanish Government. Suggestions of constitutional reform, particularly relating to Article 26 were announced, but they did not come to fruition. Lerroux's government failed to make substantial changes to the Spanish Republic in 1935. The government twice tried to change censorship laws in February and May, but the constant divide between defending civil rights versus weakening radical politics remained insurmountable. Leftist parties actively worked to undermine any attempts by CEDA Ministers to create new legislation and a wave of political and financial scandals occurred during the end of the year. With this backdrop, Lerroux or the CEDA majority were unable to pass any serious legislation or economic reform, which was badly needed. The left dubbed this governmental period the *bieno negro* (black biennium), and claimed Lerroux and CEDA had destroyed reformist legislations, but in fact, "none of the major Republican reforms were annulled by law, except the drastic reduction of what had never been a very extensive agrarian reform."[37] Overall, the radicalization of the political left and political right, combined with the lack of support for the Radicals, pushed the government to collapse at the start of 1936.

The CEDA electoral victory of 1933 and attempt to reform the Republic did spark a shift in the attitude of the political left. Liberals, socialists, and communists acknowledged that their fracturing in 1933 allowed CEDA to win the election.[38] To reestablish their political influence, leftist groups unified under the banner of the Popular Front (*Frente Popular*), like the political left in France.[39] Supporters of the left believed this unification was reasonable in order to defend Spain from conservatism and fascism, but conservatives viewed the Popular Front as nothing more than a puppet from Moscow, even though the communist party in Spain remained generally small and not influential until the start of the Civil War.[40] Gabriele Ranzato asserts that the Spanish version of the Popular Front did choose to align itself with more radical views, pushing away moderate viewpoints after their victory.[41] In the February 1936 election, the Popular Front garnered a slim victory in votes cast, but due to the Spanish electoral system, they earned a majority in the Cortes.[42] The results were highly contentious, as claims of voter fraud occurred, and a full recount was never officially completed. Once in power, the government of Manuel Azaña attempted to reinstitute the radical reforms promised during the first period. On the left, radical supporters viewed this victory as the return of social change and some allies initiated a new series of violent attacks against symbols of conservatism. Similarly, supporters of the radical right initiated violent attacks against supporters of the Republic.[43] The violence in Spain had reached a critical level with the state unable to regain control. It appeared that a larger and more violent conflict was the only possible end to the Republican crisis. The political and social pendulum in Spain began to swing more violently, leading to a Civil War.

The Radicals Inherit the Government

By the summer of 1933, Manuel Azaña's coalition of the left began to crumble. Radical leftist parties demanded greater social reform, while parties in the political middle preferred a slower pace. By August, the Azaña government was ready to fall, as votes of no confidence and judicial setbacks doomed his authority. By September 1933, President Alcalá Zamora negotiated the resignation of Azaña and the formation of a government by Alejandro Lerroux and the centrist Radical Party.[44] Although the Holy See and the Catholic Church would prefer the CEDA coalition as leaders in Spain, the center Radical party was still a better option than the radical left. On 10 September 1933, following the collapse of Azaña's government and two months before the election, the liberal Catalan Cardinal Archbishop of Tarragona,[45] Vidal i Barraquer wrote to Cardinal Pacelli to discuss the most-likely outcome of the upcoming elections, acknowledging that President of the Republic Alcalá-Zamora would be much more willing to accept the possibility of a new leader other than the radical Azaña: "It would seem that the President of the Republic was not in favor of the behavior of the Azaña Government and its allies, and by revealing the conflicts that will be caused by the application of the secularization laws and the difficulties of a sectarian policy of religious persecution, I sent to him copies of the communications directed to the President of the Council, signed by the Cardinals."[46] Vidal i Barraquer believed that Alcalá Zamora, who had the power to nominate the Prime Minister of Spain, would choose anyone other than radical leftist supporters of Manuel Azaña. The news that the moderate and Catholic President would work to move Spain away from the radical left must have been refreshing for the Spanish Catholic Church and its allies. At the same time, this language shows that the Archbishop viewed Alcalá Zamora as a stabilizing factor in politics and that the Republic could be saved.

Vidal i Barraquer continued to discuss the possible electoral results and placed his hopes in Radical leader Alejandro Lerroux: "Lerroux is a secular man, but not sectarian like some of his party. I believe he will have a more tolerant criterion, and if he convokes the new elections and elements of his party and of the center win, we can expect an understanding with the Holy See."[47] The Archbishop believed Lerroux would be a calming influence for Spain. Azaña's Cortes majority had collapsed, and the November elections would change the country. Vidal continued, "In conclusion, the Church is going to win something with the change."[48] The Archbishop believed that this next election cycle would succeed in changing Spain. Interestingly, Vidal put his faith in Alejandro Lerroux as the man who could change the country, even though his allies might not have been trustworthy. As a political moderate, it makes sense that Vidal i Barraquer chose the political middle rather than the right-wing CEDA coalition. Frank Coppa has suggested Pius XI grew suspicious of radical right parties in Europe, such as the German National Socialists, and it made sense for some Catholic leaders to avoid fully supporting the radical right.[49] At the same time, because the Archbishop was Catalan and represented the Catholic Church in Cataluña, he supported a political leader who did not speak out against regionalism. After the November 1933 elections, extreme right-wing members of the Cortes (most in CEDA) supported legislation that would "temporarily suspend" Catalan autonomy for fears the region had become too radicalized and was not working with the central government. The Bill was eventually defeated, but CEDA representatives began to introduce small anti-autonomy bills in the Cortes for months to follow.[50] Lerroux was the least of all evils; he was not sectarian or atheistic like the political left and he did not speak of removing important autonomy rights like the *Cedistas*. The Archbishop's letter clearly supported the leadership of Alejandro Lerroux, and he sought to gain Vatican support, or at least acceptance for the political leader.

On 12 September 1933, Alejandro Lerroux announced the formation of his new government, which had been negotiated following the failures of the Azaña coalition. Lerroux wanted to nominate a completely Radical cabinet, but this was not possible, as the left demanded positions until elections could be called.[51] Still, the Radical Party held its largest percentage of Ministerial posts in the government. Nuncio Tedeschini, however, did not completely welcome these new Ministers, as some of them were deemed "Mason," casting particular suspicion on Interior Minister Diego Martínez Barrio, who had risen in the ranks of the Spanish Masons.[52] Due to this connection, Tedeschini suggested that the new Lerroux government could not be trusted completely and he was uncertain if the government would make any changes.[53]

On 22 September, the National Catholic Welfare Conference (USA) Legal Department Director William F. Montavon compiled a report regarding the new Lerroux government and sent the information directly to the Holy See stating, "The government which Alejandro Lerroux formed in Spain this week may be expected to be as hostile to Catholic interests as was the Azaña cabinet which it succeeded."[54] While only a lay Catholic report, this foreign reaction to Lerroux's government was clearly aimed at provoking the Vatican to form a greater association with the political right. According to Montavon, the largest threat for Catholic interests in Spain continued to be the secularization process in the Spanish public schools: "There is no reason to expect that the new government will fail to go ahead with the program of Laicism which involves the suppression of teaching by religious Orders and the prohibition of religious instruction in all schools. Indeed, while the Constitution was under discussion the Radical Socialists deemed complete laicism in all schools under a state monopoly and marched in a body out of the Cortes in protest when the article was defeated."[55] While Archbishop Vidal i Barraquer viewed the possibility of a Lerroux government as a success for the Second Republic, other religious leaders and organizations believed the Lerroux government was too willing to follow Azaña's path. On 15 October, Nuncio Tedeschini wrote Pacelli to outline further problems with the new government. Lerroux had been unable and/or unwilling to stand up to the Cortes and make any serious changes to the state in order to improve the condition of the Catholic Church.[56] For the Nuncio, the Cortes continued to act aggressively, "The Cortes, the diabolical Cortes, that we have suffered for almost two and a half years, and that has carried out an incomparable and ferocious persecution, doesn't grant any person or reason in the world the possibility of being, let alone heard and satisfied, but not even admitted to dispute."[57] Tedeschini looked forward to the end of this "diabolical" Cortes, and hoped that new elections would finally change the direction of the Spanish state.

Vatican archival materials from 1931–1933 clearly show the hierarchy's discontent with the Republican government of Manuel Azaña, as it tried to persuade the regime to change or abate its anticlerical behavior, without avail. When it appeared that the Azaña government would collapse, some Catholics welcomed the possible formation of a centrist government of Alejandro Lerroux. The problem, however, was that the new government included Ministers of the radical left, like Diego Martínez Barrio. The threat of anticlericalism did not disappear with the fall of Azaña, and some in the Vatican hierarchy still harbored doubts. The Vatican must have wanted the removal of dangerous extreme political ideologies—most importantly communism—and the return to the traditional and influential role of the Catholic Church.

In November 1933 Spaniards voted in the second Parliamentary elections of the Second Republic. While the CEDA coalition and its allies won a majority, President Alcalá Zamora negotiated a compromise that would allow Alejandro Lerroux to form a centrist Radical Government. CEDA leader Gil Robles admitted that his coalition was not necessarily ready to govern. Therefore, Alcalá Zamora looked to the second largest winner to form the government. The Centrist Radical leadership had a history of corruption, but the large variety of political ideologies of its leaders made the party a possible calming force.[58] Radical leftist parties rejected a CEDA coalition government, and spoke out against that possibility, frequently promising violence if CEDA entered the government. Since the CEDA coalition was recently formed, and most likely not consolidated enough to form a complete government, the Radical Party appeared to be a reasonable compromise.[59] The problem was the Radical government failed to make substantial changes as the leftist groups threatened violence and retaliation.

The question of regionalism in Spain created serious concerns for the Holy See during the first year of the Lerroux Government. Following the death of Catalan President Francesc Macià on Christmas 1933, former Barcelona mayor Lluis Companys became leader of the Catalan Generalitat.[60] Companys did not share Macià's close relationship with the centrist President Alcalá Zamora. Cataluña had been a center of regionalist feelings in Spain for decades, and the Republic had allowed the Catalans greater autonomy over their own affairs. Autonomists in Cataluña, however, were not politically radical on either the left or the right, but all parties agreed to protect regionalism at all costs. While a center for industry, Cataluña also had a large agricultural sector. In April 1934, the Generalitat passed the *Llei de Contractes de Conreu* (Law of Cultivation Contracts) to help poor farmers access land. The Spanish Constitutional Courts ruled this law, and others concerning Catalan agriculture passed over the summer of 1934, as unconstitutional, creating conflict with Madrid.[61] Manuel Azaña could not resist becoming involved in this conflict in the summer of 1934, as he called Cataluña "the last bastion remaining to the Republic."[62] As this conflict between Barcelona and Madrid grew, so did the radicalization of certain agricultural and workers groups in Cataluña, sparking new class-based concerns for the Holy See.

Following the declaration of the Second Republic in 1931, Papal Nuncio Tedeschini wrote Pacelli to express his concerns about regionalism in Spain, as the historical demand for autonomy in various regions could become dangerous for the Church. During this 1934 conflict, Tedeschini again expressed alarm at the threat of an alliance between regionalists and socialists, and the effect it could have on the safety of the Catholic Church. Stronger, or even autonomous regional governments would force the Catholic Church to send other representatives to these regions, as well as force the Church to worry about radical political sentiments, hostile to the Church, that might develop in these regions. A strong central government meant the Church would be treated the same way throughout the country. On 12 September 1934, Tedeschini wrote to Pacelli about new regionalist concerns, stating the radical left "saw Cataluña as a fortified camp of resistance of the forces of the left."[63] When some in the Catalan leadership attempted to take greater regional control, the central government responded aggressively. This response angered many in Cataluña, pushing many away from the moderate regionalist feelings of 1931 to a more radical stance, startling the Catholic Church.

As the summer of 1934 was coming to a close, new regionalist concerns began in País Vasco in north-central Spain. New national regulations on wine taxation angered the Basque leadership, as they saw this new tariff as a direct attack on historically guaranteed regional rights. In response to this tax, some Basque leaders called for the first regional elections under the Second Republic. In the lead-up to those elections, parties of the political left attempted to form a pact with the *Partido Nacionalista Vasco* (Basque Nationalist Party, PNV), but the PNV rejected this possibility.[64] This fight over taxation and new elections created a reinvigorated regionalist problem for the Lerroux government. The PNV—which was Catholic and generally conservative—had been a moderate political party, but with the possibility of regionalist taxation threats, the party became increasingly cautious of the central government of the center-right. The Holy See became concerned as the devoutly Catholic Basque began to move away from the Centrist national government, and began joining forces with the political left, like in Cataluña.

Nuncio Tedeschini's 12 September letter continued with a discussion of the threats of regionalism and anticlericalism in País Vasco, as the Nuncio suggested that extreme leftist and regionalist parties and groups from Cataluña had begun influencing the politics in the Basque region. For the Spanish political right, this newfound connection was "*blasfemo impenitente*" [unrepentantly blasphemous] as this devoutly Catholic region was being influenced by outsiders and their anticlerical beliefs.[65] For the Catholic hierarchy, a closer connection between the Catalan left and the PNV could further threaten the Church's security. Tedeschini quoted an unnamed member of the Spanish Catholic hierarchy who viewed the PNV's alignment with the left as dangerous and feared "we will have in the Basque region a repetition of the painful situation of Cataluña. And that is the most painful point for the Church in the question at hand, also being equally painful the interference and even the initiative by the Clergy and the Religious in this eminently political and scandalously anti-Spanish issue."[66] The threat of anticlerical ideologies entering País Vasco was the next great problem the Catholic Church would have to overcome, "The regionalist question that will produce the next political crisis."[67] Once again, threats to the territorial or political integrity of the Spanish state posed serious problems for the Catholic Church's ability to have a singular and unified plan for dealing with Spain.

The growing pressures of regionalist violence, threats from the political left, and pressures from the CEDA coalition weakened Lerroux's ability to govern Spain. Beginning in September 1934, the northern region of Asturias experienced a violent outburst against the Republican Government led by small armed groups. According to the Nuncio, bombs had been exploding in Asturias and the government had seized a boat with weaponry before it could be unloaded.[68] In an attempt to strengthen his leadership, Lerroux included some members of the CEDA coalition in his list of Ministers, but in doing so, radical leftist organizations struck out against the government during October 1934. The Vatican received numerous reports form Nuncio Tedeschini in October explaining what had been occurring throughout Spain. According to the Nuncio, the growing pressure from Catalan regionalism was the final straw for Lerroux, pressuring the President of the Government to reorganize the new CEDA Ministers.[69]

In a report for the Holy See from 8 October 1934, Archbishop Vidal i Barraquer discussed the new organization of Lerroux's government, and he suggested that the Holy See should work to support the new Radical-CEDA leadership as it could "preserve the center-right policies . . . the ones that can provide better results for the Church with a patient and sagacious evolution that might lead to the moment of constitutional revision."[70] For the Archbishop, backing the new coalition of the center-right could be beneficial to the Catholic Church, especially if the new government would support constitutional changes: "From the point of view of the high interests of the Church, it is not hasty to trust that the New Government constitutes a greater guarantee of stability and understanding."[71] The Archbishop urged the Catholic Church and the Holy See openly to support this new government. Vidal suggested that the Vatican begin a series of negotiations with the new Spanish government in order to improve religious conditions in the state.

Vidal i Barraquer continued his report by blaming the political left for agitating more violence in Spain—especial those like Manuel Azaña who "was already threatening or instigating a violent solution to save the democratic Republic."[72] The Archbishop blamed "the ex-President Azaña and the socialists allied with the communists" for the growing tensions in the state, as the former Prime Minister and his allies worked to produce serious problems for the government.[73] Vidal worried about the serious violence led by leftist militias in Asturias, Galicia, and Cataluña, with particular attention being paid to symbols of the Church:[74] "It is not possible at this time to have an accurate view of the ravages; it can be sensed, however, the great volume and extent of the organizations in arms, which for many months were preparing themselves for the right moment in which they could seize power in order to reestablish the most extreme political-social-antireligious radicalism, and even the dictatorship of the proletariat . . . " Vidal continued "the bond of the union of all the extremists of the left and the occasion, repeatedly announced, of realizing a violent and armed attack against the President of the Republic, the Parliament, and the rightwing government."[75] The Archbishop clearly identified all violence against the government as directed by the political left. At this moment, the center-right Republican government was not the enemy of the Church, and men like Vidal i Barraquer wanted the Holy See to be aware of these threats.

Most importantly for Vidal i Barraquer, the Archbishop of Tarragona, was the threat of radical violence in Cataluña. Like other regions in Spain, Vidal believed leftist influences were seeping into Cataluña, and therefore, destroying the traditional character of the region:

> In Cataluña, whose autonomous Government was conserved by the Esquerra (Left) by means of political violence and social agitation by farmers, is where the mentioned character of leftist extremism offers the movement in all of Spain most clearly, while in Madrid the socialist direction of the revolution was acting, in Barcelona the ex-President Azaña, with his most personal political and technical elements, directed the connection of the regionalist Esquerra with all the Spanish

leftists ... the authentic Cataluña was to be sacrificed by leftist radicalism, thus jeopardizing its own autonomous regime.[76]

The Archbishop believed Cataluña became a testing ground for the importation of radical ideals from the left in order to make a social revolution. Vidal thought the region suffered because these foreign ideals created social upheaval in the cities and the countryside. The Archbishop had supported a closer working relationship between the State and Church during this period, and saw many radical ideologies as confrontational. The people of Cataluña were not hostile towards the political right or the Catholic Church, but the lies and agitation spread by revolutionary ideology infected the community. In truth, due to the center-right's distrust of regionalism, Cataluña would be hostile towards any government that worked to undermine autonomy. At the same time, some Barcelona workers and Catalan farmers supported parties of the left for decades for economic and social reasons. Leftist sympathies, therefore, were not new to the region, but agitation by radical men like Manuel Azaña made matters more dramatic.

On 17 October 1934, Nuncio Tedeschini wrote to the Holy See to summarize the widespread recent violence in Spain, and to explain that the Spanish state needed to act swiftly and forcefully to avoid further radicalization. For the Nuncio, the revolutionary actions in Barcelona, and especially Asturias, represented a threat for the future: "similar to Asturias, it could be maintained that they were preparing the vastest and greatest revolutionary movement that Spain has seen in many years."[77] While the Nuncio must have been exaggerating, the growing revolutionary actions in Spain represented a potentially dark future for the state. Therefore, the central government needed to act forcefully to repress these movements: "If it had not been for this providential gesture, Spain would have turned into a fratricidal battlefield, with the inconceivable horrors that private news affirms took place in Asturias."[78] He praised the actions by the Republic against the workers' revolutionary actions in Asturias, asserting them beneficial and even providential for the state. This "providential gesture" by the state, however, led to serious bloodshed in Asturias, with over 2000 civilians dead at the hands of the military.[79] According to the Nuncio, the state needed to act swiftly and certainly, and if not, Spain's traditional order would be changed: "If the central Government will not succeed in resolving energetically these problems, for Spain there will not be the awaited hour of salvation, and the bloody days of this October will reproduce quickly, devastating always further this poor nation."[80] The reaction of the Nuncio towards the central government in 1934 contrasted sharply with his reaction during the period of the first government. Earlier, under the leadership of Manuel Azaña, the Nuncio hoped the government would act decisively to protect Church interests, but it did not. In 1934, the Nuncio praised the government's forceful behavior. The Nuncio, and others in the Catholic Church, wanted the state to put down these revolutions, even if military force was needed. The Nuncio did not have a problem with the Centrist government using force to put down leftist attacks. Unlike May 1931, the Nuncio must have believed this government had the strength to put down these actions and guarantee security for Catholics and conservatives. The Nuncio supported the Republican government as long as the Church was being protected. At this moment, Tedeschini accepted the legitimacy and authority of the Republic because revolutionary movements with "class-warfare" ideology threatened the Church and the Lerroux government. The Nuncio understood that the Republic and the Church had a shared enemy, and if the Republic needed to act to defeat radical leftist ideology, then so be it.

According to Nuncio Tedeschini, by 25 October 1934, the serious revolutionary conditions in Cataluña had ended as the central government's forces had been able to put down any violent actions, and many of the more "radical" elements, who had led the revolt, had fled to France.[81] After acknowledging the end of that regionalist conflict, the Nuncio began a discussion about the Asturias Revolution: "That entire unhappy region was plagued by the cruelties that are only reflected in the most gruesome episodes of the ages of the most barbarous wars. Towns and villages were devastated, and the poor inhabitants who were not part of the revolutionary movement, have been subject to the harshest of punishments, from which not even small children have escaped, some of whom were blinded."[82] Of course, he blamed the violence exclusively on elements of the left in the region. While innocent people were attacked and many killed, the violence directed at the Church drew particular interest for the Nuncio. Numerous priests had been attacked and killed, and the Nuncio noted they "are true martyrs, killed in hatred of the faith."[83] The Nuncio spoke of missing clergymen, like Don Juan Puertes, who had not been heard from since the end of the activity. Tedeschini reported that many priests had been murdered:

> In Oviedo there have been many killed, including the Pastor of the Corte, the Canonico Baztan, the father Eufrasio from Infante Jesus, two Fathers from the Missionary Seminary, and 12 seminarians. In the province there have been executed the parsons of Sama, Rebolleda, Olloniego, Valcuna, Murias, and Moreda; the Father Innocenzo Passionista, eight brothers of the Christian Schools, four novice priests, the Father Martinez, Jesuit with a brother of the Society.[84]

These victims proved that the revolutionary elements in Spain had become dangerous and violent again. Religious buildings were not spared from this violence—and echoes of May 1931 resonated throughout Spain. The Nuncio was surprised that despite the revolutionaries' destruction of the holy chamber, they did not completely destroy the Cathedral of Oviedo, but he wrote of numerous damaged churches in the region like the Church of San Tirso.[85]

Even though the Nuncio reported on the violence directed at the Church and clergy, he must have been well aware of the repression used by the army against these rebellions. At the same time, the Nuncio must have suspected that the political right tried to instigate some confrontation to use the military to attack the left. According to Paul Preston, CEDA's demand to add new cabinet members to the government was a "Trojan horse" plan to undermine the Radical's control. Once the revolutionary atmosphere began, CEDA leader, José María Gil Robles, called upon the army to use "the harshest policy possible against the rebels" and to close parliament until the rebellion ended while Conservatives demanded the Army of Africa, Spain's most violent force, which was under the command of Francisco Franco, be used to put down the rebellion.[86] Preston writes, "The African Army unleashed a wave of brutality that had more to do with their normal practice when entering Moroccan villages than any threat from the defeated Asturian rebels."[87] Preston asserts the actions taken by the Army of Africa went far above what was necessary to defeat the rebellion, and the move was instead an open repression campaign against the left. When the campaign ended, Preston estimates 256 army personnel died and 639 were wounded, while over 2000 civilians—most from the working class—died.[88] While the Nuncio heralded these soldiers for protecting the Republic, it would have been impossible for him to overlook these civilian deaths. For the Nuncio, these rebels' lives did not seem to equal those of the priest murdered.

Nuncio Tedeschini asserted, "The horror of the killings and devastations has exceeded the most pessimistic forecast. The hatred accumulated over many years of propaganda of incendiary doctrines has provoked an explosion that will mark one of the most painful and shameful pages of this nation."[89] After that conclusion, the Nuncio explained how such a revolutionary movement could possibly happen. He believed that workers had been saving their earnings from 1931–33, pooling their monies, and buying illegal weaponry overseas. Once the government had shifted to the center-right, these individuals smuggled the weaponry to Asturias aboard ships and distributed them among their allies. Miners in the region expropriated explosives used at their work to launch numerous attacks.[90] Therefore, these attacks had been well-planned and these miners and workers were going to lead this type of revolutionary action no-matter-what. The Nuncio, therefore, suggested that no one should have been surprised that these uncontrollable groups struck out against the government and civility. The Nuncio applauded the government's military actions because "Only military strength has been able to win, but if this had been missing, as has occurred in some few cases, today Europe would have at its extreme western border a Bolshevik nation, the same as that which closes the eastern borders, but immensely more barbarous and ferocious."[91] For the Nuncio, if these revolutionary activities had been allowed to continue, or even gain momentum, then Spain clearly would become a Bolshevik regime—even though communism was never the primary threat to the country.[92] It was necessary, therefore, for the Spanish government to do whatever was necessary to end this possibility—even with military action. The Nuncio did not openly call for any form of violence, but he did approve of the results. Was it contradictory for a Church representative to credit the violent military actions of the center-right government against this radically revolutionary movement? Or, was the Nuncio correct to honor those individuals and support actions that saved the lives of priests and ended the threat of uncontrolled violence in Asturias? The Holy See was not supposed to call for warfare, but the Catholic Church was finally grateful for the Spanish Republic to protect its interests. Ironically, the military action taken to end the uprising was an attempt to save the Republic from the political left. This military action, however, was brutal and the army was responsible for a larger amount of blood than the rebels. The Nuncio supported the preservation of the Republic from a leftist threat. It can be argued the Nuncio had already chosen sides in any future conflict—choosing the right over the left—but this support can also be understood as a support for the survival of the Republic, as long as the Republic rejected leftist ideology. As a post-script to the Asturian Revolution, Nuncio Tedeschini wrote that the Second Republican government compiled an official report regarding the violence, but that nothing of serious novelty had been included in the final draft, leaving everyone to rely on previous discussions and articles to understand the conflict fully.[93]

The center-right government of Lerroux began to reestablish connections with countries the Azaña government had ignored. The Lerroux government was interested in problems in Europe, Africa, and the Mediterranean. By January 1935, states like Nazi Germany and Fascist Italy had begun to make more aggressive moves in order to expand their power, obtain land and increase their spheres of influence. Lerroux's Minister of State, José Rocha, attended League of Nations meetings to work on a compromise concerning the Saar region of Germany. Following sabotage of French coal mines by retreating German troops at the end of World War I, France had been granted the right to mine Saar coal for fifteen years to be followed by a plebiscite.[94] At the same time, Rocha initiated a series of discussions with the Italian, French, and British governments concerning control of the Mediterranean, as all states had serious interests in the region.[95] The Nuncio seemed impressed by the

Lerroux government's willingness to become more active in the international arena and Spain's working to act as an international moderator, rather than an agitator, like during the Azaña regime. Lerroux's centrist government might be able to negotiate international crises better than governments of the right or left. At the same time, these international negotiations did not include the USSR, most likely a great relief for the Nuncio. In the end, however, Spanish international involvement did not change the outcome of any of these conflicts.

The Spanish Catholic Church, Holy See, and Vatican hierarchy were all happy to see the Manuel Azaña government collapse. Alejandro Lerroux represented a possible political middle ground in Spain, and a hopeful end to political and physical attacks against the Catholic Church. When Lerroux first came to power, men like the Archbishop of Tarragona, Vidal i Barraquer, believed he could calm the country. A change in leadership, however, did not do enough to change the radical activities and regionalist demands of certain groups. Leftist parties worked to undermine the Lerroux regime, and parties of the right pushed the Prime Minister to include their allies. Nuncio Tedeschini appeared to support the actions of Alejandro Lerroux and his government, and hoped that his leadership would save Spain and reduce violence against the Church. The Nuncio could support definitive Republican action as long as conservatives influenced the decision and leftists were undermined. The greatest problem for Lerroux, however, was that Asturias foretold of increasing threats to the Republic's survival. Elements on the far left threatened revolution, while the repression by elements of the Army under Franco's leadership was savage. Prior to the Asturian Revolution, conservatives pressured the government for more representation, even though they were well aware of the tense political situation. While the Nuncio seemed relieved with the Lerroux regime, the Catholic Church was aware of the gravity of the situation and acknowledged the possibility of full-blown violence.

THE COLLAPSE OF THE SECOND REPUBLIC, 1936

The elections of February 1936 were important for the future of Spain as the centrist Radical government had failed in its leadership, and the country continued to radicalize. CEDA and its allies had gained support from the wealthy, military, and Spanish religious leaders, while the left had unified under the Popular Front in order to prevent conservatism's victory. The Holy See feared the inclusion of communists in the Popular Front, and the Church dreaded communist influence in the government. This section will explore the weeks leading up to the February 1936 election, the election results, and the continuing deterioration of the Spanish political arena. The Vatican hierarchy worried that communists in the Popular Front coalition would lead a "revolution of the proletariat" and they would destroy Spain, even though they represented a small percentage. Once the Popular Front won the elections, the Vatican hierarchy seemed aware that a civil war would begin in Spain, and seemed concerned about this possible result.

On 15 January 1936, Nuncio Tedeschini discussed the deterioration of the Spanish government. Alcalá Zamora's announcement dissolving the Cortes and calling for February elections was serious for the Holy See and Spanish Catholics, as the victorious side—the left or the right—would direct Spain in one ideological direction or another. The Popular Front "umbrella" coalition posed a major threat, and the Nuncio worried that leftist parties would undermine Spain and unleash a more serious class-revolution. Tedeschini believed the left worked to undermine the stability of the Republic but, "Thus now it appears that it is the Republicans who, doing everything to destroy the Republic with errors, scandals and abuses, have taken on the task to give life and popularity in the country to the royalist parties."[96] The newfound Popular Front growth coupled with the corruption of the Radicals seemed to persuade conservatives to become more active. The Church clearly was willing to support or work with the Republic, as long as the state did not allow violence to occur against the Church. The Nuncio, though, did think that the CEDA coalition might be able to win these upcoming elections, and change Spain for the better: "If the right wins, we will not only have the Constitution reformed but, it is to be believed, a new Constitution: if, God forbid, the Left wins, we will surely get the revolution and the dictatorship of the proletariat."[97] The Nuncio hoped a victory by the CEDA coalition would allow for constitutional changes, most likely concerning Article 26. For Tedeschini, however, the only result that could occur from a Popular Front victory would be a radical revolution, and more threats to the Catholic Church.

On 20 January, Nuncio Tedeschini wrote to the Holy See to explain the formulation of the Spanish Popular Front coalition, with some shocking reactions about the group's new policies. According to Tedeschini, Largo Caballero, the head of the leftist workers' union UGT, staged various public appearances to outline the Popular Front's goals. Many on the Spanish right, and the Nuncio, expected the Popular Front to take a very radical and communist agenda that would call for complete revolution: "Instead, it was surprising his relatively moderate tone. In fact, he no longer speaks of the abolition of capital, the division of lands, and the abolition of the system and, even less, of the dictatorship of the proletariat."[98] Tedeschini was also very surprised that Caballero said nothing regarding the religious problems in Spain, something that radical leftists frequently spoke of in order to inflame supporters. Even though Caballero's views appeared more moderate than before, the Nuncio still had serious suspicions. Tedeschini explained that this moderation was not independently constructed, but he believed the Soviet Komintern had instructed communists to "trick" parties of the left to join this coalition.[99] Even though Caballero had seemed to moderate his views, Tedeschini regarded this change in opinion as a "Trojan Horse" initiated by the Soviets to continue to destabilize Spain.

Members of the Vatican and Spanish hierarchies worried about the February elections. On 22 January, Nuncio Tedeschini explained a new plan developed by the Spanish Metropolitan of Bishops in order to bolster electoral support for the political right. During the 1933 elections, the Spanish Metropolitan allowed its clergy, even those cloistered nuns in convents and nunneries, to cast votes. The Bishops believed that this support from the clergy gained a great deal of votes for the CEDA coalition, and they wanted this new tradition to continue. Therefore, cloistered nuns voted (or should vote), "in those cases and places in which the triumph of the candidates of the right could depend on the votes of the nuns for being their number great and the contending forces tied."[100] The Spanish Catholic hierarchy, therefore, actively promoted its clergy voting for the political right. The Church, therefore, was not impotent during these elections, and rallied a large number of supporters to go to the polls. Archbishop of Toledo, Isidro Gomá y Tomás, also wrote to Cardinal Pacelli on 22 January expressing Spanish Catholics were concerned about the possibility of a Popular Front victory, and the Spanish Catholic hierarchy wanted to satisfy "the wishes of His Holiness to see all the Catholics united in the defense of Religion."[101] The Archbishop wanted his subordinates to push their followers to support the right in its battle against the "Marxists," and a possible public Papal message could help, even though none ever arrived.

Even though Tedeschini and Gomá y Tomás believed Catholics would help the right win the elections, the political actions of the Basque Nationalist Party, the PNV, still confounded the Church. The Spanish archbishop wrote, "It is, certainly, strange the attitude of this party, whose leaders, while they proclaim their purpose to form a new nation—breaking therefore the national unity— in which the rights of the Church would be completely recognized and respected, go hand in hand, when it suits their political plans, with the parties most hostile to the Church."[102] The Archbishop opposed the PNV's willingness to align itself with leftist political parties rather than the right. The PNV valued regional autonomy as their highest position, and they would work with any party to support it. Similar to the revolutionary period of October 1934, the Catholic hierarchy in Spain questioned the rationale of the Basque—how could their leadership proclaim to be good Catholics when they worked with parties that attacked the church? This question would continue to haunt the relationship between the Holy See and País Vasco throughout the battles and requests for mediation during the Spanish Civil War.

On 16 February, the Spanish electorate went to the polls, and 72% of Spain's eligible voters chose candidates. After the votes were counted, the Popular Front coalition earned the support of 34.3% of the electorate, the Center-Right (CEDA) earned 32.2% of the electorate, and the largest losers were the Center, with only 5.4% of the electorate.[103] The Republican constitution allowed the party or coalition earning the largest percentage of votes to form a new government. Even though the Popular Front won with a very small plurality, the proportional representational system gave the coalition 263 seats in the Cortes. The *Bloque Nacional* (Center-Right) earned 156 seats, and the Center earned 54.[104] According to Nuncio Tedeschini, the Bloque Nacional believed they had enough support to win the 16 February election, and were shocked by the final results.[105] The Nuncio worried about the Popular Front coalition, including its communist allies, would form a new government within days.

On 21 February, the Spanish Embassy to the Holy See wrote a letter to the Vatican identifying the new Spanish government, and acknowledging that Manuel Azaña would once again become the political leader of Spain.[106] While this letter from the Spanish Embassy was matter-of-fact, Nuncio Tedeschini's letter of 22 February offers great insight into the Catholic Church's opinions and reactions to the new government. The Nuncio spoke of panic in Spain after the formulation of the new government, especially because the left initiated the revolutionary atmosphere in Cataluña and Asturias during the fall of 1934.[107] At the same time, the Nuncio acknowledged that many of the leaders in this new government had participated in the 1931 government, which was responsible for many of the anticlerical laws.[108] According to Tedeschini, with the return of the left came the return of violence against the Church and its property with "vandalism: burning of churches, destruction of newspapers, threats, insults, etc" in many provinces throughout the country.[109] A 22 February note from Juan de Dios Ponce, apostolic administrator of Orihuela-Alicante, explained the increase in anticlerical violence that had occurred since the elections in Elche, Alicante Province. The parish churches of Salvador and San Juan had been completely burned, the Temple of Santa María sacked, and the Convent of Clarisas attacked with a great deal of force and destruction.[110] This violence against the Church eerily resembled the major attacks of May 1931, obviously frightening the Catholic and Vatican hierarchies. Even with this violence occurring in Spain, Tedeschini was pleased that he had scheduled a meeting with Manuel Azaña in the hope of influencing the government to moderate its reactions towards the Catholic Church and to prevent violent outbreaks.[111]

Nuncio Tedeschini wrote to Cardinal Pacelli on 22 February to outline his meeting with the new President of the Government, Manuel Azaña, about "the Holy See, the Church and the religious problem in general."[112] The most important question for the Nuncio concerned religion, and Tedeschini wanted Azaña to make some promises, but reached no agreements. Most frighteningly for Tedeschini, Azaña suggested that he had not even thought of the religious question: "Mr. Azaña responded to me: I do not know anything: we have not spoken about it: we should consider it; but I do not know when we will be able to do it, because now we have so many things to deal with, and all of the greatest importance; with this I do not mean to say that the religious problem is not important."[113] For Azaña, "the question of workers' unemployment" posed the most important problem facing Spain, along with "agrarian reform," while the religious question existed lower on the list.[114] Azaña focused on issues relating to the lower-classes in Spain, and these class issues seemed more important than questions of the Church. When the conversation switched to a discussion of what the Nuncio wanted, especially regarding a possible change in the Republican constitution, "Isn't it, interrupted the President, because the Holy See wants the Constitutional reform first? Because in that case you would have to wait quite long."[115] For the Nuncio, the most important concern was religious reform. For Azaña, the primary concern regarded the working-class. The Catholic Church and the Popular Front government had two distinct world visions about what had to be done to help Spain, and this distinctive difference meant disagreement on the constitutional issue.

Archbishop Isidro Gomá y Tomás compiled a report of his "personal impressions" concerning the February election, in order to explain why the Popular Front won and what this victory would mean for Spain.[116] According to the Archbishop, the Popular Front took advantage of a particular political and social climate to win: "On the leftist side: (a) Their unity, (b) Their way of acting directly upon the people, exploiting these resources: workers' unemployment, the stagnation of wheat, (c) The sudden entry of the unions in the elections, against their principles and practice, two hours before they closed, (d) the decomposition of the Radical party, e) the government's failed efforts to form a centrist party."[117] The right lost because: "(a) A generous and effective unity has been missing, (b) The form of propaganda: With much less contact with the people than the Left, especially in the press. Catholic newspapers enter little in the working classes, (c) the ineffectiveness of the legislative work of the last Parliament in order to improve the working class, which has been attributed to the right . . . (d) misunderstanding and lack of charity of the rich, right-wingers who, at the advent of the right parties to power in the last term, returned to the regimen of derisory wages . . . "[118] The Popular Front took advantage of the center-right's failures in order to snatch a narrow victory. It is important to note that Gomá did not just fault the left, but he blamed the right for not working together and for ignoring many in the lower-classes, almost pushing them towards the more radical parties. If the right had been more interested in the condition of the poor, these circumstances may not have occurred.

After explaining why the left won, the Archbishop outlined the future worries that would affect the Catholic Church in Spain. First, this new Popular Front government could once again use the Law of Confessions and Religious Congregations to attack the Catholic Church, making "*una situación difícil a la Iglesia.*"[119] Second, the government could seize other finances and properties owned by various dioceses throughout the country, hurting the Church's finances.[120] Third, the new government could use its position to sway public opinion in the Spanish country-side against members of the clergy.[121] At the same time, if the environment turned against the Church, then the clergy might not be able to spread its religious message in the country.[122] Finally, with the burning of Churches already done in cities like Elche, Alcoy, Valencia, Murcia, and Béjar, the government might turn a blind eye to future physical violence, like during May 1931.[123] The Archbishop offered a grim view of the future condition for the Church in Spain. When combined with Nuncio Tedeschini's concerns, one can conclude that much of the Catholic leadership feared this new government. Whereas in 1931 some in the Vatican hierarchy thought the Republican leadership might moderate, the Popular Front government of 1936 was viewed as radical and revolutionary from its inception.

In the final section of his report, Gomá y Tomás wrote of the most dangerous concerns for Spain and the Catholic Church. According to the Archbishop, representatives of the communist Komintern had been in Spain to follow the elections of 1936, and reported on how the new Popular Front government would be able to lead a full revolution:

> The Komintern delegates who have been to Spain to study the possibilities of a communist action in our country, have sent to Moscow a pessimistic report on the revolutionary masses and their leaders. The report is extensive and lavish in anecdotal detail to substantiate the thesis that there is nothing to expect from the revolution in the street . . . The informants believe that municipal elections would have caused an overflow of passion in the people with the circumstantial proclamation of communism in a few thousand rural municipalities where they would hoist the red flag, they would burn the church, and murder the priest, the pair of Civil Guards, and the rich men of the village . . . They say that in Spain all are scared: the rightists and the leftists.[124]

The Komintern learned that in order to lead a full revolt, all members of the political left needed to work together, unlike in Asturias and Cataluña. Due to the Komintern's presence in Spain, Gomá believed *all* Spaniards had become nervous about the future of their country, and many had begun to take up arms.[125] In fact, the Spanish military, according to the Archbishop, had stated it would work to prevent any overthrow of the Spanish government (ironic, as the Spanish military overthrew the Republican government months later).[126] Socialist leader Largo Caballero had been calling for the creation of "armed workers' militias" and Spain was falling further into disarray.[127] The Archbishop concluded that the environment in Spain had become toxic, and that some form of revolutionary action was going to happen. When Spain was to fall into disarray, the Popular Front would suspend the Cortes, take emergency actions, and the complete communist revolution would occur.[128] The Archbishop was pessimistic about the future of Spain, envisioned some form of violent upheaval, and blamed the political left. This hatred of the political left distorted the view of many Church representatives about possible future danger. As Sid Lowe discusses, the combination of CEDA and the *Juventud de Acción Popular* (JAP) had been discussing plans for an overthrow of the Republic since the February 1936 election, so why did the Vatican not worry about them equally?[129]

The communist threat in Spain remained real for Papal Nuncio Tedeschini. The February elections earned the communists fourteen seats out of 263 in the Cortes, the largest number ever—yet still insignificant. On 29 February and 1 March, communists took to the streets of Madrid to celebrate their successes and show their force. Although small in size, the Nuncio regarded the manifestation on Saturday, 29 February, as much more threatening to the peace. First, the crowds celebrated the release of prisoners associated with the revolutionary activities from October 1934. Later, one of the leading voices of the Spanish Communist Party, Dolores Ibárruri (La Pasionaria), who was elected to the Cortes in 1936 as a Communist delegate,[130] called for further revolutionary activities, including the deaths of political leaders on the right.[131] The masses of men, women, and children wearing red and waving red flags scared Tedeschini, and he worried about the possibility of true communist revolution. For the Nuncio, *all* parties of the political left represented a real threat and he believed they would work together for a radical revolutionary environment: "And since, practically, between communism and socialism there is no difference."[132] Because he saw little difference between the two groups, and because communists had gained their largest number of seats in the Cortes, the Nuncio believed the communists would be able to influence the government to go in whichever direction they wanted.[133] Interestingly, the Nuncio was either unable or unwilling to understand the political differences inherent in socialist and communist parties. Manuel Azaña stated that he was not going to agree always with communists, but Tedeschini regarded Azaña and his Ministers were too weak or too unwilling to stand-up to the communists, and these radicals would be able to get their way.[134] For the Nuncio, the growing presence of communists, both on the streets and in the government, posed a serious threat to the Spanish Republic, as it appeared more and more each day that these radical groups would take some action against the state.

Violence continued to occur in Spain during the spring and summer of 1936. Two-hundred seventy political killings occurred in Spain from January-July 1936, much more than any period excluding October 1934. The 12 July assassination of Socialist José del Castillo was followed by the assassination of FE y de los JONS ranking-member Calvo Sotelo on 13 July. These were the final major assassinations before the start of the Civil War.[135] Communist parties and workers' unions took to the streets in strikes and violent clashes with the police, churches continued to be looted and burned in the cities and the countryside, farmland was occupied in southern and central Spain, and political groups on both sides used their militias to strike out against each other in gangland-style violence.[136] The Nuncio wrote about this growing violence and outcome on 24 March 1936: "I learn from a reliable source that a military coup is being prepared which would not be foreign to the President of the Republic. I am being advised to take refuge in an embassy at the first signs. I will keep the Holy See informed."[137] The Nuncio did not state which side would lead this possible overthrow of the government, but by viewing his previous conversations with the Holy See, it would appear that he believed the communists and their militias would be the group to act. Conservatives might have spread a rumor of a leftist coup, to create fear in the Church and possibly justify their own actions. In a 6 April letter to the Holy See, Tedeschini explained why he believed this overthrow would occur and blamed Manuel Azaña for allowing the state to collapse. First, the Nuncio was angered that Azaña "condemned" attacks against religious institutions, but did not use the state to prevent these attacks:

> Mr. Azaña also says that he of course condemns burnings of Churches and the like; but to obtain oratorical effect, he opposes to violence of this kind another violence perpetrated in Madrid last March, when an attempt was made on the life of a Socialist University Professor, Jimenez de Azúa, who enjoyed to incite socialist students at school against other students: by whom this attack was committed I do not know, they say by fascists, but at any rate by people with whom the still smoking poor Churches do not have and will never have anything to do. It is just and fair to condemn also this second violence, and no one

more than the Church condemns it. But it is nothing other than rhetoric to excuse or to mitigate this first sin.[138]

The Nuncio accused the President of the Government of whitewashing these serious crimes and allowing these horrible attacks to continue. At the same time, Azaña did not take the threat of communists and Soviets seriously enough as "The rumors about the coming of Communism in power, and that one of these days Spain is going to establish a successful Soviet. . . . this already seems to pass the limits of what is lawful and what is tolerable and constitutes an assault![139] The President seemed to be ignoring these threats and attacks against conservatives in Spain, almost allowing the communists to build support. The passivity of Azaña was the real crime—he was not defending either Spain or the Republic from an outside attack.

On 29 May, Archbishop of Tarragona Vidal i Barraquer expressed his views of the deteriorating conditions in Spain since the victory of the Popular Front in February. Vidal believed that the CEDA coalition could not have won the February elections because both extremes, the radical left *and* radical right had been working to undermine the normal electoral process, and both groups had attacked CEDA.[140] As a consequence of the election, both extremes began a series of violent attacks against political enemies, as well as innocent individuals and property.[141] As expected, the Archbishop warned of the extreme violence committed by the left against symbols of the Church, but most interestingly, Vidal i Barraquer also had concerns about the actions of the right: "I had the honor to ask the Holy See to place its attention, always vigilant, to the dangers contained in the campaigns of the rightwing extremists."[142] While the Archbishop had hoped for a government of the center-right, he worried about the radical views of the extreme right, as they too were responsible for negative propaganda and dangerous violence. By 1936, the Vatican saw the radicalization and racial laws of extreme right-wing states, like Nazi Germany, and the Holy See might have feared these attitudes spreading to Spain. Pius XI, too, worried about the spread of paganistic Nazism and its attacks on Catholicism. Overall, Vidal i Barraquer was most concerned with "the division" that had been occurring in Spain, and he feared the possible repercussions.[143] The Archbishop did not directly speak of the possibility of a civil war, but his pessimism about the ability of Spaniards to work together seemed to signal his premonitions that something radical was about to happen.

Days before the military uprising, Cardinal Pacelli wrote Archbishop Gomá about plans for the upcoming Conferences of Spanish Bishops, scheduled for October 1936. Cardinal Pacelli was anxious about the relationship between the Popular Front and the Catholic Church, and he hoped this Conference could clearly outline the primary concerns of the

Church. On 14 July, Pacelli wrote, "The Holy Father preferred your august attention to matters relating to schools, religious teaching and to the consistent defense against threatening communist propaganda."[144] The Vatican was unaware that an uprising against the Popular Front would soon occur, and the Church prepared to continue on with its normal schedule of events. The Pope's primary interest for Spain was to fix the national schools and again allow religious education. Once again, the Vatican most feared communist influence in Spain, but as previously explained, communists remained a small percentage of the Popular Front. Even with the serious deterioration of the Second Republic, the Pope interestingly chose the public schools as the primary issue that needed to be resolved.

THE FAILED SECOND REPUBLIC?

In comparison to the first government of the Second Spanish Republic, the period of Alejandro Lerroux's leadership was much less perilous for the Roman Catholic Church and Holy See. When Lerroux formed a new government, Papal Nuncio Tedeschini seemed hopeful that this new opportunity would decrease anti-clerical legislation and prevent violence. To some extent, the Lerroux government provided a great improvement for the Catholic Church, as it ignored the Law of Confessions and Religious Congregations and clergy could once again teach in schools. These improvements, however, offered small victories, as a new period of political and social violence broke out in Spain. Social revolutionary groups, like communists and anarchists, struck out against the government with armed militias, especially in Cataluña and Asturias where violent battles occurred. Some political leaders of the left, like Manuel Azaña and Largo Caballero, instructed their followers to disobey the centrist government and push for further social revolution. Finally, regionalist interests in places like Cataluña and País Vasco weakened the state's ability to control all its territory. The political right used these perceived leftist threats as rationale for their own aggression. Conservatives called upon harsh repression of regionalist uprisings, and they supported Francisco Franco's violent campaign to repress the Asturian miners in 1934, going further than the central government wanted. Nuncio Tedeschini saw the military's actions as less destructive than those of the miners, highlighting his paranoia of the left and appreciation of the right. When these rightist or leftist threats occurred, the Papal Nuncio and other Catholic leaders worried for the survival of the Second Republic. The Catholic Church experienced a dilemma in Spain: support centralized authority or regionalist interests, and this was not always done consistently. This interesting twist in clerical conversations shows some important changes in Catholic discussions. First, clerical leaders began to speak about the survival of the Republican structure of government, showing that at least some vocal Catholic leaders seemed resigned to accept the authority of the Republican structure of government, as long as it did not attack Catholicism. Second, these same clerical leaders began to support, at least in private communications, the ideas and concepts espoused by parties of the center-right. Finally, these religious leaders warned that political groups from the radical left were working to destroy the Second Republic and install an atheistic and Bolshevistic regime in order to carry out a class and social revolution. Even with these possible threats to the stability of the Second Republic, Vatican archival materials contain few, if any, responses directly from the Holy See about these problems or directions to the Nuncio and the Catholic hierarchy in Spain. Even with the revolutionary and oft-violent attacks carried out by members of radical leftist parties and organizations, the hopeful promise of some form of stability and non-anti-clerical legislation were reasons enough to support the actions of Lerroux and his government.

While the Lerroux government might have offered some hope to the Catholic hierarchy in Spain, it was unable to create social and political stability. It was within this atmosphere of social and political upheaval that the February 1936 elections occurred. This toxic atmosphere startled Catholic leaders in Spain. With all political parties of the left united under the umbrella organization, the Popular Front, the threat of communist representation in the government became a serious concern for the Church because Catholic leaders associated all leftist parties with the actions of communists, even if this was not true. In order to prevent a Popular Front victory, the Spanish Metropolitan of Bishops instructed clergy to vote; even cloistered clergy were supposed to go to the polls. The Catholic Church in Spain worked to support the CEDA coalition, and the Holy See did nothing to prevent this behavior. While the Vatican did not make any public or private statements in support of CEDA, the fact that it did nothing to instruct the Catholic clergy to avoid political involvement is interesting. The Spanish Catholic Church, by 1936, became active in the political process in order to prevent the left from winning. Even with this political involvement, the Popular Front narrowly won the 1936 elections, and fourteen communist deputies joined their allies in the Cortes. Manuel Azaña, the controversial President of the First Republican Government and political agitator during the Lerroux regime, once again led Spain. Azaña's radical agenda threatened the Catholic Church, and Nuncio Tedeschini hoped he could talk to the President and find some common ground. In the end, though, Azaña had neither an interest in restoring any social authority to the Catholic Church, nor promised to protect the Church, as he was more concerned about the plight of workers and farmers—which can be interpreted as class-consciousness over religion.

Of all the Papal Nuncio's concerns about Spain, the most serious and timely prediction was that following the Popular Front victory of 1936, a coup d'état was on the horizon. The Nuncio believed that the Azaña regime would act passively towards the communists, and allow the Soviet Union and its allies to overthrow the government. In reality, the communists represented a small percentage of the Popular Front coalition, but after witnessing the revolutionary atmosphere of October 1934 and seeing the increasingly violent environment of 1936, the Nuncio could understandably be afraid of some radical leftist activity. The Nuncio had done his job, and alerted the Holy See that the Second Spanish Republic was weak, and pressures from the left and the right undermined the government. The Nuncio appeared paranoid of a threat from the left, and seemed to sympathize with the right and its actions during this period. In the end, the Holy See could not have been surprised that a civil war did begin months later. The Second Spanish Republic and all its political leaders had failed, pushing the state to a bloody conflict. The Vatican hierarchy was a witness to these failures, and none should have been surprised with how serious and devastating the Spanish Civil War of 1936–9 would become. The Church's representatives in Spain wanted its followers to participate and defend Catholicism's special place in Spanish society, and once again, members of the political left may have understood this as an attack against the state.

IV

The Uprising Begins, The Republic Reacts, and the Vatican Protests

The Vatican hierarchy remained well-informed of the atrocities during the first months of the Spanish Civil War, as Republican militias massacred conservatives and Rebels slaughtered government supporters. Even with this information, the Holy See often remained publicly silent concerning the carnage of war. The majority of the Spanish Catholic hierarchy had clearly sided with the Rebel cause, but the Holy See continued to express a public façade of political non-involvement. The archival material evaluated in this chapter explores the major anxieties of the Holy See towards the Republican Government during the first months of the Spanish Civil War. To explain these problems experienced in the Republic, the Holy See spoke of possible communist and anarchist infiltration in the government as the most serious problem, even though it would have been nearly impossible for the communists to overthrow the government in 1936. According to William J. Callahan, Bishop Enrique Plá y Deniel of the Spanish Catholic hierarchy "shifted his attention away from the Socialists, long perceived as the Church's principle enemy, to the Communists for reasons that are not entirely clear, given the party's relative political weakness during the summer of 1936."[1] The Spanish Catholic hierarchy associated the failures of the Republic with the most radical communist, and anarchist elements of the government, even though they could not affect all political actions. The Church explained the violence it experienced was unprovoked and that the Holy See was unable to assist a government that could not control radical anticlerical elements.

This chapter will identify the Vatican's major concerns at the outbreak of the war, especially relating to the condition of the Spanish Catholic Church. From the beginning, these documents show that the Holy See was most interested in the violence occurring against clergy and property. These troubles seemed to supersede the Church's concerns about the growing civilian death toll or the destruction of Spanish infrastructure. While the evidence does not suggest that the Vatican was uninterested in the conditions of all Spaniards, the archival sources show the Holy See was primarily concerned with the condition of the Catholic

Church, its hierarchy, and its laity in Spain. The Vatican feared becoming overly involved in Spain could lead to increased anticlerical violence during and after the War by making the Church a political target. According to the conservative historian Gonzalo Redondo, the first goal of the Holy See and the Catholic Church was supposed to guarantee the salvation of its parishioners and support peace in Spain.[2] The Holy See feared supporting the Insurgents could result in increased Republican violence, or supporting the Republic could result in Rebel attacks against the Church Leadership. The Holy See could not protect everyone and everything in Spain, so its priority turned to trying to protect those elements most closely associated with the Church. The Vatican hoped to defend members of the clergy and Catholic followers, but the Republican Government considered this concern unnecessary. The Holy See chose to follow the same plan it used during the pre-war years—avoid official public commentary, but attempt to use its representatives in Spain to present its opinions and concerns to the government.

The political back-and-forth and bloodshed during the Second Republic in Spain made the Catholic Church uncomfortable because violent attacks appeared possible at any moment. Leading to the Civil War, "Catholics and Socialists helped prepare the way for military intervention by abandoning parliamentary methods of achieving their respective aims."[3] An unwillingness to work within the governmental system by all sides weakened the state, pushed for war, and increased the general confusion regarding who was actually in control of Spain. Concerning violent actions during the Second Republic once the Spanish Civil War began, the Vatican and its representatives needed to determine the specifics of the conflict and explain the War in terms consistent with the Vatican's mission. At the start of the conflict, Vatican representatives in Spain appeared most concerned about the violence of Republican militias against symbols of the Church.[4] This chapter will examine how the Catholic hierarchy in Spain began to suggest that the Republican Government had been commandeered by the most radical political elements in the state—socialists, communists, and anarchists—and these "reds" had become a threat to the safety of Catholics.

THE POPE, THE SECRETARY OF STATE, AND CONFLICTS

In order to explore the relationship between the Vatican hierarchy and Spain during the period of the Civil War, it is necessary to explain the diplomatic goals and procedures favored by the two highest ranking Vatican officials, Pope Pius XI and Vatican Secretary of State Eugenio Pacelli (later Pope Pius XII). Thanks to the recent opening of files from the Vatican Secret Archives, historians such as Frank Coppa, Emma

Fattorini, Hubert Wolf, Lucia Ceci, and Alessandro Duce have each explored the diplomatic behavior of the Holy See during the period of Pope Pius XI (1922–39). These historians have highlighted the different goals and behaviors of the Pius XI and Pacelli, which are necessary for understanding how the Holy See would act concerning the Spanish Civil War, generally agreeing that Pope Pius XI was not willing to compromise on questions of Catholic doctrine. Due to this unwavering religious attitude, Pius XI was much more willing to speak out publicly, release encyclicals condemning behavior he did not approve of, and negotiate Concordats with foreign states in order to guarantee the position of the Catholic Church in the state.[5] On the other hand, Pacelli was the apprentice of former Secretary of State Pietro Gasparri—an ardent supporter of negotiations in order to avoid serious religious conflict. Pacelli could be described as more silent than Pope Pius XI, and Pacelli appeared willing to negotiate with any state in order to prevent increased problems for the Catholic Church.[6] Pius XI, therefore, was the more vocal individual, ready to speak out publicly against attacks on Catholicism, but Pacelli was reserved and willing to negotiate privately to prevent threats to the Church.

The Spanish Civil War of 1936–9 was not the only diplomatic crisis facing Pius XI's Vatican. Pius XI was interested in creating Concordats with the Soviet Union in 1922–7, Italy in 1929, and Nazi Germany in 1933. At the same time, Pius XI's Vatican was concerned about the 1935 Italo-Abyssinian war, German racial laws, and Fascist Italy's racial laws. Each of these events outlines the different opinions and behavior used by Pius XI and Pacelli in diplomacy. As for the Soviet Union, Pius XI wanted to formalize a Concordat to protect the rights of the Church. The Pope was willing to negotiate with the communist government if the church could maintain religious control over ecclesiastical questions, but Pacelli appeared more open to make concessions to the Soviet leadership in order to prevent further antagonism.[7] An agreement was never reached, but this diplomatic behavior showed that Pius XI firmly believed in the authority of Concordats as guarantees for the practice of the Catholic religion, but Pacelli was more pragmatic and realized the Holy See could not always obtain what it wanted from treaties. The Lateran Accords with Italy in 1929 established the physical borders of the Holy See while making Catholicism the official religion of Fascist Italy. Pacelli's negotiations helped this Concordat succeed, but the Catholic Church did have to make some concessions to Italy. Most importantly, according to Frank Coppa, was that the Vatican needed to "remain impartial in internal state matters as well as in international affairs."[8] According to Coppa, Pope Pius XI did not welcome this impartiality in political affairs, but his Secretary of State explained it was the best treaty possible. The 1933 *Reichskonkordat* was negotiated by Pacelli to guarantee the freedom of the

Catholic Church in Germany, yet the Catholic Church needed to promise not to become involved in political activities in Germany, which Pacelli saw as reasonable.[9] Pius XI wanted strong Concordats to project Church authority on religious life, but his Secretary of State believed the Church could give up political authority in order to gain religious stability.

The Italian war in Ethiopia presented another serious problem for the Vatican hierarchy as Pius XI had been critical of this Italian behavior, yet Benito Mussolini suggested the Pope should not speak critically of the war in public.[10] Pius XI refrained from public comments about this conflict, raising questions about whether or not he was complicit in these Italian activities. Lucia Ceci's research explains that the Pope remained silent about this war not because he condoned it, but because other pressures affected his actions. First, due to the Lateran Accords, the Holy See was supposed to remain silent about political issues, and Pacelli did not believe it would behoove the Catholic Church to speak out against this military action and risk the Vatican's position. Second, the majority of Italian religious figures supported the military action as a civilization campaign in Ethiopia, and it would be very difficult for the Pope to speak out against the war and contradict his religious leadership in Italy.[11] This second concern shares similarities with what happened in Spain: the local religious leaders supported the conservatives in the conflict, yet the Pope never gave public support to these belligerents and their behaviors.

Concerning German and Italian racial laws, questions have been raised as to why the Pope did not condemn them more publicly. Pius XI released *Mit Brennender Sorge* in March 1937, condemning racism, but other statements did not follow the encyclical raising the suspicions of some scholars as to the interaction of the Catholic Church and Nazi Germany. Emma Fattorini, Hubert Wolf, and Alessandro Duce have used Secret Vatican Archival materials to investigate the problem, and these historians have concluded that the Pope desired to speak out against these racial laws enforced in both states, but Secretary of State Pacelli seemed gravely concerned that commentary about these laws could damage the delicate relationships with these aggressive states. Pacelli spoke with German and Italian leaders about these laws, but he wanted the Pope to avoid these contentious topics.[12] These events highlight the problems faced by the Holy See in international diplomacy: Pope Pius XI did not support war or racial laws, but his Secretary of State feared contentious language could irreparably harm the Church in Italy and Germany. Neither man supported these Fascist and Nazi actions, but they had very different plans to deal with these concerns, and Pacelli's cooler strategies won out.

Finally, it is necessary to discuss the professional interactions between Pius XI and his Secretary of State. According to Hubert Wolf's research, the Pope and Pacelli met almost every day, and Pacelli would take brief notes concerning the Pope's wishes, but he also self-censored these materials, and destroyed other documents by burning them in his kitchen. Wolf suggests Pacelli may have destroyed more controversial materials in the possibility he was elected Pope and the notes that did survive were often short and unspecific about what had been discussed.[13] It is also important to understand that not all material sent to the Office of the Secretary of State reached the Pope—like the very personal letter from Edith Stein or from German-Jewish rabbis who wrote the Holy See for assistance with Germany's racial laws.[14] According to Hubert Wolf, it was common for Pacelli not to share all materials with the Pope and it was also quite common for the Secretary of State to respond to important communications from foreign Nunziature with a simple "thank-you" or other receipt acknowledgement.[15] Thus, while Pacelli and the Pope met often, they did not share all their ideas or concerns with each other. I would argue that these men had independent ideas about how to handle international crises, and they did not always agree on the best solution. When the Vatican responded with a direct public response, one could argue that Pope Pius XI was directly involved in the debates, but when quieter negotiations were used, one can clearly see the influence of Pacelli. Overall, however, historians must view these materials—especially those directly concerning warfare—as a coded conversation of a larger discussion—both within and outside of the Vatican.

The First Weeks of War

On 17 July 1936, members of the Spanish military, under the leadership of General José Sanjuro and General Emilio Mola, initiated an uprising against the democratically elected Popular Front government in the name of restoring traditionalism to Spain.[16] Frances Lannon explains the Rebel forces used Catholicism as a symbol for their uprising, but it was not a central factor in the military action as "There was no formal ecclesiastical involvement, no bishop-conspirators, no prior deal with the insurgent generals, and the primary motivation of the rising's military leaders was not religious," as the central reason was "the insurgents' disgust at decentralizing policies that seemed to them tantamount to a dismembering of Spain, their fear of a disintegrating public order, and disapproval of 'communist' social reforms. With the exception of General Mola they did not mention religion."[17] William Callahan explains that during an early radio address, Francisco Franco supported the "apparent commitment to an aconfessional government, as well as warning that the regime would not permit clerical interference."[18] The Rebels promised not to attack religion like the Republic did, but they did not clearly define what role Catholicism would play. Hilari Raguer explain, "Whoever wishes to analyse the genuine motives behind the uprising must read the edicts of the pronunciamiento itself... from none of the groups, not even once, was the call to defend religion given as the reason for the coup."[19] By claiming to defend traditional Spain the Rebels wanted to gain prominent Catholic allies, like in the Vatican, but they did not make specific promises to the hierarchy. Historian Paul Preston suggests the Insurgents were more concerned about maintaining the traditional connection of "Religion, Fatherland, Family, Order, Work, and Property" against the invasion of "anti-Spanish" ideals.[20] The Republic had reduced these traditional connections, and the Rebels believed this attacked what it meant to be "Spanish." Preston suggests eventual leader Francisco Franco most worried about the international "Jewish-Masonic-Bolshevik conspiracy" that needed to be rooted out in any way possible—including a violent uprising against the state.[21] Therefore, for the Rebels, their fight was for salvation and redemption of Spain from the sins of the Republic. The Republic viewed the uprising as an illegal coup d'état against the legitimately elected government, yet the Rebels and their supporters viewed the conflict as an attempt to restore conservative order and defeat the Leftist agenda. While the Insurgency had hoped for a quick military victory, their plan did not succeed because of Republican and militia resistance in major Spanish cities and certain autonomous regions, such as País Vasco and Cataluña. The Rebels managed to occupy large portions of Spanish territory during the first weeks of the war, yet Madrid, País Vasco, Cataluña, and Valencia remained strong in their resistance.

Officially, the Vatican did not openly support either belligerent during the Spanish Civil War. This section will explore the reactions of the Holy See and Republican Government towards each other in the first months of the war. Beginning in September 1936, foreign states developed a Non-Intervention Pact to prevent international aid from entering Spain, yet as time passed, evidence supported the fact that certain states had been interfering in the conflict. The Insurgents received diplomatic and military support from Nazi Germany, Fascist Italy, and Corporatist Portugal. States like the Soviet Union and Mexico acknowledged the legitimacy of the Republican government and sold some military supplies to Madrid, with the USSR sending advisors and volunteers. The Republic bought (by selling their gold reserves to Moscow) about 648 planes and 340 mortars from the USSR, the Rebels received more than 1,200 planes and 7,000 mortars from Germany and Italy, primarily on credit.[22] France, Great Britain, and the United States remained "neutral" in the conflict, but their lack of support was detrimental to the democratically elected Republican government.[23] Due to the 1929 Lateran Accords, the government of the Holy See was required to remain neutral in all international conflicts and not intervene unless all belligerents agreed.[24] The Republic still seemed to hope they could either receive Vatican acceptance during the war, or at least persuade the Holy See not to support openly the rebellion.

The Spanish Catholic hierarchy, however, was not willing to support the Republic due to the government's controversial secularizing legislation and ideological considerations. Officially, the Vatican did not support either side for the duration of the Civil War, and Gonzalo Redondo states there were four main concerns that prevented the Holy See from taking action: (1) The Rebels promised to end the legislation of the Second Republic, but it was unclear when this could occur, (2) The Rebels promised a religious state, but Franco also promised an aconfessional state, (3) In a period of growing totalitarian ideologies, both communism *and* fascism could be threatening, and (4) A war between Catholics, like in the Basque Country, could threaten attitudes toward the Church.[25] A closer investigation of Vatican reactions towards the Second Republic, especially during the first months of the Civil War, will better illuminate how the tension between Madrid and the Holy See did not subside even as the Republic found itself on the defensive against the rebel army.

During the first days of the Civil War, members of communist and anarchist militias looted and burned symbols of conservative ideology and attacked its supporters.[26] Approximately seven hundred Catholic priests, nuns, monks and other clergymen were killed in the first days of the conflict.[27] Between 6,775–6,832 ecclesiastical personnel died during the Civil War, with 4,000 priests, 2,360 monks, 285 nuns, 86 seminarians, and 12 bishops falling victim. Of those victims, 53% died during the first six weeks of the conflict.[28] According to Paul Preston, Republican sympathizers killed 49,272 conservatives, and Rebel forces killed 130,199 Republicans—possibly up to 150,000—during the violence surrounding the conflict.[29] The Civil War created a clear division within the Spanish state, as conservatives reported being arrested or attacked in the Republican zone and Republicans suffered in the Franquista zone. Madrid remained in the hands of the Republic, and militias expropriated Catholic property for their own use. Papal Nuncio Federico Tedeschini alerted the Holy See to the uncontrollable violence in the city through a 22 July telegram to Secretary of State Eugenio Pacelli, explaining the devastation of Catholic Churches in the city and blaming the Republic for a lack of protection. He described the attacks as being carried out by "Armed bands of Reds," grouping all leftist parties together of the moniker of communistic sympathies—even if this was not the case.[30]

The Office of the Vatican Secretary of the State responded to this letter and other news from Spain with a heavy-heart, but its primary concern came from the destruction of Church property and the loss of the lives of clergy. The Office of the Secretary of State wrote to Tedeschini on 31 July to express its concern:

> From different parts of Spain came and still come sad and painful news about the situation of clergy and ecclesiastical property. In Barcelona and throughout almost all of Cataluña, clergy in no way involved with the revolution are killed in the most barbarous ways; the nuns are driven out of hospitals where they do their charitable work and are wickedly insulted; they systematically destroy and burn churches and convents and go so far as to violate the graves and desecrate the corpses.[31]

The fact that uncontrollable mobs seemed to have free-rein in Spain's Republican major cities remained a frightening and real threat for Spain. Paul Preston asserts that Republican militias may have used governmental supplies to kill and pillage, but they were never under the direct authority of the state. He suggests the Republican government did all it could to try to reign in these militias over the following months as their actions harmed the Republic's international image, but the serious destruction had already occurred.[32] Even though the Republic tried to regain control over these militias, these attacks highlighted the deep-seated hatred of some Republicans towards conservatives, and the uprising presented their opportunity to strike. Preston also demonstrates throughout his work that Rebel troops murdered, brutalized, and raped thousands upon invading various regions throughout the country,[33] but the Vatican did not send many notes about these attacks against Republicans and leftists. Possibly, for many in the Church hierarchy, open attacks against symbols of religion were more telling of the Republic's true intentions for a post-war Spain, and therefore were the greater concern.

For the Church, the violence in Republican cities appeared unstoppable. The Holy See had enough proof to blame militias and mobs, but the Vatican had important questions about how this violence could be allowed to occur. Much like the sacking of Catholic sites in the weeks following the declaration of the Second Republic, the Vatican blamed the Republican government because it did not stop the destruction, even though the Republican leadership appeared disorganized and ill-prepared for any military response—even being unable to keep control over its supporters. Lannon and Callahan explain that the Republic claimed this violence was not the responsibility of the state, due to the uncontrollable actions of these mobs as the worst anti-clerical violence occurred as the Republican state apparatus was on the verge of collapse.[34] Violence, too, happened in the capital as "In Madrid, despite being the seat of the Central Government, the same heinous crimes are committed, without the authority intervening to prevent them; public worship has been prohibited and they try to impede it with all means even in private houses." Much like the 1931 violence, the Nuncio blamed the Republican Government as, "All this takes place under the eyes of the same government that claims that it still holds the power and is in control of the situation. Even accepting that the government has serious difficulties in controlling these excesses, it cannot be understood how they can be acquitted of their responsibility in the aforementioned events, which render intolerable the situation of the Church in Spain."[35] According to the Holy See, the Madrid Government was not only unwilling to prevent the violence occurring against the Catholic Church in Spain, but the Republic had made a point to prevent clergy and laypersons from publicly expressing their faith. By not protecting the rights of Catholics, the Vatican suggested the Republic was allowing its militias to victimize Christians purposefully, which would make it nearly impossible for the Vatican to align itself with the Republican government before or during the war. The argument could be made, however, that the Republic's image was being harmed by both sides—the radical left and the right— and the Republican government was never able to present its full and clear case to the Holy See.

The majority of clerical deaths occurred between the July start of the War until the end of 1936. In Barcelona there were 197 ecclesiastical deaths in July and 233 deaths in August alone.[36] As for the perpetrators, they were varied in nature, but anarchist unions like the *Federación Anarquista Ibérica* (Anarchist Federation of Iberia/FAI) and *Confederación Nacional del Trabajo* (National Confederation of Labour/CNT), and the dissident communist party, *Partido Obrero de Unificación Marxista* (Worker Party of Marxist Unification/POUM), were responsible for a great deal of this violence. *Partido Socialista Obrero Español* (Spanish Socialist Worker Party/PSOE) dominated regions like Castilla Nueva, however, also experienced high levels of anticlerical assassinations in the early weeks of the War. As Julio de la Cueva suggests, leftist groups identified perpetrators as "irresponsible" or "out of control" to avoid responsibility for these actions.[37] Richard Maddox explains that anticlerical violence by militias and discontented workers occurred due to a combination of three reasons: (1) many of these attacks were spontaneous due to the threat of an "immediate revolutionary crisis" initiated by the uprising, (2) 19th and 20th century Spanish conservatives had used the Church to maintain political authority making religious sites and personnel targets for "political agitation," and (3) these attacks were meant to undermine the long-term "inequality" based on the combination of "religion, honor, and patronage" seen by the lower classes.[38] Maria Thomas suggests the anticlerical behaviors were not new to Spain, as decades of conservative repression exploded against symbols of the right.³⁹ The Republic, however, continued to claim it could not control all actions of all allies throughout its territory given that the military coup had plunged the state apparatus into disarray and, in particular, had weakened its coercive machinery. Just because these militias fought with the Republic, it did not mean that they all agreed upon why they took-up arms. The Popular Front Government included many left-leaning parties, and they did not all agree on what Spain was supposed to look like. For the Catholic Church it was a similar and frightening comparison to the violence endured in May 1931. The Republic, therefore, could be seen as allowing radical violence to occur against the Church on two (if not more) major occasions within a five year period. For the Republican Government, however, this violence always seemed to occur when it was at its weakest or most vulnerable—soon after its declaration, during election failures, in Asturias, or when the "Uprising" began. The Republican Government did not call for all the violence against the Church, but it also appeared impotent in trying to prevent these attacks.

The Office of the Vatican Secretary of State offered more advice on how the Papal Nuncio in Madrid should proceed. In Pacelli's 31 July letter, the Nuncio was instructed to initiate a series of protests by the Catholic Church to the Madrid government. Like the early protests from 1931, these complaints were to be sent formally and remained within the bounds of diplomacy—showing the Vatican wished to continue the normal diplomatic protocol with the Republic:

> And all the more because in the past, in spite of the repeated protests of the Pontifical Representative in Madrid, they have not duly repressed nor punished the violence committed against the Church, allowing the suspicion of tolerance and conniving with the worst enemies of religion to be sustained in public opinion. The Holy See is therefore obligated to elevate its highest protest and expects that the government intervene energetically where it can to stop such excesses and at least not avoid deploring the excesses of such sacrilegious acts and separate its own responsibility from that of their authors.⁴⁰

Even though there were more failures than successes for the Church, the Holy See appeared to be willing to rely upon its representatives again, being consistent with Pacelli's previous activities in Europe. The Holy See believed it was the unfair victim of the Republic's attacks, yet it never broke off formal diplomatic channels with the Madrid government—possible proof that the Vatican still hoped for the Republic to change or because the Holy See was just as uncertain as to what was really happening throughout Spain—as all sides appeared in a state of utter confusion at the start of the uprising.⁴¹ The primary concern for the

Vatican appeared to be the destruction and violence against clergy, the Church, its property, and dozens of churches sacked and looted—especially in regions with large anarchist sympathies.[42] On 10 August 1936, *L'Osservatore Romano* published an article to express the Vatican's protests against the anticlerical violence in Spain.[43] The article contained much of the 31 July letter of the Vatican Secretary of State to the Nuncio to highlight the Holy See's fears about the deteriorating conditions in Spain, but it never suggested how the Catholic audience should respond, most likely because the Holy See did not know the best course of action.[44]

The 31 July letter from the Office of the Vatican Secretary of State sparked an important exchange between the Spanish Republican Embassy and the Holy See. The former responded to the complaints of the Holy See regarding the perceived failures of the Republic, through a 2 August letter:

> The Spanish Embassy is honored to answer the Note dated 31 July, addressed by the Secretary of State of Your Holiness. It should state before all, regarding the reprehensible violence that the Note alludes to, that the Spanish Government deplores profoundly any acts of such kind that might have actually occurred. It is well-known, however, that the Spanish authorities, and even those of Catalonia, have intervened in numerous occasions to avoid cruel excesses, protecting the lives of priests and clergy. But the Spanish Government cannot but point out to the Holy See that the painful fact that in the course of the events provoked by the military rebellion there have been victims invested with the ecclesiastical character is largely due to the attitude adopted by a considerable part of the Spanish clergy. Within your members, there are those who have taken arms in the fascist ranks, as could be verified in the collection of the dead and wounded after the combat. Some priests made themselves strong in their respective churches, being later attacked. Many clergy and religious men have provided their support to the armed rebellion against the legitimate government and to the cruel attack against the Republic, over the perpetrators of which ultimately lies the responsibility of all the evils that they have unleashed. Various Prelates appear now in relation with the fascist Junta of Burgos, and the Bishops of Palma de Mallorca, Pamplona and Vitoria have tried to exercise their influence on Catholics to dissuade them of their loyal attitude to the Government, even threatening them with spiritual punishments, as it was broadcasted on August 7 by the station of the aforementioned fascist Junta. In spite of all these facts, that could only provoke an inevitable reaction in the popular mind, the Republican Government, not only laments the acts of violence that unjustifiably might have occurred, but it also contained them as much as possible, adopting measures for the protection of temples and clergymen, and is

likewise willing to avoid them in the future. The temporary suspension of religious cults, to which the Note from the Secretary of State refers, does not respond to a hostile purpose of the Government against Catholic sentiments, guaranteed within the Constitution, but is only a temporary preventive measure precisely directed to avoid possible abuses, thus allowing the conservation of temples and religious objects and protecting your priests and ministers.[45]

The Spanish Embassy not only addressed the Vatican's public conversation about the Republic, but it raised serious issues relating to the behavior of the Church leadership in the country. For many in the Spanish Catholic hierarchy, "The idea of a war of absolutes between Christian civilization and the forces of barbarism, the exclusive identification of Spanish nationalism with Catholicism, and the appeals to providentialism tinged with Old Testament prophetism echoed the arguments directed against the French invader by an earlier generation of episcopal militants."[46] For the Republican Government, the concerns of the Holy See were generally unfounded. The Republic acknowledged that some violence had occurred in Spain against the Church, but asserted that the Vatican's claims that the Republic had done nothing to protect their property were untrue. The Republic believed this violence occurred because some members of the clergy had aligned themselves with the military rebellion and it was difficult for the Government to protect these individuals due to their political antagonism, blaming members of the Church for the violence they experienced. While religious leaders did not specifically call for their clergymen to take up arms, the Republic believed the words of certain bishops condemned the Republic and supported the Insurgents. Beginning on 23 August 1936, Bishop D. Marcelino Olaechea called the Civil War a "crusade" against atheism and a just war, Bishop D. Roberto Doménech of Zaragoza seconded this opinion on 26 August, and Archbishop of Santiago, D. Tomás Muniz Pablas publicly called the war a crusade on 31 August. These leaders did not "fight" in the war, but their words may have offered support to the Rebel cause.[47] Therefore, the Republic clearly discredited Vatican concerns, which could never help their future interactions.

Needless-to-say, the Holy See did not appreciate the Republic's statement that the clergy was possibly responsible for, or at least encouraged violence. The Republic took a more aggressive path in its communications with the Church. When Catholic leaders in Spain became more vocal in their protests against the Republic, Madrid's words to the Holy See became more aggressive. Finally, the Republic maintained that the suspension of Catholic practices in Spain was based on the protection of the Church and was allowed under the Constitution of 1931, and the Republican Embassy explained that Church rights were reduced in order to protect it from violence. If the Church used its masses to condemn the Republic's actions, it would not be a surprise for the government to suspend the actions of the Church, harkening back to the *Ley de Defensa de la República*. For the Republic, reducing the Church's public prominence was doing the Church a favor. The Republic did not consider its actions as being aggressive or hostile towards the Church, rejecting the Holy See's claims because members of the Spanish Catholic Church had chosen sides at the start of the war.

Communications such as these highlight the major problem between the Holy See and the Republican Government, or any secular government. The Holy See remained formally neutral in the War and did not offer support to either side. Some members of the Spanish Catholic hierarchy did, however, support the rebellion. This is the problem—how could the Republican Government separate the actions of the *Spanish* Catholic hierarchy from the official positions of the Holy See? As Lucia Ceci has shown, Italian priests supported the war in Ethiopia, but the Pope did not.[48] At the same time, how could the Holy See separate the actions of some Republican militias from the Republican Government? The Republic tried to contain its militias in order to regain some international legitimacy.[49] Both Madrid and the Vatican claimed radical individuals did not speak on their behalves, but how could this ever be clearly proven? Even if the Catholic Church clearly sided with the Rebels, was that a legitimate reason to kill defenseless and unarmed priests? Clearly the Vatican hierarchy would not trust the Second Republic's Popular Front Government while members of the Republican leadership would not have trusted the Catholic Church, but the inability—whether intentional or not—to separate real enemies from perceived troublemakers, prevented any space for early understanding between the two entities.

The Holy See regarded the Republic's claims of protecting the Church as untrue. The Office of the Vatican Cardinal Secretary of the State wrote to the Papal Nuncio on 21 August 1936 to express its concerns about the seemingly uncontrollable violence in Spain, "The Holy See mostly takes note of the condemnation expressed by the Madrid Government for the grave sacrileges committed against sacred persons and properties, not of the promise to adopt measures to stop them in the future." But the Cardinal remained untrusting of Madrid, "While it would want to trust its declaration, it cannot fail to notice at the same time how unfortunately the constant repetition of the same painful actions is far from the verification of the aforementioned assurance."[50] The Holy See could trace the Republic's inability to stop the violence to its broken promise to the Catholic Church to protect all Spaniards, including Catholics. The Republic admitted this violence had occurred, which was obvious, yet it supposedly declined to work to prevent further similar events. The issue was, of course, that the Republic was not completely in control, so how could they stop these behaviors? At the same time, the Church had the right to ask for assistance, even from the Republic.

The Office of the Secretary of State denied the Republican government's suggestion that the actions of Republican militias were a surprise or that the Republic had no idea of the widespread violence. The Secretary of State's letter continued, "The attitude of the press, that even under the eyes of the Government of Madrid occur violent attacks against the Church, the Clergy, and the Religious men; the numerous invasions; the arrests and barbaric killings of people dedicated to the Lord . . . all these contribute to spread in public opinion a suspicion of tolerance and connivance with the worst enemies of Religion."[51] According to Pacelli's office, the Republic knew of and condoned this violence and he suggested these were direct attempts to create a hostile environment against Catholicism. Unlike previous notes of the Holy See, this letter directly connected the violence against the Church's property and clergy in Spain to the activities of the Second Republic. Before the Civil War began, the Holy See frequently protested the lack of help from the Republic, but in this case, the Holy See was openly blaming the Government for these crimes. Was the actual government responsible?—no. But, again, how does one separate a field of uncomfortable allies during a time of bloody conflict.

The Republic could not prevent radical militias to roam the streets and act violently. In fact, according to the Holy See, these militias were Republican means to initiate violence, "Instead, fanatic and radical elements have been armed and then set free and unpunished in their wicked mania of destruction." The Nuncio continued, "The Government of Madrid should be especially invested in effectively repressing these crimes, in that honest people of all the world cannot fail to notice any longer the fact that such anti-religious atrocities, which bring dishonor to such a noble Nation as Spain, are committed and allowed to be committed only in those regions in which the Government of Madrid exercises its authority."[52] At the start of the Spanish Civil War, the Republican Government armed numerous citizens, particularly in large cities, to defend the Republic. These Republican militias were meant to defend the Government against the insurrection because a majority of the state's military leadership had sided with the Rebel movement.[53] These militias were not completely under the control of the Government, and they frequently acted in whatever manner they wanted—especially those of the ideologically unique Spanish Anarchists.[54] The Republican Government had armed these groups to protect the Republic, yet the Government was not able to control them.[55] The Holy See correlated this lack-of-control over the militias as the Republic's direct attempt to quash the influence of the Church in the Republican Zone. According to the Vatican, just as the Republic seemed uninterested in stopping the violence at the onset of the new regime, the Civil War-era Government was both unable and unwilling to control groups it viewed as necessary to defend the state. The Rebels, too, unleashed savage attacks against their enemies,[56] but fewer notes exist in the Secret Archive condemning these attacks.

On 20 August 1936, the new Papal Nuncio to the Madrid Government, Silvio Sericano,[57] sent his compiled report to the Holy See regarding the conditions in the Republican zone from the start of the war. Nuncio Sericano's report addressed the four major concerns of the Church in Spain during the first month of the Civil War: the Churches, the Convents, the Clergy and the Religious Organizations. As for the Church "About twenty burned relatively easily; a good many sacked; all the others closed with the exception of a few churches of foreigners, occupied by the red militias. The Church of Carmine was converted into a macabre and nauseating museum of the antireligious; while those of S. José and 'de las Calatravas' were particularly profaned."[58] Sericano's statement that "red militias" occupied some churches is of particular importance because there was no separation between supporters of the Republic and communists and anarchists, something that could affect the Holy See's view of the Madrid Government. The militias destroyed the sanctity of many churches by converting them into symbols of atheism and antireligious beliefs, a direct attack against the sovereignty of the Church's property and a destruction of its religious practices.[59]

The Republican militias did not just attack churches, but they also turned their attention to religious convents and other buildings owned by prominent Catholic organizations. These convents, homes of clergy and nuns in Spain, were not immune from the Republican assaults "Some burned; a good many sacked and the others occupied by the reds; the Episcopal palace and the seminary, the quarters of the Catholic organizations and the printing presses of all the Catholic periodicals were occupied by the reds."[60] Once again, Sericano noted the sacking and occupation of these religious locations by militias of the "reds." The occupation and closing of Catholic periodicals prevented the supporters of the Church from disseminating their ideas to the populace. Those periodicals that survived the *Ley de Defensa de la República* did not survive these attacks. According to Sericano, even though the militias did not occupy the Nunziatura, it was damaged in the early days of the Uprising: "The Nunziatura has been, up to now, relatively respected; saying relatively, because during the heavy shooting on 20 July this house was hit by a good number of fired bullets."[61] Because the Nunziatura was the *de facto* embassy of the Holy See in Spain, it was the responsibility of the Republic to protect it. Monasteries, publishing houses, and the Nunziatura did not receive respect and protection, which was a dangerous sign for the Papal Nuncio.

Sericano was not only interested in the condition of the Church's buildings in Spain, but he was also concerned for the lives of the clergy. The Holy See had received notes from other Papal representatives in Spain about the violence towards clergy, and Sericano's letter reestablished these concerns for "secular and regular clergy forced to seek refuge in houses of acquaintances or friends and changing continually the houses in the hope of not falling into the hands of the reds who search systematically the houses, arresting seculars whom they consider political opponents, clergy men in general, and even nuns." According to Sericano, red militias inhumanely executed numerous members of the clergy in the streets and in religious homes and "We know of many cases of clergy brutally murdered in homes, on public roads and in the churchyards . . . Many others and even numerous nuns are detained in the prisons of Madrid."[62]

The violence was uncontrollable and Sericano expressed concern for the safety of the clergy because these militias assassinated clergymen and women for no apparent reason, other than their religious beliefs. As the Spanish Embassy told the Holy See at the start of the Civil War, the Republic believed the majority of clergy supported the insurgency, but the Nuncio did not agree with this assessment and thought no seditious crimes were carried out, yet the Republican militias saw the Church as a social enemy and believed it was time to remove religious influence and punish the clergy. The reasons surrounding the arrests and "penalties" directed at clergy remained a major problem for both sides throughout the conflict.

At the start of the Civil War, religious practice was reduced in public and in private "As a consequence of this, the complete suppression of public religious worship in Madrid: the administration of the Holy Sacrament is practically impossible; the Holy Mass is celebrated only in few private chapels and in some private houses on the sly, with great caution and not without grave danger."[63] Public masses in Madrid could not occur because of the constant surveillance by the Republican militias. Sericano's letter explained to the Vatican hierarchy that religious life in Madrid had ceased and the Republic had attacked and destroyed every aspect of the Catholic Church: its property, its people, its power and its practices. The Church was not safe in Madrid because of the Republic's lack-of-control over its own supporters. From this explanation, it is understandable why the Catholic Church was so concerned with the actions of the Republic. This note, however, does not address the fact that many members of the Catholic clergy had been outspoken critics of the Republican regime, like Cardinal Gomá during the War and Cardinal Segura and Bishop Múgica during the early period of the Second

Republic.⁶⁴ The information the Holy See received from its main representative in the Republican zone condemned the Republic for its irrational actions while making all members of the clergy, no matter their political actions, victims of the state. Regarding the Republic, Sericano ended his letter by stating, "The Government is not only absolutely impotent in preventing these atrocities but it allows the reds to behave this way in public."⁶⁵ For the Nuncio, the Republican Government was unable to prevent these attacks and had sided with communists and anarchists above all other groups. Therefore, the Republic was defined as "red," a clear threat to the safety of Catholic practices in Spain.

The Holy See and its hierarchy received communications emphasizing the highly deteriorating condition of the Catholic Church in Madrid and the Republican zone, which helped to reinforce the Church's concerns about the Republican government. The behavior of the Rebel army, however, presented different issues for the Holy See. The Insurgents won many quick victories in southern Spain, with the major city of Sevilla falling in the first days of the war. After the Rebels entered Sevilla, Jesuit Ignacio Zurbano wrote a letter to the Vatican hierarchy on 11 August to explain the changing conditions in the city by describing his happiness with the arrival of the Rebel troops because they could return the free practice of Catholicism to the city.⁶⁶ The troops, according to Zurbano, were able to remove the Republican militias, supported directly by "Moskow."⁶⁷ The military victory of the Rebels also ushered in a spiritual change to the city, "It is admirable the religious spirit that was awoken in the troops, initiated by the Requetés: Almost all the soldiers wear on their chest the shield of the Sacred Heart: from the beginning they requested chaplains and Mass is already said in the Quarters and many soldiers can be seen confessing and taking communion in the Churches."⁶⁸ To Zurbano, the fact that these soldiers went directly to the Churches of Sevilla for confession and communion was important because he could report their adherence to Catholicism. This message, however, may be overstated because these armies frequently relied on Moorish Muslim soldiers, especially in Southern Spain.⁶⁹ Historically, the use of Moorish soldiers in Spain was problematic, because the battles of the Reconquista created a great deal of animosity towards Muslims fighting on Spanish soil.⁷⁰ Stating that the soldiers went to Catholic Mass, Zurbano might have been trying to "Christianize" the image of the Rebel forces.⁷¹ According to Zurbano, "now the militants look at us priests with great respect and veneration; they greet us and even kiss our hand publicly in the streets, with great affect."⁷² Zurbano was pleased to announce the improved conditions for clergy in Sevilla, with the help of the soldiers, showing this priest's distrust of the Republic. The priest, however, failed to speak of widespread violence unleashed against the working class, especially in the neighborhood of Triana. Paul Preston suggests that while

447 Rebels were killed in Sevilla, 12,507 Republicans were murdered by the rebel forces during the Civil War.[73] Obviously, Republican supporters faired much worse in Sevilla than their adversaries.

The Holy See received letters from its Nuncio and other representatives condemning the Republican Government and militias, while expressing gratitude for the actions of the Rebel troops during the war. On 10 September 1936, the Vatican Secretary of State wrote to the Papal Nuncio in Madrid to announce a Papal radio broadcast about the Civil War. The broadcast, scheduled for 14 September, was to "show Catholic exemplary suffering, denounce the inhuman persecution, deplore the civil war and the venom of Bolshevik propaganda."[74] The Pope's message was meant to show the Church's support for its Spanish brethren in this time of warfare. The summary of the Pope's broadcast suggested the message was to remain politically neutral, but it specifically acknowledged the Pope's disdain for Bolshevik propaganda. While the message did not openly support the Republican or the Rebel side in the war, the Holy See's greatest concern was the communist actions in Spain.[75] This radio broadcast did fit Pius XI's personality, as he publicly challenged the situation in Spain, condemning this violent ideological war, but he focused his ire on the communists. These communists, as other reports showed, were the supposedly primary supporters of the Republic. Therefore, even though the Pope's message was not meant to be an attack against the Republic, the criticism against communist supporters in Spain created a larger divide between the Holy See and the Republican Government. Still, however, the question remains as to where these communists actually were?

REACTING TO THE REBELLION

At the start of the War, the Vatican worried about the Madrid Government's lack of interest in protecting Catholic buildings from the sacking of communists and anarchists, and the increasing dangers for their clergy in Spain. Catholic representatives in Spain sent the Holy See numerous communications stressing the serious and grave condition in the state. These representatives identified a perceived connection between the supporters of the Republic with communists and anarchists. The majority of the communications highlighted the fact that "reds" were responsible for the majority of the violence and chaos, but the Republic was either unable or not interested in alienating its allies for the sake of the Church. The information the Vatican hierarchy received established a clear and increasingly frightening connection between Red ideology and the Republic. At the same time, however, the Vatican had to worry about the increased Spanish Catholic hierarchy's support for the

Insurgents—even as the Vatican tried to remain neutral. This support drove the Republic to view numerous Church leaders in Spain as enemies of the state. Rather than try to identify points where the Republic and the Holy See could agree—such as in the restoration of peace in Spain—both sides focused on information that blamed the other for the growing tensions and atrocities. The Republic's desperation prevented it from condemning actions from possible internal allies. At the same time, the Holy See could not condemn the actions of the Spanish Catholic hierarchy, who had been vocal for the uprising, as they remained part of the universal church. One must admit that the confusion of the insurgency and the following war made a clear understanding of each group's true opinions difficult to identify clearly.

V

Humanitarian Concerns Increase as the War Continues

As the Spanish Civil War continued, representatives of the Madrid Government and the Basque Government both tried to increase conversations with the Holy See in the hopes of persuading the Vatican to act on their behalves. For many in the Spanish Catholic hierarchy, the Republic continued to ignore the crises affecting the Church throughout the country, with some going as far as to increase claims of anticlerical environments to try to persuade the Holy See to accept the Burgos Government. Meanwhile, the Insurgency continued to spread falsehoods about the behaviors of their enemies, but most importantly, to spread half-truths about their actions. This chapter will scrutinize the hierarchy's reaction to both sets of belligerents as the Rebel forces overpowered the Republic. Next, this chapter will investigate the reaction of the Vatican hierarchy towards the region of País Vasco. The Basques were a devotedly Catholic people, but they sided with the Madrid government. Here I explore how the Vatican attempted to explain the relationship between the Madrid government and País Vasco—something most troubling for the Church. Similarly, this section will define how the Vatican hierarchy attempted to separate "good Catholics" of País Vasco from the communists and anarchists who had infiltrated the region.

Information relating to the first half of the Spanish Civil War will help to explain how the Vatican used its network of representatives to gain much-needed information about the conflict, yet the Vatican hierarchy took a reserved position and was reluctant to make itself a possible target for either side in the War. The Vatican diplomatic corp hoped to communicate with both sides during the conflict, but it soon realized the complex nature of the Civil War and the varied ideological stances of the belligerents complicated any possible Vatican strategies. The multiple messages from the Republic seemed to stand no competition to the unified and singular messages of the Franquistas—even if Burgos often lied.

The Civil War Continues

In October 1936, the Rebel forces turned their attention towards Madrid, hoping to take the city quickly and possibly force an end to the War; however, they failed as Republican allies defended the city from invading forces. With the Rebels moving towards Madrid, the Catholic hierarchy's concerns grew as Republican militias supposedly increased their attacks against perceived conservative allies. This section will explore the periods of growing violence in Spain as the war continued, as well as the conversations between Republican representatives and the Catholic hierarchy outside of Spain. News of the deteriorating conditions in Madrid continued to reach the Holy See, and the Republic failed to persuade the Vatican hierarchy that they were not the Church's enemy. The Republic wanted the Holy See to support the government against the rebellion, but how could they do so with this type of violence against religious targets continuing in the country?

Nuncio Sericano initiated a series of communications with the Holy See in October 1936 to update the Vatican on the religious and military conditions in Madrid. A 14 October telegram began "Religious situation unchanged,"[1] explaining that the dire situation for the Church at the start of the war continued in Madrid, and Vatican complaints regarding the treatment of clergy and property seemed ignored by the Republic. The Papal Nuncio updated the Holy See about the changing military conditions in the city: "From the front, recent notes of the red organizations having reacted by intensifying arrests and perpetrating new assassinations of elements of the right, among which some clergymen."[2] The proximity of Franco's forces had sparked worry in Madrid, and militias retaliated against the political right and clergy. These militias identified enemies of the Republic and detained or killed many, including many members of the Church. It should not be surprising, therefore, that the Spanish Catholic hierarchy remained hostile to the Republican cause as the war continued.

By 28 October, the rebels had reached the edges of Madrid and began a series of aerial bombardments of the city—likely flying under German and Italian flags. In Madrid, the presence of their planes above the city increased apprehension for the denizens.[3] The Papal Nuncio was also concerned about these bombardments, but for different reasons; as the Rebels "cut every railroad communication Madrid is practically besieged by the Nationalist army whose aviation each day systematically bombards fortifications and improvised trenches of the government loyalists in the surroundings of the city."[4] The memo claimed that the Insurgents forces had been "systematically" bombarding Republic military installations around the city, but it did not include information about civilian casualties.[5] This 28 October note ended with information about a rally of

Madrileña women supporting the Republic. Sericano wrote, "Manifestations of women, organized by the initiative of the Russian Ambassador, have taken place in the past days in the streets of Madrid asking for all able-bodied men to be sent to the frontlines and for the killing of all political prisoners."[6] The Nuncio appeared most concerned because he believed the Soviet Ambassador Rossenberg—under the auspices of a communist revolution—had initiated these protests in the streets. According to Sericano, the influence of Soviet Bolshevism could not be separated from the actions of these women. Therefore, the Papal Nuncio discredited the validity of the protests, but he was extremely concerned about Rossenberg's ability to organize such a rally in Madrid. Of greater worry for the Nuncio was the rally's call for the killing of detained prisoners in Madrid—some being priests. According to Sericano, the Soviet Union was using women and children to push its Bolshevik agenda—which included violence against the Church.

By the final days of October the situation in Madrid had deteriorated and the Papal Nuncio considered evacuating the city. The President of the Republic fled, as Madrid was "Completely besieged" by the Rebel army.[7] The concern for the Nuncio, however, was not the siege of the Insurgent forces on the Madrid border, but the threat of the "Red Committees" made it unsafe for clergy and the Nuncio.[8] Sericano believed it was difficult to guarantee the security of the Nunziatura in Madrid. The French *Chargé d'Affaires* in Madrid offered the availability of a French plane to evacuate the Nuncio and his staff to Toulouse, yet Sericano believed it was best to stay in the city.[9] The Nuncio hoped to initiate serious communications with the approaching Insurgent forces to assist religious leaders captured by the Republic, "I would add that in the likely event that the Rebel army enters Madrid, the Representative of the Holy See, if still present, would be morally constrained to express his sympathies with the Burgos Government, thus causing great danger for the lives of a great number of ecclesiasticals detained by the reds in the provinces in their power."[10] If the militias felt threatened by the Rebels' approach—or if the Church openly expressed support for the approaching army—then they might kill prisoners—many of whom were likely religious figures. While the Holy See did not fully acknowledge the authority of the Government of Burgos during the war, the willingness of the Vatican's leadership in Spain to communicate with the Rebels for their own interests could highlight why the Republic was so distrustful of the Catholic Church. On the other hand, the Republic's inability to control its militias and their violence against the Church may have driven the Papal Nuncio to search for assistance from the approaching army. The Republic and the Holy See shared neither the same interests nor concerns nor beliefs, making any common ground scarce.

The situation in Spain did not remain only a "Spanish crisis," especially as military supplies and soldiers from other states entered the country.[11] The greatest concern for the Holy See, as frequently mentioned, was the invasion of atheistic Bolshevism into traditionally Catholic Spain. While the Holy See's communications with the Madrid Government expressed its concerns about this external assistance, the Holy See was also aware of foreign aid assisting the Rebels. On 23 November 1936, Papal Nuncio to Italy Cardinal Borgongini Duca met with Benito Mussolini, during which *il Duce* clearly stated he and Adolf Hitler had serious problems with the spread of Bolshevism in the Mediterranean region. Both fascist leaders used the "threat of communism" as a political tool to gain support from conservatives. Borgongini Duca reported that he "Confirmed to me that Italy is helping Spain with men and materials, 'and already we have had some deaths'."[12] This confession to the Holy See shows that the Vatican hierarchy knew clearly that Italy was openly supporting the forces of Franco during the war. The Nuncio's letter concluded with the Italian rationale for entering the war: to protect the Mediterranean from Bolshevik influence. The Holy See was obtaining information about the condition of the war from Nuncios outside of Spain, showing that the Vatican had the ability to access a wide network of fact gathering due to its large international presence.

In December 1936, the Spanish Minister Antonio Fabra Ribas of the Spanish Socialist Workers Party (PSOE) met with the Papal Nuncio of Switzerland, Felipe Bernardini, in Bern to discuss the situation in Spain. The meeting occurred as Fabra Ribas prepared to attend meetings at the League of Nations in Geneva on the Spanish Civil War. Bernardini described Fabra Ribas as a "militant socialist and does not make a mystery his ideas" in his 10 December 1936 letter to the Holy See.[13] With that description, there should be no doubt that complete common ground between Fabra Ribas and Bernardini would be difficult to find. Regarding the war in Spain, Fabra Ribas told Bernardini, "The fault is of the monarchy, the aristocracy and partly of the clergy that at least in the major cities lost contact with the population, ignored the discontent of the working class and the gravity of the immanent reaction."[14] The representative of the Madrid Government placed blame on the traditional elements in Spain, including some clergy and maintained that the Republic simply reacted to this increasingly violent atmosphere.

Although Fabra Ribas was a Socialist, he did attempt to separate his government from the violence occurring against the clergy in Spain. Bernardini reported, "The same minister concludes that the horrors and the carnage carried out by the reds were completely inexcusable."[15] The Republican Minister admitted violence against the clergy was occurring in Spain, agreeing with the Holy See and acknowledging Vatican worries, but he explained rogue militias were responsible. The Spanish Minister, however, did not believe Republican allies were the only groups responsible for violence. Bernardini reported Fabra Ribas "told me frankly that the reds and the whites will be equally losers even if they are apparently successful. Poor Spain will need many years to recover internal peace in order to be able to regain its place as a great nation."[16] According to Fabra Ribas, the Republic was not the only perpetrator, as violent actions were occurring from both sides, and civilian populations were being targeted. At the end of their meeting, Fabra Ribas stated "In Spain only one religion is possible, and that is Catholicism; that whatever government, even of the extreme left, will have to recognize this fact together with the impossibility of replacing the Catholic religion with any other moral system that can educate the populace in the observance of the law."[17] Even though Bernardini began his letter by identifying Fabra Ribas as a "militant" Socialist, it is worth noting that the Spanish Minister acknowledged the historical power and position of the Church in Spain. The fact that Fabra Ribas noted that no other ideology would be able to replace the helpfulness of Catholicism in creating good citizens showed that he (even begrudgingly) had to acknowledge the influential power of the Catholic Church. The Spanish Minister was trying to soften the position of the Republic against the Church, and attempted to use such language to gain the Holy See's support. In fact, Bernardini received a letter from the Holy See on 27 December 1936, stating the Vatican was pleased that the Spanish Minister had acknowledged the helpfulness of Catholicism, but it did not offer further plans or comments.[18] The Republic needed to stop its antagonistic communications with the Holy See, but had too much damage already been done?

Bernardini's December letter to the Holy See not only contained information regarding the Spanish Minister's conversation, but it exposed the important concerns of the Spanish Republic regarding foreign intervention in the Civil War. Because Bernardini was located in Switzerland, it gave him first-hand knowledge of the ongoing debates at the League of Nations. The Republican Government had filed a formal protest to the League about the Rebels' use of Italian and German aid.[19] In response, the Italian representative in the League suggested the Republic should avoid such claims because the German and Italian Governments were attending discussions in London regarding Non-Intervention.[20] In fact, the Italian representative stated that Soviet support for the Republic had been the most egregious. The Republican representative questioned the ability and the rationale of the London Conference because it appeared not to be working.[21] This debate at the League of Nations highlighted the increasing international tensions of the Civil War. At the same time, the Vatican's representative witnessed complaints from Republican and Rebel supporters. The Vatican, therefore, knew the Republic's anger regarding Italian and German assistance for the Insurgency, but the Holy See also was able to confirm the actions of the Soviet Union.

The final portion of Bernardini's letter highlighted a conversation between the Nuncio and Giuseppe Motta, Conservative Member of the Swiss Federal Council. Because of Switzerland's close proximity and cultural ties to Germany and Italy, and because the Swiss were predominantly Catholic, Motta and his allies would not and could not support the Republican government and he wanted to see a favourable end to the Civil War that would benefit the Rebels.[22] Motta came to Bernardini and asked about:

> The Spanish situation and the possibility of stopping hostilities. Mr. Motta had read in newspapers that the Holy See was interested in taking the initiative for peace, or at least for an armistice. He recognized all the difficulty of the undertaking, but to my question as to whether he believed that a word of peace pronounced from the Holy Father would have made, in this moment, a good impression, he responded that he was convinced that this word, even if not heard, would have made in the world an excellent impression. The same was repeated to me also by non-Catholic diplomats.[23]

While not an official request, a representative of the Holy See was asked about the possibility of a Vatican peace plan for the conflict in Spain. The Swiss political leader thought the Holy See was the only entity that could construct a plan for a peaceful solution. This statement by Motta showed that other European States, in this case Switzerland, considered the Holy See a viable diplomatic state that could create political change on the continent. The 27 December letter from the Holy See to Bernardini, however, did not contain a response about Motta's idea. What this request does show, however, was that while some states had previously grown suspicious of Vatican mediation—particularly as a result of its action in WWI—others still considered the Holy See as the strongest and most moral proponent of peace.

The autumn and early winter of 1936 were very active periods in the Spanish Civil War as the Rebel forces had made serious gains in Spain, but remained unable to take Madrid. Even though the Republican Government fled to Valencia, Madrid remained in the hands of Republican supporters and militias. As the Rebels continued to win battles, "red" militias took their anger out on conservatives in their zone, with particular violence directed against the clergy. Franquistas continued to repress leftists in their newly occupied zones, yet the Nuncio's reports often associated the Republic with the communist and anarchist militias. It cannot be completely determined if the Nuncio purposefully identified all Republican militias as communists and anarchists, but the mentioning of this connection may have influenced the decisions of the Vatican throughout the conflict. Internationally, Republicans attempted to stress the widespread violence of both extremes—Reds and Whites—but used positive language about the role of the Church in Spain. The Republic, however, appeared unable to disconnect itself from the violent actions of the militias. When Republicans complained of Fascist support, Italy reminded the League of Nations about Soviet interference. True, the Republican military did receive military support from the Soviet Union, but it was nowhere close to the aid Burgos obtained. The Republic also lost its gold reserves—sending them to Moscow. Even as the violence continued to grow in Spain, the Holy See avoided public comment on the situation, apparently hoping that formal diplomacy through the League of Nations and the London Conference could fix the situation. Pius XI might have wanted to make some public commentary about this conflict, but his Secretary of State must have pushed for restraint. This "silence" by the Vatican shares similarities with the Italo-Abyssinian war, but Secretary of State Pacelli might have considered silence a better response than possibly creating more contention. As the War continued, the Vatican sorted through an ever-growing number of communications from numerous individuals—each hoping to influence the reaction of the Vatican on the international arena. With all this material, it appeared obvious that the Holy See did not want to act too quickly and appear to support a belligerent during open-warfare.

THE INSURGENCY MOVES ON THE BASQUE COUNTRY

While the forces of Franco and his troops made quick advances throughout southern Spain and reached the outskirts of Madrid, other units and Carlist forces began their attacks on the north-central region of Spain, known as País Vasco. The region was the home to an ethnically and linguistically independent people known as the Basque, who tried to maintain their unique cultural identity within the confines of the Spanish state. With the declaration of the Second Republic and the creation of the Constitution of 1931, various regions in Spain hoped for autonomous status. The leaders of the new "Basque Republic"—declared after the start of the Civil War—supported the legitimacy of the Republican cause, due to Madrid's support for autonomous rights in October. Even though the Basques were a devoutly Catholic people,[24] the prize of autonomous control over their own region was a key for their decision to side with the Republic during the Civil War. Frances Lannon explains, "When war broke out these devout, orthodox, but nationalist Catholics remained loyal to a republic that eventually, in October 1936, granted them the long-delayed statute of autonomy . . . They wanted from the Vatican—but did not get—some recognition of the specific traditions and needs of the area, some protection from the centralist bishops and anti-nationalist religious orders active in the Basque Provinces."[25] Francisco Franco and his followers wanted to end the autonomous rights of these regions and return control to a strong central government in Madrid.[26]

During the Civil War, Basque Nationalists, along with members of Leftists parties, tried to defend País Vasco from Rebel forces. The War in the Basque region presented numerous concerns for the Catholic Church in Spain. On one hand, the Basque were devoutly Catholic and extremely faithful to the teachings of the Church, but on the other hand the Basque Nationalist leadership had chosen to side with the Republic, even though socialists, communists, and anarchists worked with Madrid. Some members of the clergy in the Basque region aligned themselves with the regional government against the Insurgent forces. While the Holy See received numerous communications on the horrible conditions for clergy within the Republican zone, Rebel forces also arrested, detained, and killed sixteen pro-Basque priests in northern Spain. According to Paul Preston, Rebels specifically targeted priests who were politically influential for assassination.[27] Father Eladio Celaya of Cáseda near Pamplona spoke out against the violent repression against Republicans as the war began, and the Insurgents beheaded him on 14 August 1936.[28] The Bishop of Vitoria, Mateo Múgica, occupied a unique position; he was a self-proclaimed Monarchist but he acknowledged the strong Catholic faith of most Basque Nationalists.[29] Múgica did not openly support Basque Nationalism, yet Cardinal Gomá and the Spanish Catholic hierarchy pushed for Múgica's return to Rome due to the tension he created with the Rebel forces.[30] Monsignor Marcelino Olaechea—one of the first to call the war a *cruzada* and a contemporary of Múgica—appealed for "No more blood" in November 1936, but the Franquistas did not abide by this pastoral comment.[31]

From the start of the war until the surrender of Basque forces to the Insurgents in October 1937, País Vasco represented a serious problem for the Holy See. First, this section will investigate the Vatican's concerns relating to Bishop Múgica and his pro-regionalist agenda. The Secret Archive of the Vatican contains letters regarding this issue that can more clearly explain why and how Múgica left. Next, this section will explore the Vatican's attempts to separate truth from fiction regarding the violence in the region. A closer examination of the Civil War and the Holy See's interests in País Vasco is necessary to explain how the conflict between the Republic and Rebels was not as clear as the Vatican might have previously thought, or how the Insurgents wanted it explained. Finally, this section will explore communications and publications that attempted to influence the attitudes of the Catholic World. The Basque leadership wanted to define the people of the region as strong Catholics trying to protect their autonomy. Cardinal Gomá attempted to explain that the Basque Nationalists were not simply "good" Catholics trying to defend their state, but also a mixture of communists and anarchists looking to overthrow religion in the region. All these reports contained bits of truth, but also misleading statements.

On 4 September 1936, Cardinal Gomá[32] drafted a long note to Cardinal Pacelli to discuss the conditions within País Vasco, writing on behalf of the *Junta de Defensa Nacional de Burgos* that defined many of Gomá's and the Rebels' concerns about the violence of "*nacionalismo vasco.*"[33] Gomá wrote about the Catholic condition in Republican territories and highlighted the perceived connections between the Basque Nationalists and communists in the Republic.[34] Gomá's letter continued with a discussion regarding the actions of Bishop Múgica stating the Government in Burgos had invited Bishop Múgica to attend a meeting to discuss their position in the War.[35] Múgica, however, did not attend the scheduled meeting in Burgos, raising suspicions in their minds. Gomá explained that the Bishop would not attend the meeting due to his perceived sympathies for the Basque. General Dávila of the Burgos regime wrote to Gomá to express his concerns about the actions and attitude of Múgica,[36] demanding the actions of Múgica should be more closely watched and suggested that the Bishop should travel to the French border and leave Spain.[37] Gomá explained he was also concerned for the safety of Bishop Múgica if he made any trips within Spain, due to the anticlerical atmosphere of the Civil War.[38] Gomá seemed to wonder whether Rebels might kill Múgica due to his political leanings. General Dávila's forces had executed fourteen Basque priests in the region, but Francisco Franco often blamed miscommunications with underlings when clergy were killed by Rebels—could Múgica become a target, and was it better for him to leave?[39]

In his postscript to the letter, Gomá summarized the 5 September response from Bishop Múgica. Gomá sent an earlier letter to Múgica to suggest the Bishop leave Spain and return to Rome. In his response, Múgica stated if he was to leave Spain, the action "would be interpreted as an event of political character produced by the military authority in favor of one political sector, especially traditionalists and Falange, and against other [Basque] Nationalists."[40] For Bishop Múgica, leaving Spain would symbolize a Franquista political victory over the Basques. The Rebels and the Republicans had been keeping a very close eye on the actions of all religious leaders, and both sides interpreted almost any action as possibly political in nature. For Gomá, however, the removal of this Bishop could lessen regional tensions between the Church and Rebels, and possibly aid the latter.

The Marquis Antonio de Magaz, Rebel "confidential agent to the

Vatican,"[41] wrote to Vatican Cardinal Secretary of State Pacelli on 17 September 1936, explaining the political conditions in País Vasco to the Secretary of State. The Marquis's letter condemned the alliance of the Basque Nationalists with the Republic and argued that the Rebels were acting in the best interest for the entire country. Magaz hoped to demonize the Basque leadership in order to persuade the Holy See to give its full support to the Insurgent government.[42] The Marquis expressed his sadness that the Basque government had sided with the "*socialista-comunista-anárquico*" government of the Popular Front.[43] His letter acknowledged the problematic position of Bishop Múgica,[44] who sided with the Basque Nationalist cause against the perceived best interests of Spain.[45] This letter highlights two of the main worries for the Holy See in the Basque region: the role of socialist, communist, and anarchist support for the regional government and the role of the clergy in País Vasco.

On 25 September, Cardinal Pacelli wrote to Gomá about what to do with Bishop Múgica. While it is known that Gomá wanted Múgica to return to Rome, what has not been evaluated is the role the Holy See played in Múgica's removal.[46] Pacelli wrote (with hand-written corrections), "In the meanwhile, however, news has been gathered according to which, it seems necessary (to His Holiness [Pius XI]) that Monsignor Múgica ~~leaves the~~ (withdraw provisionally from his) diocese, not finding another way to resolve the delicate situation that has been created."[47] Pacelli appeared worried about the safety of the bishop, but the Rebels were the danger in this instance. News had begun to spread that the Vatican hierarchy was pushing for Múgica to leave Spain: "The Holy See trusts you with the delicate position to convince Monsignor Múgica ~~to abandon the~~ (to leave from) his diocese."[48] Pacelli made it clear, Cardinal Gomá needed to convince Múgica to leave Spain and go to Rome. Múgica's politics created tensions for the Holy See with the Rebels, especially as they appeared to be winning the War, and "The Nationalists were adamant, and after a report to the Holy See, Gomá was finally able to persuade Múgica to go to Rome at the behest of Pope Pius XI on the pretext of attending a missionary congress."[49] In a 9 October letter to the Holy See, Gomá stated that General Dávila favored Múgica's departure. Gomá wrote that Múgica leaving would not "add a new motive to the many factors of discord today in existence."[50] After this Rebel pressure, the Vatican helped Múgica return to Rome under the guise of a conference.

Múgica's departure from Spain was based on two important positions. First, as the Rebel army appeared to be making serious advances in Northern Spain, the Burgos Government began to pressure the Spanish Catholic Church to remove clergymen who sided with the Basque Government. The Rebel Government had the ability to pressure the Spanish Catholic Church—and possibly the Vatican—to remove its representatives with whom it did not agree. Second, the Spanish Catholic hierarchy, particularly Cardinal Gomá, listened to the Burgos Government and accepted certain advice. When Insurgents forces took Toledo on 28 September 1936, Gomá was overjoyed as, "He proclaimed the rebel capture of Toledo to be the high point of the 'clash of civilization with barbarism, of the inferno against Christ.' He thundered against 'the bastard soul of the cons of Moscow' and 'Jews and Freemasons who poisoned the nation's soul with absurd doctrines, Tartar and Mongol tales dressed up as a political system in the dark societies controlled by the Semite International."[51] On 1 July 1937, Spanish Bishops released the *Carta colectiva de los obispos españoles a los obispos de todo el mundo con motivo de la Guerra en España* (Collective Letter of the Spanish Bishops to All the World about the Spanish Civil War), signed by almost all Spanish bishops and aimed to explain the Spanish Catholic Church's opinions about the Civil War. The bishops stated that they did not like war, nor did they give aid to the initial "Uprising," but due to the Republic's antagonistic legislation, they now sided with the Rebel forces. Burgos, according to the Bishops, fought to "save the principles of religion and Christian justice."[52] The bishops stated that the Popular Front Republic had been manipulated by the Soviet Union, and needed to be defeated. Of interesting note, Cardinal Gomá was the first to sign this letter. The Burgos Government did not have complete control over the Spanish Catholic Church, but on certain issues the two groups worked together. Significantly, in 1945, years after fleeing Spain, Múgica asserted that "there was no formal collaboration between autonomists and the 'communists': 'not the unity of the common goal, but rather the unity of being attacked by a common enemy' . . . He denied allegations that the autonomists placed their ethnic and cultural interests above those of religion . . . and he said that 'none of the 2,020 priests in the diocese of Vitoria ever put politics before religion'."[53] While the Catholic Church was attempting to resolve the pressures of Burgos and Gomá regarding Bishop Múgica of Vitoria, the Vatican Office of Affari Ecclesiastici Straordinari (AES) was compiling a report about Basque Nationalism and the War and tried to explain why the Basque Nationalists sided with the Republic during the war. The Basque were devout Catholics, yet their cultural and social differences from dominant Castilla encouraged the Basque support for regionalism.

The AES report began by asserting the central problem for the Basque was that they were good Catholics but allegedly other immoral groups influenced the Basque Nationalist Party (PNV).[54] According to the AES, "*El Partido Nacionalista Vasco es por su fé religiosa Católico, Apostólico y Romano.*"[55] The report explained that the PNV had traditionally worked to support the ideals of the Catholic faith in Spain for over fifty years, however, despite this it had sided with the Madrid (Popular Front) Government at the start of the war:

> It is a fact the participation of the Party [PNV] in the fight that today is debated in the Peninsula; it agrees, in fact, to fight with the POPULAR FRONT against the Civic-Military uprising of arms against the Government of Madrid. This Popular Front has committed crimes and sacrileges against persons and things in all of Spain. Now, how does one explain this coincidence of a Catholic Party such as the PNV with the Popular Front?[56]

To the Vatican, it seemed illogical for these two groups, the PNV and Popular Front, to work for the same goals. From there, the report wanted to explain this problematic alliance by drawing specific conclusions.

Two reasons explained why the PNV did not align itself with the Rebellion and instead worked with the Popular Front. The first was the issue of regionalism: "The PNV, even with its Catholic beliefs, is divorced from the so-called Spanish Right [Falange] by its program of Basque patriotism."[57] According to the AES, the goals of Basque Nationalism did not allow the PNV to side with the Insurgency because of the latter's belief in territorial integrity and distrust of regionalism. The Basque had historically fought for their regional independence, and they would side with the group that would protect those rights. The second reason given for the PNV's support for the Popular Front was its social makeup. The PNV was a group of Basque workers and members of the middle-class who attempted to take more control over the region's industry. While the Spanish Right had sided with the conservative leaders of industry, the PNV found support with the workers, pushing the PNV towards socialist organizations.[58] Therefore, the PNV, according to the Holy See, were devout Catholics who supported regionalism yet found support from the lower, working class.

After explaining the socio-political reasons for the PNV to side with the Popular Front, the report listed the specific actions relating to the uprising that influenced the PNV. The report addressed the issue of the ideology of the Rebels: "This movement had from the beginning a militarist and somewhat of a fascist character, although there was no completely clear ideological program."[59] The uprising, therefore, was clearly understood as a movement of the political right. The military had initiated the action, but other elements, even those with fascist principles, did take part. According to the Holy See, though, the movement was not fascist in nature; in fact no clear ideological stance was seen at the start of the movement. The leaders of the Rebellion did support "the so-called Spanish national unity against all autonomous aspirations by a ferocious centralism."[60] The Rebels' call for a strong, central government against the rights of regionalists clearly defined a central reason why the Basque region might oppose the uprising.

The AES report continued with an explanation of the confusing circumstances surrounding the first days of the Civil War explaining the PNV had no real knowledge of the uprising and therefore was unclear as to what was really happening in the state. When the uprising began, "Did one think of a civil war or a mere military revolt?"[61] The PNV, therefore, did not know what actions to take concerning the military. The Rebels did not share their plans with the PNV, and the leadership of the PNV had to rely either on rumors or newspaper reports in the first days of the conflict.[62] As the Rebels did not share their plans with the Basque leadership, it is clear that the Insurgents had no intention of ever looking for support from Euzkadi. The lack of knowledge in the Basque region about the uprising, according to the AES, led to the PNV taking drastic steps to defend the region. The rumors crystallized in the language of a battle between "the citizenry against fascism and the Republic against the Monarchy."[63] As the PNV militarized the region against possible Rebel attacks, more radical elements, like Socialists, Communists, and Anarchists infiltrated the region and took prominent roles in the Basque leadership.[64] According to the AES, the socialist elements in the region, because they had become more vocal and active than the Catholic organizations, began to commandeer the direction of the PNV during the war.[65] The swirling rumors in the Basque region about the start of the war initiated concerns about what was actually happening during the summer of 1936, and the regional government needed to react to calm the situation and prevent an uprising there. The AES concluded that the PNV took up arms for two reasons: "(a) Primarily for the defense of the threatened public order and (b) for the defense of their invaded territory."[66]

The AES appeared to understand that while the Basques were strong Catholics, they demanded their regional autonomy within the state and the Holy See seemed not to condemn the Basques' interest in regionalism. Second, according to the AES, at the start of the war the PNV only acted to maintain control and peace in the region, while the rest of Spain descended into bloody conflict. In the end, the AES's reaction to the PNV shows the awkward and difficult position between the two groups. The Holy See accepted demands for autonomy from this highly Catholic region of Spain, and understood why they would have sided with the Popular Front. If not for the influx of foreign leftists, the AES assumed the Basque region would have not deteriorated into such violence.

The AES report contained a consolidation of discussions from the Diocese of Pamplona and Vitoria (the Diocese of Bishop Múgica). The report suggested that the PNV had been helpful for the rights of Catholics by preventing "*los marxistas*" from taking serious control over the Basque region.[67] In fact, according to the report, the PNV had helped the clergy in the region and they permitted Catholic Churches to remain open even during the worst parts of the conflict.[68] As Hilari Raguer identifies, President Aguirre's leadership protected churches and masses continued in the region.⁶⁹ The PNV had also been able to maintain peace in the region, with only three anarchists shot during the early tumult.⁷⁰ The PNV had done a wonderful job dismantling the leadership of the "*Anarco-sindicalistas*" and disarming their supporters.⁷¹ The PNV did not behave like the rest of the Popular Front as they were not responsible for any sacrilegious attacks against the clergy and its buildings.⁷² Even though the Basques sided with the Popular Front, the strong Catholic beliefs of the Basque people created a powerful connection with the Holy See. This traditional connection between the Holy See and País Vasco was a central concern in the war. How to help Euzkadi was a constant anxiety for the Holy See, but the Rebels would not budge in their demands. The Insurgency did not kowtow to the Vatican. José Sánchez writes, "Even before the Nationalist offensive began, Gomá and the Vatican tried to find a way to mediate an end to the war against the Basques. Franco wanted a papal condemnation of the autonomists for their support of the anticlerical Republicans. Pacelli responded that the Pope would only do so if the Nationalist leader would offer concessions to the autonomists and be lenient in the treatment of their leaders." Like with other calls for moderation "Franco rejected this as impractical and difficult. As the war continued, Gomá came to believe that the autonomists would not fight a hopeless struggle and that they would surrender if offered favorable terms. The Vatican agreed and, along with the Italian government, attempted mediation again. Cardinal Pacelli offered a plan for a conditional surrender and appealed to the Nationalists to be moderate in their treatment of the conquered Basques. But mediation aims were not realized."⁷³ This failed mediation, however, seems to be the fault of the Rebels, as they possessed a great unwillingness to make any compensation, even to the Holy See. As the Rebels gained territory in the Basque region, the attitude and actions of the Holy See towards the PNV shifted away from acceptance, as seen in the report regarding the PNV, to concern, like the debates regarding Bishop Múgica. The Insurgency's success in the region must have had some influence over interactions with the PNV.

On 19 December 1936, Cardinal Pacelli wrote Archbishop Gomá concerning possible negotiations with General Franco for the future of the Catholic Church in Spain. Pacelli's letter highlighted that the Vatican wanted "to have good relations with his Excellency the Generalissimo,"⁷⁴ but it was important for Gomá to fight for the authority of the Church. Pacelli wanted Gomá:

> In the confidential negotiations, that your Eminence should develop, will have to be firm in defending freedom of the Holy See regarding the appointment and removal of bishops, with a clear understanding that this is, especially in our days, a matter fundamental to the Holy See and

also a benefit to the Nation largely because such freedom will be a sure pledge that the prelates and churchmen will not be adherents of political parties.[75]

While Pacelli wanted good relations with Franco, he was adamant in his belief that Catholic bishops should only be appointed by the Vatican. Pacelli believed Vatican appointments could remain free of political influence, and would therefore act as representatives of the Church and not a political party. This note highlights an important point—Cardinal Pacelli saw Burgos as possible allies against atheism in Spain, but certain powers must remain in the hands of the Catholic Church.

By the final weeks of 1936, the Government of País Vasco used the channels of the media and propaganda to influence the opinion of the outside world. As expected, the question of religion frequently lay at the center of the discussion. In December 1936, the Basque newspaper *Tierra Vasca* interviewed the President of the Basque Region, José Antonio Aguirre, who offered some explanations for the Basque involvement in the Civil War. According to Aguirre, "The war that has unfolded in the Spanish Republic, the entire world should know, is not a religious war, as many have wanted you to see it; it is an economic war, and an archaic type of economic war."[76] Aguirre removed the question of religion from the conflict's context. By making the war one of economic disparity between the rich and poor in Spain and not religion, Aguirre had hoped to gain international sympathies and hoped to foster support and recognition from religious leaders, particularly the Pope. The same article asked, "And here, the President of the Government of Euzkadi, a Catholic, asks with a pained heart, Why the silence from the hierarchy?"[77] According to Aguirre, the Vatican Hierarchy had remained silent about the conflict and he wondered "why?" Aguirre, like most Basques, claimed to be devoutly Catholic and wondered why the Holy See had not tried to intervene to protect the Basque people. Even though Aguirre tried to explain that the Civil War was not one of religion, but one of economics, the Holy See was not willing to buy such an explanation.[78]

Cardinal Gomá sent a letter to the Vatican Secretary of State on 15 January 1937 to challenge Aguirre's previous explanation of the war. According to Gomá, the Basque had been successful in establishing foreign support and propaganda systems, yet communist influence had been growing within the Basque cause.[79] Communists had begun to replace "good" Basques in the leadership:

> The preponderance of the communist elements that have arrived from outside have upset the equilibrium of a situation that until now has been favorable for the Catholics, with the terrible situation of street fighting between the two bands that had been until now united,

arriving a few days ago to the point that the revolutionary elements invaded the prisons in which distinguished members of the right were detained, and in only one day they killed with hand bombs two hundred and eight of the imprisoned, among them persons most distinguished in all the region. What is occurring in Vizcaya is the same that happened in Cataluña: the elements affiliated with the communists and the anarchists have overwhelmed the elements of order, and it is to be feared that the same will happen in Vizcaya with priests, temples, and distinguished persons of Catholicism as has occurred in other regions, especially in the east and the south.[80]

Due to País Vasco's, as well as Cataluña's, proximity to the French borders, international communists and anarchists had been supposedly able to infiltrate the region and attack property of the Church. The internationalization of the conflict, on the side of the Popular Front, had increased the carnage. No mention, however, was made about the increase of Italian and German fascist troops in the region, nor the Rebel violence. The loss of control by the "good" Basque Catholics and the increase of communist power can be seen as Gomá's rationalization for not supporting the Basque, like Aguirre had expected.

Communist supporters had become visible in País Vasco, and it was not a surprise to the Basque that Gomá targeted their visibility as a reason to not support the PNV. These communist groups, however, did not remain silent and initiated a propaganda campaign via their newspapers and periodicals for the outside world. On 6 February 1937, the Basque communist periodical *ERI*—published in Bilbao—printed an article about the role of the Spanish Catholic Church in the Civil War: "Everyone knows that in the Spanish Civil War Catholics have not remained neutral. By one part, the bishops, a great number of priests and a large portion of their adherents have taken part on the side of the rebel generals; on the other hand, eminent and irreproachable Catholics defend the cause of the Spanish Government."[81] Ironically, the Communist Party of Euzkadi believed that the real and honest Catholics of the region had supported the government of the Republic, while those with something to gain had sided with the rebel forces. The communist literature stated that the Spanish Catholic Church followed a process of suppressing the poor Spanish for the benefit of the rich. The article continued, "For the great majority of Spanish Catholics the Church had become, for a long time, a purely political institution that fought against the social and economic aspirations of the majority of the people."[82] It should come as no real surprise that the communist party of the region spoke out against the power and influence of the Catholic Church. Just as Gomá had attacked the PNV for succumbing to communist influence, communists demonized the Church for supporting the social status quo.

The Basque women's periodical *Mújeres* also published numerous articles about the role of religion in the Civil War. Like *ERI*, *Mújeres* contained articles that attempted to spread the ideal that communists and "good" and "honest" Catholics in País Vasco were on the same side fighting against tyranny and the Rebels' status quo. Three articles, "Christo, es 'Rojo'?", "La Libertad Religiosa en la Zona Leal" and "Mensaje de las mujeres de Euzkadi a Eden, Blum, y Roosevelt, Representantes de los Países Democráticos", suggested that the legal government of País Vasco had actually guaranteed freedom of religion and prevented repression, in opposition to Cardinal Gomá.[83]

One event that did obtain a great deal of international coverage during the war was the 26 April 1937 bombing of the Basque cultural capital, Guernica. Supporters of the Republic and the international media correctly blamed the bombing on the German *Luftwaffe* and the Insurgency's supporters, while Franco and his supporters blamed the event on communist insurgents lighting incendiary bombs.[84] Some of the international Catholic media took this as an opportunity to lash out against the Republic after this attack. William Parsons, S.J. wrote the essay, "Atrocities Made to Order," for the Knights of Columbus magazine *Columbia*:

> As for Guernica, it bids fair to take its place as the greatest propaganda hoax (after Badajoz) in the whole merry game of misleading the public. The Basques evacuated it, because of a strategic move of Franco's armies. When General Mola moved in, he found it in ruins. Those are the facts. The next day the whole press flared out with the lurid story that Hitler's planes had bombed it flat and killed nobody knows how many women and children (never any men). The world apparently believed and Foreign Secretary Eden made a speech in the House of Commons about it. It was certainly exploited to the limit, and perhaps many of Franco's sympathizers still sorrowfully believe that it occurred.[85]

In short, Parsons argued Guernica was nothing more than a propagandistic stunt created by the Republican Government. While the Holy See did not sanction or support this article, the author agreed with Franco's interpretation of this attack and tried to delegitimize the Republican cause and prevent international sympathies.

The day before the Guernica bombing, Rebel radio in Salamanca warned, "'Franco is about to deliver a mighty blow against which all resistance is useless. Basques! Surrender now and your lives will be spared.'"[86] The Franquistas had been relying more on the German *Luftwaffe* in attacks in Northern Spain. This radio address shows the Rebels were about to do something major and highly destructive to the

Basque, pre-admitting to the following day's attack. On 27 April, Father Alberto Onaindía wrote to Cardinal Gomá to express his deepest sorrow about this attack, and he pleaded the Cardinal would help prevent other like it. In response to this impassioned plea, Gomá responded "I regret, as anyone would, what is happening in Vizcaya. I have suffered for months, God is my witness. I particularly regret the destruction of your towns, where the purest faith and patriotism once dwelt. But it was not necessary to be a prophet to foresee what is now happening . . . People pay for their pacts with evil and for their perverse wickedness in sticking to them."[87] Gomá's cold response to this priest clearly highlights the Cardinal's lack of sympathy for those Basque who sided with the Republic. At the same time, this comment shows that even the Cardinal expected something like Guernica could happen, and that the Rebels would be responsible.

The Basque region represented a serious problem for the leadership of the Catholic Church in Spain and the Vatican. The Basques were devoutly Catholic, yet their sympathies for the Popular Front Government were based on historical demands. Regionalism was the key element for the Basque, and the Catholic Church realized this fact. According to the Catholic leadership, País Vasco was Catholic, but by siding with the Republic, communist and anarchist elements began to influence and finally commandeered the PNV. The leadership of the PNV tried to foster Vatican sympathies, but reports of radical revolutionaries prevented that from happening. The Basque and communist media attempted to present their case to the world as just, but the Catholic leadership of Cardinal Gomá would not accept this explanation. The Church's justification to discredit the Basque cause was not based on culture or identity, but on those foreign influences and ideologies that had managed to infiltrate the region. Following chapters will explain the role the Catholic Church and Holy See attempted to play in ending the conflict in the region as Franco's victory became assured.

Concluding Remarks

By the middle of 1937, Spain looked very different than it did at the start of the Civil War. Although suffering occasional defeats or disappointments (the failure to capture Madrid in 1936 and the defeat at Guadalajara in March 1937), Insurgent forces had made major advances throughout the country, the Madrid Government had fled to Valencia, and País Vasco appeared ready to fall. The rapid and ever-changing Spanish environment created a variety of diplomatic pressures for the Holy See. When the first shots were fired, the Madrid Government and the Basque Republic were not sure about the exact events. Because of the collapse of the Republican state apparatus, the Republic's early reliance on armed militias created serious tensions with the Holy See, as symbols of the Church were attacked. The Republican leadership did not initiate these attacks, but the Republic became associated with this orgy of violence.

The Vatican hierarchy initiated protests to the Republic to state that these militias were unfairly targeting the Church. The hierarchy's primary concern at the start of the Civil War was the condition of the Church. The Vatican saw similarities between these attacks and anticlerical violence from May 1931 and October 1934. Because these militias fought with the Republic, the Vatican hierarchy naturally considered them to be part of the Republican structure. In reality, the Republican Government had an equally difficult time trying to control these militias, and it was not until the end of October 1936 that these militias were incorporated into the Popular Army. As Spanish Minister Fabra Ribas mentioned in Switzerland, the Republic rejected the uncontrollable violence of the "Reds" towards the Church. The Vatican hierarchy made the assumption that militias fighting on the side of the Republic held the same ideological beliefs as the government. Even though the Popular Front coalition had worked together to win the election, the various parties did not always share the same ideological ideals. Also, due to the wide spectrum of political views, the Republican Government was not ready to present a unified front at the start of the Civil War. Conservatives in Spain shared the Church's assumption that the Popular Front was a unified political entity, and began to associate all Republicans with Bolshevism, atheism, and anarchism. The Vatican hierarchy followed the diplomatic path most associated with Secretary of State Pacelli—it relied on private dialogue and initiated a series of formal protests with the Republic asking for assistance and blamed communism for the violence. Similarly, as a Rebel victory became more likely, it would have behooved the Holy See to try to work more directly with Franco and his supporters. The Vatican, however, continued not to recognize Burgos as the legitimate government. The Pope must have regarded Franco with some suspicion, as the Rebels continued to use Nazi and Fascist aid, they continued to attack the Catholic Basque, and they failed to make clear promises about the future role of the Church in Spain.[88] Pius XI, who worried about radical ideologies of the left and right, would have been uncomfortable recognizing a regime that could not make promises to the Church and worked with a paganistic ally. Cardinal Pacelli would not have wanted the Pope to press these issues, and instead, must have wanted the Holy See to negotiate for better terms for the Church as the War progressed. However, the Republic was offended by the Church's use of blanket terminology and blamed various clergy members for working with the Insurgents. Cardinal Gomá seemed to support the

Rebels' definition of the conflict, as a battle against communism and atheism, but this was not completely the case. Many in the Republic were not radical leftists—and some still Catholics—so the definition of all Republicans as communists or "reds" was simply unfounded. When Church leaders suggested the Republic was controlled solely by "reds," the Republic had a responsibility to clarify this untruth.

The complex situation surrounding the start of the Civil War was also shared in País Vasco. The Catholic hierarchy needed to explain to the Vatican why the Basque would fight with the Republic rather than the more pro-Catholic Insurgents. However, the hierarchy appeared to understand the correct answer regarding the Basque: regional autonomy trumped the political affiliations of their supporters. The Church blamed the influx of non-Basques and their foreign ideologies as the reason País Vasco became radicalized. Blaming foreign ideologies over the behavior of Basque Catholics created a neater solution for the Holy See, as these "good" Catholics could be returned to the flock after the War. País Vasco represented a very difficult case for the Holy See as it needed to reiterate the region's religious culture, yet it explained that the only reason the region was fighting was because foreigners had corrupted the honest views of the people. The removal of Bishop Múgica from Spain shows that the Holy See was influenced by Rebel pressures, but the Vatican worked to create its own rationale for his departure, and not publicly acknowledge Franquistas' demands. Múgica's recall showed a clear Vatican choice of the Rebels over the Basques, although the Vatican attempted to spare the Basques the full weight of Rebel revenge, albeit with seemingly little effect. The final question relating to all actions in the war was: How could the Holy See—the earthly representative of the Prince of Peace—side with *any* belligerent in a war? The Spanish Catholic hierarchy voiced their opinions due to their proximity to the bloodshed, but negotiations between Vatican representatives in Spain and the Republican Government offered no success.

VI

Foreign Requests for Vatican Intervention

The Hope of a Spiritual Authority?

Foreign governments worried about the growing violence in Spain's Civil War and hoped the Holy See could possibly initiate some mediation plan, but the Vatican was hesitant to act in conjunction with other states. The Holy See remained consistent in its actions, reviewing international requests for mediation, yet declining to take a public stance about the conflict. Privately, some in the Vatican hierarchy must have supported the Rebels' goals to restore traditional society to Spain, and pushed the Holy See to remain silent. Others in the Vatican must have worried a public statement from the Holy See concerning the Civil War could anger fascist Italy—which encircled the Vatican, and Nazi Germany—where Church practices were already being restricted by the government. While Britain and France had publicly pushed for Non-Intervention in Spain, privately they hoped the Holy See would mediate a truce.

As previously discussed, the 1929 Lateran Accords required the Holy See to remain neutral in all conflicts unless all belligerents requested mediation, and the Insurgents never supported Vatican mediation. Vatican representatives did communicate with Franco concerning mediation and truces, but the Holy See was never aggressive in its quest for a cessation in hostilities—possible evidence the Holy See appeased Franco in the hopes of gaining greater social authority in a post-war society or evidence the Vatican feared Franco's unclear plans for the future that possibly included Nazis and Fascists. The Vatican's agenda in Spain was for Catholics to practice freely, but more importantly, to reestablish the Church's traditional authority in Spain and to return to pre-Republican legal codes when Catholicism influenced numerous social, cultural, and legal practices. The combination of Franquista attitudes against mediation, Vatican interests in Spain's future, and the variety of foreign requests to end the War created a complex environment for the Vatican hierarchy as it attempted to make decisions regarding Spain. Also, many in the Spanish Catholic hierarchy, such as Isidro Gomá y Tomás, Enrique

Plá y Deniel, and Pedro Segura Sáenz, publicly supported the Rebel cause against the Popular Front government. While the Vatican leadership remained publicly silent, tensions with Republican secular ideology and violence against clergy at the start of war must have affected the attitudes of the Vatican hierarchy. If the Uprising had been led by communists, and a Catholic resistance tried to defend the country, would the Vatican have likely called upon all Catholic states to defend the Church in Spain? If the Holy See became involved and succeeded in establishing a truce, would other countries blame the Vatican for meddling in national affairs? If the Holy See became involved and failed in its mission, would the Vatican lose international influence? Would the Vatican weaken its future position in Spain after the Rebel victory? True, these questions are hypothetical, but they begin to expose the overwhelming complexities tied to Vatican diplomatic concerns in a contentious 1930s environment.

The foreign plans for Non-Intervention during the Spanish Civil War did not work as both sides received international aid (the Insurgency from Germany and Italy and the Republic from the USSR and other small states). The British and French Governments claimed the London Agreement for Non-Intervention worked—as states supposedly remained neutral regarding the Civil War. According to Douglas Little, the plan could be viewed as a success as it was meant to isolate the political left from the dangers of communism while keeping the political right away from direct fascist influences.[1] Contemporary scholars, like Helen Graham and Paul Preston, have shown British and French economic and political concerns primarily drove Non-Intervention.[2] Even though French and British national interests inspired these actions, it did not mean that European states lacked concern about the violence and bloodshed in the Spanish Civil War. This chapter will explore communications between foreign governments and the Holy See regarding the Spanish War as multiple states explained to the Vatican their interests in ending the Civil War for humanitarian reasons, but political and economic concerns were always close-by. While many governments had interests in the outcome of the Civil War, this chapter focuses primarily on those states and organizations that presented direct opinions relating to mediation of the conflict to the Vatican hierarchy. The first section will explore the communications between representatives of the British Government and the Holy See. While Britain had serious economic and political interests in Spain, as the War progressed and the death toll grew, the British attempted to persuade the leadership of the Catholic Church to intervene and mediate a truce. The second section will explore French attempts to gain Vatican support for mediation and hope the Holy See could use its moral authority to end the conflict. Next, this chapter will investigate communications from a sampling of other states concerning Spain. The Civil War had grown into a major international concern, and various governments had opinions about how the Holy See should mediate the crisis because they viewed the Vatican as influential enough to end the conflict. Finally, this chapter will explore calls for mediation from a few private organizations with social and cultural interests in Spain. These groups, with Republican sympathies, wanted the Holy See to use its influence to end the loss of life, but the Rebels had serious suspicions about their ideological connections. Before investigations can occur, a brief synopsis of Non-Intervention and its sponsoring states will be presented.

Non-Intervention

From the start of the Spanish Civil War in the summer of 1936, the international community's attention focused on Spain. The conflict in Spain shared similarities with the ideological tensions simmering throughout Europe before and during the 1930s—the rise of fascism, the possible spread of communism, and the erosion of liberal democratic ideals as economies weakened. Foreign actors who had involved themselves in the Spanish Civil War became belligerents in World War II. In order to avoid turning this "civil war" into an "international war," Europe's leading powers met in London to draft a Non-Intervention Agreement to forbid foreign aid for either side in Spain. This plan was not developed out of sympathy for Spain, but to maintain the political and economic status quo on the continent and avoid a larger European war of international ideologies. Enrique Moradiellos explains the four major reasons influencing Non-Intervention: economics, military fears, diplomatic weakness, and internal political fragility.[3] The French Popular Front Government of Léon Blum had originally wanted to supply the Spanish Popular Front Republic with aid, but as Paul Preston explains, if the French actions had provoked a response from Nazi Germany or Fascist Italy, then Britain would have left France to deal with the repercussions.[4] To avoid getting involved in a large-scale conflict, the French shifted their opinion and along with the British Government pushed the majority of European states to sign an agreement promising not to arm or financially support either side in Spain, establishing the plan of Non-Intervention.[5]

To understand why countries agreed on Non-Intervention, Spain's relationship to certain states needs to be briefly explained. Even though France eventually publicly suggested the idea of Non-Intervention in Spain, Britain feared the effects of an international war beginning in Spain and spreading to the rest of the continent. Britain worried most about the possibility of European destabilization.[6] The British proposed the system of Appeasement towards Nazi Germany to prevent a continent-wide war, and the British Government tried to avoid conflict at all cost.[7] Economic interests in Spain posed the second major concern for the British, namely "mines, sherry, textiles, olive oil and cork."[8] Due to these commercial assets, the British believed a socialist, or even communist political environment would devastate their financial dominance.[9] In order to maintain economic influence in Spain and keep the status quo on the continent, Britain took the lead in drafting the plan for Non-Intervention to isolate the Republic from radical leftist governments.

British and French Non-Intervention was not established for the benefit of the Spanish Republic, but in the best interests of the UK and France. The Civil War began in July 1936, and the League of Nations had not returned from its summer hiatus. Rather than allow multiple nations with varied ideologies to debate what should happen in Spain, the British Government hoped to take the international lead and create its own policy for all international actors.[10] After persuading France to follow Non-Intervention, these two powers "had decided to use a different forum for their diplomatic efforts to limit and control international aspects of the war."[11] Rather than meet in Geneva, this Non-Intervention Committee met in London, and was directed by the British Foreign Office. By establishing and hosting the Non-Intervention Committee, Britain, and to a lesser extent France, hoped to show Europe which states still controlled European policy.

British economic interests in Spain feared the possibility of communism spreading and nationalizing private corporations. According to Douglas Little, Britain feared the spread of communism more than other ideologies, "Even as Hitler's and Mussolini's aggressive designs grew more obvious in Spain and elsewhere, then, many British policy-makers still regarded Bolshevism as a greater threat to world peace than fascism."[12] In June 1936, a month before the war, Spanish Leftist unions attacked British owned corporations throughout Spain over perceived low pay and poor conditions, with the most violent occurring against the mining company, Rio Tinto.[13] The British Foreign Office considered these attacks as signs the Popular Front government grew unstable and was unable to prevent the increase of radical leftist movements in Spain. When the Civil War began in July, the British government did not rush to support the uprising against the state, but it did not seem concerned that the Popular Front might collapse. By taking the lead in Non-Intervention, the British Government hoped to maintain control over European diplomacy while supporting British corporations against the threat of leftist ideology in Spain.

France regarded the question of Non-Intervention based on other priorities. The British explained to the French Popular Front Government that French military or financial support for the Second Republic could antagonize its powerful neighbor, Nazi Germany, and to avoid this complication, France needed to deny any assistance.[14] Following the first actions of the Civil War, French Popular Front Prime

Minister Léon Blum wanted to assist the Spanish Republic, but Blum soon learned this would not be possible. Politically, France was experiencing growing pressures from the left and the right, and the Spanish Civil War exacerbated these problems.[15] Due to possible political instability, the British persuaded Blum to avoid supplying the Republic materials and champion the cause of Non-Intervention. The French government, therefore, could rely on Britain to establish Non-Intervention, and France could follow. As Geoffrey Warner writes, "If Blum had been leading an undivided Government and an undivided country, he could have successfully defied the British. Unfortunately, neither the Government nor country was undivided."[16] The British plan of Non-Intervention offered an excuse for Blum *not* to act, but French politics was the real concern. Warner continues, "It was not the attitude of the British Government that first persuaded Blum and his colleagues to 'go slow' over their plans to send aid to Spain, but opposition within France, from the President of the Republic down through his own government. Opponents on the right certainly used the British attitude as an excuse for their own, which was rooted in a hatred of 'Communism' but also, above all, in the fear of another war."[17] Non-Intervention appeared to be a solution for France's major fears, and not a way to help the Spanish Republic during this military uprising. If Blum had sided with the Spanish Republic, fears existed that French Conservatives might initiate their own political uprising, pushing France towards civil war and fascism.[18] As Robert O. Paxton notes, however, France never truly had the ingredients for a true fascist regime to develop.[19] Due to both internal and external pressures, France chose not to aid the Republican Government in Spain, and therefore had to follow the feeble plan of Non-Intervention.

The British and French plans for Non-Intervention were not established to help either side in Spain, but were developed to maintain the status quo in Europe, keep the UK and France as diplomatic leaders, and prevent the spread of communism—even though Bolshevism was not a major threat in Spain. Following the 26 April 1937 Rebel/German aerial attack on the Basque city of Guernica, the Republican representative at the League of Nations demanded more be done to stop foreign involvement in Spain. In response to this obvious foreign attack, the French and British Foreign Ministers "responded, as usual, by stating that what was needed was to make the work of the Non-Intervention Committee more effective, and in particular to obtain agreement in the Committee on the withdrawal of all foreign combatants."[20] Again, the Non-Intervention proponents stated they would do something concerning the illegal actions in Spain, but once again, nothing happened. Both the British and French, however, requested the Holy See do something to mediate the conflict in Spain. The British and French governments were unable to prevent foreign involvements in Spain, but they thought the Catholic Church could succeed.

Britain and France agreed Non-Intervention was the best plan, but other states needed to be convinced. The USSR, Germany, and Italy all signed the Agreement, but each frequently broke the accord whenever they chose. For the Soviet Union, the Spanish Civil War represented a possible revolutionary element to continue breaking the chain of international capitalism. The War, though, did create problems for the USSR. The Soviets wanted to aid the small communist party in Spain, but they had to do so without pressing Britain and France to act against them. In the end, the Agreement prevented the Soviets from sending their own troops to Spain, but they supplied enough support for the Republic to keep Nazi Germany in an extended conflict.[21] Interestingly, the Soviet Communist International had directed the Spanish Communist Party (PCE) to moderate and work alongside the Popular Front to win the elections of 1936 and avoid talk of international communist revolution in order to legitimize its ideals in Western Europe.[22]

For Nazi Germany, Non-Intervention represented both an opportunity and a problem. On one hand, the Agreement prevented Germany from testing all its military practices in Spain. On the other hand, by aiding the Rebels the Nazis could test the British–French appeasement plans concerning Nazi aggression to understand how far they would let Germany go, even when the *Luftwaffe* attacked Republican cities.[23] For the Italians, Spain was a priority as it was geographically important to Italy; it represented a possible fascist ally in the Mediterranean; and could act as a bulwark against the British in the region.[24] By intervening in Spain, the Italians showed their German allies their military aptitude and constantly tested the reactions of the French.[25] The Italians reluctantly signed the Agreement like other states but Italy recognized that this plan had no real teeth. The Vatican would be continually worried about the German and Italian manipulation of the Spanish Civil War, but it knew it could do nothing to prevent it.

BRITAIN SEEKS VATICAN ASSISTANCE

Soon after the start of the Spanish Civil War, the British Governments of Stanley Baldwin and later Neville Chamberlain, along with Léon Blum's French Government worked to establish a Non-Intervention Agreement that would prohibit foreign states from sending material aid to either side in the Spanish conflict. Following their initial meetings in September 1936, the signatories of the Agreement promised to avoid assisting in the conflict, but evidence showed Nazi Germany, Fascist Italy, the Soviet Union, and private organizations sent assistance to both sides. In reality,

Non-Intervention failed to work and a great deal of material and manpower flowed into Spain.²⁶ For the most part Britain and France continued to honor the agreement, but at the same time both became increasingly interested in finding some cessation to the war, most likely due to their own political and economic interests. The British saw two main possibilities: either push for a peace accord to end the war or organize a truce and attempt to schedule national elections in Spain, but both options would be difficult to accomplish by the British or French Governments alone.²⁷ One outlet for the British Government appeared to be the Holy See. The Vatican did not sign the Non-Intervention Agreement—due to its international political neutrality defined by the 1929 Lateran Accords—and the British Government began to explore the possibility that the Holy See's Catholic influence over the Spanish people could help resolve the conflict. This section will explore the delicate relationship between the British Government and the leadership of the Holy See. Britain gently pushed the Holy See to work for peace in Spain, but the leadership of the Holy See never broke from its original decision to remain neutral regarding Spain. The Vatican appreciated the growing British concern for peace in Spain, but did the constraints of the Lateran Accords seriously restrain Vatican involvement?

Francis D'Arcy Osborne, the British Minister at the Holy See, investigated the Vatican's reactions to the start of the Spanish Civil War, and reported to Anthony Eden in September 1936. Following the initial uprising and militia violence, Osborne reported to the Foreign Office:

> When I suggested that the Vatican might exert its influence to deter the nationalists from acts of violence and brutality and reminded [the Pope] of the article in the 'Osservatore Romano' which asserted that, whichever party in Spain was ultimately victorious, the Government that emerged could not be recognized as an equal by other European Governments if its partisans had been guilty of atrocities, he replied with an expression of indignation at the idea that the nationalists should be put on the same level as the murderers and iconoclasts who were their opponents.²⁸

Central to the Vatican's views, the Holy See did not consider Rebel actions as equal to the Republicans', even though Rebels were responsible for greater casualties throughout the War.²⁹ If the Holy See did not see Insurgents' attacks as equivalent to those of Republicans', this attitude can show possible Vatican sympathy towards the Rebels. However, after experiencing the violent militia reactions towards members of the clergy following the uprising, this reaction is understandable. With the fast advances of the Rebel army, the Holy See might have expected a quick overthrow of the Popular Front regime, but this was not the case. In the same note Osborne wrote "Cardinal Pacelli was equally afflicted by the events in Spain and mentioned the constant receipt at the Vatican of authoritative reports of atrocities. He expressed approval of the principle of non-intervention, but observed that it was being wildly evaded. I suggested to His Eminence, too, that the Vatican might at least try to restrain the nationalists from discrediting their cause by atrocities and he expressed agreement."[30] Violence against clergy affected the Holy See's views about this civil war, but Pacelli was willing to acknowledge that Non-Intervention might have been the best policy. True, this policy would have hurt the Republic, but it would have prevented paganistic Nazism from influencing the Rebels.

Not all members of the Vatican hierarchy, however, seemed to be sympathetic to Spain's suffering. Osborne wrote of an unnamed Assistant Under-Secretary of State "who made the interesting assertion that the Spaniards had never been a really Catholic people in the full implication of the term. They had always been, and remained a very superstitious race and so they flock to religious processions and demand the last sacrament when they were dying." He continued, "The very Communists who were now murdering priests and nuns and burning churches were calling for the sacrament when their own time came. But, generally speaking, the Spaniards had never achieved the moral ideal and discipline that is the essential core of Catholicism for all their devotions to its outward forms and ceremonial."[31] Even though this statement does not unequivocally explain the attitude of the Vatican hierarchy towards Spain and the Civil War, it does show that the Holy See's relationship with Spain was complex and that not everyone in Rome would agree about how to deal with the war.

The British Government and its Foreign Office communicated with the Holy See regarding the conflict in Spain and updated the Vatican on British plans to mediate the War. As País Vasco was about to fall to the Rebels in spring 1937, the British Government hoped to initiate a new plan to push for peace in Spain. Both sides in the Civil War protested the involvement of foreign troops, volunteers, and materials in Spain, but a compromise could not be found. The Non-Intervention Committee in London planned for a brief stoppage in fighting in Spain to organize the withdrawal of all foreign volunteers in the country. As Peter Brownfeld explains, British citizens fighting in International Brigades in Spain represented a serious problem for Anthony Eden and his plans for Non-Intervention adding, "Britons fighting in Spain would show a weak British commitment to non-intervention, which was believed to be the key to preventing a European war, and achieving rapprochement with Italy."[32] This agreement would affect those governments that signed the Non-Intervention Agreement, and a note went to Monsignor Giuseppe Pizzardo at the Holy See on 24 May 1937 "in which I am sure His Holiness will be interested." First, the Non Intervention Committee opened a "technical advisory sub-committee" to work on recommendations to remove foreign fighters. After the sub-committee finished its work, the British government hoped others would cooperate as the committee was "in favor of approaching the two parties at once" and work to remove foreign soldiers from Spanish soil.[33] By keeping the Vatican up-to-date with international plans regarding Spain, the British acknowledged the Holy See's religious influence over some portions of Spain and hoped the Vatican might use its connections to assist with this plan.

Communications between the Holy See and Britain regarding a possible solution to the Spanish Civil War continued into 1938 as the British Government suggested that increased pressure from the Vatican on the Burgos Government would influence the Rebels. In reality, however, the Burgos Government appeared unwilling to accept negotiations from any external powers, including the British or the Vatican, even as German and Italian aid streamed to help Burgos. On 28 May 1938, the British Legation to the Holy See wrote to London to summarize a meeting with the Vatican to explore the possibilities of further avenues for peace: "Nevertheless, His Majesty's Government trust that the Vatican will continue to exert their influence with General Franco in this direction and that, should a suitable opportunity arise for His Majesty's Government to take such an initiative, either alone or in conjunction with other Governments, they may count on receiving wholehearted support of the Vatican" and the UK instructed "the British Agent at Burgos to keep in close touch with the Vatican representative in Spanish Nationalist territory in regard to this matter."[34] What is most important is the fact that the British Legation to the Holy See requested that the Vatican support any possible avenues to stop the violence in Spain and acknowledged that the Vatican remained cordial with Burgos. This communication shows that the British Government relied more and more on the Holy See to support peace and persuade Burgos, something other states had been unable to do. This note does allude to a British belief that the Holy See might have an influence over the Nationalist leadership, yet it was never clear how much influence the Holy See really had over Nationalist actions, or if these actions fit with the Vatican's agenda. The Vatican would have had less interest in British influence in Spain and would have cared much more about Catholic traditionalism and conservatism returning following the Civil War.

Following this meeting, Burgos responded to the increased actions by the British Government to push for a negotiated ending to the Civil War with the help of the Holy See. In response, the Rebel Embassy of Spain to the Holy See sent a message to the Vatican regarding this situation. Burgos rejected any rumored peace initiative developed by the British Government and/or the Holy See. The embassy stated on 4 June that it "reiterates its unwavering intention to reject all attempts of mediation that do not encompass the surrender of the enemy, without pride."[35] In response to this letter, the Office of the Vatican Secretary of State announced on 9 June that Burgos would not accept any plans presented by the British unless it entailed unconditional Republican surrender.[36] The Rebels had been able to influence the Vatican's decision. On one hand, the Vatican was forced to respect the Insurgency's demands due to the Lateran Accords, which had required the Vatican to remain neutral in conflicts unless all belligerents agreed upon mediation. On the other hand, one could also argue that the Holy See did not want to become directly involved in mediating this conflict as its representatives in Spain and throughout Europe could become political targets of communists and fascists.

The British Government was not solely interested in a conclusion to the Spanish Civil War, but also addressed anxieties about aerial bombings of Spanish cities to the Holy See. During the Civil War, reports of bombardments of numerous cities, especially the Basque city of Guernica on 26 April 1937, had become widely reported by the foreign press. In 1938, these aerial attacks by Rebels and their foreign allies had turned to cities like Barcelona and Madrid. The British Government again considered the Holy See as the only outlet capable of preventing the Insurgents from continuing these tactics. In response, the Holy See addressed these British concerns in a 7 June 1938 memo: "the Holy See gladly takes note of this new and authoritative evidence of the interest of His Britannic Majesty's Government in preventing or at least limiting aerial bombardments of open cities in Spain which have caused the slaughter of so many innocent victims and which give new occasion to hatred and to increasing desire for revenge." The Vatican seemed supportive of British actions and claimed "the fact that the Holy See itself, faithful to its mission of justice and charity, has not failed to reiterate to competent authorities, for this same noble purpose, counsels of moderation and forbearance." But, when it came to a joint statement "even the slightest appearance of political action, with consequent prejudice to its own mission, and desirous of preserving in its activities that character of supernatural charity which derive from its divine mandate, considers that it should take this step independently of other initiatives, even while recognizing and appreciating in the highest degree the lofty humanitarian sense which inspires the action taken by other Powers."[37] The Holy See agreed with the British Government that the aerial bombardments of cities needed to be stopped or at least be greatly reduced. In this situation, both powers agreed on the disastrous nature of these attacks that would lead to further violence. Second, and quite importantly, the author of this letter admitted the Holy See, due to its spiritual nature, needed to avoid any actions that were considered "political"—even though not "acting" could be construed as taking a political stance. After centuries of political involvement, the Vatican of 1938 suggested it would not act in a political manner. This statement, however, offers clearer insight into the primary interests of the Holy See as it explained that political actions would offer "prejudice to its own mission." While the letter suggested that the Holy See's main mission was its "supernatural charity" and "divine mandate," it is unclear how speaking out against these aerial bombardments would damage Vatican missions. As discussed in Chapter 4, Pope Pius XI was willing to speak out against "wrongs" he saw in European political actions as long as they were direct violations of Catholic doctrine, but his Secretary of State, Eugenio Pacelli, worked to defuse possible confrontation between the Vatican and other European states privately in order to avoid possible retribution against the Church. The Vatican, however, could not identify the exact reason "why" the British wanted a public response from the Holy See. Was it for altruistic reasons, to maintain appeasement, or for economic interests? It can be assumed, however, that the Holy See understood that if it became publicly involved in an open conflict, Catholic privilege and influence in post-War Spain could be affected if Franco was angered. Finally, this note shows the Holy See understood it needed to act independently from other governments during the conflict. The British Government had hoped to rely on the Holy See's unique nature to reduce the carnage in Spain, but the Vatican believed its unique and special nature meant it had to act independently and avoid any perceived influence from foreign states. As the War progressed, the Holy See would try to initiate its own plans for mediation and negotiations, but Chapter 8 will highlight how the Rebels rejected any involvement. How could the Holy See take a public step regarding Spain—due to British prodding—if Non-Intervention was still the approved plan? Would the Vatican suffer repercussions if it acted and other states or Franco were not happy with the action?

The British Government next wrote a letter to the Holy See regarding the exchange of prisoners by both sides in 1938. The British Minister at Barcelona, Mr. John Leche,[38] authored a letter to the British Legation to the Holy See about prisoner exchanges, and this material was condensed and sent to the Vatican on 26 June 1938 suggesting Republican forces in Barcelona appeared willing to continue a series of prisoner exchanges, but the Burgos Government would not accept individual prisoner exchanges and would only continue exchanges of groups numbering more than twenty-five people.[39] According to the British representative, the Burgos Government had become difficult to work with, and Mr. Leche needed more assistance with these prisoner transfers, especially for those wrongly imprisoned, but "he would be sincerely grateful if the Vatican could exert any influence at Burgos to induce them to adopt a more helpful attitude and thereby to display a more humane interest in the fate of their supporters in Loyalist territory. Mr. Leche adds that he has seen so much suffering by innocent people on both sides that it is impossible not to take this humanitarian work very deeply to heart."[40] The Vatican Archival file does not contain a response from the Holy See regarding this note, but another representative of the British Government regarded the Holy See as one of the only powers capable of influencing Burgos to act in a different manner.

From the start of the Spanish Civil War, the British Government championed the idea of Non-Intervention in the conflict, a plan created to prevent the interference of other European states and hopefully prevent the Civil War from becoming a full-scale European war; still Germany, Italy, and the Soviet Union openly participated in the fight. As the war escalated, the British hoped to find some entity capable of intervening in the conflict—most likely the Vatican. The British believed the Holy See might be able to influence the Burgos Government as the Rebels had preached their strict adherence to Roman Catholicism, and the British Government hoped the Vatican—as the head of the Universal Catholic Church—would be able to influence the Franquistas and work towards a peaceful conclusion to the conflict. While the Holy See frequently admitted to the British that they supported an end to the conflict, the Vatican appeared either unwilling or unable to influence Burgos. The Vatican could not determine "why" the British really wanted the Holy See to act—maintain appeasement, protect economic interests, help the Rebels, end a war, or protect lives? The British may have claimed humanitarianism, but this was never clearly proven. In order to avoid possible political threats, the Holy See stated it had to remain apolitical in this and all conflicts, as the Lateran Accords clearly stated. If the Holy See supported a foreign call for peace, then the Vatican believed it would be ideologically tied with that state and have its legitimacy undermined. The British Government wanted the Holy See to act, but the Vatican needed to protect its own interests in Spain, namely its social and religious capacity. The British believed the Holy See had more power and greater influence than it really had—or was willing to use—in the political realm of Spain. In the end, the Vatican rationale appeared to be to avoid negotiations initiated by Britain, especially as they could anger the Rebels.

France Outlines Non-Intervention

France, as well as the United Kingdom, had serious concerns about the Spanish Civil War. Britain's interests in Spain were centered on the economics of accessing raw materials necessary for Empire to continue its worldwide dominance. At the same time, Britain would not want other states—like the USSR, Italy, or Germany—gaining influence in the Mediterranean.[41] Unlike Britain, France shared a border with Spain, and the French Government was concerned the "Civil War" could possibly spill across the Pyrenees.[42] In addition, the French Government worried the conflict in Spain could either hamper or outright prevent clear communication between the métropole and its important North African colonies.[43] Finally, like Spain, France's government was a coalition of leftist parties known as the Popular Front and French politics were deeply polarized. President Léon Blum faced a dilemma—while the more radical parties in his political coalition supported the Popular Front Republican Government of Spain, British plans for neutrality in the conflict appeared more powerful.[44] Even though the French did not push for Non-Intervention in Spain first, once Blum's Government accepted neutrality on 25 July 1936, French representatives worked to communicate its position throughout Europe. After April 1938, Édouard Daladier's government maintained the policy of non-intervention, but conservative members of the French army wanted to recognize Franco's government. The French army hoped a Rebel victory would prevent any possible spread of Bolshevism in the western Mediterranean—but still France avoided direct involvement. The Spanish Civil War became an internal problem for the Third Republic's stability and warranted a quick solution.[45] This section will explore the communications between French representatives and the Holy See surrounding the conflict in Spain. Like Britain, the French believed that the Holy See, as the worldwide leader of the Roman Catholic faith, might have been able to influence the trajectory of the Civil War. The French wanted the Vatican to support Non-Intervention to help the French first, and protect the Spanish second.

French Minister of Foreign Affairs Yvon Delbos,[46] along with his British counterpart Anthony Eden, had been working on plans for Non-Intervention throughout the late summer and autumn of 1936. Once the British and French Governments had finalized the plan, they sent copies of the Non-Intervention Agreement to leaders throughout Europe, including the Vatican hierarchy in Rome. On 4 December 1936, Delbos sent a copy of the Non-Intervention plans, along with a personal telegram to the Vatican leadership. The plans for Non-Intervention—which were agreed upon by the governments of France, Great Britain, Italy, Germany, Portugal and the USSR—outlined the goals as well as the rationalizations for the document. The six states would continue to meet at the Committee of London in order to prevent foreign involvement in Spain and try to create an international plan to mediate the crisis and push for peace.[47] Despite the Holy See's lack of direct involvement in the planning of the Non-Intervention Agreement, the French Foreign Minister had forwarded a copy of it to the Vatican as responses from the

Vatican could be debated and might affect the final outcome of the approach. The Vatican's unique position and connection to Spain meant that the Committee regarded the Vatican's opinions relating to Spain as necessary.

Delbos sought advice from the Holy See regarding plans for Non-Intervention, but he also hoped for a public statement by the Holy See. Five days after the original telegram, the French Foreign Minister wrote again to the Holy See about Spain: "Please inform with urgency . . . the Cardinal Secretary of State of the proposition of the French and English Governments . . . You will be able to denote that the French Government would be pleased that the Holy See, by its favorable action, as well as by the public expression of its sentiments, could find the occasion to give the support of its moral authority to the chances of success of an enterprise only inspired by the highest preoccupations of humanity and peace."[48] Even though Delbos seemed confident in the structure of Non-Intervention for the Spanish conflict, the Foreign Minister desired the public acknowledgement of the Holy See for the plan. Delbos emphasized the great "preoccupations" about humanitarianism and peace as themes shared by both the Holy See and the Non-Intervention Committee. True, the Holy See would want to support a plan for peace, but Non-Intervention also involved Fascist Italy, Nazi Germany, and Soviet Russia, each of which posed threats to the Church. On the other hand, how could a clear abandonment of Spain be humanitarian? The French Government continued its pressure on the Holy See over the following days to support publicly the provisions created by the Non-Intervention Committee in London. On 12 December, the Vatican Nuncio to France sent a telegram to the Office of the Cardinal Secretary of State to highlight Yvon Delbos's personal call to the Nuncio and remind him of their good relations, and hope the Holy See would work for peace.[49]

The French Government also communicated its desire for Vatican support of Non-Intervention through the Papal Nuncio in Paris, Luigi Maglione (who would later be nominated to be Cardinal Secretary of State under Pope Pius XII). On 14 December 1936, Maglione sent a letter to Cardinal Pacelli relating to his previous meeting with French Foreign Minister Delbos. Like the direct communication between Delbos and the Holy See, the Foreign Minister structured this meeting to convince the Vatican hierarchy to support Non-Intervention, "He asked me, therefore, to express to Your Excellency the desire of the French government to see the Holy See join the Franco-British efforts to finish the war in Spain and thus to reduce, among other things, the danger of international complications. The immediate goal of the plan of action should have been that of reaching an armistice." He continued "Afterwards the strategy to regularize such a complicated situation could have been considered. Mr. Delbos, in fact, did not seem to harbor any illusions on this point, considering the profound differences that exist in both camps; he pointed, however, to the possibility of creating an international commission. He added . . . account the addition of Italy, it could have made the action of the Holy See easier."[50] Once again, a representative of the French Government requested the support of the Holy See to push the idea of an armistice in Spain. Most importantly, the note acknowledged "the danger of international complications" relating to the Civil War. French representatives, like the British, wanted to prevent the internationalization of the conflict, and suggested the Vatican could help accomplish this feat. Yet, Maglione responded to Minister Delbos that the Holy See should be discreet and not make too many public comments.[51] Even though the French Government put a great deal of effort in trying to persuade the Holy See to announce its support for the Non-Intervention Agreement, the Vatican hierarchy avoided making any public statements on the issue.

The French Government was unable to persuade the Holy See to announce its support for Non-Intervention publicly, but it did not mean Paris stopped its communications with the Vatican regarding the Spanish Civil War. Over the following months, Delbos and others reminded the Holy See of the importance of the conflict in Spain and tried to convince the Vatican to take a more public role regarding the war. On 5 June 1937, an internal Vatican memo acknowledged an upcoming meeting in Brussels concerning Spain, and mentioned that Delbos would be reminding the Vatican leadership that the Holy See could take a more prominent role in trying to quell the violence.[52] Pressure, although light, from the French Government continued in the hopes of ending the conflict, but the Holy See still appeared unwilling to take a more public step, forcing the religious entity to become more political.

In the late summer of 1937, the Vatican hierarchy shared concerns with French Ambassador to the Vatican, François Charles-Roux, concerning foreign involvement in Spain. The greatest threat was German Nazism and its violent and pagan behavior, "The Cardinal [Pacelli] said, 'Now, I think the Germans capable of anything . . . I wonder of what they are not capable'."[53] Whether or not Pacelli had sympathies for the Rebels, he feared the growing influence of Nazism and its violent streak. In September, Charles-Roux wrote, "The Holy See has finally been put on guard by this work of defamation; where it believes to discern the hand of Hitlerian agents, seeking to alienate the Catholics of Nationalist Spain from it by making it appear in their eyes as acquired by their adversaries."[54] Pacelli believed Nazis wanted to create a wedge between the Catholic Church and the Rebels, possibly hurting Church-Rebel relations. Nazi Germany had worked to reduce the influence of Catholicism in Germany, and the Church feared it could happen in Spain, too. The Vatican found it hard to support the Insurgency if they rejected

Catholicism for Nazism—destroying Spain's historical connection with the Church.

Papal Nuncio in France, Valerio Valeri, sent other information concerning French attitudes towards Cataluña to the Office of the Cardinal Secretary of State Pacelli. On 30 March 1938, Valeri sent a note to the Holy See about a meeting at the Quai d'Orsay focused on French attempts to send military ships to Barcelona to evacuate a wide variety of residents, including priests.[55] The letter mentioned that France would like to send more ships to other locations along the Catalan coastline to help in evacuations as Insurgents bombarded the region. At the end of the meeting, Political Director of the Ministry of French Foreign Affairs René Massigli commented to Nuncio Valeri that France could not evacuate civilians alone and needed British help, "But above all, the Holy See might possibly arise in such capacity with its high moral authority," to find a way to intervene.[56] In the attitude of Massigli, in order to save the lives of numerous Catalans, the Holy See would have to use its moral authority. Interestingly, Valeri stated that he did not respond directly to this comment, instead sending a message to the Holy See indicating that foreign governments still pressed the Holy See for increased public action. Even French pressure placed on the Holy See for humanitarian concerns could not force the Vatican leadership to change its stance against public comments regarding Spain.

Information from France regarding the Spanish Civil War, the aerial bombardments of Barcelona, and the condition of Spanish citizens continued to be sent to the Holy See. Meetings between Papal Nuncio Valeri and members of the French Government continued in the hopes of coming to an agreement about how to deal with Spain. Valeri sent a note on 28 March 1938 to the Holy See regarding an appointment between the Nuncio and the French Minister of Foreign Affairs Paul Boncour to discuss the political situation in France, which turned into a serious conversation about Spain as Boncour "was grateful that the Holy Father wanted to speak to General Franco and he added that he hoped that, as soon as a ceasefire had been verified between the two parties, the Holy Father with His prestige would be able to intervene in order to find finally a way to make a peace agreement for turbulent Spain." Valeri however "responded nothing, limiting myself to deploring the situation of the poor Spanish nation. However, given today's military situation of the two parties in conflict, I wonder if the words of Mr. Paul Boncour are able to give the key concerns of the Government about the affairs of Spain at this time."[57] Still, the French Office of Foreign Affairs believed the Holy See to be the state most capable of reducing the violence in Spain. The French and British plan to intervene in Cataluña and Minorca still appeared to be in the early stages, but Vatican approval or at least tacit support of such an idea would make it more plausible.

Valeri once again discussed the possibility of a French and British plan to push for mediation of the Spanish Civil War in hopes of ending hostilities on 1 April. The French requested the Holy See to support such a mission, and in response, Valeri stated, "I responded to him that if it was a question of making a humanitarian gesture, such as for example advising the winner to behave with moderation, forgiveness and reconciliation among the sons and classes of the same country, I thought that the Holy See would not have refused."[58] Valeri's response is significant as the Papal Nuncio rejected the idea of a public comment regarding mediation during the Civil War, but he did promise that the Holy See would work for Spanish reconciliation following the conflict. When the War would end, the Vatican would become more vocal concerning Spain. Was the Holy See enthused to see a Rebel victory, or was it just happy to see the War was soon ending?

At the end of 1938, the French Embassy to the Holy See reported that the Vatican still worried about the Civil War in Spain, but saw no possibility of a mediation plan. Jean Rivière, French Counsel to the Ambassador, wrote to Paris about further Vatican attempts to push for mediation, but "the result of these openings was negative."[59] The Vatican Secretary of State stated the Holy See was unable to affect the attitudes of Franco, and Pacelli grew concerned about the "*l'influences hitlérienne*" and the condition of Spain after the war ended.[60] This note does not suggest whether Pacelli supported the actions of Franco in the war, but it does show that the Secretary of State did have some apprehensions about the future of Spain even if Franco won. In December, French Ambassador to the Vatican, François Charles-Roux, wrote to Paris about a last-ditch effort for negotiations, but the Vatican stated any more plans would fail, like previous attempts: "There is not a chance that the Pope is ready now to address the Spanish for a call for suspension of hostilities of any duration, neither mediation nor armistice, for he made a diplomatic intervention in this sense to General Franco that received an immediate and categorical rejection."[61] By this time, the Holy See appeared to understand that Franco would reject any form of mediation, no matter who made the attempt.

French attempts to affect the attitude of the Holy See concerning Spain appeared to be more aggressive than those of the British, relying on formal meetings with the Papal Nuncio in Paris. At the start of the Civil War, the French pushed the Holy See to support publicly Non-Intervention in Spain, but the Vatican would not take steps that might seem political. As the war progressed, the French tried to influence the Holy See in the hopes the Vatican would support British and French plans for an armistice, but again the Holy See avoided making a serious commitment. The problem was, however, that the Vatican—in theory—could only support a peace plan if all belligerents requested action. This may have been a Vatican excuse not to act, but it is what the Holy See told Britain and France was the primary reason. French and British plans for mediation did not represent what the Rebels wanted. The Papal Nuncio did suggest the Holy See would support a post-war and humanitarian action in Spain, but nothing beforehand. Like the British, the French regarded the Holy See as one of the only foreign powers capable of influencing the crisis in Spain. The French and the British had created the plans—Non-Intervention, mediation, even sending military personnel to the Catalan coast—and they appeared willing to carry them out, but they wanted to receive some public acknowledgement from the Holy See. Both the British and French had mentioned the special "moral authority" of the Vatican as necessary for either state to take serious actions in Spain.

News from Other States

Britain and France, which had taken the lead with Non-Intervention and planned mediation in Spain, were not the only states interested in announcing their views to the Vatican during the Civil War. The Spanish conflict became a major concern for countries throughout the world because radical ideologies might occupy the majority of Iberia. Discussions regarding the Civil War, as well as plans constructed to deal with the conflict, made their way to the Holy See through Papal Nuncios' communications, official governmental letters, and personal notes. This section will explore a sampling of communications sent to the Vatican about Spain from a variety of states throughout the world. While some of these letters might not specifically have called upon the Holy See to act in Spain, the Vatican maintained them in their archives regarding the Spanish Civil War. These letters, no matter their content, offered the Holy See greater insights into the thoughts of other states concerning the Spanish Civil War as they begin to highlight the growing political, rather than humanitarian, concerns for Spain by numerous actors.

The world reacted to the first months of the Spanish Civil War with special attention coming from Iberoamerica. Due to Iberoamerica's historical and cultural connections to Spain, it is clear that the region would have a great deal of interest in the Civil War. Some of these states, like Mexico, Uruguay, and Chile held sympathies for the Republic and tried to act to support it. In the end, however, open physical and financial support for the Republican Government was prevented by the Non-Intervention plans constructed and maintained by European powers.[62] The Papal Nuncio in Rio de Janiero, Benedetto Aliosi Masella, wrote to the Holy See on 31 August 1936 focusing on the reactions of Uruguay and Brazil to the conflict. The Uruguayan Minister of Foreign Affairs announced his state's support "in favor of friendly intervention of American countries in Spain to be able to end the civil war."[63] The Uruguayan Government believed states with similar cultural identities as Spain would be able to work together in order to push for peace. The Nuncio's letter also contained reactions and opinions from Brazil. Unlike Uruguay, which had called to end the fighting in Spain, Brazil's reaction to the conflict differed as it called its ambassador home after the start of the Civil War as a protest against the fighting. The central rationale for the Brazilian decision came from the "the atrocities of the communists in Madrid."[64] As discussed in Chapter 4, reports of revolutionary militias' attacks against symbols of Catholicism in Madrid had been widely reported to the Holy See and other governments. While Uruguay pushed for an active role to quell the violence in Spain, the Brazilian Government took a more passive action in order to protest violence against the Catholic Church. This note showed not all Latin American and Catholic states agreed on the best solution for Spain; therefore, it is not surprising the Vatican also had difficulties making decisions.

The Catholic and Corporatist state of Portugal also had interests regarding the possibility of Vatican interactions and mediation during the Spanish Civil War. The Portuguese Estado Novo, which came to power in 1926, had developed close ties with other dictatorial regimes of the political right—including Fascist Italy and Nazi Germany—in the years leading to the Spanish Civil War. Once the War broke out, Salazar's regime was invited to participate in the Non-Intervention Committee but Portugal was frequently accused of offering aid to the Franquistas. In 1937, the Salazar regime openly recognized the legitimacy of the Franco regime.[65] On 17 May 1937, the Portuguese State Minister sent a note to the Papal Nuncio in Lisbon concerning the possibility of Vatican mediation of the Spanish Civil War. The note tried to establish a connection between the Republican Government and the Soviets, discussing the increasingly closer relations between Paris and Moscow were becoming problematic for Germany and Italy. The growing pressure from France, according to Portugal, was based on Soviet interests in Spain.[66] Moscow's connections with the Valencia Government endangered the interests of Catholics in Spain, and the Portuguese Government believed the Holy See should be aware of such a connection.[67] The Estado Novo suggested the Holy See should defend the interests of "*nacionalismo-catolico*" rather than try to protect the communist elements in Spain.[68] Overall, the Portuguese Government told the Papal Nuncio that mediation, by any entity like the Holy See, did not appear to be the best solution to the end of the Spanish Civil War.[69] While the French and British Governments had called for the Holy See to mediate the conflict in the hopes of preventing a humanitarian disaster, the rightist Portuguese regime wanted the Holy See not to participate in plans to end the war. The Estado Novo—which had tried to use Catholicism to unify its state—wanted to influence the Holy See by portraying the central focus of the war as a battle between Catholicism and Communism, and that it needed to be played out until the end without foreign mediation and a complete Franquista victory. While it cannot be determined how influential this document or any like it had been, the Estado Novo felt it necessary to suggest the Vatican to do nothing.

The Italian Government, like the Portuguese, had a major interest in the politics of the Second Spanish Republic and the battles of the Spanish Civil War. The Fascist dictatorship of Mussolini offered massive military assistance to the Rebels in order to assist a Franco victory.[70] Italy signed and nominally supported the ideas of Non-Intervention; however, Italy systematically broke this agreement to support Franco. Duplicitously, the Italian Government spoke out in favor of Non-Intervention while breaking it. On 12 December 1936, the Holy See obtained a note from the Italian Government supporting the ideas for a complete Non-Intervention in the hope of moving towards a quick peace.[71] The Italians stated that a lack of foreign involvement would allow the Spanish to deal with the crisis themselves.

On 9 July 1937, the Italian Ambassador for the International Committee for the Application of the Agreement Regarding Non-Intervention in Spain released a detailed statement, and the Vatican Archive obtained a copy of the letter. On the surface, the statement appears to suggest the Italian Government wanted to increase the neutrality of foreign states regarding Spain, but after closer investigation, the note also tried to influence groups like the Holy See by openly portraying the battle in Spain as one between Catholicism and Bolshevism, much like the 17 May note from Portugal. The statement called for more states, not just France and Britain, to have the right and option to patrol the Spanish coast in order to protect neutrality.[72] The Italian Government claimed to be fighting for Christian values by pushing for Non-Intervention, and not allowing the "Bolshevik menace" to gain a foothold in Spain.[73] According to the Italian Government, twenty-six of the twenty-seven signatories of the Non-Intervention Agreement were still proud of their Christian heritages and therefore must work to maintain neutrality. The one exception, of course, was the Soviet Union.[74] While not directed solely for the Holy See, by continually mentioning the differences between the Nationalist and Republican supporters, the Italians attempted to build greater international sympathy for Franco's regime.

While the Italian fascists supposedly supported Franco due to their political and religious similarities, it did not mean Italy would agree with every action and opinion of the Holy See. In fact, the diary of Galeazzo Ciano—Mussolini's son-in-law and Minister of Foreign Affairs—offers examples of Mussolini's anger and dislike towards the Holy See, with an exceptionally angry note from 14 December 1938. Following a meeting between Ciano and the Italian Ambassador to the Holy See, Count Pignatti, concerning Vatican opinions, Mussolini "burst out violently against the Pope, whose death he hopes for in the near future . . . He said that in Romagna the Churches were locked and bolted when Fascism began and that if people go to them now it is only because they know the Duce desires it. He ended, however, by affirming the importance of not provoking a crisis with the Vatican at the present moment, and he authorized me to deny the report about divorce and sterilization."[75] Even though the Lateran Accords gave the Catholic Church a monopoly over the spiritual concerns of Italy, at any point Mussolini could have struck out against the Holy See and Pope. The Vatican, being a tiny physical state surrounded by Italy, must have thought often about what would happen if Italian fascists moved into the city. The Holy See, therefore, needed to remain careful when dealing with possibly controversial political or social questions that could anger the Duce—like Spain.

In July 1937, the Holy See received notes from its representatives in Japan about discussions regarding the Spanish Civil War. In 1937, Japanese forces occupied Chinese Manchuria and established the puppet-regime of Manchukuo. Japan was also a signatory of the German Anti-Comintern Pact—established to fight the spread of communism and to facilitate the expansion of the three countries. According to Florentino Rodao, General Franco saw the possibility of gaining an ally in Japan: if Nationalist Spain would acknowledge the legitimacy of Manchukuo, then Franco hoped the Japanese regime would acknowledge the authority of the Rebels in Spain. Manchukuo had only been acknowledged by El Salvador, the Vatican and Japan, but Franco worked to establish recognition—which laid the groundwork for German and Italian recognition.[76] When the Spanish Civil War began in 1936, the head of the Spanish legation to Japan, Santiago Mendez de Vigo, accepted the legitimacy of the Rebel authority, leaving the Republic without a representative in Japan. In order to rectify this scenario, the Republic anointed language-instructor José Alvarez to be the new Republican charge d'affaires. Alvarez was instructed to occupy the Spanish embassy in Tokyo, but he was unsuccessful. While occupying the Spanish embassy, Nationalist supporters attempted to gain Japanese support and recognition. As Rodao writes, "The demand was supported by most of the small number of Spaniards resident in Japan, most of them members of the Catholic missionary community, many of these being Jesuits in Japan's Pacific islands."[77] In November 1936, the Japanese Government recognized the Franquistas as the official government of Spain. In a meeting with representatives of the Holy See in Japan, Alvarez admitted that there had been violence against clergy and symbols of the Church in Spain, but that the Republic had not supported or helped these actions.[78]

The Republican Government had attempted to initiate a public relations campaign around the world in order to improve its condition in the eyes of the Church. Unfortunately for the Republic, governments sympathetic to the Nationalist cause, like Germany, had used their representatives to highlight their views.[79] Various states used their international representatives in order to persuade other governments to support their beliefs. Spain had not only become a military conflict, but a public relations battle for the ideologically diverse states of the 1930s.

The Government of the United States of America remained neutral during the War, and with the exception of private volunteers for the Abraham Lincoln Brigade, took little direct and formal action in trying to influence the outcome of events. This, however, did not mean that Americans ignored the Civil War and passionate opinions were expressed on both sides. On 2 August 1938, a New York Attorney named Robert J. Stratton sent a formal letter to Cardinal Pacelli about the Spanish Civil War, claiming the Rebels had "sold out" to Hitler, and therefore, the Roman Catholic Church had become "indifferent to the suffering of the masses of the people and is interested in material rather than spiritual matters."[80] Of course, this letter did not represent the formal beliefs of the American Government, nor did it speak for the majority of Americans, but the language in this letter is certainly damning of the Vatican hierarchy and its lack of action in Spain. Did the author know of the many letters to and from the Holy See that tried to find a way to increase Vatican involvement in the mediation? He would not. However, in the mind of some, the Holy See was not doing its job and was politicizing the Spanish Civil War and supporting the increase of fascist dictators in the world. For men like Stratton, it appeared as if the lack of action by the Holy See was direct support for Franco. Just as it had been difficult to define the position of the Vatican years after the Civil War, the Holy See's actions were even more difficult to interpret during the event.

Not all Americans, however, believed the Spanish Civil War would end with fascist influence in Spain. For some, the Church had been nothing but a victim and the fact that the Holy See had remained silent showed a great deal of integrity held by the Church. In reaction to the question of German and Italian influence in Spain, the Knights of Columbus periodical *Columbia* expressed a different opinion. Paul McGuire wrote in May 1938 "I do not believe for an instant that the Germans and Italians will dominate Spain. Italy went into Spain because she can no more afford to have Sovietism in Spain than she could afford it on the Brenner Pass."[81] The following March, McGuire continued, "If Franco refuses concessions to Mussolini, what is Mussolini to do in that situation? Plunge into war against Spain which could be immediately united on that one issue and which would immediately have help from

France and England? Il Duce is not a lunatic."[82] While Stratton alleged the Church allowed the rightist dictators of Europe to gain more influence in Spain, McGuire justified these actions by Italy and Germany as understandable and necessary to prevent the spread of atheistic communism. For McGuire, Vatican restraint was the remarkable action and it appeared best that the Spanish Civil War play out to the end. Fascism, therefore, was not the major threat for men like McGuire and his lay Catholic organization.

The debates at the personal or organizational level continued, but the Government of the United States did have some serious and choice words for the Holy See concerning Spain. On 15 January 1939, Nuncio Cicognani sent a note to Cardinal Pacelli concerning the opinions of the President of the United States of America. As mentioned in a discussion with the Archbishop of Chicago, Roosevelt "Is no longer favorable to a Franco victory."[83] The Nuncio's letter also mentioned that the American Government still worried about the lack of assistance for the people in Barcelona, and contemplated offering assistance, something Cicognani described as "dangerous."[84] The possible change in the attitude of the American Government about ending the embargo to Spain was based on rumors in the United States about the actions of the Rebels. Monsignor Michael Ready, General Secretary of the National Catholic Welfare Conference in the US, sent a note to the Holy See regarding a conversation among Dr. Maurice Sheehy, Bishop Ryan, and President Roosevelt on 31 December 1938. During the meeting Ready reported that the American Government had changed its opinion about a Franco victory.[85] Roosevelt based his conclusions on an earlier conversation with Cardinal Mundelein. Ready wrote, "The President said that other Catholic leaders in the United States and some Catholic publications held the view that a Franco victory would be harmful to world peace."[86] Sheehy and Ryan tried to explain that the President "could have misunderstood the Cardinal" and advocated to the American President a continuation of the embargo for Spain as the best path; they maintained the majority of American Catholics were almost unanimous in condemning the Barcelona regime as Communistic and they characterized the situation in Spain as a war of Christianity against atheism.[87] In order to further persuade the American Government that lifting the embargo was a bad idea, the National Council of Catholic Men scheduled a mass meeting for 9 January 1939 in Washington, D.C. This committee began a national campaign to continue the embargo towards Spain by scheduling this meeting that was "filled to capacity—4,000—and a crowd estimated variously from 2,500 to 7,000 was turned away."[88] The meeting was not the only plan, as "the National Council of Catholic Men has received reports of petitions containing 1,518,000 signatures having been forwarded to the Congress" to support the continuation of the embargo.[89] Once the

American Government appeared to waver on the continuation of the Spanish embargo, American Catholic organizations began their own campaign to prevent aid from reaching the supposedly atheistic Barcelona Government.[90] The Holy See did not direct these protest and petition drives, but they were well aware of the process. American Catholic leadership supported and worked for the continuation of the embargo, and these attempts seemed to have paid off, as the US did not change its stance on aid to the Republic.

The Holy See received information about the international attitudes concerning the Spanish Civil War from a variety of states. While France and Britain appeared consistent in their message of Non-Intervention and possible Vatican mediation, other states had varying opinions. Republican and Rebel allies around the world tried to persuade states to take stances that would be beneficial for their own side. Papal Representatives and State Officials sent numerous letters to the Holy See to try to update them on the international opinions, but as this section has shown, these reports varied. Rarely, if ever, did any of these countries seem to agree on the proper course of action in Spain. This flood of information appeared to make the situation even more complicated for the Holy See. If secular states could not agree on how the international community should behave, then the Holy See would also have serious problems in making a concrete decision. Each of the states mentioned in this section identified the proper role of the Vatican, and the Vatican chose to remain not directly involved in the conflict.

At the same time, what were the Vatican's interests concerning this war? While not explicitly stated, one could argue that some in the Vatican hierarchy might have been willing to let the Civil War proceed without intervention to assist Rebel goals. Many states tried "to use" the Vatican to support political actions. The Vatican did not consider itself a "political tool" but the leader of the Catholic world, devoid of foreign ideological influence. In this conflict, the Holy See worked to present a public face of neutrality, but it is clear that the hierarchy would have had its own opinions about how to act. The safest and best long-term solution for the Holy See appeared to be continued silence. By not taking a public stance, one way or another, the Holy See would not anger any of these secular states—like Germany or Italy—and possibly allowed the Holy See to have greater influence in post-Civil War Francoist Spain. No "complete truth" was sent to the Vatican by any state or any representative, and making an incorrect decision concerning this War might have been worse than not making any decision at all as it might have weakened Vatican influence following the conflict. The Vatican pursued its interests in Spain, and did not let conflicting reports change their opinions.

Pressure from Private Organizations

The private organizations based outside of Spain, like the *Comité Espagnol pour la Paix Civile* (Spanish Committee for the Civil Peace) and the *Jeunesse Ouvrière Chrétienne* (Young Christian Workers), sent communications to the Vatican with the hopes of persuading the Holy See and Pope to begin the process of mediation. All sides in the conflict, however, did not appreciate these messages as Burgos made its opinions well known to the Holy See about international calls for mediation from all groups. These private groups and the Franquistas both tried to use the language of good Christianity versus barbarous totalitarianism in order to influence the Holy See's decision. This section will explore the letters sent to the Holy See from these private organizations as well as responses from the Rebels in order to explore the bombardment of information received by the Vatican concerning Spain.

From 30 April until 2 May 1938, the *Comité Espagnol pour la Paix Civile* met in Paris in order to construct a plan for mediation and armistice in Spain. Alfredo Mendizábal and Joan B. Roca i Caball founded this organization in 1937 to speak out for the Republican cause.[91] The first step of the plan was to sign an armistice until a final treaty could be completed.[92] During this period each side was supposed to maintain order, prohibit demonstrations against the other side, prohibit demonstrations against peace, repatriate foreign fighters, facilitate the work of an International Commission, give freedom of movement for citizens between zones, not purchase military weaponry and disarm all citizens.[93] The armistice was supposed to guarantee the liberation of all prisoners and support public freedoms. Similarly, the armistice would allow for the reconstruction of commerce in the two zones to improve lives.[94] In order to finalize the peace, an International Commission would be created in order to create a provisional government that was supposed to be acceptable for both sides.[95] During this period, the Spanish state would be neutral. The Plan of the *Comité* goes on to explain how the Spanish Provisional Government should be organized and finally explained that after much international mediation, Spain would once again become a normal state. This statement did not specifically call for the Holy See to become active in this plan, but in order for it to work a great number of foreign states would need to be willing to participate and follow the outlined steps. In reality, however, this plan was clearly untenable and could never end Spain's debacle.

On 13 May 1938, the Rebel Embassy to the Holy See sent a message to the Vatican to warn the Church about *Comité Espagnol pour la Paix Civil*, which was allegedly nothing more than a group with Masonic influence that was attempting to end the War in Spain before the Rebels had the ability to remove negative influences from the state.[96] The Burgos leadership bluntly outlined its agenda to the Holy See, and therefore, the Vatican was clearly aware of Franco's goals to end the war. The Rebels painted the Society as a group that wanted to hurt the interests of the Right in Spain while trying to gain sympathy for international mediation that would assist the Republicans in the War.[97] In response to the actions of this Society, the Rebels believed a military triumph would be the only way to save Spain in response to organizations that wished to "to decrease the independence of Spain" by inviting other states to intervene.[98] For the Rebels, the idea of any foreign intervention to mediate the Spanish crisis was paramount to a foreign invasion of Spanish soil. Ironically, while the Insurgency had openly accepted aid from Germany and Italy during the Civil War, foreign mediation for peace was an attack against sovereignty. In response to this letter, the Holy See sent a memo to the Rebel Embassy to confirm it had received the note about the Society in Paris, but it gave no concrete information about how it would react to the Rebels' or Society's interests concerning mediation.[99] Once again, two ideological entities pulled the Holy See in different directions.

The *Comité Espagnol pour la Paix Civil* increased its international communications, including direct letters to the Holy See. On 24 September, the *Comité's* President and prominent Catholic theologian, Jacques Maritain, sent a letter to the Vatican, attempting to persuade the Holy See, and specifically the Holy Father, to become active regarding Spain and push for peace: "The Voice of the Holy Father is understood as in favor of peace."[100] According to Maritain, the Holy Father would be able to push through British plans for mediation, help with the exchange of prisoners on both sides, and reconcile the traumas of Spain.[101] The President of the *Comité* believed that the Holy Father might be the only one capable of sending this message and gaining acceptance of the British plan by the Burgos Government.[102] The message concluded with, "It is with the anxiety that this situation inspires in us and with a great hope in the Apostolic See that we come respectfully to solicit the charitable intercession of the Holy Father."[103] The privileged position of the Holy See in its relationship (or at least perceived one) with the Burgos Government was viewed as a very powerful bargaining tool with the Rebels. However, the Holy See accepted this letter from the Comité, but did not release a public statement about the subject. It cannot be determined if the previous communication from the Rebel Embassy was the reason that no action was taken concerning this statement, but more likely, the Holy See continued to follow its plan of international silence when concerning Spain.

Even though the communications from September did not result in action by the Vatican on behalf of the *Comité*, the organization continued to communicate with the Holy See in the hopes that action would be taken. On 9 December 1938, the *Comité* wrote once again to the Office of Cardinal Pacelli because, "The tragic situation of our country moves us to elevate our request to the common Father of Christianity."[104] The *Comité* stated that the increase of violence and starvation in Spain required some form of foreign assistance. The problem, though, was that "*la diplomacia de las grandes potencias*" had been unable to prevent these serious conditions and the only way to solve this situation was to believe in "*las fuerzas espirituales y en el poder supremo de la caridad fraterna.*"[105] There was also a specific reason for the timing of this note. The Comité had hoped that due to the proximity of Christmas both sides could agree upon a one-month long armistice. Whereas the other foreign powers had been unable to establish such an accord, the Comité believed that the Holy Father was the one voice that could succeed "demanding an end at once to the horrible war in Spain and that the killings among brothers that take place against the majority's will, be substituted by a peace settlement. Or, at least, that both belligerents accept a truce of one month, starting from the 24th of December—a truce from God for Christians—during which all acts of war or military readiness would be prohibited."[106] According to the beliefs of the Comité, the Holy Father could force the two belligerents and others involved in the war to establish a truce for the holiday. The Comité's reliance on the Holy Father, stating that all Christians relied upon this peace initiative, illustrates once again that certain organizations hoped to rely on the Vatican; however, the Vatican did not announce a plan based on these statements.

The Comité Espagnol pour la Paix was not the only group to write to the Holy See to express its desires for a truce for the Christmas holiday of 1938. On 15 December, the *Jeunesse Ouvrière Chrétienne* of Brussels, Belgium wrote to the Holy See to support this idea. The JOC was formally established in 1925 with the idea to act for social change but under the auspices of Catholic teachings.[107] The Chaplain General of the organization stated that he was writing to the Pope on behalf of young Spanish Catholics who had been forced to relocate to Brussels, "It is an action by the Holy Father addressed to the two belligerent parties in Spain, in order to obtain a break in hostilities during the feasts of Christmas. All the young Spaniards would be able to thus unite with their brothers from all countries to celebrate in tranquility the birth of the Prince of Peace."[108] The JOC believed that the Holy Father would be able to force through such a plan. Like the Comité, this organization used the words and themes surrounding the Christmas holiday to try to convince the Holy See to take action. According to the JOC, all Christian youth deserved to celebrate the tranquility of the Christmas holiday, especially those from Spain. At the end of the letter, however, the Chaplain General stated that he was not trying to pressure the Pope into making any specific decisions, but actions would be very helpful. Like the letter from the Comité, it appeared as if no direct action was taken by the Holy See concerning the Christmas cessation of hostilities, other than recognizing that yet another organization with Christian values had asked for intervention.

A 19 December note from the *Comité* tried to explain how a cessation of hostilities could be completed in Spain if the Holy See took a more public step. The letter begins, "I am not sure about the attitudes in Barcelona, but after some serious intelligence, received second hand, I believe that the Republican Government is ready to accept all propositions of peace."[109] According to the note, the Republicans were ready for mediation, but the Rebels were not, as the Insurgents viewed the necessity to reject mediation to regain "prestige" for Spain, as the country could handle this issue on its own. On the other hand, it was suggested that the Franquistas might be willing to accept help in "reconciliation" for all the children of Spain.[110] The following page of the note contained information about how this hope of reconciliation could occur, and more importantly, who could assist in such a process:

> From whom can this call come? This cannot be from a foreign nation. The Spaniards –despite everything that happened at home!– proclaim that their war is an internal affair that only involves themselves and that they want to solve among themselves. Besides, no power can effectively intervene. If it is a government of French-English agreement, Spain will face the hostility of the Rome-Berlin axis, in which it is in part already trapped. If it is a government of the Axis, Spain will lose the financial resources of the agreement that are essential to it. If the Holy See is the one that intervenes, all the objections will disappear. It is not a foreign government that interferes in the affairs of Spain, it is the Common Father who calls his children to fraternal unity. Moreover, as the Holy See has no material interests to protect in Spain, the issue of international rivalry does not arise.
>
> What advantages could the Holy See not derive from such an intervention![111]

Again, the Holy See is mentioned as the only possible government that could intervene in this conflict. The author separated the governments of the secular states from that of the Vatican. According to the note, the Vatican had no material or financial interests in Spain, and could be the only power rational and unbiased enough to work for peace.

The note also discussed the attacks against Christianity that had occurred in Spain during the Civil War. It admitted that the "*rouges*" had been responsible for attacks against religion, but that not all Republicans were reds. On the other hand, it alluded that Franco's forces were not completely innocent. They had been receiving aid from the Nazis, who, according to the memo, had been antagonistic towards the practice of

Christianity.[112] What, then, could the Pope do to bring these two sides together in order to overcome these concerns? "First, the moral call to reconciliation and the proposal of an immediate armistice. Then, to enter the practical domain, the meeting of representatives of the major forces in the country: Republican Government, Falangists, Requetés, Catalan, Basque, and maybe offering a legate who should be the Cardinal-Secretary of State?—to chair the meeting and arbitrate."[113] The organization believed that the Holy See had the power to call a truce and then bring together all the forces involved in the War together for a compromise. At the meeting, the goal would be to establish a federal system that would give regional freedoms to minority groups in Spain, but would also restore the monarchical powers of Don Juan—son of Spanish Bourbon King Alfonso XIII—to avoid a situation similar to that of Nazi Germany.[114] The note ends by explaining if this scenario could occur under the leadership of the Holy See, then the condition for Catholics and all Spaniards would be greatly improved. Like previous international calls for mediation, there is no evidence the Holy See actively worked on such an idea. Maybe the Holy See found such a plan impossible and believed there was no reason to even acknowledge it. A private organization, and not a foreign government, had given the Holy See a possible mediation plan, but the Vatican assumed these plans might not be "neutral"—or they might not coincide with the Holy See's interest in Catholic practice in Spain.

The *Comité Espagnol* and the JOC had close connections or at least ideological leanings with the Spanish Republican Government. Both groups supported the idea of Vatican mediation in order to end the fighting in Spain, but the Rebels did not want such a plan. In order to prevent this from occurring, the Rebels sent the Holy See information libeling the Comité Espagnol as nothing more than an appendage of the Republican Government. It cannot be clearly determined how influential either of these arguments was for the Holy See, but it can be established that the Holy See had obtained information from both sides and had chosen to avoid taking any public stance. Foreign Governments had been unable to persuade the Holy See to act publicly, and so had these private organizations.

THE END OF FOREIGN PRESSURES?

The Vatican received numerous calls to mediate the Spanish Civil War and to initiate a truce between the warring factions. The British, French, and private groups believed that only formal Vatican mediation could end the conflict. The Insurgents, Portuguese, and Italians opposed mediation so that Franco's forces could remove all atheistic elements from the state—war and executions were the only way to do this. Both sides used religious appeals to try to persuade the Holy See to take their side.

In the end, the Holy See remained publicly silent. Massive amounts of material arrived at the Holy See but it represented a wide spectrum of ideas. The Vatican was concerned about the humanitarian situation in Spain, but it was inundated with opinions and persuasive arguments that tried to convince the Holy See to behave in one way or another. What was the central reason behind these new and sudden interests in Vatican mediation: British appeasement and economics, French stability, Portuguese Corporatism and rightist ideology, Italian Mediterranean ambitions, Nazi war games, Soviet interference, or Republican legitimacy? Any Vatican action would please some groups but anger others—what could be done? At the same time, some members of the Vatican hierarchy must have privately supported Franco's promised restoration of tradition in Spain, and these men would want the Holy See to avoid shaming the Rebels, and possibly angering their allies. Similarly, others must have feared fascist and Nazi repercussions in Europe should the Holy See take a public stance these dictatorships saw as distasteful. As explained in Chapter 4, Pius XI might have wanted to speak more, but Pacelli would have supported a quieter approach in order to avoid conflicts in other states. How could the Vatican support some foreign opinions while ignoring others? By choosing to follow a certain plan, the Holy See would be choosing sides in a much larger European conflict. Even by exploring archival materials relating to the possibility of Vatican mediation proposed by foreign states, one can see the major difficulty in trying to determine the genuine interests in mediation by foreign states and what the best action for the Holy See would be. At the same time, however, the Vatican would have an agenda for a future Catholic Spain, in which the Church had authority of many social, cultural, and even political behaviors. The Rebels could give the Vatican what it wanted, but the Holy See could not publicly condone this war. Instead, the Vatican tried some passive diplomacy with Burgos, and some could argue the Holy See appeased Franco as it never pressed any issue too strongly. Had communists overthrown the Republic and established an atheistic dictatorship, the Vatican surely would have pleaded for international action. In this case, supposed communists were losing, supposed Catholics were winning, and the Church did not have to exacerbate other tensions. The Vatican had the ability to create its own plans if it wanted, but when foreign states prodded, the Vatican remained silent.

VII

How to Save the Basque
Vatican Mediation Meets Rebel Opinions

The Vatican had interests in Spanish Civil War mediation, hoping to influence the future Spanish state, but the Rebel leadership would not accept any plan to end hostilities—highlighting the Insurgency's desire for a complete and bloody military victory. The Vatican sympathized greatly with the plight of the devoutly Catholic Basque and hoped to mediate a cessation of hostilities to the northern campaign but Vatican mediation was never strong enough to force the Rebels to end their attacks and they continued a campaign of war and repression. The Vatican could have been more public in its condemnation of the Insurgency's attacks through encyclicals or Papal messages, or even threatened the excommunications of murderous generals, but it avoided all these actions. The Franquistas were poised to win the Civil War, and the Holy See would have to work with this new government in the near future, and the Church wanted a better relationship in Spain than it had with the Republic.

Franco spoke of a crusade to restore Catholicism's central character in Spain, but he never clearly outlined what position the Church would occupy in the post-war environment. This role appeared contingent on the Church's actions during the conflict. When the Holy See did voice concern over atrocities, the Rebels quickly denied these actions and requested the Holy See avoid such statements, even if true. Because promises were not clearly defined, because the Franquistas reacted so forcefully against mediation, and because the Rebels still killed thousands in the conflict, the Holy See declined to recognize the new government during the War.[1] At the same time, while Pope Pius XI viewed the War with great sadness and wanted more direct communications with Franco concerning atrocities, his Secretary of State Eugenio Pacelli likely tempered Vatican messages not to anger the future Spanish leader or powerful states—like Germany and Italy—that backed the rebellion. The Vatican leadership never disputed the Insurgent victory in the region—in fact, many Spanish Catholic leaders, like Cardinal Isidro Gomá y Tomás, supported the Republic's defeat—but the Vatican suggested peace settlements as the war appeared all but over. Was there a way to help the Spanish people and favor a Franquista victory while allowing the Republic to lose? The answer appeared to be maintenance of open dialogue with Franco during the conflict, but not to create serious pressures on the general in the fear he might turn on the Church. The Rebel leadership spared a few lives in the Basque region, but wanted a complete military extrication of the Republican leadership and sympathizers. The Holy See could express that it did something during the Civil War to spare some lives, but a moral authority like the Vatican could have done more.

This chapter explores calls from various Republicans for assistance from the Vatican, especially those with interests in the Basque region. The Basque, who were devoutly Catholic, sided with the Republic due to regionalist concerns. Due to the region's adherence to Catholicism, the Spanish Catholic Church leaders were interested in ending the hostilities there. The Basque Government demanded reassurances from Franco that he and his armies would not suppress or attack the Basque once the War was over, yet the Rebels claimed they would never repress them and appeared insulted by the accusation.[2] Yet the Insurgents reneged on such promises. The Holy See sent numerous communications to Burgos to request a cessation in hostilities in País Vasco, but the Rebels rarely cooperated. At the start of the conflict, members of the Spanish Catholic Church aligned themselves with the conservatives to end the Republic's secularization campaign and a large ideological divide existed with hostility to liberal democracy, socialism, communism, and anarchism. The Republic had expropriated church lands and buildings, closed church schools, and turned a blind-eye to violence against priests. The Franquistas promised to restore the Church's privileged position in Spain and protect it from secular activities even if the right never clearly identified how they would do this. How could the Vatican leadership ignore the Spanish Catholic hierarchy's support for the Rebels? The Spanish Catholic Church seemed to need the Insurgents more than the Insurgency needed the Church. Religion had been a rallying cry for the Rebels, but they did not kowtow to the Church's demands. As William J. Callahan explains, "On balance, the Church saw its fortunes improve under the Nationalists, but, as so often in the past, it found itself dependent upon a regalist government whose view of civil-ecclesiastical relations left little room for the kind of institutional autonomy sought by the clergy for generations ... The cost to what one historian has appropriately called a 'mortgaged-church' proved high."[3] The Church found protection with the Rebels, but the Spanish Catholic hierarchy remained indebted to the uprising's leaders. Callahan continues, "During the Civil War, the Nationalists identified religion and government more thoroughly than any government since the waning days of absolute monarchy over a century earlier" but most importantly the Rebels wanted "to accomplish more or less what nineteenth-century liberals and twentieth-century republicans had attempted, to keep the Church on a tight leash by confining it to the realm of purely religious activities."[4] The Catholic Church's two choices, Republicans or Rebels, were clear, but the Franquistas would never subjugate themselves. To assert influence, the Holy See wanted a pretense of being an honest broker in humanitarian concerns, as previous Popes had tried during other modern political and military conflicts.[5] From reviewing ASV sources, it appeared that the Holy See hoped to persuade the Rebels to reduce attacks against civilian centers, but these sources do not offer evidence of any sympathies for the Republican Government.

Foreign Governments requested that the Holy See mediate the Spanish Civil War in order to find a solution to the fighting, but the Vatican was unable to persuade either side—particularly the Franquistas—to accept these requests. When the Rebel developed a serious military advantage in the summer of 1937, Republican allies in the Basque region initiated requests for mediation from the Holy See to prevent further bloodshed. The Vatican considered mediation possibilities, but Burgos worked to prevent them. The Rebel Government claimed to be insulted that the Vatican intervened because Burgos promised to avoid arrests and executions of enemies once the battles in the region ended—even though thousands were sent to work camps or executed after "kangaroo courts."[6] The Insurgents reminded the Holy See that Burgos claimed to fight for the Catholic Church and would act responsibly to end the Civil War, and not kill innocent victims, even though they clearly did. Once the Basque region fell, the Rebels turned their complete attention to the last Republican strongholds in eastern Spain. As the fighting in this region intensified, and a Rebel victory appeared assured, representatives from the Republic hoped the Holy See would intervene and initiate a peace plan. Burgos did not appreciate these requests, rejected mediation, and wanted the War to be fought until the bitter end with a decisive military victory.

This chapter will explore the interactions among the Republic, the Rebels, and the Holy See regarding possible Vatican mediation in the Basque region. From the declaration of the Second Spanish Republic, the Holy See and the Republic had a confrontational relationship concerning the role of the Catholic Church in Spanish society and politics. As the Civil War continued, few Republicans wondered if concessions could be made with the Catholic Church in order to gain its support. One such Basque Republican, Manuel de Irujo—minister without portfolio and practicing Catholic in the Republican leadership—hoped to establish a better relationship with the Catholic Church in January 1937. Irujo wanted "normalization" as "the Spanish Catholic Church would revert to its prewar status, namely, freedom of worship within the limits imposed by the Constitution of 1931, and that these freedoms and limited rights would be protected by the government."[7] Irujo hoped that Catholics would support the Republic and the Holy See could understand the Republican ideals. For the Republican leadership, this option could not work due to Rebel threats and a perceived Vatican disinterest in the plan.[8] The Holy See wanted to help Catholics, but the Republican leadership would not promise to return to the pre-1931 legal status of the Church and "Furthermore, as time went on, the inescapable fact that the Nationalists appeared each day more likely to win the war adversely affected any possible compromise."[9] The Rebels, however, promised change and appeared ready to win the War. The Vatican hierarchy, therefore, was aware the Republican apparatus was unwilling to compromise, but the Holy See still investigated possible mediation—even if this went against Rebel or Spanish Catholic hierarchy positions. But one could still argue the bottom line for the Vatican was self-preservation and a return to pre-1931 privileges and safety.

Even though some in the Holy See worked to establish mediation plans, it can be assumed that others desired regime change in Spain. The Rebels asserted they initiated their uprising to protect the rights of conservatives, and most importantly Catholics in Spain.[10] By characterizing this Civil War as a true "crusade" against atheism and communism, the Insurgents hoped to gain the outright support of the Holy See for their actions, but they never received full recognition. In fact, according to historian Peter C. Kent, the Vatican was rather publicly ambivalent to the Rebels' cause due to the chaos and persecution that occurred in war.[11] Burgos's ploys to gain Vatican recognition did not succeed, and a surprisingly contentious relationship developed between the Holy See and Burgos. By 1937, the Rebels had won numerous battles and appeared unstoppable, but the Vatican continued not to recognize them officially. Was Burgos too violent, did Franco break promises? One can speculate the Holy See did not recognize Burgos due to the growing death toll and repression by the army, or due to a lack of promises from the Rebels concerning the future role of the Church in Spain, or due to conflict between Pius XI and Secretary of State Pacelli concerning what role the Holy See should play in this conflict and how it could affect the Catholic Church in other states.

As the Civil War continued, the Vatican decided the best solution was to remain out of the public discourse surrounding the Civil War to avoid any excuses "for escalation of the anti-Church repression—and wait for a quick end to the fighting."[12] However, multiple invitations to mediate the conflict arrived, and the Vatican sorted through these requests and developed some workable plans. Ricardo Miralles has suggested that the Republican Government was unwilling to accept negotiations from

Britain and France, but hoped the Holy See would find a workable program.[13] As the war turned dire for the Republic, its government appeared willing to accept mediation, especially from the Vatican. Repression of Republican Catholics by Rebel forces was a growing concern for the Vatican.[14] The Holy See increased its diplomatic activities in late 1937 and throughout 1938 to find some solution for the conflict in Spain, angering the Franquista Government and souring relations between the Holy See and Burgos. This growing Rebel animosity forced Count Rodenso, the Nationalist Minister of Justice, to suggest Burgos break off relations with the Holy See if the Vatican did not remove its representatives from the Republican region in September 1938.[15] When the Civil War began, the Rebels wanted to persuade the Holy See to support their cause in order to justify the "Uprising," but when the Republic was ready to negotiate, Burgos's attitude had changed. The Rebels no longer needed to garner Vatican support as victory became clear, and the Rebels rejected Vatican suggestions for mediation and continued the conflict to its decisive end.

One of Franco's greatest frustrations during the War was the relationship with the Holy See. Frances Lannon explains, "Throughout the Republic, Pope Pius XI and his Secretary of State, Pacelli, had maintained a discreet distance from constitutional matters . . . Cardinal Pacelli had seconded in every way open to him the commitment of careful negotiation pursued by the nuncio Tedeschini and Vidal."[16] Even though the Vatican had a contentious relationship with the Republic, the leadership did not overtly work to undermine the government as the Madrid Nunziatura stayed open and Burgos did not receive its Charge d'Affaires Antoniutti until September 1937, who had previously spoken to improve the treatment of the Basque. It wasn't until spring 1938 that Franco received a Nuncio, Gaetano Cicognani.[17] Therefore, the Vatican was never Franco's *ally* during the Civil War. The Nationalist leadership originally wanted Vatican support to justify its actions, but it never received *carte-blanche* approval, as the Vatican avoided making public statements. Similarly, the Vatican hierarchy would not condone Rebel behavior, even though the Holy See had an interest in mediation during certain points of the Civil War.

A Desire for Mediation Meets Rebel Mockery

Franquistas and Republicans manufactured and/or manipulated evidence to persuade the Vatican to make a public statement for their political cause. The Vatican acknowledged these communications, but the Vatican did not take a public stance for either side, even as the war was about to end. Here I explore early communications between the

Spanish Governments and the Holy See during the first period of the Civil War. As the evidence will show, the Vatican studied these communications but believed it was hampered by the Lateran Accords and relied on private contacts rather than possibly threaten its tenuous position within fascist Italy—as the Holy See was physically surrounded by this powerful and aggressive neighbor. Next, I explore the communications presented to the Holy See concerning a possible truce between the Rebel forces and the Basque Government. The generally devout Basque Nationalists had sided with the Republican Government, and many in the region regarded the Holy See as the only power that could negotiate an end to the hostilities in northern Spain. Communications from religious leaders and Basque politicians highlighted how they hoped the Holy See would negotiate a peaceful solution for the region. On the other hand, many who had sided with the Rebels believed that the Holy See should not involve itself in such activities unless the Basque would surrender completely without concessions.

The Conde de los Andes, Francisco Moreno Zuleta—a Spanish noble, Nationalist ally, and aide to the Spanish Monarch in-exile—wrote to Cardinal Pacelli on 16 September 1936 to explain the increasingly tragic condition of the people of Spain. The Conde wrote with "*la esperanza de obtener un favor*" from Cardinal Pacelli,[18] concerning the actions of South American and North American bishops who wanted to take more public action regarding the crimes of Marxists against Catholic properties and practices in Spain. The Conde aimed for the Vatican Secretary of State's Office to write a letter of introduction for these bishops to meet with the Pope in order to discuss the Spanish crisis. While the letter was meant to support the actions of foreign bishops concerning Spain, the letter came from a Rebel ally. If the Vatican allowed these bishops to meet with the Pope and make their arguments on a larger scale, they might have been able to gain further support for the Insurgency.

Cardinal Pacelli responded to the Conde's letter on 28 September 1936, acknowledging his sadness concerning the attacks against the Church and its flock in Spain, and he thanked the Conde for his interest in the matter.[19] This letter is important because it gives insight into the Cardinal Secretary of State's attitude about the public role of the Holy See:

> At this end, however, it does not seem necessary a direct intervention of the Holy See, which was necessary to avoid in other similar cases, not for minor reasons. In truth, the Holy Father, to whom I have submitted the request from Your Excellency, does not see the possibility and convenience of this intervention in the present circumstances and believes that for the noble and holy objective indicated by Your Excellency, the words of the Most Eminent Mr. Cardinal

Primate will be fully efficient as a voice that raises from the fields stained with the blood of the fight and martyrdom.[20]

The Holy See had avoided public comments concerning possible mediation of the Spanish crisis, but it did work through private-channels. Like previous communications from American bishops in 1933, the Holy See did not support formal meetings between the Pope and other representatives concerning the Civil War, but Rome did pay great attention to Spain. Audiences with the Pope were difficult to obtain for anyone, and Cardinal Pacelli might have acted as an interceptor trying to block meetings he did not want to schedule.

After the Rebel forces advanced rapidly in 1936, the Republic was split in two parts: north-central País Vasco and eastern Cataluña-Valencia-Madrid. The Basque region tried to hold out against the onslaught, but Franco's forces continued to win in 1937, leading to the surrender in October. As it became likely the Basque region would soon fall in 1937, Basque communications reached the Holy See about the idea of Catholic mediation to end the war there and return some form of normalcy for the people. The Basque had been unable to gain support for their war effort from the Holy See, but they hoped that the increased violence in the region would persuade the Vatican to take some kind of action.[21]

A memo from the Father Jacques de Bivort de la Saudée, an outspoken French critic of communism and atheism, dated 23 January 1937, spoke against the possibility of Vatican mediation in the Basque region, stating, "An intervention of the Holy See in favor of an exchange of hostages between the Insurgents and the Basques would be <u>for now and in the present circumstances</u>, in my humble and subordinated view, <u>ineffectual, inopportune, and perhaps even harmful for the interests of the Church</u>."[22] The central focus of this discussion was to show the leadership of the Holy See that becoming involved in this conflict was not in its best interest because the Basque leaderships' ideological allies were dangerous. Vatican involvement, according to the note, would be ineffectual for specific reasons. First, the International Red Cross and the British Government had become involved in the humanitarian situation in the region, and the Holy See should allow those agencies to continue their work. Second, since the Basque National Party had sided with the Republican Government—which had allowed a variety of leftists to commit acts of violence against the Church and its followers—the moral authority of the Holy See would be damaged if it assisted any Republicans. Next, evidence showed the Rebels were responsible for numerous deaths in the region, making the situation more complicated for the Holy See. Overall, the primary rationale for the ineffectiveness of Vatican mediation was centered on supposed communist influence in the Republican and Basque Governments, which would hurt the mission of the Holy See by openly working with an ideological enemy of the Church.[23] While these concerns might not have made Vatican intervention "ineffective", they certainly would have sullied the image of the Holy See to devout Catholics worldwide by cooperating or working with declared enemies of religion. Why should the Catholic Church take aggressive actions to save people interested in its annihilation?

Next, a plan for Vatican mediation in País Vasco would be "inopportune" due to foreign involvement. According to the memo, the interference of Latin American states, like Mexico, complicated the plausibility of mediation for the Holy See. Similarly, debates in the League of Nations, particularly those led by the Soviet Representative, Maxim Litvinoff, made it inopportune for the Holy See to become more active in mediation.[24] The involvement of foreigners, particularly those with communist leanings, made it difficult for the Holy See to act. Finally, involvement would be "dangerous to the interests of the Church" because the "red" Valencia Government could use Vatican involvement as propaganda. As the Rebels closed in on the region, the losing Basque troops might have turned their attention to repressing clergymen and conservatives.[25] Overall, this letter argued that the timing and reaction to any Vatican mediation would be dangerous, and the Vatican needed to think of its own interest first—namely the condition and privileges of the Catholic Church in Spain.

The Archbishop of Toledo, Isidro Gomá y Tomás, sent a memo to Cardinal Pacelli on 26 January 1937 to explore the possibilities of a more active role for the Holy See. In order to begin such a process the Archbishop needed to secure the cooperation of Franco: "Write to the Cardinal who deals personally with Franco so that he makes him understand that without concessions nothing can be done. When Franco is willing to make any concessions, which of course we would like to know what they would be, the Holy Father is not opposed to writing a Pontifical Letter to the Basque Clergy."[26] Gomá, who had been a constant critic of the Republic, believed that he could persuade Franco to make some concessions and therefore work towards mediation. Given concessions, the Holy See could send an official letter to the Basque clergy, some of whom had sided with the PNV, to work towards an end to the conflict, "But of course General Franco must make some concessions, of which we must know the scope. Good Catholics as they really are, if they were faced with a personal word from the Pope, written for them, and in so sad a condition for the Pope, it can be expected that it would have some effect."[27] While Gomá did not specify the necessary conditions, this passage illustrates that certain members of the Spanish Catholic Hierarchy believed negotiations with the Rebels could succeed in the Basque region due to Catholic faith, and the Holy See should make attempts to normalize relations and work with them in order to restore peace to the Basque region.

In response to Gomá's letter, the Office of the Vatican Secretary of State sent a note to the Archbishop dated 30 January 1937 to discuss the Holy See's opinions regarding possible intervention to mediate the conflict in the Basque region: "His Holiness therefore calls to Your Most Reverend Excellency to judge if it seems expedient to treat the matter personally with the Most Excellent General Franco, making it present to him, with the tact and skill that so distinguish you, that without concessions of some importance an intervention by the Holy See would not be possible..."[28] The Office of the Secretary of State acknowledged through communications with General Franco there could be the possibility of mediation if the General agreed. However, since the topic was still quite delicate and possibly problematic for the Holy See, Gomá needed to be careful with how he approached the subject. The letter continued:

> In the event that His Excellency General Franco were willing to make concessions of such nature and extent as to render such intervention possible, the Basques, good Catholics as they are, if they were right in front of a personal word from the Holy Father, written for them, and in conditions so painful for His August Person, one can hope that they would feel deeply moved by the Pontifical Letter and it would not fail to produce some beneficial effect.[29]

Even though the Basque had maintained an allegiance with the Republican Government, the Holy See still viewed them as "good Catholics" and appeared willing to negotiate some mediation plan for the region, but General Franco's willingness to accept some concessions was key to make a peace plan plausible. The Office of the Vatican Secretary of State was not in a serious rush to draft a Pontifical Letter to the Basque public. Previously outlined conditions for Vatican involvement needed to be maintained: all sides in the conflict needed to invite the Holy See to mediate.

While the Holy See and Archbishop Gomá continued their correspondence regarding the possibility of mediation in País Vasco, the Italian Ambassador's Office to the Burgos Government sent a letter to the Holy See concerning the same issue on 27 January 1937. Franco was willing to work with the Holy See, but he had expressed serious concerns about the Basque Government, "General Franco affirms that the Basque never took any step towards the government of Burgos to reach an agreement. On the contrary, from the start, they threw themselves into war with the reds with which they had previously had contacts and arrangements." The General denied the Basque would want a stoppage and continued, "General Franco assumed that a threat of excommunication by the Holy See could have helped the Catholics of Biscay to move away from a monstrous alliance that otherwise threatens to turn against themselves. In fact, the Basques are at risk of being taken over in their own territory by Communists and Marxists." Again, Franco's tactic was to play upon a perceived Marxist threat:

> The Government of Burgos, however, respects the reasons that, in its supreme wisdom, the Holy See might have in order not to pronounce the excommunication. Such an act would be welcomed by the true Spanish people, horrified by the crimes and desecrations that are committed. However, the Government does not insist on this suggestion, recognizing the exclusive competence of the Holy See in this field.
>
> About the treatment to be given to the Basque Country, the Government of Burgos remits to its public statement of 1 October. Through it all regions and provinces of Spain were given a power of administrative decentralization, therefore respecting their peculiarities. The Government of Burgos noted that based on the predominance of reds in the Basque province, the separatist problem will receive a radical solution because every day the Reds take on more dominance over the Basques. The latter are destined to disappear if the same state of affairs continues.
>
> The Government of Burgos noted that this point, which for it has value more in the spiritual than in the material domain, must be observed with especial consideration by the Holy See, due to its considerable importance from a religious standpoint.[30]

The Burgos Government used its Italian allies to communicate a possible solution with the Holy See regarding País Vasco, and accused the Basques of not wanting to negotiate any form of peace. This note raises an interesting issue—the Burgos Government wanted direct communication with País Vasco to negotiate a surrender with the region. The Holy See had received information from individuals like Archbishop Gomá suggesting the Holy See should negotiate a surrender by the Basques to the Rebels. Even though the note suggested the Burgos Government wanted an end to the conflict in the region, it did not rely on the Holy See to create a specific plan for mediation. If anything, Burgos wanted the Holy See to take a more active "spiritual" role by threatening to excommunicate those acting with the communists and Marxists. Once again, the Insurgents used the language of atheistic communism as reasons for the Holy See not to trust the Basque Government. True, the Burgos Government understood it could not force the Holy See to take a more active religious role—excommunication—but it hoped that the Vatican could be persuaded. Overall, Burgos believed their armies could solve this rebellion in País Vasco militarily, but it wanted to guarantee religious backing. The information from the Italian Ambassador on behalf of Burgos, as well as that from Gomá, offered two separate plans for the Holy See to take. Each relied on Franco's willingness to allow mediation in one form or another, but neither was able to persuade the Vatican from changing its stance. In both cases, it became clear that no matter what path the Vatican chose, General Franco's decision would determine if the plan would come to fruition.

Cardinal Pacelli wrote to Gomá on 10 February to respond to Burgos's opinions about the Vatican's role in negotiations for the Basque region. After speaking to the Pope, Pacelli wrote, "About the delicate issue of Basque Catholics, which he rightly points out, His Holiness does not consider it possible to intervene in the way he had wanted with the Government of Salamanca."[31] Franco wanted the excommunications of Basque leaders who had worked with the Popular Front, but the Holy See was unwilling to punish the Basque in such a manner. The Vatican may have approved of the Rebels' campaign to restore Catholicism in Spain, but the Holy See also understood the deeply religious intentions of many Basque, and would not punish them for political sins.

In his 17 February 1937 letter, Archbishop Gomá continued trying to persuade the Vatican to help negotiate an end to the conflict in the Basque region stating the Pope "who has offered so much proof of his tender love for our Spain, especially since it has been suffering the tribulations of the war that has caused us so much pain in all orders, has been moved by the indications made to Him from various parts to accept to intervene in favor of peace between the Basque Nationalists and the Spanish National Government."[32] Gomá acknowledged that the Pope had been extremely concerned as well as saddened by the Civil War in Spain, and he hoped that these reactions would convince the Holy See to work towards peace. He argued again that only the Holy See could find a solution between the Basque and the "Spanish National Government." Before sending the letter, Gomá had initiated a series of communications with Franco in hopes of finding some way for the Rebels to approve Vatican mediation, with results different from the Italian Ambassador's:

> Two times I have spoken with General Franco to interest him in the wishes of our Holiest Father. In both conversations he has been most deferential, and when the conversation drifted to the relations of the Government with the Church, and especially to the modification of the actual Spanish legislation in a purely Catholic sense, he had very laudable viewpoints, that I will have the satisfaction of expounding to Your Eminency in another letter.
>
> Concerning the concrete point of the object of the Letter to which I respond, General Franco has had words of great encomium for the position that Your Holiness adopted with respect to the Basque-

Spanish problem and for the paternal gesture that Your Eminency suggests, so in harmony with the tradition and the charitable mission of the Holy See. But, as I indicated to Your Most Reverend Eminency in cipher telegram No. 7, issued on this same date, General Franco does not deem opportune for now to offer terms of surrender of the Basques, which could cause in these people a greater disgrace than the one they are suffering, in addition to the military and political considerations that I am happy to explain in the next two sections, which explain, in the right and the actual living fact, the various points of view and conclusions derived from the conversation held with General Franco. In them, I try to give Your Eminency an overview of the various factors of the Basque problem, which becomes at times of a gravity that could degenerate in true disaster.[33]

Gomá had been actively working to find a solution to the Basque question by speaking with Franco and while the conversations had not been completely successful, he relayed the concerns of the Holy See about violence. Franco, however, while willing to listen, yet presented his own demands.

Gomá's letter to the Holy See included Franco's series of demands to end the conflict. In the first section, Gomá highlighted the "political aspects of the Basque question in negotiation."[34] First, the Insurgents concluded the Government of País Vasco, the leadership of the PNV, and the Basque populace needed to be defined and viewed as separate entities in order to understand who was speaking for the region. As described in Chapter 5, Cardinal Gomá identified important differences between these groups. The traditional Basque government and Basque people were true Catholics, but foreign ideological influences corrupted the PNV. Second, the PNV needed to be removed from the overall conversation, because unlike the rest of the Basque population, they were not good Catholics and were influenced by foreign leftists. Third, the Rebels would not negotiate with any parties that could not guarantee the protection of hostages or that would negotiate with major conditions. Burgos wanted guarantees from the Basque, but made no promises of their own. Fourth, the Insurgents would only negotiate with the historical leadership of the region (who were not defined), which according to Burgos had represented the historical integrity and culture of the Basque. The "historical leadership" was more conservative than the PNV and would be more willing to surrender to the Rebels. Finally, Burgos considered the PNV to be an illegitimate group without any historical connection to the region and considered it unable to negotiate with any entity, including the Holy See.[35]

The following section of the letter concerned "the situation of facts with respect to negotiations." The Rebels considered the "military situation" for the PNV to be grave and Burgos believed it could guarantee a victory. Next, Gomá outlined the "criteria of General Franco" relating to the PNV. Franco believed that the Basque took up arms for regional autonomy, but as time passed their allegiance with the Popular Front Government—and communists—overtook their original rationale. This being said, Franco alleged the Popular Front controlled decisions and he believed it would be extremely difficult to negotiate. Finally, Gomá explained the "criteria for the Basque Nationalists" to negotiate. Gomá explained that internal problems for the Basque, including the likely fall of numerous cities like Bilbao, left the Government desperate and willing to cooperate with the Holy See in order to find a peaceful solution to the conflict.[36] While Gomá wanted to open negotiations between the Rebels and Basque Nationalists, his findings showed even though possibilities existed, Franco refused any concessions, even to the Church. Franco questioned the authority of the Basque Government, as well as many of its members, and made it almost impossible for any acceptable representatives to be found. The Rebels listened to the possibility of negotiations but presented unattainable demands. In the end, Franco and his allies held more leverage, and brushed Gomá aside. When the Holy See received these reports and understood the Insurgents were only willing to speak on their own terms, it was understandable that the Vatican would avoid pressing the issue. Either the Insurgents would win the war outright, or the Basques would unconditionally surrender. If the war was going to end on the Rebels' terms anyway, then the Holy See could not seriously affect the outcome and Burgos had seemingly removed the Church's ability to moderate any negotiations. Because the Holy See saw itself as a moral leader, though, it should speak out to save lives in a War.

While Insurgents continued their assaults in northern Spain, a combined Rebel-Italian campaign progressed through the south, ending in the Battle of Malaga, from 3–8 February 1937. When the battle ended, hundreds of Republicans were shot, and thousands of others were imprisoned. The battle and result were remarkably cruel, and news spread to the Holy See about this attack. In response to the battle, Pacelli wrote to Gomá on 5 March 1937 "The Holy Father has learned with deep sorrow such news . . . His Holiness will therefore be grateful if Your Eminence, with that prudence and tact which so much distinguishes him, will want to take with Mr. General Franco those steps that will make possible and appropriate for such massacres not to be repeated."[37] In response to this battle and massacre against Republicans, the Holy Father requested Pacelli to direct Archbishop Gomá to ask the Rebels to avoid these types of killings. The Pope wanted to avoid these cruel massacres, and Cardinal Pacelli took orders and completed the task he was assigned. Pacelli appeared to emphasize that this opinion is the Pope's exclusively, and the Secretary of State did not seem to want this plan and these opinions directly related with him or the entire Vatican hierarchy. Pacelli did not want Franco to see this as a direct attack from the entire Vatican, but personal requests from the Pope, that could be accomplished.

Archbishop Gomá continued his reports to the Holy See regarding the situation in País Vasco over the following months. Through a series of communications with representatives from the Insurgents and the Basque Nationalists, Gomá compiled another report, which was sent from Pamplona to the Vatican on 8 April 1937. Gomá reiterated his worries about the fighting in northern Spain. According to the Archbishop, the conflict in País Vasco had become both a national and international crisis and it was starting to affect opinions of some Catholics in relation to the Church. In order to improve the opinion of the Church, Gomá believed the Holy See needed to be aware of specific information and take a stronger course in trying to alleviate the conflict.[38] Gomá first reported on the "*Momento Actual*" in the conflict. According to Gomá, General Mola—the Head of the Army in the North—announced his plans to take the Vizcaya region in the hopes of ending the war. Gomá wrote, "The victorious offensive goes on, and there will not be many days left without a definitive break in the resistance of the joint Basques and Reds."[39] Gomá considered this new action by the Rebels to be the final thrust into the Basque region, and in a short period País Vasco would fall.

In the second section of the report, "Profanities and Massacres," the Archbishop outlined the sharp increase of violence against religious individuals as the war seemed to be drawing to a conclusion in the region. Gomá insisted that "During the past months Basque Catholics have not been able to control totally the reds."[40] Once again, a representative of the Catholic Church in Spain attempted to separate the "good" Catholic Basque from the leftists who had invaded the region for their own gain. This dichotomy was extremely important because the Catholic Church was more willing to work with its followers rather than leftists. At the same time, by accusing leftists of all the crimes against the Church, it would give the Vatican a greater reason to support the complete victory of the Rebels—as long as they protected the Catholics. Gomá then discussed the recent attacks by communists against the Catholic Church and its followers. Churches had been burned and profaned, prisoners had been taken and killed, and radio broadcasts had spoken out against the Pope's previous fears about communism.[41] As desperation increased, so did the violence. Desperation may have also forced President Aguirre of the Basque Government to write directly to Gomá. Within his letter, Aguirre claimed to have contacted the Holy See numerous times in order to discuss the ongoing conflict, something Gomá did not consider to be true. Aguirre claimed that he and his government wanted to open dialogue, but it never received an answer.[42] Gomá quickly dismissed these claims and noted the President accused Catholic priests of intervening in the conflict on the side of the Rebels. Finally, for Gomá and the Minister Vicar of Vitoria, the ongoing conflict in the region had made it difficult for each diocese to properly lead their followers and spread the teachings of the Church.[43] In his report Gomá never openly called for Vatican mediation to begin, but his words gave the Holy See more details about the deteriorating conditions as the Basque region appeared ready to fall. Gomá used letters such as this to warn the Vatican about the dire possibilities that would follow. For Gomá, at least, the Holy See could never claim it did not receive reports concerning the Basque condition.

Gomá's warning of future Insurgent military activities in País Vasco did not appear to raise serious red flags at the time, but within weeks Mola and his forces had made serious gains in the region. On 26 April 1937, Rebel forces bombarded the city of Guernica on their way to Bilbao. The serious devastation to the Basque city posed a warning for the possible attacks to come.[44] Nuncio Valeri in France wrote to Pacelli on 3 May to discuss the serious repercussions of Guernica. After this bombardment, Reverend Alberto de Onaindia Zuluaga of Valladolid and the Bishop of Vitoria suggested initiating discussions between the Franquistas and Basques in order to evacuate Bilbao to prevent further civilian casualties.[45] Representatives of the Spanish Catholic Church wanted a more active role to protect lives in the region, but the Vatican did not take a stance one way or another at this time.

The bombardment of Guernica and the possible intervention from members of the Spanish Catholic Church may have protected the residents of Bilbao. According to Gomá, the Archbishop established a plan for the surrender of the city. A 7 May letter to the Holy See outlined the agreed upon terms, and his 8 May letter explained how the demands would work, with a great deal of compliments for the Rebels. First, both sides "Pledged themselves to conserve Bilbao."[46] In Gomá's follow-up letter, the Archbishop explained that Guernica had not been destroyed by Rebel planes, but by communist incendiaries used by the Republicans.[47] The Insurgents gave Gomá supposed evidence to support this falsehood, helping the Archbishop believe Mola's forces would not destroy the city. Second, Burgos agreed that they "Will facilitate the exit of all leaders."[48] According to Gomá, the Rebels had no interest in capturing or executing the leaders of the city.[49] Third, Burgos gave "Complete guarantee that Franco's military will respect persons and things."[50] Gomá believed the Rebels would not destroy any property in Bilbao, as long as no serious fighting was initiated.[51] Fourth, Franco agreed to the "Absolute liberty for the militiamen and soldiers who surrender with their arms."[52] The Archbishop believed the Franquistas would follow the international rules for warfare and allow those who surrender protection.⁵³ Fifth, "Those guilty against common law or responsible for destructions and devastations will be taken to court."⁵⁴ For Gomá, these tribunals were obvious, because they could find a legal rational for punishing those, especially communists, who had been responsible for serious crimes.⁵⁵ Sixth, "The lives and goods of those who surrender in good faith, including bosses, will be respected."⁵⁶ Even though others had expressed doubts, Gomá believed this protection would occur.⁵⁷ Seventh, "In the political realm, decentralization in the same form that is enjoyed by other regions."⁵⁸ Gomá believed that this region would be given local control, like Navarra, as a form of privilege.⁵⁹ Finally, "In the social realm, progressive justice will be made considering the means of the national wealth and according to the principles of the Encyclical 'Rerum Novarum.'"⁶⁰ By using the teachings of the Church, the Franquistas promised to offer social justice for the workers, especially the miners, in the region. By doing so, these workers would not have to turn to communism for support, but could find it in the state.⁶¹ The Rebels agreed to work towards these regulations, and Gomá certainly believed Mola and his forces would follow such rules. Gomá was either naïve—believing the Rebel would follow this plan, or he had little interest in saving the Basque—as he knew the Insurgents would lie. Either way, Gomá clearly accepted Rebel promises and did not worry too much about these repercussions. In order for these regulations to happen, however, the Rebels needed to be able to move into Bilbao and take the city.⁶² Burgos continued to send its armies towards Bilbao, and this plan could only truly work if no resistance was met, something even Gomá could not promise. Republicans did try to hold Bilbao, but they withdrew their forces, along with many civilians, on 18 June 1937. Even with the promise to not destroy the city, after the evacuation of 200,000 residents on 19 June 1937, the German *Luftwaffe* bombed the city the following day before General Fidel Dávila entered.⁶³

The same day Bilbao fell, Cardinal Pacelli telegrammed Archbishop Gomá as "Given the approaching capture of Bilbao, some people ask for the intervention of His Holiness in order to save priests, women, children, and unfortunate unmarried mothers together."⁶⁴ Pacelli wanted to inform Gomá that even though the battle for Bilbao was over, something needed to be done for those survivors. Pacelli continued, "Please Your Reverend Eminence, in regard to that Government, take steps that will be more appropriate."⁶⁵ The Cardinal wanted the Archbishop to speak to the Rebels and make sure some humanitarian aid would be sent to the city. Even though the physical battle was over, Pacelli and Pius XI appeared worried—with good reason—about the future conditions of denizens and wanted to avoid possible repercussions against these Basques.

In his letters to the Vatican, Gomá outlined ways to end the Civil War in northern Spain. On 7 July 1937 the Cardinal Secretary of State sent a letter on behalf of Pope Pius XI to Gomá, which was to be transmitted to General Franco:

> Having learned that negotiations are underway for the surrender of the Basques, His Holiness, without going into the particulars of the surrender, appeals in the name of the Divine Redeemer to your Catholic faith so that these negotiations come to fruition quickly and any further bloodshed is prevented. His Holiness rests assured that Your Excellency will not impose conditions which would lead to the ruin of a population that might have made mistakes, but that is a Christian population.[66]

The letter to Gomá ended with the lines, "In the transmission of this message Your Eminence shall make the most insistent care so that General Franco consents to what is asked by the Holy Father and does not impose unacceptable conditions."[67] According to Cardinal Pacelli, the Pope wanted to find a moral way to end the War. This message is significant because the Pope forcefully requested Franco be reasonable in his plans to end the conflict and not make any unreasonable demands on the Basque. What would have been viewed as "unreasonable" is not clear, but the Pope highlighted that the Basques were a Catholic population and should be treated as such—even though they would face repression by the invading forces. After nearly eighteen months of debate surrounding the actions of the Basques in the Civil War, the Pope acknowledged Basque adherence to the faith. Even though leftists had possibly infiltrated the leadership of the PNV, the Pope vigorously requested the bloodshed be ended in the region and this conflict come to a reasonable end. The Pope did not give support to either side in the conflict, but his message highlighted great concern over the loss of Catholic life in Spain. We are left to wonder why the Pope did not take a more aggressive role at this time. He could have taken his message public, but the Vatican had restraints, such as possible Rebel retaliation following the War or possible Italian and German restrictions on the Church. Similarly, even if the Pope wanted to speak out, his reasonable Secretary of State must have understood these dangers and pushed for silence over direct confrontation.

Gomá sent the Pope's message to General Franco, and the Archbishop sent Franco's reply to the Holy See on 12 July, "General FRANCO received with the greatest veneration the Message from the HOLY FATHER and, recognizing the call made to him by His Holiness in the name of the Divine Redeemer and of his Catholic faith, in deference to this call and to the Highest Pontiff, is willing to act with absolute graciousness and accepts purely and humbly your presented propositions."⁶⁸ According to Gomá, Franco acknowledged the Pope's proposition, but did not state what he would be willing to do to prevent bloodshed and end the conflict. He received and understood the message, but made no promises. These communications provide evidence that the influence of the Holy See and Pope over the Burgos Government was nominal. The Holy See defended its beliefs in peace and life by sending Franco this note, but the Church had no definite or physical way of guaranteeing serious results. Franco held the power in this relationship, and the Church could not "force" any group in this Civil War to behave accordingly.

The interesting relationship between the Holy See and Franco regarding northern Spain continued for months. On 26 December 1937, Cardinal Pacelli sent a note to Papal Nuncio Antoniutti concerning an increase of violence in the city of Bilbao "News has arrived that last week numerous detained people were shot in Bilbao for political motives. Anticipating new sentences, the Holy Father charges Your Reverend Eminence to intervene in His August Name to General Franco and advise him to use acts of clemency especially in occasion of the Christmas holiday."⁶⁹ For the Holy See, Christmas provided reason for the Insurgents to grant clemency for political capital sentences. On one hand, this act shows the Holy See did try to persuade the Rebels not to execute prisoners, but on the other hand it shows the Holy See had not been able to alter the sentences of those already killed. The Holy See requested its Nuncio try to persuade Franco to grant clemency for these prisoners, but it was not able to force the Rebels to change their behavior. Franco even made promises that he would stop detaining priests unless, of course, they were suspected of common crimes.⁷⁰ The Holy See needed to rely on the "kindness" of Franco in order to save these lives.

On 28 December, Antoniutti reported good news concerning this previous Papal request "His Holiness asked General Franco from the beginning of December for acts of clemency in occasion of the Christmas Holiday. General Franco communicated to me yesterday evening that, adhering to the Holy Father's invitation, he commuted the sentences of 100 condemned to death and proceeds to exchange 200 detained officials condemned to death. He says the majority of those recently executed were red criminals and agents of the armed Basque resistance."⁷¹ Franco commuted many sentences due to the Christmas holiday, something that the Pope had requested, and therefore, a success for the Holy See. According to Franco, those already executed were communists or resistance fighters who were dangerous to the state. Even though the Pope and his Nuncio appeared capable of changing the sentences of these prisoners, many executions had occurred and many would continue. Franco would only stop executions for specific cases. How could the Holy See know about each execution? Franco and the Rebels held the power in this relationship. While speaking to an Italian representative about the Basque region, Franco is reported as saying, "I am interested not in the territory but in the inhabitants. The re-conquest of the territory is the mean, the redemption of the inhabitants the end."[72] True, they would assuage the Holy See occasionally when requested, but Franco executed whomever he wished.

THE NORTHERN FRONT WAS OVER

The Civil War in the Basque region involved numerous actors: Rebels, Basque Nationalists, leftists, clergy, and many others. At the start of the conflict, allies of the former monarch hoped the Holy See would be able to influence the Basque and persuade them to avoid helping the Republic. The Holy See avoided taking any serious position at that time. The Vatican received large amounts of contradictory information which made it quite difficult to make a clear and well-informed decision. As the War proceeded, and the Rebels made serious gains in the north, men like Archbishop Gomá tried to find a way for the Insurgents and PNV to end the conflict. A Franquista victory was the obvious outcome, and Gomá would have been content with the end of the Republic. However, Gomá tried to find a way to spare more bloodshed. He wrote numerous letters to the Holy See explaining his actions, and he often believed he had found the proper solution. The problem was, however, the Rebels wanted a complete victory and the opportunity to detain, try, and execute their opponents, and would not make any serious concessions. Each agreement Burgos supported ended in a complete surrender of the Basque. Franco would get what he wanted, no matter what. The main interest of the Holy See was to try to prevent serious bloodshed at the end of the War, especially in Catholic País Vasco, which represented the most troubling and difficult aspect of the War for the Church. Nevertheless, the periods in between Vatican and Papal communications allowed the Rebels to execute prisoners. Burgos stated it was fighting a crusade, and therefore needed to do whatever necessary to win that battle—even if it meant repression, or even if the Church objected. The conflict in the Basque Country was clearly the most troubling aspect of the Civil War for the Holy See and the Church, but even Papal prodding to the Rebels was unable to affect Burgos's behavior. The fighting in northern Spain definitely highlights the real power dynamic that had developed between the Insurgents and the Holy See—the Church had become a tool for Franco.

VIII

Bombings and Civilians
Rebel Rejection of Mediation

As the Spanish Civil War appeared all but over, the Republican Government initiated a series of requests to the Holy See to mediate some truce or cessation of hostilities because the Holy See appeared to be the Republic's only hope for a negotiated surrender to the War. With a Rebel victory almost assured, the Holy See became involved in possible negotiation through communications with Burgos, but the Rebels rejected these possibilities. On multiple occasions Burgos forcefully reminded the Holy See why the Rebels fought—a supposed crusade—and they used this language to silence the Vatican. Even with these reminders, the Vatican tried to negotiate on humanitarian grounds, as cities like Barcelona were devastated by aerial bombardments, yet these seemingly reasonable requests were flatly denied. This chapter explores the final period of Civil War documents accessible in the ASV: AES (Spagna) and highlights the ways in which the Holy See believed it could affect the conflict, but most importantly, this research shows how the previous manipulation of terms and concepts by the Rebels had given a theoretically "Catholic" license to their actions in the hopes of destroying the theoretically "atheistic" Republicans. By the time the War turned to Barcelona, it was far too late for the Vatican to act; no longer did Franco require the Vatican's support to garner allies for the War—foreign airplanes and bombs gave the Rebels their true strength. For Franco, all the Church needed to do was keep silent and wait for the conflict to subside.

THE REPUBLICAN FATE WAS SEALED

Following the 24 August 1937 surrender of the Basque Nationalist Government to Franco and his allies, the Rebel forces turned their complete attention to eastern Spain. Cataluña and Valencia managed to defend their territory for the Republican Government, but once the Franquistas defeated the Basque, Burgos sent the complete strength of its armies to defeat these hold-outs. Cataluña's strong regionalist sentiments were not enough to withstand the attacks of 1938, and even Valencia succumbed to the Rebels' superior military might. In 1938, international concerns surrounding the aerial bombardments of Republican cities increased as their sympathizers tried to gain support by accusing the Rebels of indiscriminately targeting civilian populations under the guise of military objectives. In response, the Insurgents accused the Republican Government of burning its own cities and blaming it on Burgos in order to sway public opinion.[1] Most importantly, both sides tried to persuade the Catholic Church and Vatican hierarchy to understand the situation in either Rebel or Republican terms. This chapter explores the final months of 1938 when the Republic and its allies increased their demands for international mediation. Rebel military victories came quickly and the Republic knew its fate. On the other hand, the Insurgents knew a complete victory would come soon, and international mediation would only prohibit their abilities to conclude the War in the manner they wanted—meaning a complete eradication of Republican influences. The Rebels rejected the thought of international assistance, even from the Vatican, and they would not change their plans for the War even if the Church voiced an opinion. Franquista representatives made polite requests for the Holy See to remain out of the conflict,[2] even though the Vatican did appear to have sincere fears of increased violence and revenge in the final months. The Vatican could have tried to force Franco to agree to terms, but any forceful interactions might have jeopardized the Church's future role in Spain.

Rebel aerial bombardments, particularly in Cataluña, became a growing concern due to the increase of civilian casualties. On 2 February 1938 Cardinal Pizzardo, stationed at the Holy See, received a letter from the Catalan Regional Government regarding the seriousness of these attacks in the region's cities. The Catalans requested the Cardinal send a letter to General Franco—along with Nuncio Antoniutti and the French Ambassador—to protest these bombings and request that the General try to avoid using such tactics in the conflict.[3] A report entitled "*I bombardamenti aerei in Ispagna*" [The Aerial Bombardments in Spain] accompanied the letter to Pizzardo, and explained the deterioration of conditions in Spain. "The bombardments occurred during the last fifteen days have been particularly destructive and deadly, and they have become as frequent as to provoke the condemnation of the civilized world."[4] According to the Catalan note, foreign newspapers like *Messaggero* and *Temps* as well as the British Labour Party, began to speak out against this type of attack. The Catalan report continued by describing other reasons why these types of attacks were so devastating "with regard to the bombings carried out by Nationalists, we fear that they will provoke a resumption of civil and religious persecution, until now very tranquil" and Rebel assaults would push further anticlerical violence as "Towards the end of October 1936, during an alleged bombing of the port of Rosas, in Cataluña there was the biggest massacre of civilian hostages, and of priests and monks. Later, towards the end of August 1937, in the small town of Granollers near Barcelona—where there had been many murders by the end of July 1936— 50 other hostages were killed."[5] Before the Rebel planes bombed the region, the Catalans claimed they had maintained control over their people, but once attacks arrived, more radical groups in the region lashed out at perceived conservatives. The Barcelona Government tried to show the Holy See that General Franco, who had claimed to be the savior of Spain from the destruction of the Republic, represented the real danger to the Spanish people.[6] According to the Barcelona authorities, the indiscriminate violence of the Rebels bore responsibility for the increasing numbers of deaths, with 3,688 killed.[7]

Following this discussion, the report included a review of the most recent Insurgent bombings. According to the Barcelona Government, at least fourteen large bombing runs had occurred in Spain from 16 January-30 January 1938,[8] responsible for hundreds of deaths and thousands of casualties, with the majority of victims being women and children. The Catalan government stated "It should be noted that the Nationalists generally do not give exact numbers of the damage and casualties caused by the bombings of the governmental forces, perhaps in order not to demoralize the people and not to confess that, frequently, anti-aircraft defenses have been caught by surprise and also that they have often been ineffective."[9] In response, the Barcelona Government continued a series of its own propaganda films aiming to gain international sympathy for its cause. In fact, the Catalans reported that the British Labour Party offered to initiate a mediation campaign for the Catalans, and also urged a cessation of these bombings.

In response to this letter (and others like it), Cardinal Secretary of State Pacelli sent a note on 6 February to his representative in San Sebastian regarding these bombings:

> The Holy Father profoundly grieves for the numerous victims of the civil population and the destruction of artistic works caused by the two parties at war with accentuated and ever more frequent aerial bombardments of open cities, reserving himself to solicit Apostolic Nuncio in Paris [Luigi Maglione] to intervene in any way possible toward the Barcelona Government in order to cease this inhumane form of war; He trusts in the Catholic sentiment of General Franco so that also the Nationalists desist from such bombings that cause innocent victims and serve their adversaries to intensify their violent foreign campaign against Nationalist Spain.[10]

The Holy Father and the Holy See were disheartened by the violence being caused by both sides during the War, as evidence showed both sides were responsible for death and destruction. The Vatican was ready to work towards some type of intervention to prevent these aerial bombardments, even if responsibility would fall to a Papal Nuncio outside of Rome. This note represents the Vatican's problems concerning Spain: both sides communicated with the Holy See yet neither side was completely innocent, and both tried to prove the guilt of the enemy. The Vatican hierarchy was aware of the destruction in Spain, and some in Rome wanted to stop the death toll, but the negotiation process could not begin until all sides agreed. The first step was to achieve Franco's permission to begin negotiations, but this would not be easy. Second, the Vatican needed to avoid the perception that it was helping the leftist Republican politics, and was acting for humanitarian concerns, but neither would succeed.

In response to Pacelli's letter, Nuncio Antoniutti met with General Franco to discuss the Vatican's concerns about aerial bombardments. On 17 February, Antoniutti explained to the Holy See Franco's reactions:

> General Franco, showing gratitude to the paternal worry of His Holiness for the civilian victims of airstrikes, asserted that the National Aviation has always refrained and will refrain from bombing defenseless cities, having bombed only military targets which, being located in residential neighborhoods, might have caused serious consequences in spite of precautions used. General Franco assured to have appointed security zones for the civilian population, but those areas (such as in Madrid and Barcelona) were used for factories and storage of munitions.
>
> General Franco said that open cities and defenseless towns in National Spain were also very recently bombed causing numerous civilian victims.
>
> General Franco finally wants to assure His Holiness that nothing is omitted to save the civilian population.[11]

Franco promised to avoid attacking civilian populations in the future, which was wonderful news for the Holy See because civilian deaths had been on the rise—yet this promise was never kept. For Franco, this statement was likely used to fend off possible Vatican criticism, which he still found problematic, but he refused to stop bombing Madrid or Barcelona due to their military and munitions importance. According to Generalissimo, cities like Madrid had established humanitarian zones, but communists had been sneaking weapons to those areas and made them military targets.[12] In Franco's opinion, Barcelona had 180 military targets, fourteen artillery batteries, sixty-two military quarters, eleven military command centers (communist, Basque, and Catalan), three aerodromes, sixty-eight military factories, five toxic gas plants, eleven depots for combustible weapons and three radio stations.[13] All these major targets meant the Insurgents needed to continue their bombings of the city. To protect lives, the Republicans needed to close these military targets. The Vatican wanted to convince the Rebels to stop bombing cities, but Franco would not commit to cessation. Similarly, Franco claimed cities within his zone had also been attacked, and Republicans were responsible. According to the General, communist planes had attacked the cities of Algeciras, Tetuan, Granada, Sevilla, and Salamanca recently. The Republic did have a number of Soviet made planes supplied in 1936, but by the end of the War, these planes were obsolete compared to German planes.[14] Similarly, Franco blamed a recent attack of Pamplona on planes that had originated in France.[15] Overall, while Franco promised to be careful when attacking these cities, he made no guarantee as the last major targets for the Rebels were cities—like Barcelona—and the General did not promise to avoid these locations. Franco placed the blame not on his forces, but on the Republicans. The Holy See had been able to force a reaction and statement from Franco, but the General did not share the Vatican's worries.

After receiving Antoniutti's letter and report regarding his meeting with General Franco, Cardinal Pacelli passed the information concerning aerial bombardments in Spain along to the Archdiocese of Paris. Pacelli ordered the Papal delegation in Paris to negotiate terms to end these aerial bombings. Pacelli's letter stated, "The Holy Father, in fact, in occasion of the last tragic events, to which Your Eminence makes allusion, was quick to intervene with the responsible authorities in order to mitigate the terrible consequences of aerial bombardments."[16] Pacelli's letter reiterated points previously reported by Antoniutti to Pacelli as it goes on to explain that General Franco asserted he could have avoided serious destruction if the Republicans had not hidden numerous military targets inside civilian territory. This reiteration of Franco's arguments does not specifically mean that the Holy See completely believed the General's assessment, but it does show that the Holy See considered this information as it assessed the situation. Pacelli's letter ended "I have allowed myself to express to Your Eminence the above for information purposes only. However, you can easily deduce what obstacles face the work of peace and persuasion that the Holy See does not stop to deploy in order to eliminate or at least diminish the horrors of the so painful Spanish conflict."[17] The Cardinal had directed the French Papal delegation to work towards reducing this conflict; however it did not give specific instructions of how to do this.

Finding a way to end aerial bombardments in Spain not only concerned the Holy See, but organizations like the Committee for Peace in Spain, based in Paris, also discussed the issue. On 19 March, the Committee's President Alfredo Mendizábal Villalba, wrote to Papal Nuncio Valeri to express his hopes that the Holy See could do something to stop these attacks. On 24 March, Valeri relayed this message to Pacelli, "The well-known writer Mr. Mendizábal, President of this Spanish Committee for Civil Peace, has sent me, in order for me to deliver it to its destination, the attached telegram, in which, as Your Most Reverend Eminence will detect, the assistance of the Holy Father is invoked in order to end the bombings of open cities that have already killed many innocent people and accumulated so many ruins."[18] In response to this note calling for further actions from the Holy See, Cardinal Pacelli responded to Valeri by acknowledging that the Vatican had not stopped its attempts to end these attacks. Similarly, Pacelli stated that the Holy See would continue steps to negotiate with General Franco about these bombings.[19] Unfortunately for the Holy See, these continued conversations had little effect on the actions of the Rebel forces in the following months.

These bombardments of Spanish cities continued into the spring and summer of 1938. The Holy See, however, did not forget its pledge to continue speaking with Burgos regarding these attacks, even as more Rebel planes took to the skies. On 4 June, Cardinal Pacelli wrote to the Papal Nuncio in Spain: "Following the recent aerial bombardments, I plead with Your Excellency to renew, in the manner deemed most appropriate, in the name of the Holy See, the steps already made with General Franco with the scope of avoiding destructions and killings that can only harm the Nationalist cause itself."[20] The Holy See learned of further aerial bombings in Spanish cities and used this moment as another opportunity to remind the Franco regime of its great displeasure. Nuncio Antoniutti relayed this message to General Franco, who "stated that the bombing near the French border was not done by Nationalist air force."[21] Franco did not take responsibility for this attack, suggesting the responsibility of a Republican allied air force.[22] Franco's reaction asserted that Republicans were also capable of these open city attacks. The General, however, did take responsibility for bombings in Granoers and Barcelona maintaining they were "Important military objectives for enormous quantity of arms and munitions in those deposits."[23] When the Rebels did take responsibility for bombing cities, they claimed these locations were military targets. General Franco had previously established military targets in cities as viable objectives for these bombings and the Insurgents had well-timed excuses for the Vatican's concerns.

Also on 9 June, Antoniutti wrote a longer letter to the Holy See to discuss other aspects of the Rebel-Republican relationship. Antoniutti explained the Rebels had been working on propaganda to establish the guilt of the Republicans in the war and the necessity for bombing cities to root out communist influence.[24] Antoniutti explained Franco's reaction to the increase of violence located near the French border, "The Generalissimo himself wants to insist on this point: that the foreign governments, especially the French government, should realize that by helping the Republicans to resist (despite their statements to the contrary) they actively contribute to making the war crueler, because the resistance that the Nationalists are finding is harsher."[25] Franco blamed foreign governments that had been aiding the Republicans, yet this argument is dubious since the Rebels received the vast majority of foreign aid that made it to Spain.[26] The French had agreed to Non-Intervention, and its government had not sold or loaned serious aid to the Republic. However, the Burgos Government claimed that the French had not effectively closed their border, and international aid had been streaming into Republican Spain, "It is assured by neutrals from France that never has more material of war passed through the border of the Pyrenees into red Spain as in these last two months. The huge storage of weapons and ammunition in residential areas would have provoked, in the words of the Nationalists, their air raids." The letter continued, "When this aid would stop, this government says that the day when France will close the border in the Pyrenees, the bombings will stop immediately, because there will be no reason to do them anymore, and the war would come to its end soon."[27] In reality, this aid was never enough to help the Republicans "win" the Civil War as had been seen throughout the entire conflict, but Franco used it as an excuse.

On 3 June, the British Prime Minister announced before the House of Commons his Government's desire for Burgos to suspend these aerial bombings and, at the same time, the British representative "in Burgos expressed to the Nationalist authorities the horror with which His Majesty's Government regard this continuous shedding of innocent blood."[28] The British Government hoped increased international pressure would persuade Franco to end these attacks, yet the failed plan of Non-Intervention still permeated. At the end of the letter, the British Legation to the Holy See wrote, "His Majesty's Government would much appreciate any action which the Holy See might be able to take in support of these representations."[29] The British Government hoped the Holy See would attempt to diminish the violence in Spain, regarding the Vatican as the strongest and most influential power to change the actions of the Franquistas.

Even though pleased with British willingness to take steps to work to end these attacks, which had caused death and revenge, the Vatican still refused to act alongside them.[30] The Vatican's response to the British request for a shared response offers important insights into the Vatican's understanding of international conflicts—particularly Spain. First, the Holy See stated it made similar attempts to persuade the Rebel Government to avoid these bombings on previous occasions. For a longer period, the Holy See had communicated with leaders from both belligerencies about these attacks, but without success. The Vatican had suggested a possible truce in Spain, but it would not align itself with foreign plans in order to maintain political neutrality. If the Holy See worked with the British directly, then it would be connected politically with the British, something that was unacceptable because the Holy See had to maintain the appearance of international neutrality but might have also opened the concerns over working with an Anglican state over the will of a Catholic "rebellion." Finally, the Vatican concluded all of its actions were humanitarian and based on the teaching of a supernatural power, asserting the divine mandate of the Holy See was pure and true, and the Catholic Church would continue to work independently.

The Holy See chose not to release a joint statement with the British Government, and aerial bombardments continued. On 18 June, Nuncio Antoniutti communicated to the Holy See information regarding a recent Rebel bombing run in Barcelona stating they claimed the bombing was meant to destroy a large stash of arms and ammunition, along with the destruction of highly dangerous benzene. The action, therefore, was meant to protect Insurgents and find a quick end to the war. The note ended with the lines, "There is great anxiety and indignation in this government center because of the ever increasing French aid to the red army, without which the Barcelona communists would be easily won."[31] Again, Franco rationalized the bombing in Barcelona to be righteous, because foreigners had been assisting the Catalans with aid and extending this conflict. Burgos did not hide its actions from the Vatican, but they attempted to direct the attention of the Holy See in another direction. Again, they blamed communism and international interference as they were adept at finding excuses to criticize the Republic while justifying their behaviors.

The Burgos Government was angered because the international media focused on the aerial bombardments in Spain. Nuncio Cicognani wrote a letter to the Holy See on 7 July 1938 to summarize a conversation with Franco, who claimed the *Times* of London had been publishing lies about the Spanish Civil War, and the General wanted to clear away some misconceptions. First, Franco suggested a communist-Soviet alliance had been defaming the Rebel cause. Second, Franco blamed the Republic for working against the traditional interests of the Spanish people. Third, the Republic and its international allies created an environment that would continue the war. Fourth, Spanish communists had been trying to internationalize the war by crossing the French border and entering Spain. Finally, Franco continued his rationale that all aerial assaults destroyed military targets only.[32] The Civil War was a major international story, and the Rebels wanted to change the opinion of the Holy See by suggesting they were not responsible for this violence, while pointing out communists inside Spain as the true evil. By attacking the international media, Franco hoped to persuade the Holy See not to believe the numerous articles published about the violence and deaths. According to Franco, because the media had a leftist slant, most reports on the Civil War could not be believed and only official Rebel memoranda were truthful.

On 19 July, the Rebel Embassy to the Holy See wrote a letter concerning what it viewed as "inaccurate" reporting, concerned about a 10 June article from *L'Osservatore Romano*, which had discussed aerial bombings and mentioned that a recent attacks by the Rebels had "*ningún interés militar*" as no military targets were located near the attack.[33] The Embassy's note reminded the Holy See that the Insurgent air force did not attack civilians, and only bombed targets of military importance. Because this article reached the worldwide Catholic community, the Embassy wanted the Holy See to avoid writing about such speculations, "The Embassy of Spain is forced to plead with the Secretary of State of His Holiness to inform the responsible management of *Osservatore Romano* of this complaint, so that hereafter they avoid the publication of information that . . . does not match the accuracy of the facts and the profound Catholic sense that characterizes Spain's National Movement."[34] Not only did the Rebel Government speak out against international periodicals but it complained directly to the Holy See about an article published in its semi-official newspaper. Franco might have maintained most of the power in the Rebel-Vatican relationship, but the General still feared public Vatican responses that could damage his image. The article had been written by a foreign newspaper and republished, but the Rebels warned the Holy See not to believe nor republish articles such as this, because they damaged the interest of the Insurgent cause. The Rebels only had their honor that they did not attack civilian targets. Once again, the power disparity between Burgos and the Holy See appeared. The Holy See did not have complete control over what appeared in *L'Osservatore Romano*, but influenced certain commentary in it. The Rebels warned the Vatican not to publish such information, not because it was untrue, but because it tarnished the image of the Rebels in the Catholic world, which should not be done to the "defenders" of the faith.

Through conversations with the Papal Nuncio in Ireland, Paschal Robinson, Irish Prime Minister Éamon De Valera suggested that if representatives of the Catholic Church could persuade Franco to consider peace, then the Irish Government would take the lead in August. Information regarding this Irish plan was sent to the Holy See for consideration and according to Pacelli's report, De Valera believed Republicans in Barcelona would fight until the absolute end. The only way a peace plan could be negotiated, as described by Pacelli, was if General Franco assured that no repercussions, like arrests or assassinations, would occur after surrender. Pacelli stated that "His Holiness gladly would join his intercession if he did not already know that General Franco abhors any such negotiation."[35] Even though the Irish Prime Minister proposed negotiation, by 19 August 1938, Cardinal Pacelli had determined General Franco's unwillingness to accept any negotiations that contained concessions. Pacelli understood Franco was unwilling to promise not to execute Republicans.

Pacelli was not the only member of the Catholic hierarchy who believed Franco would be unwilling to agree to any conditions. On 24 August, Nuncio Cicognani explained he would speak to the Rebels concerning this plan, but expected little from it stating, "The Minister of Foreign Affairs [of Nationalist Spain] said he can predict no different response from those already given. I answer that the terms of the new proposal, which, unlike others, leaves to the generosity of General Franco to decide the conditions, should be carefully considered."[36] Franco had all the power in determining how to react to mediation and the leadership of the Holy See and its representative in the Rebel zone concluded no serious changes would be made in Franco's reactions, even if the Holy See offered plans.

After a full meeting with the Burgos Minister of Foreign Affairs Francisco Gómez-Jordana Sousa, Cicognani reported to Nuncio Robinson in Ireland on 11 September about the chances of mediation. Again, while the Holy See did not create this plan for mediation, the Irish Government used it as an intermediary:

> As I had the honor to reveal to Your Eminence, it was my care to insist to General Jordana, in order to demonstrate that in this case it is not a mediation that is being proposed to reach an agreement with the government of Barcelona, but rather the goal was to find out, even if in general, under what conditions a surrender would be possible. But even these proposals are regarded with suspicion by General Franco and hence will not be accepted. The Foreign Minister told me that of course by the Generalissimo there is no intention of revenge, and that in the punishment to those responsible for the current situation and to perpetrators of crimes authorities will proceed with a high level of justice, from which a great feeling of generosity will never be disassociated because after all they are all Spaniards. [He said] that relying on the generosity of General Franco will be the best way to make the consequences of surrender less burdensome. General Franco persists in the belief that any proposal that might tend to stipulate an agreement or to explore a settlement with the enemy, will be in favor of the army and the Marxist ideal, thus undermining the future of Spain and of the whole world, which must defeat communism definitively. This attitude

is made even firmer by widespread opinions that the conditions in which the population of Madrid are living are disastrous, and that another winter of deprivation and hardship will decimate with tuberculosis and starvation the youth and women. However, the hope of a fast victory is here slightly reduced after the events of the Ebro. There is no doubt about the final victory, but they are convinced that this might still require great efforts and months of fighting.[37]

The Rebel Government made it clear that any sort of mediation with the Republic was not possible—a victory had to be decisive and clear and it insisted any negotiations with the Republicans in Barcelona would be considered an international sign of weakness towards Marxists, and therefore, increases Bolshevik influence in the world. The Rebels also tried to present a complete victory as a possible humanitarian option, but how could this be humanitarian if cities were still bombed? According to the Franquistas, the suffering in cities, such as Madrid, would continue as long as the war dragged on and the only way to prevent this suffering would be for the Rebels to win the war. If negotiations or mediation occurred, then this suffering would continue as much time was wasted. If mediation was ruled out, then the only hope would be that the Insurgents conquer Cataluña quickly. The Holy See, in this report, was not supporting Burgos's cause, but it began to realize a quick Rebel military victory would kill less than a long and drawn-out battle.

In response to the possibility of Irish mediation, as well as the communications from Catholic representatives concerning these possibilities, the Spanish Rebel Office of Foreign Affairs defended its actions to Nuncio Cicognani. It was concerned with criticism that the Franquistas had been overly violent against supporters of the Republic, "Certainly the idea that there may be acts of revenge or others not inspired by the highest sentiments of justice is wrong. Well to the view is how this [justice] is administered in National Spain, in which, if it were the case, the law will be applied with a spirit of exact reality and, in case of doubt, inclining always to benevolence." The note continued, "To Red Spain only remains one road: the surrender offered by the generosity of Generalísimo Franco. The Generalísimo appreciates in all its value the attitude of the Holy Father and thanks him with all his heart."[38] The Rebels denied they would carry out vengeance after the conflict, but they again appeared sensitive to possible Vatican criticisms. According to the author of the report, Burgos would follow the law and act responsibly and since the Rebels had already made these promises, there was no reason for further mediation or concessions. Only Republican surrender could prevent further destruction and loss of life; the Rebel leadership thanked the Holy See for its interest in preventing violence in Spain, but rejected any form of mediation—the only solution was outright Republican surrender.

By November 1938 Republican representatives informed Parisian Nuncio, Valeri, of the desperation of the Government. Valeri learned that the emissary came to "Ask if the Pope would not have been able to act as an intermediary. I replied that no one wished more than the Holy See to end the conflict but that the mediation, to leave aside the rest, could not be taken into consideration from the moment that one of the parties, namely General Franco, did not want to consider it."[39] Valeri openly admitted to the Republican emissary the only thing stopping Vatican mediation was the reaction of General Franco. Valeri also learned of the desperate conditions of the Barcelona Government, which, given its weakness and that of its military, was not going to survive much longer.[40] Valeri was constrained—from reading his letter one could assume he wanted to pursue the possibility of serious mediation in Spain, but because the Burgos Government would not agree to any conditions, the Holy See was unable to act, as was clearly explained in the 1929 Lateran Accords. Each time the suggestion of mediation arose, the Rebels rejected it. Each time the Rebels were questioned regarding revenge, they rejected the assumption and claimed no agreements were necessary. The Franquistas did not want mediation of any sort, including from the Holy See, and they would prevent any serious plan from occurring.

On 17 November 1938, Burgos again became concerned about the international media's reporting on the conflict in Spain. According to the Rebel Embassy to the Vatican, the Republicans had been supplying false information to newspapers in order to sway public opinion, "The extraordinary escalation in the campaign that the Red Government of Barcelona carries out to give the impression to the world and very specially to the Holy See of a radical change in its policy of cruel persecution of the Catholic Church and its Ministers that has covered in blood the land of Spain." The target for the Rebels was the media as "Sometimes the articles are published in unscrupulous newspapers ... they also use radios, a very recent partner of Diplomacy, when it cannot justify the direct talks, and they use all resources available to them, thinking that they can give the world an impression of order and respect for religion, when this [religion] has always been ridiculed under their authority."[41] The Rebels claimed Republicans had utilized this campaign to try to influence the world, but most specifically the Church. If the Republic was able to influence the opinions of the Church, then maybe the Holy See would become more active in trying to end this conflict. The letter continued by highlighting "inaccurate" articles published in newspapers like *Le Temps, La Croix, El Boletín*, and others that suggested changes in the Republic and the Republic's willingness to support the rights of the Church.[42] Burgos rejected these claims and reminded the Church of the uncontrolled violence against Catholicism, claiming that the most dangerous weapon used by the Republic was its ability to manipulate the media.⁴³ Therefore, the Rebels wanted the Holy See to not believe the international media—even though many of these reports were probably accurate.

Because the Republican Government had been able to utilize the international media in France and Britain to gain sympathy, the Rebels hoped to keep the Holy See well informed about the ongoing battles in Spain, in order to prevent the Republicans from claiming any serious war crimes occurred and changing the mood of the Vatican hierarchy. On 18 November the Rebel Embassy at the Holy See sent a letter to the Vatican to report on its decisive victory at the River Ebro, allowing its army to get farther into Cataluña, cutting the region off from the rest of the Republican controlled territory, and preventing access to the French border. The letter was sent to share the "good news" with the Holy See and ended, "I believe it is my duty to turn the attention of Your Most Reverend Eminence to the transcendental character of this glorious military victory, whose consequences will reflect, without a doubt, effectively in the resolution of the war."⁴⁴ The Rebels wanted to explain to the Holy See that this victory was influenced by their religious strength yet, by stating this battle would effectively end the Civil War, the Insurgents wanted to show the Holy See the conflict was almost over and any mediation unnecessary. Burgos clearly intended to end the War with a complete victory and were concerned about a possible Vatican initiative concerning the conflict. Presumably, the Vatican realized the Civil War was almost over, and the hierarchy worried angering the Rebels could hurt the authority of the post-War Church in Spain, and they did not press the issue.

After receiving the 18 November letter from the Franquista Embassy, Cardinal Pacelli wrote to the Papal Nuncio in Zaragoza noting that the Holy See still investigated the possibility of mediation, but also indicated the Rebels refused to cooperate in this arena as "We receive from various parts new and reiterated requests that the Holy See mediate in the Spanish conflict. It has been made clear in this regard that the National Government will not accept any mediation. Still, should there be any possibility in this regard; Your Excellency must know that the Holy See in the desire to return much longed-for peace to this beloved and tested nation would always be willing to intervene."⁴⁵ Cardinal Pacelli knew that the Rebels would not accept mediation, which had been made clear over and over again, however, Cardinal Pacelli believed if any window for mediation could be found then the Papal Nuncio was to suggest action. This information reveals that even though the Holy See had been told "no" numerous times, it was still willing to work on that project if the chance arose. The Holy See did have an interest in negotiating a peaceful solution for Spain, but the Rebels had a greater interest in fighting the Civil War until the bitter end.

The public and private requests for mediation in Spain came from various groups, including the Holy See. Franco rejected these claims, but they needed to present evidence why the loss of more Spanish lives was better than peace. Burgos needed to use language and concepts familiar and comfortable with the Vatican in order to "logically" explain why mediation had to be rejected. On 7 December the Embassy of the Spanish Rebels wrote to Cardinal Pacelli to thank the Holy See for its interest about the Spanish Civil War, but the Embassy reminded the Holy See that this conflict was not just a question of human life, but of something greater:

> Against such compromise would raise the shadows of the half million innocent victims killed by the enemies of God and the Country. We continue and will continue to the end with the same irrevocable purpose, believing that justice cannot negotiate with crime or Catholic Civilization with Soviet barbarism. We will continue to the victorious end of the war, because we have the intimate and well justified conviction that only the total triumph of Franco will ensure in Spain respect for the Altar, the consciences, the human person, the family, the Spanish Society, and Catholic civilization.[46]

Mediation was not going to be a solution to the War, but would give in to the demands of the communists. Once again the Rebels wanted to explain the war in their terms: it was not a war between two groups of Spaniards, but it was a war between real Catholic Spaniards and foreign Bolsheviks. The Burgos Government needed to make it clear any intervention would weaken the state of Catholicism in Spain while strengthening the power of communism. By reiterating this dichotomy to the Vatican, the Franquistas hoped the Holy See would once again see the conflict as a "crusade," but the loss of human life still appeared to be a major concern for the Church. As José Sánchez has suggested, agreement between the Holy See and the Republic appeared untenable, as neither side was willing to compromise.[47] The Rebels promised to give the Catholic Church "favored status," and more importantly, the Insurgents appeared to be the foregone winners of the War. Because the War was almost over, for all intents and purposes, the Vatican tried to find a non-military solution through mediation. Even though the Vatican was not an ally of other side, it did appear to find moments for mediation—even if they existed at the end of the war after hundreds of thousands had already died. The Vatican could not end the War; the Rebels had to want to end the War.

Once again, Burgos discredited any attempts from the Republic to initiate mediation. While the Rebels had pushed for the Vatican to remain uninvolved in mediation, the Republic used any chance to gain the sympathies of the Church. As the Civil War continued into the Christmas season of 1938, the Republicans hoped to secure some type of mediation in honor of the holiday. Nuncio Cicognani wrote to the Holy See on 16 December to explain the conditions in Spain from a Rebel perspective:

> The Foreign Minister tells me that they know that the Barcelona Government, backed by foreign Powers, wants to communicate with the Holy Father because in occasion of the Christmas greeting speech the Spanish question was treated, suggesting mediation. The Minister qualified this as a new maneuver of the red government to try to rescue before the defeat; and . . . that mediation is firmly rejected by authentic Spain and will make . . . serious injury; the National Government is decided to give a definitive solution to the conflict and with it to give the country a secure orientation.[48]

The Rebels considered this plan for international mediation as another ploy by the communists in the Republican Government and the Republic's sudden interest in the sanctity of the Christmas holiday was based solely on political gains. Republicans would say whatever was necessary in order to gain sympathy, especially from the Vatican.

Cardinal Pacelli wrote to Papal Nuncio Valeri in Paris on 20 December about the ongoing possibilities of international mediation in Spain and acknowledged the Nunziatura in Paris had been trying to work towards mediation, but Pacelli understood that Franco would not allow anyone to push for peace: "Generalissimo Franco, following the voices running in this regard, has made known by his own initiative even in these last days, both through the Nunziatura and through the Embassy, that he does not intend to accept mediation proposals. Therefore, His Holiness does not see the possibility to intervene."[49] Cardinal Pacelli, after months of trying to find some quiet way of urging negotiations to end the Spanish Civil War, finally seemed inclined to believe nothing was going to come from this work. After numerous rejections through Nunziatura and Embassies, Pacelli understood there appeared to be no way to persuade the Rebels to allow mediation. This being said, the Vatican would be forced to allow the Civil War to play out until its inevitable end.

With hopes of serious mediation to end the Spanish Civil War seemingly dead, a chance to prevent some bloodshed in Spain would be to work towards a truce for Christmas 1938, as previously suggested by organizations like the *Comité Espagnol pour la Paix Civile* and the *Jeunesse Ouvrière Chrétienne* in 1937. For the Holy See, even a short-term cessation of hostilities would be worth something. Pacelli wrote to the Nunziatura in San Sebastian on 20 December, "It is wanted that Your Most Reverend Eminence investigate and refer with the maximum promptness whether the Government would accept favorably a call from the Holy Father to the two belligerent parties for a brief Christmas truce, even if only for twenty-four or forty-eight hours, in resemblance of what Benedict XV did in the first year of the World War."[50] By Christmas 1938, the only power the Holy See had over the conflict in Spain was to suggest a brief, maybe one-day, truce for the holiday.[51] Once the holiday ended, the conflict would continue. Whether or not the Rebels accepted this truce is less important than the fact the Holy See was only able to introduce the possibility of a one or two-day stoppage in hostilities.

The Vatican was greatly concerned about the actions in Spain during the Civil War. When the Rebels appeared assured of victory, the Holy See became increasingly worried about how the war would actually end. International and Republican calls for mediation, namely at the hands of the Vatican, became commonplace, yet the more requests made, the more the Vatican believed some sort of mediation necessary to avoid more bloodshed and vengeance. The Holy See had no way to force the Insurgents to consider mediation due to the Lateran Accords, but it frequently requested the Burgos Government to support these plans. Burgos, however, held all the serious power in the conflict. Each time the Holy See requested mediation, the Rebels responded by reminding the Vatican why the war was being fought (at least in the propagandistic eyes of the Rebels). Mediation would not happen; the only way the war would end would be with a complete and concession-free surrender of the Republic, the only way to root out communism and atheism. While the Vatican hoped to persuade the Rebels to spare blood, Franco and his supporters reminded the Catholic Church that Bolshevism was the true enemy and whatever had to be done needed to be finished, completely.

Final Thoughts

The Burgos Government, with the help of its foreign allies, defeated the Basque region by the end of August 1937 and pushed even closer to Barcelona during 1938. In both cases, representatives and supporters of the Republic requested the Holy See find a way to end the conflict and spare lives. The Republic, which had been an ideological, political, and spiritual problem for the Holy See, wanted to persuade the Vatican it was the defender of freedoms and religion in Spain, and repression and violence would follow the end of the War. As a self-proclaimed moral and spiritual leader, the Vatican was called upon to save lives. The Holy See wanted to persuade the Rebels that concessions and mediation would be the best course of action, but Burgos wanted a complete military victory. Throughout the conflict, the Rebels used the language of crusade, religion, and anti-communism as the central rationales for their actions. At the start of the Civil War, the Holy See appeared content to know that one side fought against religious repression and violence against the clergy, but as the conflict dragged on and death tolls grew, calls for mediation persuaded the Vatican to act through its private channels. The central problem, however, for Vatican mediation was not a lack of trying or a lack of interest, but it was the fact the Burgos Government no longer needed public Vatican support; the Rebels hoped to placate the Holy See for as long as possible. The longer Burgos could survive on empty promises to the Holy See, the more time Franco had to win the Civil War. The Rebels wanted to "string" the Vatican along—hoping to have the conflict already won by the time the Vatican pushed for greater humanitarian interests. On various occasions, Pope Pius XI instructed his hierarchy to negotiate with Franco to save lives in Spain, but he never released any public commentary about Insurgent actions. The Pope appeared to want a more vocal reaction from the Holy See concerning the conflict, but Secretary of State Pacelli tempered these comments and avoided a public discussion of the War. When the Vatican did speak to Franco about repression and atrocities, the Rebels responded aggressively to the Holy See, showing they vehemently opposed Vatican interference in the conflict and the Church needed to back-down for a congenial relationship in the future. The Civil War was almost over, one way or another. The Vatican was not callous and it tried to negotiate peace, but its unwillingness to act at the start of the conflict prevented the Holy See from pushing its proposals. The Vatican hierarchy knew it would have to work with this new Spanish government after the War, and the Catholic Church would want to guarantee a better environment and greater Catholic influence in the new government.

The Vatican's reactions and behavior did appear to change over time, but mainly because the Civil War's outcome seemed clear. The Vatican hierarchy waited for moments when negotiations appeared most likely to work—such as the inevitable Rebel victory in País Vasco or the fall of Barcelona. Could the Vatican have tried harder and pushed for other stoppages of hostilities? Yes, the Vatican could have been more aggressive, but this aggression could have had negative results for the Catholic Church—pushing for mediation could have threatened the Lateran Accords and could have created conflict with Franco's ally, Fascist Italy. Also, the Republic never made any promises to return privileges to the Church. Until clear promises could be made about the restoration of Catholic privileges in Spain, the Holy See avoided recognition of either side. Most importantly, the Republic and its allies were responsible for many more clerical and ecclesiastical deaths than the Rebels. Elements like communists and anarchists actively worked to undermine the Catholic Church in Spain, and the Catholic Church had no need to defend these enemies of the faith. The Vatican hierarchy acted to protect the Catholic Church and its followers, and it could not risk more enemies and more attacks from Rebels and their supporters after the war ended. A supporter of the Republic would clearly suggest the Vatican did not do enough to protect innocent casualties during the War. A supporter of the Insurgents would clearly claim the Vatican did too much to try to affect the outcome of the conflict. Both sides had developed problems with the Holy See. The primary goal of the Holy See was to protect Church interests—some may consider this act noble while others many consider it criminal, but it is what happened.

Conclusion

In the overnight hours of 9–10 February 1939, Pope Pius XI died and the Vatican initiated the conclave to choose his successor. After the proper mourning period, a relatively short debate was conducted and a new Pope was chosen. Vatican Cardinals elected Vatican Secretary of State Eugenio Pacelli, and announced him as Pope Pius XII on 2 March 1939. Meanwhile, the Spanish Civil War was drawing to a close—General Franco declared victory on 1 April 1939. With the selection of a new Pope came new archival holdings—many of which remain closed to scholars today. This new Papacy experienced the horrors of the Second World War and the Holocaust. The final conflict for Secretary of State Pacelli—the Spanish Civil War—shared many similarities with Pope Pius XII's major global crisis, World War II. With the death of the Pope also comes the closing of his Papal Archives, therefore information regarding the last few months of the Spanish Civil War will be disclosed at a later period.

Before the declaration of the Second Republic in 1931, the Roman Catholic Church maintained a powerful position within Spanish society—influencing numerous social and cultural practices in the country. The Catholic Church—along with the monarchy, large-landowners, and the military—remained symbols of a strong traditionalist state where the concerns of the poor were often overlooked for the sake of perceived historical glory. The elections of April 1931, however, inspired Republicans, with a left-leaning majority, to establish a new state with a new liberal and modern constitution and legal codes. The goals of many amendments and laws were to reduce the influence of the Church in Spain and secularize the country as much as possible. As Chapters 1 and 2 have shown, the Spanish Catholic Church did not appreciate these legal and physical attacks, and tried to undermine the state's authority. Meanwhile, the Holy See was forced to deal with these new, modern pressures in Spain. The Vatican, through its Nuncio, often requested the Republic moderate its views and attempt to protect the Catholic Church—but most importantly, the Vatican wanted the Church to maintain its influence in the state and its influential role in the country at large. The Vatican believed the Republic was unfairly targeting the Church, which maintained a vital role in early modern Spain. The Republic, however, connected Spain's serious problems of inequality and underdevelopment to traditional institutions, like the Church.

Therefore, the period of the Constitutional Convention and First Republican Government (1931–3) was a tense time between the two states as both had their own worldviews, and they did not agree on the new role for Catholicism. Pius XI's *Dilectissima Nobis* of 1933 called upon the world to acknowledge the attacks the Church faced in the new, secular democracy. The Pope wanted the Church to retain its influence and openly stated the Republic's new changes as serious attacks, but the Republic understood these adaptations as necessary and saw the Pope's message as a seditious move against the authority of the new government. Most importantly, the Vatican believed its concerns in Spain were important, the Republic was not acknowledging these problems, and that the Holy See needed to speak out and remind Spain of the important role played by the Church. Pius XI wanted to confront the Republic and push the new government to acknowledge the moral significance of Catholicism in Spanish society, but pragmatic Cardinal Pacelli must have feared further Republican retaliation. Following the release of the *Dilectissima Nobis*, Pius XI never released another encyclical about the growing chaos in Spain. Pacelli's conciliatory attitude appeared to have won, as the Holy See avoided public commentary about perceived Republican attacks against the Church. The Republic, however, believed its actions were in the best interest for Spain, the Church had too much influence over Spanish society, and the Vatican should not interfere with internal Spanish issues. With this contentious groundwork established, the future relationships with any left-leaning Spanish government were tumultuous. Leftists in the Republic grew more distrustful of the Spanish Catholic Church and Holy See, and the Church wanted a change in the Republic's leadership to moderate the government's behavior.

Following the collapse of the leftist Republican coalition, Spain held a second round of parliamentary elections in November 1933. Leading to these elections, a new rightist coalition, CEDA, campaigned hard to defeat the left and roll back many legal precedents. The Spanish Catholic Church supported the supposedly Catholic attitudes of CEDA, and worked for their victory. While the Holy See did not publicly support one group over another, it allowed its clergy in Spain to help CEDA win. Even though this coalition won the elections, the centrist Radical Party was offered the opportunity to lead Spain, in hopes of moderating the growing ideological tensions between left and right. The Radicals, however, were unable to do this, and the center-right government faced serious social and political problems. When Spain descended to revolution in October 1934, the government needed to call on the military to put down revolts in Asturias. Unlike the period of the First Government when the Holy See and Catholic Church could not trust the state, Catholic leaders supported this military action and the state's aggressive behavior. As Chapter 3 has shown, the Vatican and Catholic Church were not completely antithetical to the idea of a "Republic," as long as that Republic was politically conservative and willing to protect the Church, roll back previous legislation, and use force to put down perceived radical leftist threats. When the government worked against socialists, communists, and anarchists, the Republic could be trusted, and an open dialogue between the state and Church could be maintained.

This relationship, however, was tested in the February 1936 elections when CEDA and a new leftist Popular Front fought for control of the country. The Spanish Catholic Church openly supported CEDA, for example encouraging nuns to vote for it, and privately, the Holy See worried the Popular Front could once again restore a period of anticlerical legislation and violence in Spain. After a razor-thin Popular Front victory the Church grew more concerned. Rather than worry the right would try to overthrow the government, the Holy See worried the Popular Front would use a "Trojan-horse" plan to establish a communist dictatorship. The political right fed this fear of socialism, communism, and anarchism in Spain, even though the right would lead the nearly inevitable violent uprising. From 1933–6, the Holy See's agenda was to establish positive relations with a center-right Republic to help the Church. The Vatican and Spanish Catholic Church wanted the end of contentious anticlerical legislation and a restoration of Catholic privilege and authority over many social and cultural practices. At the same time, the growing ideological tensions that swept across Europe were growing stronger in Spain. The Holy See, through communications with representatives in Spain, knew some type of violent action was going to occur. The Church most feared violence from the left, and possibly overlooked or underestimated the possible threats from the political right. Vatican representatives did not openly confront these Republican governments; instead, the Papal Nuncio and others tried to find some middle-ground to improve the condition of the Church. Cardinal Pacelli must have understood that by maintaining an open dialogue with any Spanish governments rather than openly confronting them, the Vatican might be able to influence future Republican actions.

Following the growth of political violence in Spain from springsummer 1936, conservative Spanish Generals initiated the "Uprising" against the Republic, and began the violent Civil War (1936–9). At the start of the Civil War, repression occurred on both sides as Republican militias attacked conservatives and clergy, and Rebel troops murdered Republican allies in occupied territories. The Vatican's first priority was the safety of its clergy and property in Spain. The Vatican believed the unorganized Republican militias, often not under the control of the state, deliberately targeted the Church on the orders of the Republic. The Church appeared to believe the Insurgents' rallying-cry for a crusade against a supposed communist and anarchist threat in Spain. The Vatican would be more obliged to support the side that suggested a restoration of pre-1931 Spain—especially if the Church could regain an influential role in the state. Even though the Franquistas sounded sympathetic to the Church, some of their actions raised major concerns. The most pressing area for the Holy See was the predominantly Catholic País Vasco, which had sided with the Republic for autonomous regionalist concerns. The Holy See most worried about two Catholic forces fighting, and the possible large death toll including Basque Catholics and a small number of priests. The Holy See wanted to believe the conflict there could be negotiated and tried to influence the outcome. Pope Pius XI supported more direct Vatican responses than his Secretary of State and appeared to want the Holy See to be more frank with the Nationalists, especially in protesting their massacres and executions; for example, the Pope forcefully demanded protest to Franco about extensive executions in Málaga. The Pope wanted to push the Rebels to negotiate a truce and save lives, especially Catholic lives in the Basque region. At the same time, the more pragmatic Vatican Secretary of State, Eugenio Pacelli, appeared to want the Holy See not to become overly aggressive in negotiations in order to avoid conflict with Franco. Even by 1937, a Rebel victory seemed imminent, and Pacelli likely realized the Holy See would someday have to develop a relationship with this government. At the same time, the Holy See would not want to anger states like Germany and Italy, which had both supported the Nationalist cause and could each repress Catholics in their own states. Pius XI and Pacelli appeared to understand Article 24 of the Lateran Accords differently: the Secretary of State adhered the language of remaining "outside of any temporal rivalries" to protect the Church, while the Pope must have believed it was the role of the Holy See to take actions in a "moral or spiritual" crisis. Both men wanted to protect the interests of the Catholic Church in Spain, but their opinions varied on how this could be accomplished.

Basque Bishop Mateo Múgica, who had remained a supporter for Basque autonomy against the Rebels, represented a major problem for the Holy See. The Nationalists wanted him removed from Spain for his opinions, and they could even have endangered his life and the Vatican worked to get him out of the country. The Vatican appeared to appease Burgos when their clergy, like Bishop Múgica, criticized the uprising, but the Rebels never made concrete promises about the future of the Church in Spain. The Insurgents spoke of a return to traditional Spain, yet they had never clearly defined what role the Church would play following the Civil War. For the Vatican, and especially for most of the Catholic hierarchy in Spain, the Rebels were a much welcomed change from the anticlerical attitudes of the Popular Front, and the Vatican apparently chose to appease the Insurgents to protect potential gains after the War. Pope Pius XI must have wanted stronger conversations with Burgos to obtain clear promises about the role of Catholicism in Franco's Spain, but Secretary of State Pacelli must have supported a more moderate plan not to risk angering Burgos and its allies, and therefore not endanger the Church. Pacelli must have suspected the Rebels could change their opinions regarding the Church at any time if it became politically convenient and this dangerous possibility needed to be avoided. As Chapters 5 and 7 have shown, the Vatican found comfort in the ideals of the Insurgents, but because clear promises were not given to the Church and because the Catholic Basque were still embroiled in a major military conflict and faced revenge the Vatican chose not to recognize the Rebels as the government of Spain during the War.

The Spanish Civil War attracted the attention of many international governments. Britain and France hoped to isolate the conflict and prevent it from turning into a continent-wide ideological war that could destabilize the status quo. Even though the British and French wanted non-intervention for the Spanish Civil War, both governments requested the Holy See find some avenue for negotiations or mediation in the conflict. The British and French presented possible plans, but in each case the Vatican rejected the possibility of accepting a plan developed outside the auspices of the Church. Private organizations also requested Vatican intervention in Spain, but again the Vatican appeared unwilling to assist with these plans. As the Vatican learned of these requests, they often communicated with Burgos to gauge its response. Each time, the Franquistas expressed that no negotiations could occur, and the Civil War needed to have a military victory followed by the removal of all foreign ideological threats. The Vatican must have realized that the Rebels were likely going to win the conflict, and it would behoove the Holy See to acknowledge Insurgents' demands to create a positive working relationship in post-War Spain. Similarly, the Rebels had used Nazi German and Fascist Italian aid, and these governments had a serious interest in Franco's victory. As Chapter 6 has shown, if the Holy See became publicly involved in mediation plans contradictory to Nationalist desires, then Italy and Germany might become aggressive towards the Church and increase repression. The Vatican began to express privately its concern about the growing influence of Nazism in Spain at the expense of the Catholic Church, and Cardinal Pacelli stated this fear of Hitler's growing influence to French Ambassador, François Charles-Roux. Pope Pius XI had released the encyclicals, *Non Abbiamo Bisogno* (1931), *Dilectissima Nobis* (1933), *Divini Redemptoris* (1937), and *Mit brennender Sorge* (1937) during his papacy to express his distrust of the growing threats of political ideologies of the extreme right and extreme left and his words protested attacks against the Catholic Church. Pius XI must have wanted to find some way to negotiate this conflict and reestablish the diplomatic power of the Vatican in European affairs, but his Secretary of State would have feared vocal Vatican responses could create other serious problems for the Holy See. Pacelli never released Pius XI's final encyclical draft, *Humani Generis Unitas*, which spoke out against racism following the Pope's death, as it might have caused serious difficulty for the new Pontiff in 1939. Pacelli had learned the practice of Vatican "impartiality" in conflicts from his mentor, Pietro Gasparri, and the Secretary of State must have wanted the Pope's words not to harm the Church by creating new tensions. In the end, the Vatican chose to avoid international calls for mediation that it did not lead.

By the middle of 1937, the Nationalists had won numerous military victories throughout Spain, and the Republic was barely surviving. A Franquista victory, especially with the military aid of Germany and Italy, seemed inevitable. When the Basque were ready to fall, the Vatican initiated its own plans to help establish surrender. After the Basque fell, the Rebels turned their attention to the last Mediterranean strongholds of the Republic. The Rebels claimed falsely they would not repress the Basque following surrender, and were insulted the Holy See would even broach the subject. The Franquistas claimed they fought a crusade against communism and atheism, and that would be enough of a guarantee. The Catholic Church needed the Rebels after the Civil War to reestablish Catholic privilege, and therefore, chose not to pressure the Insurgents too much. At the same time, when the Nationalists bombed cities, they claimed they were dangerous military targets and not civilian locations. As Chapter 4 and 8 have shown, the Holy See tried to press the Rebels to change their behaviors, but the Franquistas would not accept any mediation or truces. Some could argue the Holy See could have pushed harder—the Vatican could have gone public with its complaints or even threatened excommunication of Rebel generals who launched attacks on civilians, but they never did. Pius XI must have wanted Burgos to listen and accept Vatican opinions concerning the conflict, but Cardinal Pacelli seemed to temper the Church's demands. Pacelli knew the Rebels were about to win, and the Secretary of State would not want to anger a future ally. The Holy See did not want a growing death toll in Spain, but the Vatican chose to be practical and think about the future of the Catholic Church in both Spain and Europe following this conflict. The Holy See could have intervened for "moral" reasons during the Civil War, but practical conditions in Spain and Europe outweighed this concern. Franco had spoken of a return to a pre-1931 state, and the Holy See wished to avoid jeopardizing their future influence. Even with these promises, the Rebels were never clear about what the Church would gain following the War, and the Vatican did not want to anger Franco and his leadership and risk a continued period of anticlericalism. Because the Insurgents could not promise the specific role of the Church following the Civil War and because civilians were still being targeted, and because

Nazis and Fascists still operated in Spain, the Holy See was unable to recognize Franco as Spain's leader. The Holy See thought of its own agenda and interests, but it needed to know Spain would return to a Catholic state.

Overall, the Holy See most worried about the condition of the Catholic Church in Spain during the 1930s. The First Republican Government believed its actions were beneficial to the state, but the Holy See understood them as direct anticlerical attacks. When the government did not moderate its views, the Holy See saw benefits in a rightist government that could put down any threats from the radical left. When the left returned to power in 1936, the Vatican and many in Spain were aware some type of revolutionary action would occur. The Insurgents represented a logical ally for the Catholic Church and the Holy See, but Burgos could not be controlled by the Vatican. The Church needed the Rebels more than the Rebels needed the Vatican. The Vatican found itself in the middle of a major ideological crisis, and its hierarchy worked to establish a logical route to protect Catholic interests and avoid further confrontation after the Civil War would end. This period also highlights the varying opinions of Pius XI and Pacelli concerning the diplomatic actions of the Vatican. Pius XI wanted to confront international problems relating to Catholicism when he saw them. He appeared to believe it was the Vatican's moral duty to speak against political and military evils, but his Secretary of State must have worried that any public comments from the Pope might endanger the Vatican's perceived political impartiality and create new problems for the Church. Pacelli appeared to believe that being conciliatory towards foreign powers had benefits for the future conditions for Catholicism. While the Lateran Accords allowed the Holy See "to exercise its moral and spiritual power," these men disagreed about how this influence could or should be used, even during a period of civil war.

This project set out to show the complicated nature in the relationship between Spain and the Holy See during the 1930s. Many actors worked to undermine the stability of the Second Republic and many others unleashed a violent Civil War. The Holy See did not communicate with just one or two governments or groups, but a variety of entities each of which wanted the Holy See to take a particular role. For the Holy See, trying to reestablish its pre-1931 role in a traditional Spanish society was a tempting, and often effective, rationale for its behavior during this period. The Holy See could not make each group happy, and in the end, worried more about its own survival and the survival of the Catholic Church in Spain.

Notes

Introduction

1 "Pope Benedict XVI Sees 'Aggressive Secularism' in Spain" in *BBC News Europe Online* (6 November 2010).
2 *Ibid.*
3 José María Bedoya, "Pope Francis Receives Spanish Prime Minister in Vatican," in *El País* (15 April 2013).
4 The terms "Rebels," "Insurgents," "Burgos," or "Franquistas" will be used. While Nationalists is a commonly accepted term for the political right during the Spanish Civil War, this work attempts to avoid an unnecessary contemporary political debate on "naming." As Manuel Álvarez Tardío and Fernando del Rey Reguillo suggest, Spanish history has often been infected with a "militant history" that has associated past historical events with "particular political interests." I attempt to create a study that, as these historians argue, should be "disconnected from myth, condemnations and self-interested manipulations." See: *The Second Republic Revisited: From Democratic Hopes to Civil War (1931–1936)* (Eastbourne: Sussex Academic Press, 2012), pp. 6–7.
5 Pius XI died in the overnight hours of 9–10 February 1939. With his death came the closing of his archival records even though the Spanish Civil War had not completely ended.
6 See Chapter I for an outline of tensions between the Catholic Church and Spanish liberals leading to the Second Republic and following the declaration of the new government.
7 See Chapter IV for information relating to the *Spanish* Catholic hierarchy's specific opinions and general support for the Rebels.
8 Frank Coppa, "Pope Pius XII: From Diplomacy of Impartiality to the Silence of the Holocaust," *Journal of Church and State* 55, 2 (Dec. 2011): pp. 286–306, esp. pp. 291–2.
9 *Ibid.*, p. 289.
10 *Lateran Accords*, Treaty between the Holy See and Italy, 1929.
11 Paul Preston, *The Spanish Holocaust: Inquisition and Extermination in Twentieth Century Spain* (London: W.W. Norton & Company, 2012); *The Spanish Civil War: Reaction, Revolution, and Revenge: Revised and Expanded* (New York: W.W. Norton & Company, 2006); *Franco: A Biography* (London: Harper Collins Publishers, 1993); and *The Politics of Revenge: Fascism and the Military in Twentieth-Century Spain* (London, Routledge, 1995).
12 Stanley Payne, *Fascism in Spain, 1923–1977* (Madison: University of

Wisconsin Press, 1999); *The Franco Regime, 1936–1975* (Madison: University of Wisconsin Press, 1987); *Spain's First Democracy: The Second Republic, 1931–1936* (Madison: University of Wisconsin Press, 1993); and "Fascist Italy and Spain, 1922–1945," in *Mediterranean Historical Review* 13, 1 (June-Dec 1998): pp. 99–115.

13 William Callahan, *The Catholic Church in Spain, 1875–1998* (Washington, D.C., The Catholic University of America Press, 2001) and Frances Lannon, *Privilege, Persecution, and Prophecy: The Catholic Church in Spain, 1875–1975* (Oxford: Clarendon Press, 1987).

14 José Sánchez, *The Spanish Civil War as a Religious Tragedy* (Notre Dame, Indiana: University of Notre Dame Press, 1987); Gonzalo Redondo, *Historia de la Iglesia en España, 1931–1939: Tomo II* (Madrid: Ediciones Rialp, S.A., 1993); and Hilari Raguer, *Gunpowder and Incense: The Catholic Church and the Spanish Civil War* (London: Routledge, 2007), p. 10

15 Vicente Cárcel Ortí, *Pio XI Entre la República Y Franco* (Madrid: Biblioteca de Autores Cristianos, 2008) and Raguer, *Gunpowder and Incense.*

16 See Chapter III for a discussion of Pius XI and Pacelli and their attitudes towards European ideologies.

17 Susan Zuccotti, *Under His Very Windows: The Vatican and the Holocaust in Italy* (New Haven: Yale University Press, 2000); Carol Rittner and John K. Roth (eds.) *Pope Pius XII and the Holocaust* (London: Leicester University Press, 2002); and John Cornwell, *Hitler's Pope: The Secret History of Pope Pius XII* (New York: Penguin, 2008).

18 Lucia Ceci, *Il papa non deve parlare* (Bari: Gius, Laterza, & Figli, 2010); Hubert Wolf, *Pope and Devil* (Cambridge, MA: The Belknap Press, 2010); Emma Fattorini, *Hitler, Mussolini, and the Vatican* (Cambridge: Polity Press, 2011); Alessandro Duce, *La Santa Sede e la Questione Ebraica* (Roma: Edizione Studium: 2006); and Frank Coppa, *The Policies and Politics of Pope Pius XII* (New York: Peter Lang, 2011).

19 Coppa, *The Policies and Politics*, pp. 9–12.

I A Troubled Past and a Tense Introduction: The Second Republic is Born

1 See: Peter C. Kent and John F. Pollard, *Papal Diplomacy in the Modern Age* (Westport, CT: Praeger, 1994).

2 For a brief explanation of the clerical and anticlerical divide in Spain during the 19th century, see the section: *Brief Review of Spanish Clerical–Anticlerical Divide*; Stanley G. Payne, *Spain's First Democracy: The Second Republic, 1931–1936* (Madison: The University of Wisconsin Press, 1993), pp. 12–3; Maria Thomas, *The Faith and the Fury* (Eastbourne: Sussex Academic Press, 2013), pp. 20–44; Alfonso Botti, *Cielo y Dinero* (Madrid: Alianza Editorial, S.A.: 1992), pp. 33–6; and José Luis Ledesma, "Enemigos Seculares: La Violencia Anticlerical (1936–1939), in Julio de la Cueva and Feliciano Montero (eds.), *Izquierda Obrera y Religión en España (1900–1939)* (Alcalá de Henares: Universidad de Alcalá, 2012), pp. 225–232.

3 For a discussion of Spain's clerical and anticlerical past, along with their seemingly symbiotic relationship, see: Julio de la Cueva and Feliciano

Montero (eds.), "Introducción" in *La Secularización Conflictiva: España (1898–1931)* (Madrid: Biblioteca Nueva, 2007), pp. 9–18.
4 According to José M. Sánchez, the Holy See had established a "passive policy towards the Republic" in order to avoid direct confrontation with the government. See: José M. Sánchez, "The Second Spanish Republic and the Holy See: 1931–1936" in *The Catholic Historical Review* 49, 1 (1963): pp. 47–68, esp. p. 47.
5 The historiography and research relating to the Second Spanish Republic is great and vast covering a wide variety of social, cultural, and political situations. For a *tiny* sample of some literature, see: Manuel Álvarez Tardío, *Anticlericalismo y libertad de conciencia: Política, religion en la Segunda República Española, 1931–1936* (Madrid: Centros de Estudios Políticos y Costitucionales, 2002); Gerald Brenan, *The Spanish Labyrinth: The Social and Political Background of the Spanish Civil War* (Cambridge: Cambridge University Press, 1943); Fernando de Meer Lecha-Marzo, *La Constitución de la II República: Autonomías, Propiedad, Iglesia, Eseñanza* (Pamplona: EUNSA, 1978); Sandie Holguín, *Creating Spaniards: Cultural and National Identity in Republican Spain* (Madison: University of Wisconsin Press, 2002); Gabriel Jackson, *The Spanish Republic and the Civil War, 1931–1939* (Princeton: Princeton University Press, 1965); and Paul Preston, *The Coming of the Spanish Civil War: Reform, Reaction and Revolution in the Second Republic* (London: Routledge, 1978).
6 William J. Callahan, *The Catholic Church in Spain, 1875–1998* (Washington, D.C.: Catholic University of America Press, 2000), pp. 2–3. Overall, therefore, various liberal groups reacted differently towards the Catholic Church, but no 19th century liberal movements seemed to work exclusively for the destruction of Catholicism in Spain.
7 Frances Lannon, *Privilege, Persecution, and Prophecy: The Catholic Church in Spain, 1875–1975* (Oxford: Clarendon Press, 1987), p. 2.
8 *Ibid.*
9 See: Callahan and Lannon.
10 Frank J. Coppa, *Pope Pius IX: Crusader in a Secular Age* (Boston: Twayne Publishers, 1979), p. 196.
11 *Ibid.*
12 Callahan, p. 8.
13 *Ibid.*, p. 9.
14 *Ibid.*, p. 14.
15 *Ibid.*, p. 19.
16 See: Lannon and Callahan.
17 Anarchism came to Spain in 1868 through Mikhail Bakunin's emissary, Giuseppe Fenelli. The movement grew quickly, with sixty thousand supporters in Andalucía by 1873. The anarchist workers' union, *Confederación Nacional de Trabajadores* (CNT), was the largest union by 1919, and by 1936, it had 1.6 million members. See: Martha Grace Duncan, "Spanish Anarchism Refracted: Theme and Image in the Millenarian and Revisionist Literature" in *Journal of Contemporary History* 23, 3 (July 1988): pp. 323–346.

18 Lannon, p. 20. *Tragic Week* resulted from political and union agitation in Barcelona by leftist groups. Many of Barcelona's working-class were angered by the increase of conscriptions necessary to fight Spain's war in the Rif. Tensions grew in the city. William Callahan suggests that the reason the Church became a primary target of this violence is not completely clear, but for some workers, the Church's educational and charitable organizations were obstacles "for a free, secular system of education, while the charitable organizations seemed well-financed attempts to lure the workers away from militant labor organizations," Callahan, p. 78.

19 See: Callahan, pp. 19–25, 43, 193–196; Lannon, pp. 3–4, 20; and Alejandro Quiroga, *Making Spaniards: Primo de Rivera and the Nationalization of the Mass, 1923–30* (New York: Palgrave McMillan, 2007), p. 23.

20 For examples of Socialism and Anarchism and their relationships to anticlericalism, see: Víctor Manuel Arbeloa "El Partido Socialista y la Iglesia (1879–1935), a través de Pablo Iglesias," pp. 49–70; Julio de la Cueva Merino, "Socialistas y Religión en la Segunda República: De la Liga Nacional Laica al Inicio de la Guerra Civil," pp. 71–98; and Gonzalo Álvarez Chillida, "Movimiento Liberatrio y Religión durante la Segunda República," pp. 99–128, in De la Cueva and Montero (eds.), *Izquierda Obrera . . .*

21 Callahan, p. 59.

22 *Ibid.*

23 Lannon, p. 4.

24 Quiroga, pp. 58–63.

25 A similar movement occurred in France. The leadership of Action Française saw value in the Catholic Church as a tool for order and discipline. At the start, the Catholic Church did see value in this authoritarian movement that was against the radical left. However, as the leadership of Action Française radicalized, the Catholic Church distanced itself. In 1926, Pope Pius XI instructed the French Catholic Hierarchy to condemn the works of Action Française because the movement had been "disregarding Catholic beliefs and morality." See: Joel Blatt, "Action Française and the Vatican" in *Encyclopedia of the Vatican and Papacy*" Frank J. Coppa (ed.) (Westport: Greenwood Press, 1999), pp. 3–5.

26 Quiroga, p. 134.

27 Gonzalo Redondo, *Historia de la Iglesia en España, 1931–1939: Tomo I La Segunda República 1931–1936* (Madrid, Ediciones Rialp, S.A., 1993), p. 131.

28 José Manuel Macarro, "The Socialists and Revolution" in Manuel Álvarez Tardío and Fernando del Rey Reguillo (eds.), *The Second Republic Revisited: From Democratic Hopes to Civil War (1931–1936)* (Eastbourne: Sussex Academic Press, 2012), pp. 40–57, esp. p. 42.

29 "On the thirteenth of April, [the Provisional Government] issues a statement declaring that the municipal elections had 'the value of a plebiscite' and called upon the monarchy to submit itself to the national will. Responding to the Provisional Government's call for public demonstrations, exuberant crowds took to the streets in various provincial capitals and in the larger cities, often singing the 'Himno de Riego' (anthem of early

nineteenth-century liberalism) and the 'Marseillaise.'" Payne, *Spain's First Democracy*, p. 32.
30 Manuel Álvarez Tardío and Fernando del Rey Reguillo (eds.), *The Second Republic Revisited: From Democratic Hopes to Civil War (1931–1936)* (Eastbourne: Sussex Academic Press, 2012), p. 3.
31 Telegramma de Cardinale Pacelli, 15/4/31 Archivio Segreto Vaticano (ASV): Affari Ecclesiastici Straordinari, Spagna (AES, Spagna): Fasc. 117 Pos. 784, 68r.
32 Payne, *Spain's First Democracy*, p. 34.
33 In 1900, Federico Tedeschini began working for the Vatican Secretary of State's Office following the completion of his Doctorates in Philosophy, Theology, and Canonical Rights. In 1914, Pope Benedict XV named him as a substitute for the Secretary of State. On 31 March 1921, Pope Benedict XV made Tedeschini the Apostolic Nuncio to the King of Spain. In 1936, Pope Pius XI elevated Tedeschini to Cardinal, and he returned to Rome. Tedeschini's ascension in the Office of the Vatican Secretary of State coincided with Pope Benedict XV's attempts to reestablish the Vatican as a moral leader in world political affairs, particularly during the First World War. During WWI, Pope Benedict tried to negotiate for peace, but his plans failed. On one hand, both the Allies and the Central Powers did not appreciate this revived Vatican interest in international political concerns, but on the other, the Vatican left the WWI-era as both a religious institution, and as Stewart A. Stehlin states, "an international one dealing with problems of nations and individuals alike." Tedeschini, therefore, must have been influenced by this new role for the Holy See—the Vatican became more active in international conflicts, and its mediation was frequently not appreciated by certain belligerents. See: Vicente Cárcel Ortí, *Pío XI entre la República y Franco* (Madrid: Biblioteca de Autores Cristianos, 2008), pp. 382–3 and Stewart A. Stehlin "The Emergence of a New Vatican Diplomacy during the Great War and Its Aftermath, 1914–1929" in Peter C. Kent and John F. Pollard (eds.), *Papal Diplomacy in the Modern Age* (Westport, CT: Praeger, 1994), pp. 76–7.
34 Sánchez, p. 50.
35 For detailed discussions of the life and politics of Alejandro Lerroux, see: Nigel Townson, *The Crisis of Democracy in Spain* (Brighton: Sussex Academic Press, 2000) and José Alvarez-Junco, *The Emergence of Mass Politics in Spain* (Brighton: Sussex Academic Press, 2002).
36 See: Alvarez-Junco, Chapter 9.
37 ASV: AES, Spagna: Fasc. 116 Pos. 784, 82r.
38 ASV: AES, Spagna: Fasc. 116 Pos. 784, 82v.
39 Townson, *The Crisis of Democracy*, p. 17.
40 The Republican government was comprised of numerous parties: Socialists, Radicals, Esquerra Republicana, Liberal Republican Right, Federalists, Galicianists, Republican Action, Radical Socialists, Independent Republicans, "Al Servicio de la República", and Liberal Democrats. Payne, *Spain's First Democracy*, p. 51. With all these parties having influence in the coalition, it cannot be surprising that the Holy See

did not know who would rise to what roles. As Gonzalo Redondo explains, the Provisional Government's leadership was a mixed bag: "President Niceto Alcalá Zamora (conservative republican), Secretary of State Alejandro Lerroux (Centrist Radical), Minter of Justice Fernando de los Ríos (Socialist), Minister of Army Manuel Azaña (Acción Republicana), Minister of the Navy Santiago Casares Quiroga (Galician Autonomist), Minter of Housing Indalecio Prieto (Socialist), Minister of the Government Miguel Maura (conservative republican), Minister of Public Education Marcelino Domingo (Radical Socialist), Minister of Promotion Álvero de Albornoz (Radical Socialist), Minister of Labor Francisco Largo Caballero (Socialist), Economics Minister Lluís Nicolau d'Owler (Catalan Autonomist), and Minister of Communications Diego Martínez Barrio (Centrist Radical)," Redondo, p. 131.

41 ASV: AES, Spagna: Fasc. 116 Pos. 784, 84r.
42 ASV: AES, Spagna: Fasc. 116 Pos. 784, 84v.
43 Callahan, p. 278.
44 "La composizione del nuovo Governo raccoglie repubblicani e socialisti." ASV: AES, Spagna: Fasc. 116 Pos. 784, 71r.
45 Payne, *Spain's First Democracy*, p. 27. The central focus of this pact was to unite all supporters of a Republic and undermine King Alfonso XIII's authority. Members of the Basque Nationalist Party (PNV) and Niceto Alcalá-Zamora also attended to support the movement.
46 As Manuel Suárez Cortina explains, while it is fair to say that almost all Republicans were "in one or another manner" anticlericals, it is "unacceptable to categorize" the majority as antireligious. "Clases Populares, Republicanismo y Anticlericalismo en la España del Primer Tercio del Siglo XX" in Julio de la Cueva and Feliciano Montero (eds.), *Izquierda Obrera y Religión en España (1900–1939)* (Alcalá de Henares: Universidad de Alcalá, 2012), p. 26.
47 Álvarez Tardío, *Anticlericalismo y libertad de conciencia*, pp. 133–4.
48 ASV: AES, Spagna: Fasc. 116 Pos. 784, 71r.
49 ASV: AES, Spagna: Fasc. 116 Pos. 784, 71r. Regarding Masonry, Stanley Payne summarizes the consensus about the order in Republican politics by writing, "For over a hundred years the Masonic Orders had been intensely combated in Spain by Catholic conservatives, who saw in Masonry the spearhead of liberal anticlericalism. A sizeable cross section of Republicans were indeed Masons, but historians would later point out that Masons themselves became increasingly politically divided, in some cases ending up on opposite sides in the Civil War. Spanish Masonry clearly did not represent any monolithic conspiracy, though it is also true that by the second year of the Republic the dominant sector of Madrid Masons would become strongly committed to left Republican politics, in turn provoking considerable resistance among the more moderate members of the order," *Spain's First Democracy*, p. 37.
50 Redondo, p. 135.
51 ASV: AES, Spagna: Fasc. 116 Pos. 784, 71–71v.
52 "È difficile, per non dire impossibile che queste forze così diverse possano

fare molto cammino insieme." ASV: AES, Spagna: Fasc. 116 Pos. 784, 78r.
53 See: Ludger Mees, "Clase, Religión y Nación. El Sindicalismo Nacionalista en el País Vasco hasta la Guerra Civil," in Julio de la Cueva and Feliciano Montero (eds.), *Izquierda Obrera y Religión en España (1900–1939)* (Alcalá de Henares: Universidad de Alcalá, 2012), pp. 155–178.
54 Payne, *Spain's First Democracy*, pp. 32–3.
55 ASV: AES, Spagna: Fasc. 116 Pos. 784, 78r.
56 ASV: AES, Spagna: Fasc. 116 Pos. 784, 78v.
57 "Me ha ordenado comunicar a V.E. que la Santa Sede está dispuesta a secundar al Gobierno provisional en la obra de la conservación del orden, en la confianza de que también el Gobierno respetará de su parte los derechos de la Iglesia y de los católicos en una Nación en que la totalidad del pueblo profesa la Religión Católica." ASV: AES, Spagna: Fasc. 116 Pos. 784, 86r.
58 ASV: AES, Spagna: Fasc. 116 Pos. 784, 87r.
59 For a discussion of the specific attacks against Church property and lives, see: José Ramón Hernández Figuieredo, *Destrucción del patrimonio religioso en la II República* (Madrid: Biblioteca Autores Cristianos, 2009), pp. 55–117.
60 Payne, *Spain's First Democracy*, p. 44.
61 Activities at the *Círculo Monárquico* were suspended by the police on the night of 10 May due to the threat of riots. Some monarchist supporters, like the Miralles brothers, were arrested and held in prison for two years until they were acquitted. Following the closure of the building, rumors spread that monarchists had killed a Republican taxi driver. Following this rumor, church burnings spread to other Spanish cities: 41 in Malaga, 21 in Valencia, 13 in Alicante, and 11 in Madrid. In these attacks, however, there were no reported deaths of clergy. Most attacks occurred in cities with strong anarchist unions. As a result of the violence, the Republican government created a new urban police force and arrested hundreds of monarchist agitators. See Payne, *Spain's First Democracy*, p. 46.
62 ASV: AES, Spagna: Fasc. 133 Pos. 787–788, 29r.
63 Stanley G. Payne, "Spain: The Church, the Second Republic, and the Franco Regime" in Richard J. Wolff and Jörg K. Hoensch (eds.), *Catholics, the State, and the European Radical Right, 1919–1945* (Boulder: Social Science Monographs, 1987): pp. 182–198. In his article, Payne argues that the Republic allowed its supporters to act violently, fearing loss of support from its allies if the state intervened.
64 "No si puó certamente dire che il Governo abbia provocato il movimento incendiario; ma é facile il dimostrare che non ha fatto nulla per impedirlo." ASV: AES, Spagna: Fasc. 133 Pos. 787–788, 50v.
65 "Pretesta il Governo che non poteva difendere i troppi numerosi conventi che esistono in Madrid: ma si potrebbe rispondere molto facilmente che se ne poteva difendere almeno uno." ASV: AES, Spagna: Fasc. 133, Pos. 787–788, 51r.
66 ASV: AES, Spagna: Fasc. 133 Pos. 787–788, 51v. While the threat of communists in the government was a primary concern for the Catholic

Church, Stanley Payne explains that the majority of violence against the Church and its property occurred in cities where the anarchist union FAI-CNT (Federación Anarquista Ibérica-Confederación Nacional de Trabajo) was well-represented. Payne, *Spain's First Democracy*, p. 45.
67 Nigel Townson, "A Third Way? Centrist Politics under the Republic," in Manuel Álvarez Tardío and Fernando del Rey Reguillo (eds.), *The Second Republic Revisited: From Democratic Hopes to Civil War (1931–1936)* (Eastbourne: Sussex Academic Press, 2012), pp. 97–113, esp. p. 98.
68 ASV: AES, Spagna: Fasc. 134 Pos. 788, 47r.
69. "Serena y decidida protesta ... noble y católica Nación Española." ASV: AES, Spagna: Fasc. 134 Pos. 788, 62r.

II From Caution to Contention: The Republican Constitution and Catholic Confrontation

1 The Republican coalition in the Cortes (in number of seats): Socialists 113, Radicals 87, Esquerra Republicana 36, Liberal Republican Right 27, Federalists 19, Galicianists 19, Republican Action 16, Radical Socialists 61, Independent Republicans 18, "Al Servicio de la República" 7, Liberal Democrats 4 (Total 407). The Opposition coalition in the Cortes (in number of seats): Basque Nationalists 6, Lliga Catalana 2, Agrarian Party 14, National Action 5, Traditionalists 4, Monarchists 1, Miscellaneous Rightists 19 (Total 51). Stanley Payne, *Spain's First Democracy The Second Republic, 1931–1936* (Madison: University of Wisconsin Press, 1993), p. 51.
2 *Ibid.*, p. 50.
3 Luis Arranz Notario, "Could the Second Republic have Become a Democracy?" in Manuel Álvarez Tardío and Fernando del Rey Reguillo (eds.) *The Second Republic Revisited: From Democratic Hopes to Civil War (1931–1936)* (Eastbourne: Sussex Academic Press, 2012), pp. 20–39, esp. p. 31.
4 "Da ieri sera è ricominciato allarme conventi e case religiose e regna incertezza e panico per maneggi sindacalisti e comunisti che si sforzano impedire elezioni per Cortes del 28 corrente." Archivio Segreto Vaticano (ASV): Affari Ecclesiastici Straordinari, Spagna (AES, Spagna): Fasc. 118 Pos. 784, 11r.
5 While the Nuncio's letter reported on widespread violence, historian Gabriel Jackson concluded that while workers in mining and seaport regions made their opinions well-known through demonstrations, the overall disarray of the moderate and conservative parties was responsible for the Left's victory. Gabriel Jackson, *The Spanish Republic and the Civil War, 1931–1939* (Princeton: Princeton University Press, 1965), p. 41.
6 "El Gobierno provisional, compuesto en su casi totalidad de sectarios, sigue su avance contra los derechos de la Iglesia sin detenerse en su camino." ASV: AES, Spagna: Fasc. 119, Pos. 784, 5_10.
7 "El decreto de la libertad religiosa en la enseñanza habla de *compromisos del Gobierno*? Con quien?? Hasta donde llegan estos compromisos?" ASV: AES, Spagna: Fasc. 119 Pos. 784, 5_10.
8 ASV: AES, Spagna: Fasc. 119 Pos. 784, 05_42, 05_46.

9   "Los documentos pastorales en estas circumstancias deberán ser publicados con singular cuidado por los graves peligros que encierra su interpretación" ASV: AES, Spagna: Fasc. 119 Pos. 784, 05_21.
10 Payne, *Spain's First Democracy*, p. 43.
11 José M. Sánchez, *The Spanish Civil War as a Religious Tragedy* (Notre Dame, Indiana: University of Notre Dame Press, 1987), pp. 53–55.
12 *Ibid.*
13 ASV: AES, Spagna: Fasc. 119 Pos. 784, 05_26.
14 See: Joel Blatt, "Ralliement" in *Encyclopedia of the Vatican and Papacy*, Frank J. Coppa (ed.) (Westport: Greenwood Press, 1999), pp. 350–1.
15 Sánchez, p. 53 and Hilari Raguer, *Gunpowder and Incense: The Catholic Church and the Spanish Civil War* (London: Routledge, 2007), p.16.
16 Raguer, p. 20.
17 Nigel Townson, *The Crisis of Democracy in Spain* (Brighton: Sussex Academic Press, 2000), p. 51.
18 "Una fuerza defensiva de los intereses católicos" ASV: AES, Spagna: Fasc. 122 Pos. 784, 94bis.
19 "'No existe religión de Estado. La Iglesia Católica será considerada como corporación de derecho público. El mismo carácter podrán tener las demás confesiones religiosas cuando lo soliciten y, por su constitución y el número de sus miembros ofrezcan garantías de subsistencia.'" Esaminiamo per parti questo articolo redatto in una forma assoluta e quasi aspri.
    'No existe religión de Estado.' Che si vuol dire con questo? Logicamente esaminata questa proposizione viene ad essere universale e negativa e si risolve in questa altra: la religione dello stato non esiste. Dal che si deduce che nessun stato tiene o deve tenere una religione, il che è quanto dire che lo Stato è ateo: errore condannato dalla Chiesa e dalla stessa ragione. Lo stato come l'uomo dipende da Dio nella sua esistenza e nel suo governo e deve riconoscere questa dipendenza e rendergli il dovuto culto professando la unica vera religione.
    Secondo gli autori dell'ante progetto la nazione spagnola non ha religione e si dichiara atea: espelle dunque Dio dal suo seno e commette perciò un vero deicidio sociale." ASV: AES, Spagna: Fasc. 136 Pos. 789, 58r.
20 "L'articolo in parola dice che rimane garantita la libertà di coscienza. Questo è falso, perchè quello che con tale disposizione resta garantita è la libertà dell'errore e de la irreligione." ASV: AES, Spagna: Fasc. 136 Pos. 789, 60v.
21 ASV: AES, Spagna: Fasc. 136 Pos. 789, 8r.
22 "Il Communismo Sovietico e la Rivoluzione Spagnuola," *La Civiltà Cattolica*, 10 July 1931, Volume III, p. 123.
23 "La questione che ora si dibatte nella Spagna, non è una semplice manifestizione di ostilità contro questo o quell'Ordine religioso; è una vera dichiarazione di guerra alla Chiesa Cattolica e a tutto ciò ch'essa rappresenta; guerra aperta, ufficiale senz'altre attenuazioni che non siano quella ispirate da una politica satanica, per menare più sicuramente il colpo e rendere irreparabile la rovina." "La Bufera Anticlericale Spagnuola" in *La Civiltà Cattolica*, 31 October 1931, Volume IV, p. 225.

24 "Le Changement de Régime en Espagne" in *L'Esprit Internationale*, 20 October 1931, Number 20.
25 Payne, *Spain's First Democracy*, pp. 81–2.
26 *Ibid.*
27 *Ibid.*
28 *Ibid.* and Sandie Holguín, *Creating Spaniards: Cultural and National Identity in Republican Spain* (Madison: University of Wisconsin Press, 2002).
29 Arranz Notario, p. 27.
30 Payne, *Spain's First Democracy*, 83.
31 Fernando De Meer Lecha Marzo, *La Constitución de la II República: Autonomías, Propiedad, Iglesia, Eseñanza* (Pamplona: EUNSA, 1978), pp. 131–165.
32 Socialist support helped Article 26 pass, Julio de la Cueva Merino, "Socialistas y Religión en la Segunda República: De la Liga Nacional Laica al Inicio de la Guerra Civil," in Julio de la Cueva and Feliciano Montero (eds.), *Izquierda Obrera y Religión en España (1900–1939)* (Alcalá de Henares: Universidad de Alcalá, 2012), pp. 84–5.
33 Frances Lannon, *Privilege, Persecution, and Prophecy: The Catholic Church in Spain, 1875–1975* (Oxford: Clarendon Press, 1987), p.186.
34 William J. Callahan, *The Catholic Church in Spain, 1875–1998* (Washington, D.C., The Catholic University of America Press, 2001) p. 274.
35 "Conservazione Congregazioni Religiosi è battaglia grave. Ma essa difenderà conservazione di tutte in blocco, avvertendo però che se si suscita questione concreta Compagnia di Gesù novanta probabilità su cento sono per la negativa." ASV: AES, Spagna: Fasc. 118 Fasc. 784, 33r.
36 ASV: AES, Spagna: Fasc. 118 Pos. 784, 35r.
37 ASV: AES, Spagna: Fasc. 118 Pos. 784, 68r.
38 ASV: AES, Spagna: Fasc. 118 Pos. 784, 69r.
39 "Partito socialista e radicale socialista nella riunione di ieri hanno deciso votare integralmente articolo dissoluzione ordini religiosi e confiscazione beni." ASV: AES, Spagna: Fasc. 118 Pos. 784, 70r.
40 Manuel Álvarez Tardío, *Anticlericalismo y libertad de conciencia: Política, religion en la Segunda República Española, 1931–1936* (Madrid: Centros de Estudios Políticos y Costitucionales, 2002), pp.173–195.
41 *Ibid.*
42 Nigel Townson, "A Third Way? Centrist Politics under the Republic," in Manuel Álvarez Tardío and Fernando del Rey Reguillo (eds.), *The Second Republic Revisited: From Democratic Hopes to Civil War (1931–1936)* (Eastbourne: Sussex Academic Press, 2012), pp. 97–113, esp. p. 100.
43 ASV: AES, Spagna: Fasc. 192 Pos. 808–809, 29r.
44 "Les he contestado que espero que la S. Sede nos dará instrucciones pertinentes a estos asuntos." ASV: AES, Spagna: Fasc. 192, Pos. 808–809, 30r.
45 ASV: AES, Spagna: Fasc. 192. Pos. 808–809, 32r.
46 "A hateful disparity" ASV: AES, Spagna: Fasc. 192 Pos. 808–809, 32v.
47 According to Álvarez Tardío, the Radical Socialists were well aware that the

legalization of divorce would be a clear attack against the Church's confessional rights over marriage; they were hoping to reduce the Church's social control, Álvarez Tardío, p. 231.

48   The Second Republic's attempts to legalize civil marriage were not the first in Spain. In 1870, numerous Catholic clergymen spoke out publicly against Spain's attempt to legalize civil matrimony: "Civil marriage, although limited by the Cánovas government only to those who were obviously non-Catholic, that is, those who had not been baptized in the Catholic Church." The Church used the Spanish courts to prevent civil marriage. Therefore, the battle over civil marriage was not a new problem in 1931, but had decades of previous conflict. Previously, Church pressure had won these types of battles by reiterating Spain's commitment to Catholicism, but during the Second Republic the Church failed. Callahan, pp. 171–2.

49   ASV: AES, Spagna: Fasc. 192 Pos. 809, 12v.

50   ASV: AES, Spagna: Fasc. 192 Pos. 809, 16v.

51   After the July 1936 "Uprising," Franco and his supporters frequently argued that their actions were meant to return traditional and Catholic elements to Spain, but this was not the central reason for their actions. See: Chapter IV.

52   "Mentre i piú gravi problemi della vita Nazionale incombono su questa disgraziata Nazione, ed attendono invani la loro risoluzione, il Governo Repubblicano ha avuto un'altra peregrina idea contro la Chiesa e si é affrettato a convertirla in decreto, dando con cio un'altra soddisfazione ai settarii ed ai massoni. Il nuovo aggravio verte su di un particolare che, tra le altre cose, non solo preoccupava la Spagna, ma neppure le era passato per la anticamera del cervello. Mi riferisco alla <u>cremazione</u>, che é stata legalmente disciplinata da un Decreto a firma del cattolico Presidente della Repubblica, Signor Alcalá-Zamora, e del Ministro della Gobernación, Signor Santiago Casares Quiroga." ASV: AES, Spagna: Fasc. 200 Pos. 823–824, 3r.

53   Payne, *Spain's First Democracy*, p. 73.

54   "Ed é un evidente sopruso anche il disporre che la voluntá di parenti atei possa far cremare il cadavere di un buon cristiano." ASV: AES, Spagna: Fasc. 200 Fasc. 823–824, 4r.

55   ASV: AES, Spagna: Fasc. 200 Fasc. 823–824, 4v.

56   Payne *Spain's First Democracy*, p. 83. Like civil marriage, previous Spanish governments had attempted to take control over Catholic cemeteries. William J. Callahan writes, "Conflicts over cemeteries made their way into the courts with monotonous frequency. The Church claimed that cemeteries were ecclesiastical property over which it had administrative control, meaning in practical terms that it fell to the parish priest to decide who would or would not be buried in consecrated ground. Between 1868 and 1873 the secularization of cemeteries by the government produced endless conflicts between clergy and local authorities. Cánovas yielded to ecclesiastical pressure and recognized the clergy's exclusive right to determine who was eligible for burial in local cemeteries. The Church denied intern-

ment to 'public sinners,' those who refused extreme unction, or had renounced Catholicism, or were Protestant or freethinkers." Individuals who could not find a private cemetery had to be buried outside graveyard's walls in unkempt and unprotected land—which was a severe insult. Callahan, p. 172. Following the secularization of cemeteries in 1932, "Wars of the Dead" began throughout Spain as many municipalities tore down graveyard walls. J. Albertí in *La Iglesia en Llamas: La Persecución Religiosa en España durante la Guerra Civil* (Barcelona: Ediciones Destino), p. 147, tells of the Barcelona city council ordering the walls of its cemeteries torn down—ending Church control over the land.

57 ASV: AES, Spagna: Fasc. 200 Pos. 823–824, 6r.
58 "Le Cortes, quando si tratta della Chiesa, non sentono altra misione che quella di opporsi ad essa in tutto e per tutto, rifiutandosi di esaminare qualsiasi ragione e frustrando ogni tentativo di ragionamento da parte dei cattolici. [. . .] Queste disposizione fanno tremare pensando a quelle che saranno le discussioni sul progetto di legge delle Relazioni fra la Chiesa e lo Stato." ASV: AES, Spagna: Fasc. 200 Pos. 823–824, 7v.
59 "Los católicos que hayan cumplido veinte años, si quieren ser enterrados en cementerio católico, deben firmar inmediatamente tres declaraciones como la presente. Una deben llevarla siempre consigo en la cartera o en el bolso; otra, para entregar en su parraoquia, donde la archivarán; y otra, para ponerla en la cabecera de la cama o en sitio conocido de la familia." ASV: AES, Spagna: Fasc. 200 Pos. 823–824, 19_3r.
60 "Yo [nombre y apellidos] DECLARO ser católico apostólico romano y querer morir, como he vivido, en el seno de la Iglesia Católica. RUEGO a mis familiares, amigos y a cuantos bien me quieran, tengan la caridad de avisarme cuando me vieren en punto de muerte, y me procuren un sacerdote católico que me administre los santos sacramentos, que desde ahora deseo y pido. DISPONGO de modo terminante y expreso que a mi cadáver se le dé sepultura eclesiástica en tierra sagrada, con todas las ceremonias, ritos y bendiciones de la Iglesia católica, y que sobre mi sepultura, bendecida por sacerdote católico, se ponga la Santa Cruz." ASV: AES, Spagna: Fasc. 200 Pos. 823–824, 19_2r.
61 ASV: AES, Spagna: Fasc. 200 Pos. 823–824, 41r.
62 Callahan, p. 293.
63 ASV: AES, Spagna: Fasc. 200 Pos. 823–824, 45r-v.
64 "il Governo del Generale Franco continua nella sua opera di ricostruzione cristiana e patriottica; e le disposizione su accennate sono state accolte con viva approvazione dal popolo spagnuolo, il quale ha sempre avuto per i Cimiteri, ravvivati dalle speranza della vita eterna, una pietà intima e una speciale cura." ASV: AES, Spagna: Fasc. 200 Pos. 823–824, 79v.
65 "Il Santo Padre, colectivamente informato al riguardo, ha presso conoscenza di tale legge col più vivo interesse paternamente complaciato al medesimo tempo di questa nuove prove di filiale devozione alla Chiesa data del Generalísimo Franco." ASV: AES, Spagna: Pos. 200 Pos. 823–824, 81ar.
66 Following chapters will explore the Vatican's concerns regarding

Nationalist actions during the war—especially the assassination of Basque priests and the aerial bombardment of cities.
67 Payne, *Spain's First Democracy*, p. 68.
68 *Ibid.*, p. 73.
69 *Ibid.*, pp. 73–4.
70 "La draconiana legge per la difesa della Repubblica, usata esclusivamente contro i cattolici . . . ." ASV: AES, Spagna: Fasc. 150 Pos. 791, 25r-26r. Azaña's Government used The Law of Defense of the Republic to close a wide variety of newspapers that shared opinions contradictory to the Republic. Rafael Guerrero Moreno, in his article "La Prensa en la Segunda República: breve aproximación como contexto vital de don Diego Martínez Barrio" in *Ámbito* 7–8 (2001–2002): pp. 327–337, esp. p. 331, lists conservative newspapers in Andalucia closed: *ABC* (Monarchist), *El Debate* (Catholic), *El Correo* (in Sevilla), *El Cronista* (in Málaga), *El pueblo católico* (in Jaén), and *La Información* (in Cádiz). Each of these newspapers was suspended for various periods in 1932. While many other papers were censored, this short list gives better insight into the types of papers targeted. The Government also suspended the publication of communist newspapers like *Mundo Obrero*, *Solidaridad Obrera*, *El Liberario*, and *La Tierra*. Enrique Gomez-Reino y Carnot's "La Libertad de Expresion en la Segunda República" in *Revista de Derecho Político* 12 (1981–2): pp. 159–187, esp. pp. 177–8.
71 While Catholic leaders considered the law antireligious, other groups were tried and convicted under this law. Enrique Gomez-Reino y Carnot describes the 11 February 1933 trial of the periodical *La Gaceta del Norte* at the Tribunal de Garantías. The newspaper published a photo of Catholics visiting a monument of the Sagrado Corázon de Jesús. In the background, state police were making obscene gestures. Because the newspaper had published the photo, which hurt the image of the state, the Tribunal fined *La Gaceta del Norte* 10,000 pesetas. The Tribunal also fined the newspaper *Euzkadi* 10,000 pesetas for its article "Amai-katako" [Talking with the Government] published on 28 October 1932. The Tribunal considered the article to be an encroachment into the Government's privacy. Gomez-Reino y Carnot, pp. 183–5.
72 As Manuel Álvarez Tardío explains, Socialists viewed the Law of Confessions and Religious Congregations as a major success. The law was meant to put an end to the religious problems of the Republic. The two main goals were to remove the influence of the Catholic Church over education and to finalize the process for a liberal and secular society, p. 262. William J. Callahan explains, "The law of Confessions and Religious Congregations was the most important piece of religious legislation passed by the Republic. First, it represented as coherent a statement of principles as the regime ever produced on the Church . . . Second, along with this affirmation of modern liberal thought ran another underlying theme, the necessity of keeping the Church and the clergy under government control," p. 310. Callahan continues, "The Law on Religious Confessions and Congregations embodied the fundamental strengths and weaknesses of the

Republic's policy towards the Church. The separation of Church and State and the commitment to religious liberty and freedom of conscience, although sullied on occasion by manifestations of crude anticlericalism, were by any standard significant achievements. The Republic did not intend to destroy Catholicism, nor was its legislation even remotely capable of reducing the Church to religious, social, and political impotence. But it erred in abandoning nineteenth-century republicanism's commitment to a 'free Church in a free State.' The Republic continued in more extreme form the historic regalism long associated with Spanish governments; and yet, even though, the Church profited from nineteenth-century regalism in some respects, it had always resented its restrictions. The more extreme republican version, laced as it was with strong anticlerical residues, made conflict with the Church inevitable. Having rejected a negotiated settlement with the Church and the papacy, the Republic needed to liberate itself from the ghosts of ancient civil-ecclesiastical battles through the creation of a secular State in which the Church could function free of government tutelage," pp. 302–3. The Law of Religious Confessions and Congregations, therefore, was the clearest step the Republic could have done to increase secular thought in the state. The Republic viewed the legislation as a way to protect the state. For the Church, it was a direct attack against Catholicism. This project does not intend to show that the Republic was "wrong" in its legislation, or that the Church was "wrong" in its concerns, but that the problems of clear intentions and miscommunications between the two entities made the situation worse for the Republic and for the Holy See. For a discussion of the Socialist Party's involvement, see: De la Cueva Merino, pp. 85–7.

73 Payne, *Spain's First Democracy*, p. 84.
74 ASV: AES, Spagna: Fasc. 183 Pos. 805, 40r.
75 Letter from Tedeschini 2 May 1932, "Il Ministro ascoltava con rispetto, e dirò anche con docilità. E perfino ascoltò con rispetto la diatriba con la quale io conclusi il mio ragionamento: voi state scrivendo, dissi io, una pagina indegna e che dovrà essere corretta; voi state abusando della nostra pazienza, e ne abusate a scienza Coscienza, perché sapete che la Chiesa non solo non usa mai la violenza, ma considera una virtù la pazienza e il sacrificio." ASV: AES, Spagna: Fasc. 183 Pos. 805, 42v-43r.
76 ASV: AES, Spagna: Fasc. 183. Pos. 805, 71r.
77 "The true evil" ASV: AES, Spagna: Fasc. 183 Pos. 805, 71v.
78 "E specialmente bisognerà emettere una più che energica protesta in occasione della prossima legge sulle Confessioni e sulle Congregazioni Religiose." ASV: AES, Spagna: Fasc. 183 Pos. 805, 74r.
79 "... mala y llena de pesimismo." ASV: AES, Spagna: Fasc. 151 Pos. 791, 5r.
80 ASV: AES, Spagna: Fasc. 151 Pos. 791, 5r.
81 ASV: AES, Spagna: Fasc. 151 Pos. 791, 11r.
82 "Una Enciclica sulle condizioni religiosi della Spagna (a) sarebbe molto ampia perché dovrebbe riccordare almeno le più gravi violazioni dei diritti della Chiesa e delle anime: (b) sembrerebbe piuttosto in ritardo dopo tante iniquità compiute dai nuovi governanti di Spanga: (c) data la solennità del

documento, potrebbe più facilmente esser causa di un isaprimento delle misure persecutorie.

D'altra parte sembra doversi affermare la necessità che la Santa Sede faccia udire pubblicamente la sua voce .Si potrebbe forse prendere occasione dalla nuova legge sulle Congregazioni religiose per elevare una pubblica formale protesta. Da notare che nella nuova legge sono, più o meno, contenuti i più gravi errori e le più enormi pretese dello Stato già pur troppo affermati nella Costituzione. Infatti:

(1) all'art. 1º si ricorda la Costituzione e la libertà di Coscienza.

(2) All'art 2º si ricorda la separazione dello Stato della Chiesa.

(3) Tutta la legge è ispirate al concetto di totale supremazia dello Stato sulla Chiesa: lo Stato dispone di cose e persona sacre senza alcuna limitazione: dichiara propietà pubblica chiesa, episcopi, seminarii, monastery, oggetti d'arte.

(4) Proibisco ai religiosi di insegnare, assume la tutela dei religio fridfraghi, ecc.

Schema dell'enciclica

ESORDIO. Parole di rammarico, di affetto verso la Spagna, esortazione alla preghiera

PREGIUDIZIALE. La Chiesa non è nemica di nessuna forma di governo. Anzi la Chiesa stessa è il migliore ausilio per conservare la concordia e la pace.

DEPLORAZIONE delle violenze commesse contro cose e persone sacre e delle disposizione costituzionali avverese a Dio e alla religione.

In particolare si deplora:

(a) la separazione della Chiesa dallo Stato e la forma che a detta separazione si è voluto dare.

(b) La soppressione degli assegni al clero dovuti per giustizia

(c) La soppressione della Compagnia di Gesù con una mo"vazione che offendo lo stesso Vicario di Cristo. (d) Le limitazioni fatte agli ordini religiosi, specialmente con la proibizione dell'insegnamento.

(e) Le disposizione contro la santità del matrimonio.

Si conclude esortando a far del tutto con i mezzi legittimi per far cambiar la Costituzione, a rimaner concordi, a dare impulso all'Azione Cattolica, a perseverare nella preghiera." ASV: AES, Spagna: Fasc. 209 Pos. 833, 92r–93r.

83 Pope Pius XI, *Dilectissima Nobis*, 3 June 1933, Introduction.
84 *Ibid*, Paragraph 2.
85 *Ibid*, Paragraph 4.
86 *Ibid*, Paragraph 19.
87 *Ibid*, Paragraph 26.
88 ASV: AES, Spagna: Fasc. 210 Pos. 833, 51r, 53r, 55r, etc.
89 ASV: AES, Spagna: Fasc. 210 Pos. 833, 69r.
90 ASV: AES, Spagna: Fasc. 210 Pos. 833, 75r.
91 "Ante las protestas sediciosas de la Santa Sede y del Episcopado español, de las coacciones y amenazas de los órganos de la prensa de la extrema derecha y las propagandas de los elementos reaccionarios, aconsejando actitudes de

rebeldía y de desobediencia con motivo de la ley de Confesiones y Congregaciones Religiosas ... " ASV: AES, Spagna: Fasc. 210 Pos. 833, 78v.
92 ASV: AES, Spagna: Fasc. 210 Pos. 833, 79r.
93 "Nuevas agresiones a la libertad." "La Ley de Confesiones y Congregaciones Religiosas," *Cruz y Raya*, 15 Madrid 1933, p. 122.
94 ASV: AES, Spagna: Fasc. 210 Pos. 833, 81r and 82r.
95 ASV: AES, Spagna: Fasc. 210 Pos. 833, 81v.
96 ASV: AES, Spagna: Fasc. 210 Pos. 833, 83r-83v.
97 16 November 1931, ASV: AES, Spagna: Fasc. 170 Pos. 799–800, 5r.
98 28 November 1931, ASV: AES, Spagna: Fasc. 170 Pos. 799–800, 6r.
99 ASV: AES, Spagna: Fasc. 170, Pos. 799–800, 10r.
100 ASV: AES, Spagna: Fasc. 170, Pos. 799–800, 29r.
101 Paloma Aguilar, in her monograph, *Memory and Amnesia: The Role of the Spanish Civil War in the Transition to Democracy* (London: Berghahn Press, 2002), argues that the creation of the 1978 Spanish Constitution was centered on the idea of avoiding similarities to 1931, especially the creation of a bicameral legislature to slow the passage of legislation. The Spanish state had learned a great deal from the failed period of 1931–1939. James O'Connell goes as far as to argue that moderation of religious legislation might have helped the Republican Government survive, but another problem, such as class-warfare, would likely doomed the state. "The Spanish Republic: Further Reflections on Its Anticlerical Policies," in *The Catholic Historical Review*, vol. 57, 2 (July 1971): pp. 275–289, esp. pp. 288–9.

III Republic Reorganizations: Elections of 1933 and 1936

1 Stanley Payne, *Spain's First Democracy* (Madison: University of Wisconsin Press, 1993), pp. 338–347.
2 *Ibid.*, pp. 353–359.
3 See Chapters I & II for an in-depth discussion of the Vatican hierarchy's reactions to the Second Spanish Republic.
4 Payne, *Spain's First Democracy*, pp.135–145.
5 *Ibid*, p.168.
6 *Ibid.*
7 CEDA's growth was centered on fears of secularization, especially under the leadership of Manuel Azaña. CEDA pushed for "Catholic Corporatism" in Spain, in politics and economics. Overall, the main focus of CEDA was to return Catholic influence to all elements in Spanish society. See Payne, *Spain's First Democracy*, pp. 168–171.
8 Manuel Álvarez Tardío, "The CEDA: Threat or Opportunity?" in Manuel Álvarez Tardío and Fernando del Rey Reguillo (eds.), *The Second Republic Revisited: From Democratic Hopes to Civil War (1931–1936)* (Eastbourne: Sussex Academic Press, 2012), pp. 58– 79, esp. p. 58.
9 The Revolutionary left won 2.24% of the vote, Socialists 19.84%, Left Republicans 14.13%, Center Republicans 30.01%, Moderate Right 24.25%, Extreme Right 9.15% and .38% for the Miscellaneous Parties. Payne *Spain's First Democracy*, pp. 179–180.

10 Nigel Townson, *The Crisis of Democracy in Spain* (Brighton: Sussex Academic Press, 2000), p. 194.
11 Álvarez Tardío, "The CEDA," pp. 70, 74–5.
12 Payne, *Spain's First Democracy*, pp. 178–180.
13 Álvarez Tardío, "The CEDA," p. 75.
14 Enrique Moradiellos, *1936: Los Mitos de la Guerra Civil* (Barcelona: Ediciones Peninsula, 2004), p. 56.
15 See: Townson, *The Crisis of Democracy in Spain* and José Alvarez-Junco, *The Emergence of Mass Politics in Spain* (Brighton: Sussex Academic Press, 2002).
16 Nigel Townson, "A Third Way? Centrist Politics under the Republic," in Manuel Álvarez Tardío and Fernando del Rey Reguillo (eds.), *The Second Republic Revisited: From Democratic Hopes to Civil War (1931–1936)* (Eastbourne: Sussex Academic Press, 2012), pp. 97–113, esp. p. 105.
17 *Ibid.*, p. 109.
18 Payne, *Spain's First Democracy*, pp. 183–5.
19 Political parties of both extremes prevented the Parliamentary system from working normally. Personal and political arguments trumped the normal governmental activities. *Ibid*, p. 188.
20 Townson, *The Crisis of Democracy in Spain*, p. 201.
21 Unemployment increased due to three concerns: the global depression, Republican reforms, and slow modernization of the Spanish economy. Payne, *Spain's First Democracy*, pp. 154–5.
22 Paul Preston, "Spain's October Revolution and the Rightists Grasp for Power" in *Journal of Contemporary History* 10, 4 (Oct. 1975): pp. 555–578, esp. pp. 560–1. See: Carlos José Márquez, *Cómo se ha escrito la Guerra Civil española* (Madrid: Ediciones Lengua de Trapo, SL, 2006).
23 Preston, "Spain's October Revolution," p. 569.
24 Álvarez Tardío, "The CEDA," pp. 73–4.
25 Mariano García de las Heras González, "La Revolución de Asturias, ¿Primer Acto de la Guerra Civil?" in *Ab Initio* 1 (2010): 169–194, esp. pp. 170–1.
26 José Manuel Macarro, "The Socialists and Revolution" in Manuel Álvarez Tardío and Fernando del Rey Reguillo (eds.), *The Second Republic Revisited: From Democratic Hopes to Civil War (1931–1936)* (Eastbourne: Sussex Academic Press, 2012), pp. 40–57, esp. pp. 41, 50.
27 García, p. 173
28 For a discussion of the attacks against religious sites, see: José Ramón Hernández Figuieredo, *Destrucción del patrimonio religioso en la II República* (Madrid: Biblioteca Autores Cristianos, 2009), pp. 119–190.
29 Payne, *Spain's First Democracy*, p. 213–14.
30 William J. Callahan, *The Catholic Church in Spain, 1875–1998* (Washington, D.C., The Catholic University of America Press, 2001), p. 360.
31 Payne, *Spain's First Democracy*, pp. 218–220.
32 Francisco Franco led this army during this revolt, crystallizing his hatred of the political left. Enrique Moradiellos, "Francisco Franco: The Soldier

Who Became Caudillo" in Alejandro Quiroga and Miguel Ángel del Arco (eds), *Right-wing Spain in the Civil War Era* (London: Continuum, 2012): 117–146, esp. p. 125.
33 Paul Preston, *The Spanish Holocaust* (London: W.W. Norton and Company, 2012), pp. 81–3.
34 *Ibid.*
35 Gabriel Jackson, *The Spanish Republic and the Civil War, 1931–1939* (Princeton: Princeton University Press, 1965), p. 167.
36 See: Sánchez.
37 Payne, *Spain's First Democracy*, p. 254.
38 *Ibid.*, pp. 233–260.
39 Beginning in 1934, the International Komintern developed plans for Popular Fronts to unify all parties of the political left to defeat the growing rise of fascism. The hope was a bourgeois-proletariat alliance could succeed. See: Martin S. Alexander and Helen Graham (eds.), *The French and Spanish Popular Front: Comparative Perspectives* (New York: Cambridge University Press, 1989), pp. 5–20.
40 Payne, *Spain's First Democracy*, p. 256.
41 Gabriele Ranzato, "The Republican Left and the Defense of Democracy, 1934–1936," in Manuel Álvarez Tardío and Fernando del Rey Reguillo (eds.), *The Second Republic Revisited: From Democratic Hopes to Civil War (1931–1936)* (Eastbourne: Sussex Academic Press, 2012), pp. 80–96, esp. pp. 93–4.
42 Popular Front Parties won 263 seats, representing 18 different parties—from Communists to Galicianists. The Center coalition earned 54 seats, a major drop. The rightist Bloque Nacional won 156 seats, with CEDA winning 101. Payne, *Spain's First Democracy*, pp. 274–5.
43 *Ibid.*, pp. 305–8.
44 *Ibid*, p. 145.
45 Francesc Vidal i Barraquer was born in Cambrils in Tarragona. He studied at a Jesuit university, and later earned a doctorate in 1900. In 1895, Vidal entered seminary, and he became a priest in 1899. In 1913, he was named Bishop, Archbishop of Tarragona in 1919, and Cardinal in 1921. According to historians, Vidal was concerned with Catalan regionalist questions, often giving him problems with the former monarchy and Dictator Primo de Rivera. He was much less aggressive towards the Second Republic's leadership than many others in the Spanish Catholic hierarchy. See: Vicente Cárcel Ortí, *Pío XI entre la República y Franco* (Madrid: Biblioteca de Autores Cristianos, 2008), pp. 383–4 and Mateo Madridejos, *Diccionario onomástico de la guerra civil* (Barcelona: Flor del Viento Ediciones, 2006), p. 353.
46 "Parecía que el Presidente de la República no le era actuación del Gobierno Azaña y sus aliados, y para ponerle de manifiesto los conflictos que han de acarrear la aplicación de las leyes laicizadoras y las dificultades de una politica sectaria y persecutaria de la religion, le envié copias de la comunicación dirigida al Presidente del Consejo, firmada por los Cardinales."

Archivio Segreto Vaticano (ASV): Affari Ecclesiastici Straordinari, Spagna (AES, Spagna): Fasc. 213 Pos. 835, DSCN6391.

47 "Lerroux es un hombre laíco, pero no sectario como algunos de su partido. Creo tendrá un criterio de más transigencia, y si hace las nuevas elecciones y triunfan los elementos suyos y los de centro podremos esperar inteligencia con la Sta.Sede." ASV: AES, Spagna: Fasc. 213 Pos. 835, DSCN6392.

48 "En resumen, la Iglesia va a ganar algo con el cambio." ASV: AES, Spagna: Fasc. 213 Pos. 835, DSCN6392.

49 Frank J. Coppa, *The Policies and Politics of Pope Pius XII* (New York: Peter Lang, 2011), p. 87.

50 Payne, *Spain's First Democracy*, pp. 227–8.

51 Lerroux's cabinet was a mixture of Centrist Radicals and leftists: President of the Government Lerroux (Radical), Secretary of the State Claudio Sánchez Albornoz (Acción Republicana), Minister of the Interior Diego Martínez Barrios (Radical), Justice Minister Juan Botella Asensi (Republican Socialist), Minister of War Juan José Rocha (Radical), Minister of the Navy Vicente Iranzo (Independent), Minister of Housing Antonio Lara (Radical), Minister of Public Works Rafael Guerra del Río (Radical), Minister of Agriculture Ramón Feced (Radical Socialist), Minister of Industry and Commerce Laureano Gómez Paratcha (Galician Republican), Minister of Communications Miguel Santaló (Catalan Left), Minister of Employment Ricardo Samper (Radical). ASV: AES, Spagna: Fasc. 213 Pos. 835, DSCN6399–4000.

52 Barrios was a Grand Master in the Spanish Masons, from Sevilla. He was a member of the Centrist Radical party, but in 1934, he left the party and established the Unión Republicana, which was to the left of Lerroux's party. Madridejos, p. 214.

53 ASV: AES, Spagna: Fasc. 213 Pos. 835, DSCN6400, 17/9/1933.

54 ASV: AES, Spagna: Fasc. 213 Pos. 835, DSCN6405.

55 ASV: AES, Spagna: Fasc. 213 Pos. 835, DSCN6405.

56 ASV: AES, Spagna: Fasc. 213 Pos. 835, DSCN6409.

57 "Le Cortes, le diaboliche Cortes, che abbiamo patito per quasi due anni e mezzo, e che hanno fatto opera di persecuzione incontrastata e feroce, non accordando a nessuna persona e a nessuna ragione al mondo, la posoibilità di essere, non dirò ascoltato e soddisfatto, ma neppure di essere ammesso a belligeranza." ASV: AES, Spagna: Fasc. 213 Pos. 835, DSCN6415-6.

58 Payne, *Spain's First Democracy,* pp. 183–4.

59 *Ibid.*

60 On 6 October 1934, Companys declared a Catalan State within a Republican Federation, leading to some rebellion in the region. Lerroux's government ordered the military to enter the city and end the Rebellion. Madridejos, p. 96.

61 Payne, pp. 201–5.

62 *Ibid.*, p. 203.

63 "Che mirava a Catalugna come un campo fortificato di resistenza delle forze di sinistra," ASV: AES, Spagna: Fasc. 240 Pos. 856, DSCN6430.

64 Payne, *Spain's First Democracy*, pp. 205–6.
65 ASV: AES, Spagna: Fasc. 240 Pos. 856, DSCN6432.
66 "avremo in Vasconia una ripetizione della dolorosa situazione di Catalugna. E questo è il punto più doloroso per la Chiesa nella questione in parola, pur essando tanto doloroso quello della ingerenza ed anzi della iniziativa del Clero e dei Religiosi in questa questione eminentemente politica e scandalosamente antispagnuola. ASV: AES, Spagna: Fasc. 240 Pos. 856, DSCN6433.
67 "la questione regionalista che produrrá la prossima crisi politica." ASV: AES, Spagna: Fasc. 240 Pos. 856, DSCN6434
68 ASV: AES, Spagna: Fasc. 240 Pos. 856, DSCN6427.
69 ASV: AES, Spagna: Fasc. 240 Pos. 856, DSCN6437.
70 "perseverar en la política de centro-derecha . . . la que puede proporcionar mejores resultados para la Iglesia con una evolución paciente y sagaz que conduzca al momento propicio de la revision constitucional." ASV: AES, Spagna: Fasc. 240 Pos. 856, DSCN6421.
71 "Desde el punto de vista de la los altos intereses de la Iglesia, no es temerario confiar que el Nuevo Gobierno constituya una mayor garantía de estabilidad y comprensión." ASV: AES, Spagna: Fasc. 240 Pos. 856, DSCN6422.
72 Ranzato, p. 89.
73 "El ex-Presidente Azaña y los socialistas aliados con los comunistas." ASV: AES, Spagna: Fasc. 240 Pos. 856, DSCN6423.
74 ASV: AES, Spagna: Fasc. 240 Pos. 856, DSCN6423.
75 "No es dable en este momento tener exacta visión de los estragos producidos; puédese, sin embargo, apreciar el gran volume y extensión de las organizaciones en armas, que de muchos meses veníanse preparando para el momento propicio en que pudieron apoderarse del poder a fin de restablecer el más extreme radicalismo político-social-antireligioso, y aun la dictadura del proletariado [. . .] el vínculo de union de todos los extremismos de izquierda y la occasion, repetidamente annunciada, de realizar el ataque violent y armado contra el Presidente de la República, el Parlamento actual, y las derechas gubernamentales." ASV: AES, Spagna: Fasc. 240 Pos. 856, DSCN6423
76 "En Cataluña, cuyo Gobierno autónomo conservaba la Esquerra (Izquierda) por medios de violencia política y agitación social de los campesinos, es donde más claro ha aparecido el carácter mencionado de extremism izquierdista que ofrece el movimiento en toda España, puesto que así como en Madrid actuaba la dirección socialista de la revolución, en Barcelona el ex-Presidente Azaña con sus más personales elementos politicos y técnicos dirigía la conexión de la Esquerra regional con todo el izquierdismo español . . . la auténtica Cataluña iba a ser sacrificada por el radicalismo izquierdista compromentiendo su propio régimen autonómico. ASV: AES, Spagna: Fasc. 240 Pos. 856, DSCN6424–5.
77 "come in Asturias, si sarebbe dato conto che si preparava il movimento rivoluzionario più vasto e più grave che la Spagna abbia visto da molti anni." ASV: AES, Spagna: Fasc. 240 Pos. 856, DSCN6440.

78 "Se non fosse stato questo tratto provvidenziale, la Spagna si sarebbe cambiata in un campo di lotta fratricida, con gli orrori inconcepibili che notizie particolari affermano si siano compiuti in Asturas." ASV: AES, Spagna: Fasc. 240 Pos. 856, DSCN6441.
79 Paul Preston, *The Spanish Holocaust*, p. 87.
80 "Se il Governo centrale non riuscirà a risovere con energia questi problemi, per la Spagna non sarà affatto giunta la anelata ora di salvezza, e le giornate sanguinose di questo ottobre si riprodurranno e presto, desolando sempre più questa povera nazione." ASV: AES, Spagna: Fasc. 240 Pos. 856, DSCN6445.
81 ASV: AES, Spagna: Fasc. 240 Pos. 856, 25rv-26rv-27rv.
82 "Tutta quella infelice regione è stata flagellata da crudeltà che non hanno riscontro che negli episodi più truci delle epoche delle più barbare guerre. Città e villaggi furono devastati, ed i poveri abitanti che non facevano parte del movimento rivoluzionario, sono stati assoggettati ai più duri supplizi, dai quali sfuggirono neppure i piccoli bimbi, alcuni dei quali furono acciecati." ASV: AES, Spagna: Fasc. 240 Pos. 856, 25rv-26rv-27rv.
83 "veri martiri, uccisi in odio alla fede." ASV: AES, Spagna: Fasc. 240 Pos. 856, 25rv-26rv-27rv.
84 "In Oviedo sono stati assassinati il parroco de la Corte, il Canonico Baztan, il Padre Eufrasio del Bambino Gesù, carmelitano, due Padri della Missione del Seminario e 12 seminaristi. Nella provincia sono stati giustiziati i parroci di Sama, della Rebolleda, di Ollonicgo, di Valcuna, di Murias e Moreda; il Padre Innocenzo Passionista, otto fratelli delle Scuole cristiane, quattro novizi passionisti, il Padre Martinez, gesuita con un fratello della Compagnia." ASV: AES, Spagna: Fasc. 240 Pos. 856, 25rv-26rv-27rv.
85 ASV: AES, Spagna: Fasc. 240 Pos. 856, 25rv-26rv-27rv..
86 Paul Preston, *The Spanish Holocaust*, pp. 78–82.
87 *Ibid*, p. 83.
88 *Ibid*, p. 85.
89 "L'orrore delle uccisioni e delle devastazioni ha superato ogni più pessimistica previsione. L'odio accumulato in tanti anni di propaganda di dottrine incendiarie ha avuto una esplosione che segnerà una delle pagine più dolorose e vergognose di questa Nazione." ASV: AES, Spagna: Fasc. 240 Pos. 856, 25rv-26rv-27rv.
90 ASV: AES, Spagna: Fasc. 240 Pos. 856, 25rv-26rv-27rv.
91 "Solo la forza dell'esercito ha potuto vincere; ma se questa fosse mancata, come è accaduto in ridotti casi particolari, oggi l'Europa avrebbe al suo estremo confine occidentale una nazione bolscevica, uguale a quella che ne chiude i confini orientali, ma immensamente più barbara e più feroce." ASV: AES, Spagna: Fasc. 240 Pos. 856, 25rv-26rv-27rv.
92 ASV: AES, Spagna: Fasc. 240 Pos. 856, 25rv-26rv-27rv.
93 ASV: AES, Spagna: Fasc. 240 Pos. 856, 61.
94 ASV: AES, Spagna: Fasc. 240 Pos. 856, 58rv-59r.
95 ASV: AES, Spagna: Fasc. 240 Pos. 856, 58rv-59r.
96 "Così ora pare che siano i Repubblicani che, facendo del tutto per distruggere la Repubblica, con errori, con scandali e con abusi, si siano proposti

di dare vita e popolarità nel paese ai partiti monarchici.." ASV: AES, Spagna: Fasc. 252 Pos. 876 10rv-11rv-12rv-13r.
97 "Se vinceranno le destre avremo non solo la riforma della Costituzione, ma è da credere, una Costituzione nuova: se, quod Deus avertat, vinceranno le sinistre, arriveremo alla rivoluzione e senz'altro alla dittatura del proletariato." ASV: AES, Spagna: Fasc. 252 Pos. 876 10rv-11rv-12rv-13r.
98 "Invece ha sorpreso il suo tono relativamente moderato. In esso infatti non si parla più di abolizione del capitale, della divisione delle terre, della soppressione del regime e meno di dittatura del proletariato." ASV: AES, Spagna: Fasc. 252 Pos. 876, 16rv.
99 ASV: AES, Spagna: Fasc. 252 Pos. 876, 16rv.
100 "en aquellos casos y lugares en los que el triunfo de las candidaturas de derecha pudiera depender del voto de dichas Religiosas por ser grande su número y estar equilibradas las fuerzas contendientes." ASV: AES, Spagna: Fasc. 252 Pos. 876, DSCN6448–9.
101 "los deseos de Su Santidad de ver unidos a todos los católicos en la defensa de la Religión." ASV: AES, Spagna: Fasc. 252 Pos. 876, DSCN6451.
102 "Es, ciertamente, extraña la actitud de este partido, cuyos dirigentes, mientras proclaman su propósito de formar una nueva nación—rompiendo para ello la unidad nacional—en la que serían plenamente reconocido y respetado los derechos de la Iglesia, van de la mano, cuando conviene a sus planes politicos, con los partidos más hostiles a la Iglesia." ASV: AES, Spagna: Fasc. 252 Pos. 876, DSCN6451.
103 Payne, *Spain's First Democracy*, p. 274.
104 *Ibid.*, p. 275. The Popular Front was composed of numerous parties (number of seats won): Socialists (88), Izquierda Republicana (79), Unión Republicana (34), Esquerra Catalana (22), Communists (14), Acció Catalana (5), Leftist independents (3), Unió Socialista de Catalunya (3), Galicianists (3), Federal Republicans (2), Unió de Rabassaires (2), POUM (1), Partit Català Proletari (1), Estat Català (1), Revolutionary Catalan nationalist (1), Partido Sindicalista (1), Independent syndicalist (1), Esquerra Valenciana (1)—263 total. For the Bloque Nacional: CEDA (101), Traditionalists (15), Renovación Española (13), Agrarians (11), Rightist independents (10), Conservatives (2), Independent monarchists (2), Spanish Nationalist Party (1), Catholic (1)—156 total. For the Center coalition: Centrist Party (21), Lliga Catalana (12), Radicals (9), Progressives (6), Basque Nationalists (5), Liberal Democrats (1)—total 54.
105 ASV: AES, Spagna: Fasc. 252 Pos. 876, 20r.
106 ASV: AES, Spagna: Fasc. 253 Pos. 879, DSCN6480.
107 ASV: AES, Spagna: Fasc. 253 Pos. 879, DSCN6483.
108 ASV: AES, Spagna: Fasc. 253 Pos. 879, DSCN6484.
109 "vandalisme: incendii di chiese, distruzioni di giornali, minaccie, ingiurie, ecc." ASV: AES, Spagna: Fasc. 253 Pos. 879, DSCN6486.
110 ASV: AES, Spagna: Fasc. 253 Pos. 879, DSCN6494.
111 ASV: AES, Spagna: Fasc. 253 Pos. 879, DSCN6493.
112 "la Santa Sede, la Chiesa e il problema religioso in generale." ASV: AES, Spagna: Fasc. 253 Pos. 879, DSCN6501.

113 "Il Signor Azaña mi ha risposto: Non so niente: non ne abbiamo parloto: dobbiamo occuparcene; ma no so quando lo potremo far, perchè ora abbiamo tante cose da trattare, e tutte importantissime; con che no voglio dire che non sia importante il problema religioso." ASV: AES, Spagna: Fasc. 253 Pos. 879, DSCN6502.
114 "la questione del paro obrero" and "della riforma agrariana." ASV: AES, Spagna: Fasc. 253 Pos. 879, DSCN6503.
115 "Non sarà, interruppe il Presidente, perchè la Santa Sede vuole prima la riforma della Costituzione? Perchè in questo caso dovrebbe aspettare abbastanza." ASV: AES, Spagna: Fasc. 253 Pos. 879, DSCN6505.
116 ASV: AES, Spagna: Fasc. 252 Pos. 876, DSCN6453.
117 "Por parte de las izquerdistas (a) La union, (b) Su forma de actuación, directamente sobre el pueblo, explotando estos recursos: el hecho del paro obrero; el estancamiento del trigo, (c) La brusca entrada de los sindicalistas en los comicios, contra sus principios y práctica, dos horas antes de que se cerraran aquellos, (d) La descomposición del partido radical, e) El empeño fracasado del gobierno de formar un Partido de centro." ASV: AES, Spagna: Fasc. 252 Pos. 876, DSCN6455.
118 "(a) Ha faltado lo unión generosa y eficaz, (b) La forma de propaganda: Con mucho menos contacto con el pueblo que las izquierdas, sobre todo por la prensa. Los periódicos católicos entran poco en las clases obreras, (c) La ineficacia de la labor legislativa de las últimas Cortes en orden a mejorar la clase obrera, que ésta ha atribuido a las derecha . . . (d) La incomprensión y falta de caridad de los ricos, derechistas que, al advenimiento de las derechas al poder en la pasada legislature, volvieron al régimen de jornales irrisorios de antes de la república . . . " ASV: AES, Spagna: Fasc. 252 Pos. 876, DSCN6456.
119 ASV: AES, Spagna: Fasc. 252 Pos. 876, DSCN6458.
120 *Ibid.*
121 ASV: AES, Spagna: Fasc. 252 Pos. 876, DSCN6458–9.
122 *Ibid.*
123 ASV: AES, Spagna: Fasc. 252 Pos. 876, DSCN6459–60.
124 "Los Delegados del Komitern que han estado en España para estudiar las posibilidades de una actuación comunista en nuestro país, han enviado a Moscú un informe pesimista respecto a las masas revolucionarias y a sus dirigentes. El informe es muy extenso y pródigo en detalles anecdóticos para corroborar la tesis de que nada hay que esperar de la revolución en la calle . . . Creen los informadores que unas elecciones municipales hubiesen provocado un desbordamiento pasional en los pueblos con la proclamación circunstancial del comunismo en varios millares de Ayuntamientos rurales donde se izaría la bandara roja, se quemaría la Iglesia, y asesinaría al Cura, a la pareja la Guardia Civil, y a los más ricos del pueblo . . . Dicen que en España todos tienen miedo: las derechas y las iziquierda." ASV: AES, Spagna: Fasc. 252 Pos. 876, DSCN6461.
125 *Ibid.*
126 ASV: AES, Spagna: Fasc. 252 Pos. 876, DSCN6462.
127 ASV: AES, Spagna: Fasc. 252 Pos. 876, DSCN6463.

128 ASV: AES, Spagna: Fasc. 252 Pos. 876, DSCN6464.
129 Sid Lowe, *Catholicism, War, and the Foundation of Francoism: The Juventud de Acción Popular in Spain, 1931–1939* (Eastbourne: Sussex Academic Press, 2010), pp. 124–140.
130 Madridejos, 165–7.
131 ASV: AES, Spagna: Fasc. 252 Pos. 876, Fasc. 252 Pos. 867, 31rv-32rv-33rv-34r.
132 "E siccome, praticamente, tra comunismo e socialismo non vi è differenza." ASV: AES, Spagna: Fasc. 252 Pos. 876, Fasc. 252 Pos. 867, 31rv-32rv-33rv-34r.
133 *Ibid.*
134 *Ibid.*
135 Payne, *Spain's First Democracy*, pp. 355–7.
136 *Ibid.*. 305–6.
137 "Da fonte attendibile apprendo che preparasi colpo di mano militare cui non sarebbe estraneo Presidente della Repubblica. Mi si consiglia che ai primi indizi mi rifugi in qualche Ambasciata. Terrò informata Santa Sede. ASV: AES, Spagna: Fasc. 253 Pos. 879, 72r.
138 "Dice inoltre il Signor Azana che condanna naturalmente gli incendi delle Chiese e cose simili; ma per ottener effetto oratorio, contrappone a violenze di questo genere un altra violenza che si perpretò in Madrid nel passato Marzo, quando si attentò alla vita di un Professore Universitario socialista, il Jimenez de Asua, che nella scuola si divertiva ad aizzare gli studenti socialisti contro gli altri: attentato commesso non so da chi, dicono da fascisti, e ad ogni modo da persone colle quali le povere Chiese ancora fumeggianti, non hanno e non avranno mai nulla a che vedere. E' giusto condannare anche questa seconda violenza, e nessuno più della Chiesa lo condanna. Ma non è altro che oratoria il discolpare o almeno attenuare quella prima colpa." ASV: AES, Spagna: Fasc. 253 Pos. 879, 77rv-77bisrv-78rv-79r
139 "Le voci diffuse sul prossimo avvento del Comunismo al potere, e che uno de estos dias Espana va a amenecer constituida en Soviet.... esto ya parece que pasa los limites de lo licito y de lo tolerable, y constituye una agresion!" ASV: AES, Spagna: Fasc. 253 Pos. 879, 77rv-77bisrv-78rv-79r.
140 ASV: AES, Spagna: Fasc. 252 Pos. 876, Fasc. 252 Pos. 876, DSCN6467. As for the Radical Right in Spain, the Archbishop most likely meant the FE y de los JONS, which was the organization closest to fascist ideals in Spain. In 1931, Ramiro Ledesma established the JONS movement. In 1933, José Antonio Primo de Rivera, son of the former dictator, established the Falange Española (Spanish Phalanx)—based on Italian fascism. The two groups unified in 1934, but their influence in Spanish politics was never great. Estimates claim the group had no more than 10,000 members by 1936, meaning it was not a major player in the war. The discussion about whether or not the Nationalists were *fascist* still exists today, but evidence seems to show that this claim is not necessarily true. Payne, 175–7. The Popular Front Government also faced constant threats from the anarchist extreme left. See: Enrique Moradiellos, "Francisco Franco," p. 126.
141 ASV: AES, Spagna: Fasc. 252 Pos. 876, Fasc. 252 Pos. 876, DSCN6469. For

a conversation of the violent oppression by the political right, see: Chris Bannister, "José Antonio de Primo Rivera", pp. 91–116.

142 "... tuve el honor de pedir a la Santa Sede que fijara Su atención, siempre vigilante, sobre lod peligros que encieraan las campañas de los extremistas de derechas." ASV: AES, Spagna: Fasc. 252 Pos. 876, Fasc. 252 Pos. 876, DSCN6471.

143 ASV: AES, Spagna: Fasc. 252 Pos. 876, Fasc. 252 Pos. 876, DSCN6476.

144 "Il Santo Padre ha fermato di preferenza la Sua augusta attenzione sui punti relativi alla scuola, all'insegnamento religioso e alla conseguente difesa dalla minacciosa propaganda comunista." José Andrés-Gallego and Antón M. Pazos, *Archivo Gomá: Documentos de la Guerra Civil—1: Julio-Diciembre de 1936* (Madrid: Consejo Superior de Investigaciones Científicas, 2001), p. 55.

IV The Uprising Begins, the Republic Reacts, and the Vatican Protests

1 William J. Callahan, *The Catholic Church in Spain, 1875–1998* (Washington, D.C.: Catholic University of America Press, 2000), p. 349.

2 Gonzalo Redondo, *Historia de la Iglesia en España, 1931–1939: Tomo II* (Madrid: Ediciones Rialp, S.A., 1993), p. 16.

3 Frances Lannon, *Privilege, Persecution, and Prophecy: The Catholic Church in Spain, 1875–1975* (Oxford: Clarendon Press, 1987), p. 198.

4 "The anticlerical fury, then, cannot be explained by a single reason. A number of motivations were at work. This is because at least two struggles were going on simultaneously: a war between Republicans and Nationalists—a military struggle being fought in conventional terms—and a revolution in which the left was trying to impose its aims and hopes on the right. Moreover, the struggles occurred within a century's tradition of anticlerical violence.

Thus, it seems possible to detect three basic motivations based on the perceptions of the clergy, with none of them exclusive and all overlapping in a certain context: (1) the clergy perceived as military enemies in the specific circumstances of the uprising and war; (2) the clergy perceived as part of the old regime, to be destroyed for the aims of the revolution; (3) anticlerical violence perceived as part of Spanish tradition." José M. Sánchez, *The Spanish Civil War as a Religious Tragedy* (Notre Dame: University of Notre Dame Press, 1987), pp. 23–4.

5 Frank J. Coppa, *The Policies and Politics of Pope Pius XII* (New York: Peter Lang, 2011) and Frank J. Coppa (ed.), *Controversial Concordats* (Washington, D.C.: Catholic University of America Press, 1999).

6 *Ibid.*

7 Coppa, *The Policies and Politics*, pp. 46–51.

8 *Ibid.*, pp. 66–7.

9 *Ibid.*, pp. 70–86.

10 Lucia Ceci, *Il papa non deve parlare* (Bari: Gius, Laterza, & Figli, 2010), p. 7.

11 See: Lucia Ceci.

12. Emma Fattorini, *Hitler, Mussolini, and the Vatican* (Cambridge: Polity Press, 2011); Hubert Wolf, *Pope and Devil* (Cambridge, MA: The Belknap Press, 2010); and Alessandro Duce, *La Santa Sede e la Questione Ebraica* (Roma: Edizione Studium: 2006).
13. Wolf, pp. 128–32 and Fattorini, p. 57.
14. Wolf, pp. 187–195.
15. *Ibid.*, p, 129.
16. To understand the variety of pressures leading Spain to war, see: Enrique Moradiellos, *1936: Los Mitos de la Guerra Civil* (Barcelona: Ediciones Peninsula, 2004).
17. Lannon, p. 199.
18. Callahan, p. 346.
19. Hilari M. Raguer, *Gunpowder and Incense: The Catholic Church and the Spanish Civil War* (London: Routledge, 2007), pp. 39–40.
20. Paul Preston, *The Spanish Holocaust: Inquisition and Extermination in Twentieth Century Spain* (London: W.W. Norton & Company, 2012), p. xv.
21. *Ibid.*, pp. 5–6.
22. Daniel Kowalsky, *La Unión Soviética y la Guerra Civil Española* (Barcelona: Crítica, 2003), pp. 211–240.
23. See Chapter VI and the discussion of French and British political interests in the Spanish Civil War.
24. "In regard to the sovereignty appertaining to it also in international matters, the Holy See declares that it desires to take, and shall take, no part in any temporal rivalries between other States, nor in any international congresses called to settle such matters, save and except in the event of such parties making a mutual appeal to the pacific mission of the Holy See, the latter reserving in any event the right of exercising its moral and spiritual power. The Vatican City shall, therefore, be invariably and in every event considered as neutral and inviolable territory." Lateran Accords of 1929, Article 24.
25. Redondo, pp. 191–2.
26. Forty-six churches were burned in Madrid, which was about 34.8% of all religious sites in the capital, Redondo, p. 20. For a more descriptive account of the violence against church property and individuals, see: José Ramón Hernández Figueiredo, *Destrucción del patrimonio religioso en la II República* (Madrid: Biblioteca Autores Cristianos, 2009), pp. 245–340.
27. Stanley G. Payne, "Spain: The Church, the Second Republic, and the Franco Regime," in Richard J. Wolff and Jörg K. Hoensch (eds.), *Catholics, the State, and the European Radical Right, 1919–1945* (Boulder: Social Science Monographs, 1987): pp. 182–198, esp. p. 185.
28. José Luis Ledesma, "The Enemy par excellence: Anticlerical Violence in the Spanish Civil War (1936–39)," (Salzburg, 9th Global Conference: Violence—Probing the Boundaries, 2010).
29. Preston, *The Spanish Holocaust*, xviii. As Preston also states, these numbers are clearly estimates, as files identifying the dead have been destroyed, and uncontrolled violence without documentation also occurred.

30 "bande rosse armate." Archivio Segreto Vaticano (ASV): Affari Ecclesiastici Straordinari, Spagna (AES, Spagna): Fasc. 285 Pos. 895, 4v.
31 "Da diverse parti della Spagna sono giunte e giungono tuttora tristissime e dolorosissime notizie sulla Situazione delle persone e cose ecclesiastiche. A Barcellona ed in quasi tutta la Catalogna, si uccidono nei modi più barbari ecclesiastici e religiosi in nessuna modo implicati nella rivoluzione; le religiose sono scacciate dagli ospedali dove prestano la loro caritatevole opera e vengono empiamente vilipese; si distruggono e bruciano sistematicamente chiese e conventi e si arriva persino a violare le tombe e profanare le salme." ASV: AES, Spagna: Fasc. 285 Pos. 895, 9r.
32 Preston, *The Spanish Holocaust*, p. 222.
33 *Ibid.*
34 Lannon, p. 211 and Callahan, p. 359.
35 "A Madrid, sebbene sede del Governo Centrale, si committono pure simili efferati delitti, senza che l'Autorità intervenga a reprimerli; viene anzi proibito il culto in pubblico e si tenta con ogni mezzo di impedirlo persino in privato e nella case particolari. [...] Tutto ciò si va compiendo impunemente sotto gli occhi di quello stesso Governo, il quale, come afferma, ha tuttora il potere ed è padrone della situazione. Pur ammettendo che il Governo medesimo si trovi in gravi difficoltà nel reprimere detti eccessi, tuttavia non si vede come possa del tutto liberarsi della responsabilità dei fatti sovraccennati, che redono intollerabile la Situazione della Chiesa in Spagna." ASV: AES, Spagna: Fasc. 285 Pos. 895, 9r-9v.
36 Julio de la Cueva, "Religious Persecution, Anticlerical Tradition and Revolution: On Atrocities against the Clergy during the Spanish Civil War" in *Journal of Contemporary History* 33, 3 (1998): pp. 355–369, esp. pp. 355–369.
37 *Ibid.*
38 Richard Maddox, "Revolutionary Anticlericalism and Hegemonic Processes in an Andalusian Town, August 1936" in *American Ethnologist* 22, 1 (Feb. 1995): pp. 125–143, esp. p. 128.
39 See: Maria Thomas, *The Faith and the Fury: Popular Anticlerical Violence and Iconoclasm in Spain, 1931–1936* (Eastbourne: Sussex Academic Press, 2013).
40 "E ciò tanto più perchè in passato, nonostante le ripetute proteste del Rappresentante Pontificio a Madrid non sono state debitamente represse e punite le violenze commesse contro la Chiesa lasciando così sussistere nella pubblica opinione il sospetto di tolleranza e connivenze coi peggiori nemica della religione. La Santa Sede è pertanto obbligata ad elevare la sua più alta protesta e si attende che cotesto governo dove può intervenga energicamente per frenare siffatti eccessi e almeno non ometta di deplorare tali sacrileghi atti e di separare la sua responsabilità da quella dei loro autori." ASV: AES, Spagna: Fasc. 285 Pos. 895, 9v. The redactions in this memo and those that follow were made by hand on letters.
41 Redondo, p. 85
42 According to Gonzalo Redondo, the burning of churches in Madrid began on the evening of 18 July 1936. The first burnt in Madrid were: Church San

Andrés, Church San Ramon, Convent of las Comendadores de Santiago, Church Nuestra Señora de las Dolores. Burnt on 19 July: Church San Cayento, Nuestra Señora de los Ángeles, Cathedral of San Isidro, and Convent of La Latina. From 19 July-20 July, 34 buildings were burnt. Deaths of clergy in July were as follows: 20th 3, 21st 3, 22nd 4, 24th 2, 25th 1, 26th 3, 27th 12, 28th 4, 29th 1, 30th 1. In Cataluña, 200 churches were burned in the first months. See: Redondo, pp. 19–27. Maddox, pp. 125–6.

43 Raguer, p. 80.
44 "La Santa Sede e la situazione religiosa in Spagna" in *L'Osservatore Romano*, 10/8/36. ASV: AES, Spagna: Fasc. 285 Pos. 895, 12r.
45 "La Embajada de España se honra a la Nota que, con fecha de 31 de Julio útltimo, le dirigió la Secretería de Estado de Su Santidad.

Debe manifestar ante todo, respecto a las reprobables violencias a que la Nota allude, que el Gobierno español deplora profundamente aquellos hechos de ese género que en realidad hayan podido occurir. Notorio es, por otra parte, que las autoridades españoles, incluso las de Cataluña, han intervenido en muchos casos para evitar crueles excesos, protegiendo la vida de sacerdotes y religiosos.

Pero el Gobierno español no puede menos de hacer presente a la Santa Sede que el hecho doloroso de que en el curso de los sucesos provocados por la rebelión military haya habido victimas investida de carácter eclesiástico se debe en gran medida a la actitud adoptada por un considerable parte del clero en España. Entre sus miembros, les hay que han tomado las armas en las filas facciosas, como pudo comprobarse en la recojida de muertes y heridos después de los combates. Algunos sacerdotes se hicieron Fuertes en sus respectivas Iglesias, siendo luego estas atacadas. Muchos clérigos y religiosos, han prestado su apoyo a la rebeldía armada contra el Gobierno legitimo y al cruente ataque contra la República, sobre cuyos autores recae, en el fondo, la responsibilidad de tantos males como han desencadenado. Varios Prelados aparecen ahora en relación con la Junta facciosa de Burgos, y los Obispos de Palma de Mayorca, Pamplona y Vitoria han tratado reiteradamente de influir sobre los católicos para disuadirles de su leal actitud hacia el Gobierno, llegando a amenazarles con penas espirituales, según el día 7 del corriente Agosto fué radiado por la estación emisora de la Junta facciosa mencionada.

A pesar de todos estos hechos, que habían de provocar una inevitable reacción en el ánimo popular, el Gobierno de la República, no sólo lamenta los actos de violencia que injustificadamente hayan podido realizarse, sino que los ha contenido en lo posible, adoptando medidas para la protección de templos y de religiosos, y está asimismo dispuesto a evitarles en lo sucesivo.

La suspensión temporal del culto, a la que la Nota de esa Secretaria de Estado se refiere, no responde en modo alguno a propósito hostil del Gobierno hacia los sentimientos católicos, garantidas dentro del marco de la Constiución, sino que es transisteria medida preventiva, encaminada precisamente a evitar posibles desmanes, amparando de esta suerte, en el momento actual, la conservación de los templos y objetos del culto y prote-

giendo a sus sacerdotes y ministros." ASV: AES, Spagna: Fasc. 285 Pos. 895, 19r-19v.
46 Callahan, p. 347.
47 Redondo, pp.72–3 and Callahan, p. 348.
48 Ceci, p. 7.
49 Michael Alpert, "The Popular Army of the Spanish Republic, 1936–1939" in Bowen, W. and Alvarez, J. (eds.) *A Military History of Modern Spain: From the Napoleonic Era to the International War on Terror* (Westport, CT: Praeger Security International. 2007): pp. 93–109.
50 "La S. Sede prende atto innanzi tutto della deplorazione espressa dal Governo di Madrid per i gravissimi sacrilegi commesse contro persone e cose sacre, nonchè della promessa di adottare procedimenti per impedirli in avvenire. [. . .] Mentre però vorrebbe confidare su tali dichiarazione, non può non rilevare al tempo stesso come purtroppo il continuo ripetersi di così dolorosa fatti è ben lungi dal confermare le suddette assicurazioni." ASV: AES, Spagna: Fasc. 285 Pos. 895, 26r.
51 "L'atteggiamento della stampa, che fin sotto gli occhi del Governo di Madrid muove violenti attachi contro la Chiesa, il Clero e i Religiosi; le numerosi invasioni; gli arresti e le barbare uccisioni di persone dedicate al Signore.. anno si che sempre più si diffonda nella pubblica opinione il sospetto di tolleranza e connivenze coi peggiori nemici della Religione." ASV: AES, Spagna: Fasc. 285 Pos. 895, 26r.
52 "Al contrario elementi fanatici e irresponsabili sono stati armate e lasciati poi liberi e impunity nella loro empia mania di distruzione. [. . .] E tanto più doverosa sarebbe da parte del Governo di Madrid la effettiva represione di tali delitti, in quanto che le persone oneste di tutto il mondo non possono ormai non rilevare come simili artocità con carattere anti-religiosi,—le quali finiscono per tornare a disonore di una Nazione così nobile come la Spagna—si commettano e si lascino commettere soltanto in quelle regioni in cui esecita la sua autorità il Governo di Madrid." ASV: AES, Spagna: Fasc. 285 Pos. 895, 27r.
53 Paul Preston, *The Spanish Civil War: Reaction, Revolution, and Revenge: Revised and Expanded* (New York: W.W. Norton & Company, 2006), pp. 93–103.
54 Callahan, p. 361.
55 These militias would patrol Republican cities until 30 September 1936 when they would be absorbed into the Republic's new Popular Army, See: Alpert in Bowen and Alvarez (eds).
56 Preston, *The Spanish Holocaust*, pp. 310.
57 Silvio Sericano became a priest in 1913. In 1922, he became a professor of Science, Philosophy and Theology for the Vatican. In 1925, he started working for the Secretary of State's Office in Central America, followed by his work in Austria. In 1936, he was sent to Spain. Vincente Cárcel Ortí, *Pio XI Entre la República Y Franco* (Madrid: Biblioteca de Autores Cristianos, 2008), pp.381–2. During his time in Austria, Sericano witnessed the Catholic corporatism of Dollfuss, his assassination, and the attempt to prevent the Nazi Party from gaining support in Austria, possibly influ-

encing his opinions about Nazism/Fascism and its antagonistic attitudes toward the Catholic Church.
58 "Una ventina bruciate relativa facilità; parecchie saccheggiate; tutte le altre chiuse e fatte eccezione di qualche chiesa di stranieri, occupate dalle milizie rosse. La Chiesa del Carmine è stata convertita in un macabro e nausenate museo antireligioso; Mentre quella di S. José e "de las Calatravas" sono state particolarmente profante." ASV: AES, Spagna: Fasc. 263 Pos. 889, 30r.
59 For an explanation of anarchist profanity, see: Callahan, pp. 362–3.
60 "Alcuni bruciati; parecchi saccheggiati e gli altri occupati dai rossi; così pure occupati dai rossi il palazzo e il seminario vescovile, le sedi dell'organizzazione cattolica e le tipografie di tutti i giornali cattolici." ASV: AES, Spagna: Fasc. 263 Pos. 889, 30r.
61 "La Nunziatura è stata finora relativamente rispettata; dicesi relativamente, perchè durante la nutrita sparatoria del 20 luglio anche questa casa è stata colpita da parecchie pallottole di fucile." ASV: AES, Spagna: Fasc. 263 Pos. 889, 30r.
62 "clero secolare e regolare costretto a cercare rifugio in abitazioni presso conoscenti od amici ed a cambiare continuamente di casa per non cadare nelle mani dei rossi che perquisiscono sistematicamente le case, arrestando quanti secolari suppongono loro avversari politici, ecclesiastici in genere ed anche suore. [. . .] Si sa di molti casi di ecclesiastici barbaramente trucidati nelle case, sulle pubbliche vie e nel camposanto. Moltissimi altri ed anche parecchie suore sono detenuti nelle carceri di Madrid." ASV: AES, Spagna: Fasc. 263 Pos. 889, 30r-31r.
63 "In conseguenza di tutto ciò la soppressione completa del culto pubblico in Madrid: l'amministrazione dei Santi Sacramenti è practicamente impossibile; la Santa Messa viene celebrata solo in poche capelle private e in qualche casa di nascosto, con molta precauzione e non senza grave pericolo." ASV: AES, Spagna: Fasc. 263 Pos. 889, 31r.
64 Redondo, pp. 182–4.
65 "Il Governo non solo è assolutamente impotente as impedire tali atrocità ma è schiavo dei rossi perfino nei suoi stessi atti pubblici." ASV: Fasc. 263 Pos. 889, 32r.
66 ASV: AES, Spagna: Fasc. 263 Pos. 889, 74r.
67 ASV: AES, Spagna: Fasc. 263 Pos. 889, 75r.
68 "Es de admirar el espíritu religioso que se ha despertado en las tropas, iniciado por los Requetés: Casi todos los soldados, se han puesto al pecho el escudo del Sdo. Corazón: muy desde el principio, han pedido capellanes y ya se dice Misa en los Cuarteles y se ven muchos soldados por las Iglesias confesando y comulgando." ASV: AES, Spagna: Fasc. 263 Pos. 889, 75r.
69 Paul Preston, *The Spanish Civil War*, p. 120.
70 Shannon E. Fleming, "Spanish Morocco and the Alzamiento Nacional, 1936–1939: The Military, Economic and Political Mobilization of a Protectorate" in *Journal of Contemporary History* 18, 1 (Jan 1983): pp. 27–42, esp. pp. 28–30 and Carmen T. Sotomayor Blázquez "El moro traidor, el moro engañado: varientes del estereotipo en el Romancero republicano" in *Anaquel de Estudios Árabes*" 16 (2005): pp. 233–249, esp. p. 234.

71 William Callahan tells of Cardinal Gomá's happiness to hear about religious services for Rebel soldiers. Also, Cardinal Ilundaín offered a special mass for Falange members on 15 August 1936 for their support for the Church, pp. 347 and 367.
72 "A los sacerdotes, nos miran ahora los militantes con gran respecto y veneración; nos saludan y hasta besan la mano públicamente por las calles, con grande afecto." ASV: AES, Spagna: Fasc. 263 Pos. 889, 75r.
73 Preston, *The Spanish Holocaust*, pp. 141 and 666.
74 "Esemplare sofferenza cattolici, denuncia inumana persecuzione, deplora guerra civile et veleno propaganda bolscevina." ASV: AES, Spagna: Fasc. 285 Pos. 895, 52r.
75 Gonzalo Redondo explains that according to some in the Vatican hierarchy, it was not possible to be a good Catholic and a fascist, just like a communist could not be a good Catholic, p. 34.

V Humanitarian Concerns Increase as the War Continues

1 "Situazione religiosa immutata." Archivio Segreto Vaticano (ASV): Affari Ecclesiastici Straordinari, Spagna (AES, Spagna): Fasc. 264 Pos. 889, 7r.
2 "Causa crescenti successi esercito nazionali difesa Madrid diventa ogni giorno più difficile. Di fronte noti recenti rovesci militari organizzazioni rosse hanno reagito intensificando arresti et perpetrando nuovi assassini elementi di destra tra cui alcuni ecclesiastici." ASV: AES, Spagna: Fasc. 264 Pos. 889, 7r.
3 John F. Coverdale, *Italian Intervention in the Spanish Civil War* (Princeton: Princeton University Press, 1975); Glenn T. Harper, *German Economic Policy in Spain* (The Hague: Mouton & Co., 1967); Robert H. Whealey, *Hitler and Spain: The Nazi Role in the Spanish Civil War* (Lexington: University of Kentucky Press, 1989); and Ismael Saz, "Fascism and Empire: Fascist Italy Against Republican Spain" in *Mediterranean Historical Review*, 13, 1 (June 1998): pp. 116–134.
4 "Tagliata ogni comunicazione ferroviaria Madrid è praticamente assediata dall'esercito Nazionali la cui aviazione da qualche giorno bombarda sistematicamente fortificazioni et trincee improvvisate dai governativi nei dintorni della Città." ASV: AES, Spagna: Fasc. 264 Pos. 889, 31r.
5 According to Helen Graham, as the Nationalist armies reached the outskirts of Madrid, air force assaults on the city greatly increased. Between 14–27 November 1936, the air force specifically targeted civilian in the city in order to create chaos amongst the denizens. Helen Graham, *The Spanish Republic at War, 1936–1939* (Cambridge: Cambridge University Press, 2002), p. 179. Paul Preston explains that as Nationalist troops reached the outskirts of Madrid, they were known to round-up Republican and militias leaders for assassination. At least seventy were killed on 23 August 1936 at the Modelo Prison near Madrid by Nationalists, Paul Preston, *The Spanish Holocaust: Inquisition and Extermination in Twentieth-Century Spain* (London: W.W. Norton & Company, 2012) pp. 124–5.
6 "Manifestazioni di donne, organizzate per iniziativa di questo Ambasciatore russo, hanno avuto luogo nei passato giorni nelle vie di

Madrid invocando invio alla frontiera tutti uomini validi et uccisione detenuti politici." ASV: AES, Spagna: Fasc. 264 Pos. 889, 31r.
7 "... completamente assediata." ASV: AES, Spagna: Fasc. 264 Pos. 889, 33r.
8 "Comitato rosso" ASV: AES, Spagna: Fasc. 264 Pos. 889, 35r.
9 ASV: AES, Spagna: Fasc. 264 Pos. 889, 35r.
10 "Mi permetto aggiungere che nel caso probabile di promissa entrata Madrid esercito Nazionali, il Rappresentante Santa Sede, se qui presente, si vedrebbe moralmente constretto manifestare sua simpatia Governo Burgos mettendo con ciò in grande pericolo vita numerosi ecclesiastici detenuti dai rossi nelle provincie in loro potere." ASV: AES, Spagna: Fasc. 264 Pos. 889, 35r.
11 Failures surrounding Non-Intervention will be discussed in Chapter VI. France and Britain initiated international Non-Intervention plans for Spain, but Nazi Germany, Fascist Italy and the USSR each sent a great deal of aid to their allies in Spain. As for Italy, the fascists sent 764 planes, hundreds of tanks, and soldiers to fight for the Nationalists. This aid, combined with Nazi aid sent on credit gave the Nationalists a large advantage on the battlefield. See: Brian R. Sullivan, "Fascist Italy's Military Involvement in the Spanish Civil War" in *The Journal of Military History* 59, 4 (Oct. 1995), pp. 697–727.
12 "Mi confermava che l'Italia aiuta la Spagna con uomini e materiale, 'e già abbiamo avuto alcuni morti." ASV: AES, Spagna: Fasc. 264 Pos. 889, 74v.
13 "socialista militante e non fa mistero delle sue idee." ASV: AES, Spagna: Fasc. 265 Pos. 889, 6r.
14 "La colpa su la monarchi, l'aristocrazia e in parte sopra il clero che almeno nelle grandi città, perduto il contatto con il popolo, ignorava il malcontento della classe operia e la gravità dell'imminente reazione." ASV: AES, Spagna: Fasc. 265 Pos. 889, 6r.
15 "Lo stesso Ministro concluse che gli orrori e le stragi compiute dai rossi erano pienamente inescusabili." ASV: AES, Spagna: Fasc. 265 Pos. 889, 6r-6v.
16 "Mi dichiarò francamente che i rossi e i bianchi sarano ugualmente vinti anche se apparentemente vincitori. La povera Spagna avrà bisogno di molti anni prima di riacquistare la pace interna per poter riprendere il suo posto tra la grandi nazioni." ASV: AES, Spagna: Fasc. 265 Pos. 889, 6v.
17 "In Spagna non è possibile che una religione e questa è la cattolica; che qualsiasi governo anche di estrema sinistra dovrà riconoscere questo fatto insime all'impossibilità di sostituire alla religine cattolica qualche altro sistema morale che valga ad educare il popolo all'osservanza delle leggi." ASV: AES, Spagna: Fasc. 265 Pos. 889, 6v.
18 ASV: AES, Spagna: Fasc. 265, Pos. 889, 10r-11r.
19 ASV: AES, Spagna: Fasc. 265, Pos. 889, 7r.
20 ASV: AES, Spagna: Fasc. 265, Pos. 889, 7r.
21 ASV: AES, Spagna: Fasc. 265, Pos. 889, 7v.
22 Elena Rodríguez Ballano, "Un socialista y una atalaya del SIDE en Berna" in Viñas, A. (ed.), *Al Servicio del la República: Diplomáticos y Guerra Civil* (Madrid: Marcel Pons, Ediciones de Historia, 2010), pp. 177–206, esp. p 205.

23 "La situazione spagnola e la possibilità di arrestare le ostilità. Il Sig. Motta aveva letto nei giornali che la S. Sede era state interessata a prendere l'iniziativa della pace o almeno di un armistizio. Egli riconosceva tutte le diffcoltà dell'impresa; però ad una mia domanda se credeva che una parola di pace pronunciata dal S. Padre avrebbe fatto in questo momento una buona impressione, mi rispose che era pienamente convinto che questa parola, anche se non ascoltata, avrebbe produtto nel mondo una impressione eccellente. Lo stesso mi è stato ripetuto anche de diplomatici non cattolici." ASV: AES, Spagna: Fasc. 265 Pos. 889, 8r-8v.
24 Hilari M Raguer. *Gunpowder and Incense: The Catholic Church and the Spanish Civil War* (London: Routledge, 2007), p. 115.
25 Frances Lannon, *Privilege, Persecution, and Prophecy: The Catholic Church in Spain, 1875–1975* (Oxford: Clarendon Press, 1987), p. 213.
26 Graham, pp. 240–253. Chris Bannister also explains that territorial integrity was a goal of the political right in Spain, "Antonio Primo de Rivera: Catholic Fascism," in Quiroga, Alejandro and Miguel Ángel del Arco, eds., *Right-wing Spain in the Civil War Era: Soldiers of God and Apostles of the Fatherland, 1914–1945* (London: Continuum International Publishing Group, 2012): pp. 91–116.
27 Preston, *The Spanish Holocaust*, pp. 184–5.
28 Gabriel Jackson, *The Spanish Republic and the Civil War, 1931–1939* (Princeton: Princeton University Press, 1972), p. 377. When Nationalists did kill Basque priests, Gomá protested to Franco directly, José M. Sánchez, *The Spanish Civil War as a Religious Tragedy* (Notre Dame, Indiana: University of Notre Dame Press, 1987), p. 80.
29 Jackson, pp. 375–6.
30 *Ibid.*, pp. 377–8.
31 Preston, *The Spanish Holocaust*, p. 185.
32 Cardinal Isidro Gomá y Tomás was named Bishop of Tarragona in 1927, then Archbishop of Toledo in 1932 to replace Cardinal Pedro Segura y Sáenz, who was expelled from the Second Republic in June 1931. Gomá was made Cardinal in 1935. See: Vincente Cárcel Ortí. *Pio XI Entre la República Y Franco* (Madrid: Biblioteca de Autores Cristianos, 2008), p. 377.
33 "Basque Nationalism" ASV: AES, Spagna: Fasc. 287 Pos. 896, 11r.
34 ASV: AES, Spagna: Fasc. 287 Pos. 896, 11r.
35 ASV: AES, Spagna: Fasc. 287 Pos. 896, 13v.
36 ASV: AES, Spagna: Fasc. 287 Pos. 896, 13v.
37 ASV: AES, Spagna: Fasc. 287 Pos. 896, 14r.
38 ASV: AES, Spagna: Fasc. 287 Pos. 896, 14v.
39 Lannon, p. 214 and Gonzalo Redondo, *Historia de la Iglesia en España 1931–1939* (Madrid: Ediciones Rialp, S.A., 1993), p 141.
40 "Sería interpretada como un suceso de carácter político producido por la autoridad militar en favor de un sector político, specialmente tradicionalistas y falange, y contra otro, nacionalistas." ASV: AES, Spagna: Fasc. 287 Pos. 896, 15v.
41 Raguer, p. 78.
42 Redondo, p. 163.

43 ASV: AES, Spagna: Fasc. 287 Pos. 896, 7r.
44 "The actions, endorsements, retractions, and musings of Bishop Mateo Múgica of Vitoria are probably the most difficult to make any sense of. He was persecuted and threatened by the Nationalists, yet he stoutly defended their cause; he was a Basque and he defended his clergy and laity, yet he criticized their political decisions," Sánchez, p. 81. Múgica was a monarchist in 1931, and requested his followers not vote for Republicans. He was expelled from Spain in 1931, but allowed to return in 1933. He was a supporter of Basque autonomy, but was a monarchist who had certain problems with the Partido Nacionalista Vasco (PNV), Sánchez, pp. 81–3.
45 ASV: AES, Spagna: Fasc. 287 Pos. 896, 7v.
46 Redondo, pp. 61–67.
47 "Intato però sono giunte notizie in base alle quali sembrato (a Sua Santità) necessario che Monsignor Múgica ~~lasci la~~ (si allontani provvisoriamente dalla sua) diocesi, non vedendosi altro modo di risolvere la delicata situazione che si è venuta creando." ASV: AES, Spagna: Fasc. 287 Pos. 896, 19r.
48 "Le affida il delicato incarico di convincere Monsignor Múgica ~~ad abbandonare la~~ (a partire dalla) sua diocesi." ASV: AES, Spagna: Fasc. 287 Pos. 896, 19v.
49 Sánchez, p. 83.
50 "Añadir un nuevo motivo a los muchos factores de discordia hoy existentes." ASV: AES, Spagna: Fasc. 287 Pos. 896, 56r.
51 Preston, *The Spanish Holocaust*, p. 185.
52 "salvar los principios de religión y justicia Cristiana." *Carta colectiva de los obispos españoles a los obispos de todo el mundo con motivo de la Guerra en España.*
53 Sánchez, p. 84.
54 ASV: AES, Spagna: Fasc. 289 Pos. 896, 9r.
55 "The Basque Nationalist Party is in its faith Catholic, Apostolic and Roman." ASV: AES, Spagna: Fasc. 289 Pos. 896, 10r.
56 "Es un hecho la participación de este Partido [PNV] en la lucha que hoy se debate en la Peninsula; coincide, de hecho, en combatir con los del FRENTE POPULAR al conjunto Cívico-Militar levantado en armas contra el Gobierno de Madrid. Este Frente Popular ha cometido crímenes y sacrilegios en personas y cosas en toda España. Ahora bien ¿cómo se explica esta coincidencia de un Partido Católico como lo es el P.N.V. con el FRENTE POPULAR?" ASV: AES, Spagna: Fasc. 289 Pos. 896, 11r.
57 "El P.N.V., a pesar de su condición de católica, está divorcido de las llamdas Derechas Españoles por su programa patriótico vasco." ASV: AES, Spagna: Fasc. 289 Pos. 896, 11r.
58 ASV: AES, Spagna: Fasc. 289 Pos. 896, 13r.
59 "Este movimiento llevaba desde un principio un carácter militarista y algún tanto 'fascista', aunque no un programa ideológico completo claro." ASV: AES, Spagna: Fasc. 289 Pos. 896, 13r.
60 "La llamada 'unidad' nacional española contra toda aspiración autonómica por un feroz centralismo." ASV: AES, Spagna: Fasc. 289 Pos. 896, 13r.

61 "¿Se pensó en una guerra civil o en una mera rebelion militar?" ASV: AES, Spagna: Fasc. 289 Pos. 896, 14r.
62 ASV: Fasc. 289 Pos. 896, 14r.
63 "La ciudanía contra el fascismo y por la República contra la Monarquía." ASV: AES, Spagna: Fasc. 289 Pos. 896, 14r.
64 ASV: AES, Spagna: Fasc. 289 Pos. 896, 15r.
65 ASV: AES, Spagna: Fasc. 289 Pos. 896, 15r.
66 "(a) primordialmente para la defensa del orden público amenazado, y (b) para la defensa de su territorio invadido." ASV: AES, Spagna: Fasc. 289 Pos. 896, 16r.
67 ASV: AES, Spagna: Fasc. 289 Pos. 896, 19r.
68 ASV: AES, Spagna: Fasc. 289 Pos. 896, 20r.
69 Raguer, pp. 68, 250.
70 ASV: AES, Spagna: Fasc. 289 Pos. 896, 21r.
71 ASV: AES, Spagna: Fasc. 289 Pos. 896, 22r.
72 ASV: AES, Spagna: Fasc. 289 Pos. 896, 23r.
73 Sanchez, p. 87.
74 "tener buenas relaciones con S.E. el Generalísimo." José Andrés-Gallego and Antón M. Pazos, *Archivo Gomá: Documentos de la Guerra Civil—1: Julio-Diciembre de 1936* (Madrid: Consejo Superior de Investigaciones Científicas, 2001), p. 450.
75 "Por eso en las negociaciones, confidenciales, que Vuestra Eminencia deberá desarrollar, tendrá que ser firme en la defensa de la libertad de la Santa Sede respecto al nombramiento y remoción de obispos, haciendo comprender claramente que ello constituye, especialmente en nuestros días, una cuestión fundamental para la Santa Sede y beneficiará tambien grandamente a la Nación, porque tal libertad será una prenda segura de que los Prelados seran hombres de Iglesia y no adeptos de partidos politicos. *Ibid.*
76 "La guerra que se desenvuelva en la República española, sépalo el mundo eterno no es una guerra religiosa, como ha querido haberles ver; es una guerra de tipo económico y de tipo económico arcaico." "Discurso de S.E. el Presidente del Gobierno vasco" in *Tierra Vasca* 23 December 1936 (MF/R 2226).
77 "Y aquí, el Presidente del Gobierno Euzkadi, católico, pregunta con el corazón dolorido ¿Por qué el silencio de la jerequia?" "Discurso de S.E. el Presidente del Gobierno vasco" in *Tierra Vasca* 23 December 1936 (MF/R 2226)
78 The conservative historian Luis Suárez has made the suggestion that Pacelli was very interested in negotiating with Aguirre, but the Basque President was the problem, *Franco y la Iglesia* (Madrid: Homolegens, 2011), p. 22.
79 ASV: AES, Spagna: Fasc. 289 Pos. 896, 106r.
80 "La preponderancia del elemento comunista que viene de fuera altera el equilibrio de una situación que hasta ahora era favorable a los católicos, y se da el caso terrible de luchas callejeras entre los dos bandos hasta ahora unidos, llegando hace pocos días los elementos revolucionarios a invadir las prisiones en que estaban detenidos destacados derechistas y matando en

un solo día y con bombas de mano a doscientos ocho presos, entre ellos personas destacadísimas de toda esta region. Ocurre en Vizcaya lo que ha pasado en Cataluña: los elementos afiliados al communismo y anarquismo han desbordado a los elementos de orden, y es de temer que ocurra en Vizcaya con sacerdotes, templos, y personas destacadas del catolicismo lo que ha pasado en otra regions, espacialmente de levanta y sur." ASV: AES, Spagna: Fasc. 289 Pos. 896, 106v. The new Prime Minister and Minister of War for the Republic, Largo Caballero, sent communist militias to the Basque region to fight against the Nationalists. These PNV did not support the import of communist militias. Similarly, as the Confederación Nacional de Trabajo (CNT) radicalized during spring 1937, the relationship between the PNV and the anarchist union deteriorated rapidly. Graham, pp. 246–8.
81 "Todos saben en la guerra civil española los católicos no han permanecido neutrales. Por una parte, los obispos, un gran número de sacerdotes y la mayor parte de sus adheridos han tomado netamente parte en pro de los generales rebeldes; por otra parte, los católicos eminentes e irreprochables defienden la cuasa del Gobierno español." "Editorial por el Partido Comunista de Euzkadi: La Iglesia Católica en la Guerra Civil" in *ERI* 6 February 1937 (MF/R 2263).
82 "Para la gran masa de católicos españoles la Iglesia había venido a ser, después de largo tiempo, una institución puramente político que luchaba contra las aspiraciones sociales y económicas de la gran mayoría del pueblo." "Editorial por el Partido Comunista de Euzkadi: La Iglesia Católica en la Guerra Civil" in *ERI,* 6 February 1937 (MF/R 2263).
83 "Christ, he is 'Red'", "The Freedom of Religion in the Loyal Zone" and "Message from the Women of Euzkadi to Eden, Blum, y Roosevelt, Representatives of the Democratic Countries" in *Mújeres,* 20 May 1937 (MF/R 1415).
84 Graham, p. 308.
85 William Parsons, S.J. "Atrocities Made to Order" in *Columbia* July 1937.
86 Preston, *The Spanish Holocaust*, p. 434.
87. *Ibid.,* 435.
88. Raguer, p. 86.

VI Foreign Requests for Vatican Intervention: The Hope of a Spiritual Authority?

1 Douglas Little, *"Malevolent Neutrality:" The United States, Great Britain, and the Origins of the Spanish Civil War* (Ithaca: Cornell University Press, 1985), p. 261.
2 Helen Graham, *The Spanish Republic at War, 1936–1939* (Cambridge: Cambridge University Press, 2002), p. 125 and Paul Preston, *The Spanish Civil War: Reaction, Revolution, and Revenge* (New York: W.W. Norton & Company, 2006), pp. 136–7.
3 Enrique Moradiellos, *1936: Los Mitos de la Guerra Civil* (Barcelona: Ediciones Peninsula, 2004), pp. 151–158.
4 Preston, *The Spanish Civil War*, pp. 136–7.

5   For a discussion of the French lack of unity on how to react to Spain's war, see: David Wingate Pike, *The French and the Civil War in Spain* (Eastbourne: Sussex Academic Press, 2011).
6   Graham, 125 and Preston, *The Spanish Civil War*, p. 139.
7   Little, *"Malevolent Neutrality,"* p. 262.
8   Preston, *The Spanish Civil War*, p. 139.
9   International economic worries had grown since the declaration of the Republic in 1931. The UK and US feared the nationalization of foreign companies in Spain. See: Little, *"Malevolent Neutrality"*, pp. 26, 32, 63, 66.
10 Richard Veatch, "The League of Nations and the Spanish Civil War, 1936–9" in *European History Quarterly*, 20 (1990), pp. 181–207.
11 *Ibid.*, p. 181.
12 Douglas Little, "Red Scare, 1936: Anti-Bolshevism and the Origins of British Non-Intervention in the Spanish Civil War" in *Journal of Contemporary History* 23, 22 (1998): pp. 291–311, esp. p. 306.
13 *Ibid.*, p. 298.
14 Graham, p. 125.
15 Geoffrey Warner, "France and Non-Intervention in Spain, July-August 1936" in *International Affairs* 38, 2 (1962): pp. 203–220.
16 *Ibid.*, p. 219.
17 *Ibid.*, p. 220.
18 Preston, *The Spanish Civil War*, p. 144.
19 Robert O. Paxton, *The Anatomy of Fascism* (New York: Vintage Reprint, 2005), pp. 68–72.
20 Veatch, pp. 192–3.
21 Preston, *The Spanish Civil War*, p. 149.
22 Aviva and Isaac Aviv, "The Madrid Working Class, the Spanish Socialist Party, and the Collapse of the Second Republic" in *Journal of Contemporary History* 16, 2 (1981): pp. 229–250, esp. p. 238.
23 Preston, *The Spanish Civil War*, p. 151.
24 *Ibid.*, p. 156.
25 *Ibid.*, p. 158.
26 Tom Buchanan, *The Impact of the Spanish Civil War on Britain: War, Loss, and Memory* (Eastbourne: Sussex Academic Press, 2007).
27 Antonio Marquina, "Planes Internacionales de Mediación durante la Guerra Civil" in UNISCI Discussion Papers (2006): pp. 229–248, esp. p.234.
28 Mr. F. D'A. G. Osborne at the British Legation to the Holy See to Mr. Eden, September 3, 1936, *British Documents on Foreign Affairs* (Great Britain: Foreign Office Confidential Print: British Documents, 1960).
29 Paul Preston, *The Spanish Holocaust: Inquisition and Extermination in Twentieth-Century Spain* (London: W.W. Norton & Company, 2012), pp. 665–671.
30 Mr. F. D'A. G. Osborne at the British Legation to the Holy See to Mr. Eden, September 3, 1936, British Documents on Foreign Affairs (Great Britain: Foreign Office Confidential Print: British Documents, 1960).
31 *Ibid.*

32 Peter Brownfeld, "London's Policies towards British Volunteers for the International Brigades: An Attempt to Safeguard her Precarious Diplomacy" in *International Journal of Iberian Studies* 15. 1 (2002): pp. 14–29 esp. p. 15.
33 Archivio Segreto Vaticano (ASV): Affari Ecclesiastici Straordinari, Spagna (AES, Spagna): Fasc. 268 Pos. 889, 99r–101r.
34 ASV: AES, Spagna: Fasc. 303 Pos. 899, 54r.
35 "reiterar su propósito inquebrantable de rechazar todo intento de mediación que no envuevla la rendición del enemigo, sin vanagloria." ASV: AES, Spagna: Fasc. 303 Pos. 899, 58r.
36 ASV: AES, Spagna: Fasc. 303 Pos. 899, 59r.
37 ASV: AES, Spagna: Fasc. 341 Pos. 929, 76r.
38 John Leche replaced Ogilvie-Forbes as British Chargé d'Affaires in Valencia. Before arriving in Valencia, Leche had been sympathetic to the Nationalist cause, but after viewing the uncontrollable violence of the situation, Leche attempted to continue humanitarian work. As Tom Buchanan writes, "For all of Leche's gaffes and unfortunate manner, however, it should be recorded that he not only continued Ogilvie-Forbes's humanitarian work, but also strove to enhance the conditions and terms of service for those working under him in increasingly perilous circumstances," Tom Buchanan, "Edge of Darkness: British 'Front-line' Diplomacy in the Spanish Civil War, 1936–1937" in *Contemporary European History* 12, 3 (2003): pp. 279–303, esp. p. 291. Therefore, one could argue that these British Chargés d'Affaires in Valencia were honest in their actions and willingness to help humanitarian causes. The inclusion of these men in any plans to evacuate civilians, therefore, should have come as a comforting reassurance.
39 ASV: AES, Spagna: Fasc. 311 Pos. 904–5, 89r.
40 ASV: AES, Spagna: Fasc. 311 Pos. 904–5, 90r-91r.
41 Antonio Manuel Moral Roncal, *Diplomacia, humanitarismo y espionaje en la Guerra Civil española* (Madrid: Editorial Biblioteca Nueva, 2008), p. 374.
42 *Ibid,*, p. 324.
43 *Ibid.*
44 *Ibid.*
45 Peter Jackson, "French Strategy and the Spanish Civil War" in Christian Leitz and David J. Dunthorn (eds.), *Spain in an International Context* (New York: Berghahn Books, 1999): pp. 55–79.
46 Delbos was sworn in as Foreign Minister in May 1936, following the Popular Front victory. During his tenure as Foreign Minister, Franco-Soviet relations greatly improved and conservative French generals were uncomfortable with this new relationship as it might anger Nazi Germany—posing a greater threat to the country. When Anthony Eden suggested talks between Britain and Italy concerning Spain in October 1937, Delbos insisted France join the talk. However, Italy rejected French involvement in these discussions. According to Glyn Stone, it appears that France was the junior partner to Britain's diplomatic actions and Delbos frequently tried to show Eden that France could be a reliable equal. See:

Glyn Stone, "Yvon Delbos and Anthony Eden: Anglo-French Cooperation, 1936–38" in Glyn Stone and Thomas G. Otte, eds., *Anglo-French Relations since the Later Eighteenth Century* (London: Routledge, 2009), pp. 165–186.
47 ASV: AES, Spagna: Fasc. 302 Pos. 897–9, 81r–82r.
48 "Veuillez donner d'urgence . . . au Cardinal Secrétaire d'Etat connaissance de la proposition dont les Gouvernements français et anglais . . . Vous pourrez indiquer que le Gouvernement français serait heureux que le Saint-Siège par son action favorable, aussi bien que par l'expression publique de son sentiment, put trouver l'occasion d'apporter l'appui de son autorité morale aux chances de succès d'une enterprise inspirée suelement par les plus hautes preoccupations d'humanité et de paix. ASV: AES, Spagna: Fasc. 302 Pos. 897–9, 85r.
49 ASV: AES, Spagna: Fasc. 302 Pos. 897–9, 74r.
50 "Il Sig. Ministro accennò al progetto di mediazione franco-inglese per la Spagna ed aggiunse che, a suo modo di vedere, al successo di ale iniziativa la Santa Sede avrebbe potuto contribuire in modo definitivo. Mi pregò, pertanto, di farmi interprete presso l'E.V. del desiderio del Governo Francese di veder la Santa Sede associarsi agli sforzi franco-inglesi nell'i-tento di poter arrivare ad estinguere la guerra in Spagna ed allontanare così, tra l'altro, il pericolo di complicazioni Internazionali. Lo scopo immediate dell'azione da svolgersi avrebbe dovuto esser quello di arrivare ad un armistizio. [. . .] In seguito si sarebbe potuto considerare il da farsi per regolare una questione tanto complicata. Il Sig. Delbos, infatti, non mostrò di nutrire illusioni su questo punto, atesse le divergenze profonde che esistono nei due campi; accennò, tuttavia, alla possibilità di nominare una Commissione internazionale. Mi aggiunse . . . anche dell'adesione dell'Italia, avrebbe potuto render più facile l'azione della Santa Sede." ASV: AES, Spagna: Fasc. 303 Pos. 899, 3r-3v.
51 ASV: AES, Spagna: Fasc. 303 Pos. 899, 4r.
52 ASV: AES, Spagna: Fasc. 303 Pos. 899, 8r.
53 "Le Cardinal disait <Maintenant, je crois les Allemands capables de tout . . . Je me demande de quoi ils ne sont capables>." François Charles-Roux to Paris, *Documents Diplomatique Français*, 4/7/1937.
54 "Le Saint-Siège a fini par être mis sur ses gardes par ce travail de dénigrement, où il croit discerner la main d'agents hitlérliens, cherchant à lui aliéner les catholiques d'Espagne nationaliste en le faissant apparaître à leurs yeux comme acquis à leurs advaersaires." François Charles-Roux to Paris, *Documents Diplomatique Français*, 18/9/1937.
55 ASV: AES, Spagna: Fasc. 303 Pos. 899, 29r.
56 "Ma la S.Sede sopratutto potrebbe forse presentarsi in tal veste con la Sua alta autorità morale." ASV: AES, Spagna: Fasc. 303 Pos. 899, 29v-30r.
57 " . . . si disse grato che il Santo Padre avesse voluto intervenire presso il Generale Franco ed aggiunse di sperare che, non appena si fosse verificato un momento di tregua fra le due parti, il Santo Padre col Suo alto prestigio sarebbe potuto anch'Esso intervenire onde trovare finalmente una via d'accordo e dar la pace alla tormentata Spagna. [. . .] il Santo Padre, io non risposi nulla limitandomi a deplorare la situazione della povera nazione

spagnola. Data però la situazione militare odierna delle due parti in conflitto, mi domando se le parole del sig. Paul Bancour non possan dare la chiave delle preoccupazioni del Governo in questo momento circa gli affari di Spagna. " ASV: AES, Spagna: Fasc. 303 Pos. 899, 32r-33r.

58 "Gli ho risposto che se si trattava di compiere un gesto umanitario, come per esempio di dar consigli al vincitore di moderazione, di perdono e di riconciliazione fra i figli e le classi di uno stesso Paese, pensavo che la Santa Sede non si sarebbe certo rifiutata." ASV: AES, Spagna: Fasc. 303 Pos. 899, 35r.

59 "Le résultat de ces ouvertures a été négatif." J. Rivière to Paris, *Documents Diplomatique Français*, 24/11/1938.

60 *Ibid.*

61 "Il n'y a aucune chance que le Pape se prête maintenant à addresser aux Espagnols un appel en vue d'une suspension d'hostilités de quelque durée, non plus que d'une mediation ou d'un armistice, Car il vient de faire dans ce sens auprès du general Franco une intervention diplomatique qui s'est heurtée à un refus immediate et catégorique." Jean Charles-Roux to Paris, to Paris, *Documents Diplomatique Français*, 19/12/1938.

62 See: Moral Roncal, Chapters II–V.

63 "di una intervenzione amichevole dei paesi americani in Spagna per porre termine alla guerra civile." ASV: AES, Spagna: Fasc. 285 Pos. 895, 44r.

64 "atrocità dei comunisti di Madrid" Fasc. 285 Pos. 895, 44v.

65 Moral Roncal, p. 422.

66 ASV: AES, Spagna: Fasc. 267 Pos. 889, 33r.

67 ASV: AES, Spagna: Fasc. 267 Pos. 889, 34r.

68 ASV: AES, Spagna: Fasc. 267 Pos. 889, 35r.

69 *Ibid.*

70 See: Ismael Saz, "Fascism and Empire: Fascist Italy Against Republican Spain" in *Mediterranean Historical Review*,13, 1 (1998) pp. 116–134 and John F. Coverdale, *Italian Intervention in the Spanish Civil War* (Princeton: Princeton University Press, 1975).

71 ASV: AES, Spagna: Fasc. 302 Pos. 897–9, 94r.

72 ASV: AES, Spagna: Fasc. 268 Pos. 889, 61r.

73 ASV: AES, Spagna: Fasc. 268 Pos. 889, 76r.

74 ASV: AES, Spagna: Fasc. 268 Pos. 889, 79r.

75 Andreas Mayor (translator), *Ciano's Diary 1937–1938* (London: Methuen & Co. Ltd., 1952), p. 204.

76 Florentino Rodao, "Japan and the Axis, 1937–8: Recognition of the Franco Regime and Manchukuo" in *Journal of Contemporary History* 44, 3 (2009), pp. 431–447.

77 *Ibid.*, p. 436.

78 ASV: AES, Spagna: Fasc. 268 Pos. 889, 52r.

79 ASV: AES, Spagna: Fasc. 268 Pos. 889, 53r.

80 ASV: AES, Spagna: Fasc. 303 Pos. 899, 69r.

81 Paul McGuire, "After the Storm: The Nationalist Government of Spain Works for Reconstruction in the Sane and Christian Spirit" in *Columbia* (May 1938), p. 1.

82 Paul McGuire, "Storm in the Mediterranean" in *Columbia* (March 1939), p. 7. While this project is not interested in the mental state of Il Duce, it is interesting to note this reaction to Mussolini only months before the start of WWII, but after the invasions of Ethiopia and Albania.
83 "non è più favorevole vittoria Franco." ASV: AES, Spagna: Fasc. 303 Pos. 899, 76r.
84 *Ibid.*
85 ASV: AES, Spagna: Fasc. 303 Pos. 899, 87r.
86 *Ibid.*
87 *Ibid.*, 87r–88r.
88 ASV: AES, Spagna: Fasc. 303 Pos. 899, 90r.
89 ASV: AES, Spagna: Fasc. 303 Pos. 899, 91r.
90 *Ibid.*
91 Hilari M. Raguer, *Gunpowder and Incense: The Catholic Church and the Spanish Civil War* (London: Routledge, 2007), p. 214.
92 ASV: AES, Spagna: Fasc. 303 Pos. 899, 50r.
93 *Ibid.*
94 ASV: AES, Spagna: Fasc. 303 Pos. 899, 50v.
95 *Ibid.*
96 ASV: AES, Spagna: Fasc. 303 Pos. 899, 39r.
97 *Ibid.*
98 "mermar la indepenencia de España." ASV: AES, Spagna: Fasc. 303 Pos. 899, 39v.
99 ASV: AES, Spagna: Fasc. 303 Pos. 899, 41r.
100 "la voix du Saint Père s'est fait entendre en faveur de la paix." ASV: AES, Spagna: Fasc. 303 Pos. 899, 72r.
101 *Ibid.*
102 ASV: AES, Spagna: Fasc. 303 Pos. 899, 72v.
103 "C'est dans l'anxiété que cette situation nous inspire et dans un grand espoir en le Siège Apostolique que nous venons respectueusement solicitier la bienfaisante intercession du Saint Père." ASV: AES, Spagna: Fasc. 303 Pos. 899, 73r.
104 "La trágica situación de nuestra patria nos mueve a elevar nuestra suplica al Padre común de la Cristianidad." ASV: AES, Spagna: Fasc. 347 Pos. 938–940, 108r.
105 "the diplomacy of the great powers" ... "the spiritual forces and in the supreme power of fraternal charity." *Ibid.*
106 "reclamando que cese de una vez la espantosa guerra de España y sea sustituítra poe un arreglo pacífico la matanza entre hermanos que contra la voluntad de casi todos ellos se prosegue. O, el menos, QUE SE ACEPTE POR AMBOS BELIGERANTES UNA TRUEGA DE UN MES, A PARTIR DEL 24 DE DICIEMBRE—truega de Dios para los cristianos—durante la cual todo acto de guerra o de preparativos bélicos quedería prohibido." ASV: AES, Spagna: Fasc. 347 Pos. 938–940, 109r.
107 See: Gonzalo Redondo, *Historia de la Iglesia en España 1931–1939, Tomo I* (Madrid: Ediciones Rialp, S.A., 1993), 95–98.
108 "Il s'agit d'une demarche du Saint Père auprès des deux parties

belligérantes en Espagne, afin d'obtenir une trêve des hostilités pendant les fêtes de Nöel. Tous les jeunes Espagnols pourraient ainsi s'unir à leurs frères de tous les pays pour célébrer dans la tranquillité la naissance du Prince de la Paix." ASV: AES, Spagna: Fasc. 347 Pos. 938–940, 99r.

109 "Je ne sais rien sur les dispositions de Barcelone, mais, d'après des renseignements sérieux, quoique de seconde main, je crois que le gouvernement républicain est prêt à accepter toute proposition de paix." ASV: AES, Spagna: Fasc. 347 Pos. 938–940, 101r.

110 ASV: AES, Spagna: Fasc. 347 Pos. 938–940, 102r.

111 "De qui peut vient cet appel? Ce ne peut être d'une nation étrangère. Les Espagnols—malgré tout ce qui se passé chez eux!—proclament que leur guerre est une affaire intérieure qui ne regards qu'eux et qu'ils veulent régler entre eux. D'ailleurs aucune puissance ne peut afficacement intervenir. S'il s'agit d'un gouvernement de l'entente franco-anglaise, l'Espagne se trouvera en butte à l'hostilité de l'axe Rome-Berlin dont elle est déjà, en partie, prisonnière. S'il s'agit d'un gouvernement de l'axe, l'Espagne se privera des resources financières de l'entente qui lui sont indispensables. Si c'est le Saint-Siège qui intervient, toutes les objections disparaissent. Ce n'est pas un gouvernement étranger qui s'immisce dans les affaires espagnols, c'est le Père Commun qui appelle ses fils à l'union fraternelle. D'autre part, comme le Saint Siège n'a pas d'intérêts matériels à faire prévaloir en Espagne, la question de rivalité internationale ne se pose plus.
Que d'avantage le Saint-Siège ne retirerait-il pas d'une pareille intervention!" ASV: AES, Spagna: Fasc. 347 Pos. 938–940, 103r.

112 ASV: AES, Spagna: Fasc. 347 Pos. 938–940, 104r.

113 "D'abord l'appel moral à la conciliation et la proposition d'un armistice immediate. Puis, pour entrer dans le domaine pratique, la reunion des représentants des principales forces du pays: Gouvernement républicain, phalangistes, requetes, Catalans, basques, en offrant puet-être un légat qui devrait être de premier plan—le Cardinal Secrétaire d'Etat?—pour présider et arbitrer la reunion." ASV: AES, Spagna: Fasc. 347 Pos. 938–940, 105r.

114 ASV: AES, Spagna: Fasc. 347 Pos. 938–940, 105r–106r.

VII How to Save the Basque: Vatican Mediation Meets Rebel Opinions

1 Hilari M. Raguer, *Gunpowder and Incense: The Catholic Church and the Spanish Civil War* (London: Routledge, 2007), p. 86.

2 According to Paul Preston, the Spanish Nationalists went on to arrest and execute tens of thousands of Republican sympathizers after the war ended. During the whole civil war, Preston suggests the Republic was responsible for 49, 272 casualties, and Nationalists caused officially 130,199 and probably at least 150,000. Paul Preston, *The Spanish Holocaust: Inquisition and Extermination in Twentieth-Century Spain* (London: W.W. Norton & Company, 2012), p. 666.

3 William J. Callahan, *The Catholic Church in Spain, 1875–1998* (Washington, D.C., The Catholic University of American Press, 2000), pp. 379–80.

4   *Ibid.*
5   John F. Pollard, *Money and the Rise of the Modern Papacy: Financing the Vatican, 1850–1959* (Cambridge: Cambridge University Press, 2005), pp. 56, 81.
6   Preston, *The Spanish Holocaust*, pp. 428–468.
7   José M. Sánchez, *The Spanish Civil War as a Religious Tragedy* (Notre Dame: University of Notre Dame Press, 1987), pp. 132–4.
8   *Ibid.*
9   *Ibid.*
10 Antonio Marquina Barrio, "El Vaticano y el Estallido de la Guerra Civil: El Cardinal Gomá Reparó el Fracaso Diplomático del Marqués de Magaz" in *UNISCI Discussion Papers* 12 (2006), pp. 229–244, esp. p. 231.
11 Peter C. Kent, "The Vatican and the Spanish Civil War" in *European History Quarterly* 16, 4 (1986), pp. 441–464 esp. pp. 441–6.
12 Tadeusz Milkowski, "The Spanish Church and the Vatican during the Spanish Civil War" in *The Polish Foreign Affairs Digest* 3 (2004), pp. 207–242, esp. p. 211
13 Ricardo Miralles, "The International Policy of the Second Republic during the Spanish Civil War" in *Mediterranean Historical Review* 13, 1 (1998), pp. 135–149, esp. pp. 146–7.
14 Milkowski, p. 229.
15 *Ibid.*, p. 231.
16 Frances Lannon, *Privilege, Persecution and Prophecy: The Catholic Church in Spain 1875–1975* (Oxford: Clarendon Press, 1987), p. 207 and Preston, *The Spanish Holocaust*, pp. 236–7.
17 *Ibid.*, 207.
18 "The hope of obtaining a favor." Archivio Segreto Vaticano (ASV): Affari Ecclesiastici Straordinari, Spagna (AES, Spagna): Fasc. 302 Pos. 897–9, 68r.
19 ASV: AES, Spagna: Fasc. 302 Pos. 897–9, 70r.
20 "A este fin, por los demás, no parece necesaria una intervención directa de la Santa Sede, que fué preciso evitar en otros casos semejantes, por no leves razones.
    A la verdad, el Santo Padre, al que he sometido el deseo de V.E. no ve la posibilidad y conveniencia de esta intervención en las presentas circumstancias y cree que para el noble y santo objeto indicado por V.E. será plenamente eficaz la palabra del Eminentísimo Señor Cardenal Primado como voz que se levanta de los mismos campos ensangretados por la lucha y por el martirio." ASV: AES, Spagna: Fasc. 302 Pos. 897–9, 70r.
21 For Preston, the Rebels represented a much more repressive group. Preston, *The Spanish Holocaust*, p. 665.
22 "Un intervento della Santa Sede in favore di uno scambio di ostaggi tra i Nazionalisti ed i Baschi sarebbe per ora e nelle attuali circostanze, a mio unile e subordinato modo di vedere, inefficace, inopportune e fors'anche dannoso per gli interesse della Chiesa." ASV: AES, Spagna: Fasc. 311 Pos. 304–5, 6r.
23 ASV: AES, Spagna: Fasc. 311 Pos. 304–5, 6r.
24 ASV: AES, Spagna: Fasc. 311 Pos. 304–5, 6v.

25 *Ibid.*
26 "Scrivere al Cardinale che tratta personalmente con Franco e gli faccia capire che senza concessioni non si può far nulla. Quando Franco fosse disposto a fare qualche concessioni, che naturalmente vorremmo sapere quali fossero, il Santo Padre non è alieno dalle scrivere una Lettera Pontificado al Clero basco." ASV: AES, Spagna: Fasc. 290 Pos. 896, 8r.
27 "Ma naturalmente bisogna che il Generale Franco faccia qualche concessione e che noi ne conosciamo la portata. Buoni cattolici come sono realmente, se proprio si trovassero davanti a una parola personale del Papa, scritta per loro, e nelle condizioni cosi penose per il Papa, si può sperare che non mancherebbe una qualche effetto." ASV: AES, Spagna: Fasc. 290 Pos. 896, 8r.
28 "Sua Santità rimette pertanto all'E.V.Rev.ma di giudicare se Le sembra espediente di trattare personalmente la cosa coll'Eccmo Sig. Generale Franco, facendogli presente, con quel tatto ed abilità che tanto La distinguone, che senza concessioni di qualche importanza non sarebbe possibilie un intervento della Santa Sede . . . " ASV: AES, Spagna: Fasc. 290 Pos. 896, 9v.
29 "Qualora poi Sua Eccellenza il Signor Generale Franco fosse disposto a fare delle concessioni di tale natura ed entità da rendere possible detto intervento, i Baschi, buoni cattolici come essi sono, se proprio si trovassero davanti ad una parola personale del Santo Padre, scritta per loro, e nelle condizioni così penose per la Sua Augusta Persona, si può sperare che se ne sentirebbero profondamente commossi e non mancherebbe la Lettera Pontificia di produrre qualche benefico effetto." ASV: AES, Spagna: Fasc. 290 Pos. 896, 9v-10r.
30 "Il Generale Franco afferma che i baschi non facero mai alcun passo verso il Governo di Burgos per arrivare a un accordo. Al contrario, dal primo momento, si buttarono in guerra con i rossi con I quali avevano avuto previamente contatti e intese. [. . .] Il Generale Franco supponeva che una minaccia di scomunica della Santa Sede avrebbe potuto auitare i cattolici di Biscaglia a svincolarsi da una mostruosa alleanza che del resto minaccia di ritorcersi contro essi. Infatti i baschi corrono pericolo di essere sopraffatti, nel loro stesso territirio, da comunisti e da marxisti. [. . .] Il Governo di Burgos rispetto tuttavia le ragioni che, nella Sua Suprema saggezza, la Santa Sede possa avere per non pronunciare la scomunica. Tale atto sarebbe accolto con favore dal vero popolo spagnuolo, inorridito per i crimini e le profanazioni che si commettono. Comunque il Governo non insiste sul suo suggerimento, riconoscendo la esclusiva competenza della Santa Sede in questo campo. A proposito del trattamento da farsi alla provincia basca, il Governo di Burgos si rimette alla sua dichiarazione pubblica del 1º Ottobre u.s. Con essa si concedeva a tutte le regioni e provincie spagnuole di potere di un decentramento amministrativo, rispettando la loro peculiarità. Il Governo di Burgos osserva che in dipendenza del predominio dei rossi nella provincia basca, il problema separatista riceverà una radicale soluzione in quanto che i rossi acquistano ogni giorno più il predominio sui Baschi. Questi ultimi sono destinati a sparire, se

continuerà il presente stato di cose. Il Governo di Burgos osserva che questo punto che ha per esso valore più nell'ordine spirituale che materiale, deve essere oggetti di particolare considerazione per la Santa Sede per l'importanza notevole che ha sotto l'aspetto religioso." ASV: AES, Spagna: Fasc. 290 Pos. 896, 11r.

31 "Circa la delicata questione dei cattolici Baschi, con'Ella giustamente rileva, Sua Santita non ritiene possible d'intervenire nella forma che aveva desiderato il Governo di Salamanca." José Andrés-Gallego and Antón M. Pazos, *Archivo Gomá: Documentos de la Guerra Civil—3: Febrero 1936* (Madrid: Consejo Superior de Investigaciones Científicas, 2001), p. 163.

32 "que tantas pruebas tiene dadas de tierno amor nuestra España, especialmente desde que sufre la tribulación de la guerra que tantos daños nos ha causado en todos los órdenes, se ha conmovido ante las indicaciones que de varias partes se le han hecho para que se sirva intervenir en favor de la paz entre los Nacionalistas Vascos y el Gobierno Nacional Español." ASV: AES, Spagna: Fasc. 290 Pos. 896, 16r.

33 "Dos veces he hablado con el General Franco para interesarle en los deseos de nuestro Santísimo Padre. En ambas conversaciones ha Estado deferentísimo, y cuando la conversación ha derivado hacia las relaciones del Gobierno con la Iglesia, y especialmente a la modificación de la legislación española actual en sentido netamente católico, ha tenido puntos de mira laudabilísimos, que tendré la satisfacción de exponer a Vuestra Eminencia en otro escrito.
Por lo que atañe al punto concreto que es objecto de la Carta que correspondo, el General Franco ha tenido palabras de gran encomio para la posición que adopta Su Santidad con respecto al problema vasco-español y para la gestión paternal que insinúa V.E. en Su nombre, tan en consonancia con la tradición y con la misión de caridad de la Santa Sede. Pero, según le indicaba a V.E.R. en telegrama cifrado Número 7, expedido en esta misma fecha, no juzgaoportuno por ahora el General Franco ofrecer una condiciones de rendición, por parte de los vascos, que podrían causar en aquel pueblo maypr desgracia de la que sufre, a más de las consideraciones de carácter militar y político que tengo el gusto de concretar en los dos apartados siguinetes, que explican, en el derecha y en el hecho vivo actual, los diversos puntos de vista y las conclusions que derivan de la conversación habida con el General Franco. En ellos procuro dar a Vuestra Eminencia una visión de conjunto de los distintos factores del problema vasco, que adquiere por momentos una gravedad que puede degenerar en veradera catástrofe." ASV: AES, Spagna: Fasc. 290 Pos. 896, 17r.

34 ASV: AES, Spagna: Fasc. 290 Pos. 896, 18r-19r.

35 *Ibid.*

36 ASV: AES, Spagna: Fasc. 290 Pos. 896, 20r-22r.

37 "Sua Santita sara pertanto grata all'Eminenza Vostra Rev.ma se, con quella prudenza e tatto cha tanto La distinguono, vorra fare presso il Signor Generale Franco quei passi che credera possibili ed opportuni affinche tali eccidii non abbiano piu a ripetersi." José Andrés-Gallego and Antón M. Pazos, *Archivo Gomá: Documentos de la Guerra Civil—4: Marzo 1936*

(Madrid: Consejo Superior de Investigaciones Científicas, 2001), p. 94.
38 ASV: AES, Spagna: Fasc. 292 Pos. 896, 34r.
39 "Sigue la ofenisva victoriosa, y no habrán de pasar muchos días sin que quede definivamente quebrantada la resistencia de vascos y rojos manconumados." ASV: AES, Spagna: Fasc. 292 Pos. 896, 34r.
40 "Durante los pasados meses los católicos vascos no han podido controlar totalmente a los rojos." ASV: AES, Spagna: Fasc. 292 Pos. 896, 34r.
41 ASV: AES, Spagna: Fasc. 292 Pos. 896, 34v.
42 *Ibid.*
43 *Ibid.*
44 As discussed in Chapter V, Burgos gave a warning of a serious attack in the Basque country for 26 April. In response, Monsignor Onaindía wrote to Cardinal Gomá to discuss these attacks, and Gomá responded that "People pay for their pacts with evil and for their perverse wickedness in sticking to them." Preston, *The Spanish Holocaust*, pp. 434–5.
45 ASV: AES, Spagna: Fasc. 293 Pos. 896, 10r-10v.
46 "Se empeñen en conservar intacto Bilbao." ASV: AES, Spagna: Fasc. 292 Pos. 896, 52r.
47 ASV: AES, Spagna: Fasc. 292 Pos. 896, 54r-54v. Franco's forces frequently claimed Republican forces had destroyed the city as they evacuated it, and not the Nationalist troops.
48 "Facilitarán la salida de todos los dirigentes." ASV: AES, Spagna: Fasc. 292 Pos. 896, 52r.
49 ASV: AES, Spagna: Fasc. 292 Pos. 896, 54v.
50 "Completa garantia que el ejercito de Franco respetará personas y cosas." ASV: AES, Spagna: Fasc. 292 Pos. 896, 52r.
51 ASV: AES, Spagna: Fasc. 292 Pos. 896, 54v.
52 "Libertad absoluta para los milicianos y soldados que se rindan con las armas." ASV: AES, Spagna: Fasc. 292 Pos. 896, 52r.
53 ASV: AES, Spagna: Fasc. 292 Pos. 896, 54v.
54 "Serán sometidos a los tribunales los culpables contra derecho común devastaciones y destrucciones." ASV: AES, Spagna: Fasc. 292 Pos. 896, 52r.
55 ASV: AES, Spagna: Fasc. 292 Pos. 896, 54v.
56 "Será respetada la vida y los bienes de aquellos que se rindieran de buena fé aun para los jefes." ASV: AES, Spagna: Fasc. 292 Pos. 896, 52r.
57 ASV: AES, Spagna: Fasc. 292 Pos. 896, 54v-55r.
58 "En el ordén político decentralizacion administrativa en la misma forma que la disfrutan otra regiones." ASV: AES, Spagna: Fasc. 292 Pos. 896, 52r.
59 ASV: AES, Spagna: Fasc. 292 Pos. 896, 55r.
60 "En el orden social justicia progresiva teniedo en cuanto los medios de la hacienda nacional según los principios de la 'Enciclica Rerum Novarum.'" ASV: AES, Spagna: Fasc. 292 Pos. 896, 52r.
61 ASV: AES, Spagna: Fasc. 292 Pos. 896, 55r.
62 ASV: AES, Spagna: Fasc. 292 Pos. 896, 55v.
63 Preston, *The Spanish Holocaust*, p. 436.
64 "Alcune personalita domandano intervento Sua Santita affinche prossimo prendere Bilbao siano risparmiati sacerdoti, donne, fanciulli et madre

nubile disgraziate combinazioni." José Andrés-Gallego and Antón M. Pazos, *Archivo Gomá: Documentos de la Guerra Civil—6: Junio-Julio de 1937* (Madrid: Consejo Superior de Investigaciones Científicas, 2001), p. 179.
65 "Prega V.E.R. far in proposito presso codesto Governo raggiungendo passo che credera piu oppotuno." *Ibid.*
66 "Avendo saputo che sono in corso trattative per la resa dei baschi, Sua Santità, senza entrare nei particolarri della resa, fa appello nel Nome del Redentore Divino alla vostra fede di cattolico affinchè tali trattative giungano celermente a buon fine e si evite così ogni ulteriore spargimento di sangue. Sua Santità è sicuro che Vostra Eccellenza non imporrà condizioni che porterebbero alla rovina di una popalazione che può aver errato ma che è una popalazione cristiana." ASV: AES, Spagna: Fasc. 296 Pos. 896, 45r.
67 "Nel trasmettere tale messaggio Vostra Eminenza faccia le più insistenti premure affinchè il Gernale Franco accondiscenda a ciò che domanda il Santo Padre e non imponga condizioni inaccesttabili." ASV: AES, Spagna: Fasc. 296 Pos. 896, 45r.
68 "Generale FRANCO ha ricevuto colla massima venerazione Messaggio SANTO PADRE et riconoscente dell'appello fattogli da Sua Santità nel nome del Redentore Divino e della sua Fede di cattolico, in ossequio a questa ed al Sommo Pontefice, è disposto as agire con assoluta benigntità et accetta da parte sua puramente et semplicemente proposizioni presetate." ASV: AES, Spagna: Fasc. 296 Pos. 896, 46r.
69 "È giunta notizia che settimana scorsa furono fucilati Bilbao numerosi detenuti per motivi politici. In previsione nuove condanne Santo Padre incarica V.E.R. intervenire Suo Augusto Nome presso Generale Franco consigliando specialmente occasione feste natalizie atti clemenza." ASV: AES, Spagna: Fasc. 297 Pos. 896.
70 Raguer, p. 188.
71 "Interpretando paterno desiderio Sua Santità fin dal principio dicembre chiese Generale Franco atti clemenza occasione festività Natale.
Generale Franco mi ha fatto comunicare ieri sera che aderendo invito Santo Padre commuta sentenza 100 condannati a morte et procede scambio 200 ufficiali detenuti condannati a morte. Maggiorenza fucilati recentemente dicesi siano stati criminali rossi et agenti resistenza armata basca." ASV: AES, Spagna: Fasc. 297 Pos. 896, 61r.
72 Preston, *The Spanish Holocaust*, p. 434.

VIII Bombings and Civilians: Rebel Rejection of Mediation

1 Brian R. Sullivan, "Fascist Italy's Military Involvement in the Spanish Civil War" in *The Journal of Military History* 59 (1995): pp. 697–727, esp. p. 723 and Michael Alpert, "The Clash of Spanish Armies: Contrasting Ways of War in Spain" in *War in History* 6 (1999) pp. 331–351, esp. p. 343.
2 Archivio Segreto Vaticano (ASV): Affari Ecclesiastici Straordinari, Spagna (ASV: AES, Spagna): Fasc. 347 Pos. 938–440, 94r.
3 ASV: AES, Spagna: Fasc. 341 Pos. 929, 4r.

4 "Sono stati singolarmente distruttore e mortiferi i bombardamenti avvenuta durante gli ultimi quindici giorni, e sono divenuti così frequenti da provocare la condanna del mondo civile." ASV: AES, Spagna: Fasc. 341 Pos. 929, 5r.

5 "per quanto riguarda i <u>bombardamenti</u> effettuati dai <u>nazionali</u> è da temere che essi provocheranno una ripresa della <u>persecuzione religiosa</u> e civile, ora assai pacata. [. . .] Verso la fine di ottobre del 1936, in occasione di un preteso bombardamenti del porta di Rosas, vi fu in Catalogna, ovunque, il più grande massacro di ostaggio civile, e di sacerdoti e religiosi. Più tardi, verso la fine di agosto 1937, nella piccola città gi Granollera presso Bacellona,—dove erano stati numerosi gli assassini fin da luglio 1936— furano assassinati altri 50 ostaggi." ASV: AES, Spagna: Fasc. 341 Pos. 929, 5r-6r.

6 ASV: AES, Spagna: Fasc. 341 Pos. 929, 6r-7r.

7 According to Paul Preston, Republicans detained 8,352 conservatives, while Nationalists were responsible for 3,688 deaths and casualties in Cataluña. Paul Preston, *The Spanish Holocaust: Inquisition and Extermination in Twentieth-Century Spain* (London: W.W. Norton & Company, 2012), p. 665.

8 ASV: AES, Spagna: Fasc. 341 Pos. 929, 8r-9r.

9 "Conviene notare che i nazionali generalmente non danno le cifre esate dei danni e delle vittime causate dai bombardamenti dei governativi, forse per non demoralizzare le popolazioni e per non confessare che, sovente, le difese antiaere sono state sorprese e che inoltre sono spesse volte inefficaci ASV: AES, Spagna: Fasc. 341 Pos. 929, 9r.

10 "Santo Padre profondamente addolorato per numerosi vittime popalazione civile el distruzione opere artistiche causate dalle due parti in lotta con accentuati et sempre più frequenti bombardamenti aerei città aperte, riservamdosi di sollecitare Nunzio Apostolico Parigi intervenire nel modo che gli sarà possibile presso Governo Barcellona per far cessare tale inumana forma guerra, confida nei sentimenti cattolici Generale Franco affinchè anche Nazionale desistano da tali bombardamenti che causando vittime innocenti servono agli avversari per intensificare violenta campagna estera contro Spagna Nazionale." ASV: AES, Spagna: Fasc. 341 Pos. 929, 12r.

11 "Gen. Franco mostrandosi grato preoccipazione paterna Sua Santità per vittime civile incursioni aeree affermò aviazione Nazionale essersi sempre astenuta et si asterrà da bombardamenti città indifese avendo bombardato solo obiettivi militari che per essere situati dentro quartieri abitati hanno potuto causare gravi conseguenze non ostante precauzioni usate.
Gen. Franco assicurò avere segnalato zona sicurezza per popolazione civile ma tali zone (come a Madrid et a Barcelona) furono usate per fabbriche et depositi di munizioni.
  Gen. Franco dichiarò che città aperte et paesi indifesi Spagna Nazionale furono assai bombardarti anche recentemente causando numerouse cittime civile.
  Gen. Franco desidera infine assicurare Sua Santità nulla omettere per

risparmiare popolazione civile." ASV: AES, Spagna: Fasc. 341 Pos. 929, 30r.
12 ASV: AES, Spagna: Fasc. 341 Pos. 929, 34v.
13 ASV: AES, Spagna: Fasc. 341 Pos. 929, 35r.
14 Michael Alpert, "The Popular Army of the Spanish Republic, 1936–39" in Wayne Bowen and José Álvarez (eds.), *A Military History of Modern Spain* (Westport: Praeger, 2007), pp. 331–351, esp. p. 105. Republican forces were capable of their own attacks, including the December 1937 Battle of Teruel. Victories such as this, however, were not the norm. George Esenwein, "Spanish Civil War: Franco's Nationalist Army in Wayne Bowen and José Álvarez (eds.), *A Military History of Modern Spain* (Westport: Praeger, 2007), pp. 68–92, esp. p. 88.
15 ASV: AES, Spagna: Fasc. 341 Pos. 929, 34v.
16 "La Saint Père, en effet, à l'occasion aussi des derniers èvènements tragiques, auxquelles Votre Eminence fait allusion, s'est empressé d'intervenir auprès des Autorités responsables pour atténuer les terribles conséquences des bombardements aériens." ASV: AES, Spagna: Fasc. 341 Pos. 929, 26r.
17 "Je me suis permis de faire connaître à Votre Eminence ce qui précède à seul tître d'information. Elle pourra toutefois aisément déduire quels obstacles rencontre l'oeuvre de paix et de persuasion que le Saint Siège ne cesse de déployer pour éliminer ou au moins diminuer les horreurs du si douloureux conflit espagnols." ASV: AES, Spagna: Fasc. 341 Pos. 929, 27r-27v.
18 "Il noto scrittore sig. Mendizabal, Presidente di questo Comitato spagnuolo per la Pace civile, mi ha inviato, perchè io lo facessi pervenire a destinazione, il qui accluso telegramma con il quale, come l'Eminenza Vostra Reverendissima rileverà, viene invocato l'intervento del S. Padre onde far cessare i bombardamenti di città aperte che han già provocato la morte di tanti innocenti e accumulate tante rovine." ASV: AES, Spagna: Fasc. 341 Pos. 929, 64r.
19 ASV: AES, Spagna: Fasc. 341 Pos. 929, 67r.
20 "In seguito ai rcenti bombardamenti aerei prego V.E. rinnovare, nel modo che crederà più oppotuno, a nome della S.S. i passi già fatti presso Generale Franco allo scopo di evitare distruzioni e uccisioni che non possono non nuocere stessa cuasa nazionale." ASV: AES, Spagna: Fasc. 341 Pos. 929, 75r.
21 "dichiara che bombardamento fronte francese non essere stato fatto da aviazione nazionale." ASV: AES, Spagna: Fasc. 341 Pos. 929, 75r.
22 The Nationalist air force received a great deal of German Ju-52s and Italian Savoia-Marchetti SM.81s. These planes had been used to bomb other Spanish cities, most notably, Guernica. Esenwein, p. 82.
23 "Importante obiettivo miltare per enore quantità armi e munizioni in esse depositate." ASV: AES, Spagna: Fasc. 341 Pos. 929, 75r.
24 ASV: AES, Spagna: Fasc. 341 Pos. 929, 79r-79v.
25 "Lo stesso Generalissimo volle insistere su questo punto: che i governi esteri, specialmente il Governo Francese, dovrebbero rendersi conto che aiutando i repubblicani a resistere (nonostante le loro dichiarazione in contrario) cooperano attivamente a rendere più crudele la guerra, perchè

più aspra è la reistenza che i Nazionali vanno incontrando." ASV: AES, Spagna: Fasc. 341 Pos. 929, 79v-80r.

26 Esenwein, p. 84.
27 "Si assicura, da persone neutrali provenienti dalla Francia, che mai è passato, attraverso la frontiera dei Pirenei, tanto materiale da guerra, a destinazione della Spagna rossa, come in questi due ultimi mesi. L'ammasso ingente di armi e munizioni in locatità abitate, avrebbe provocato, al dire dei Nazionali, le loro incursioni aeree [...] Questo Governo dichiara che il giorno in cui la Francia chiuderà la frontiera dei Pirenei, i bombardamenti cesseranno subito, perchè non ci sarà ragione di farli, e la guerra volgerebbe presto alla fine." ASV: AES, Spagna: Fasc. 341 Pos. 929, 79v-80r.
28 ASV: AES, Spagna: Fasc. 341 Pos. 929, 91r.
29 ASV: AES, Spagna: Fasc. 341 Pos. 929, 92r.
30 ASV: AES, Spagna: Fasc. 341 Pos. 929, 93r.
31 "Si nota grande eccitazione et indignazione in questo centro governativo per sempre crescenti aiuti francesi all'esercito rosso, senza i quali aiuti comunisti Barcellona sarebbero facilmente vinti." ASV: AES, Spagna: Fasc. 341 Pos. 929, 83r.
32 ASV: AES, Spagna: Fasc. 341 Pos. 929, 86r-86v.
33 "No military interest." ASV: AES, Spagna: Fasc. 341 Pos. 929, 90r.
34 "La Embajada de España se ve obligada a rogar a la Secretaria de Estado de Su Santidad que tenga a bien dar a conocer a la dirección responsible del Osservatore Romano, esta queja, para que, en lo sucesivo, sea evitada la publicación de informaciones que, aunque tomadas de otros periodicos . . . que no se compadece con la exactitud de los hechos y el profundo sentido católico que caracteriza al Movimiento Nacional de España." ASV: AES, Spagna: Fasc. 341 Pos. 929, 90r-90v.
35 "Sua Santità unirebbe volentieri sua intercessione se già non sapesse che Generale Franco rigugge da ogni simile negoziato." ASV: AES, Spagna: Fasc. 347 Pos. 938-440, 43r.
36 "Il Ministro Esteri [of Nationalist Spain] . . . dice poter prevedere risposta non differente da altre già date. Contesto siano considerati attentamente termini nuova proposta che, diversamente da altre, lascia alla generosità del Generale Franco inidicare le condizioni." ASV: AES, Spagna: Fasc. 347 Pos. 938-440, 44r.
37 "Come ebbi l'onore di manifestare a Vostra Eminenza, fu mia cura insistare con il Generale Jordana, per dimonstrare che nel caso presente non si proponeva una mediazione per giungere ad un accordo col Governo di Barcellona, ma si trattava di conoscere, sia pure in linee generali, a quali condizioni sarebbe possibilie una resa. Però anche simili proposte sono considerate dal Generale Franco con diffidenza e per questo non sono accolte.

Il Ministro degli Esteri naturalmente mi dichiarò che da parte del Generalissimi non vi è nessun proposito di vendette, e che nel castigo ai responsabili dell'attuale situazione e ai colpevoli di delitti si procederà con un elevato concetto di giustizia, dal quale non andrà mai disguinto, poichè dopo tutto si tratta sempre di spagnuoli, un grande sentimento di generosità. Che anzi affidarsi alla generosità del Generale Franco sarà il modo migliore per rendere meno gravosa le conseguenza della resa.

Il Generale Franco persiste nella convinzione che ogni porposta, la quale tenda a stipulare un accordo o a tentare una intesa col nemico, sia a favore dell'esercito e dell'ideale marxista, quindi di pregiudizio per l'avvenire della Spagna e del mondo intero che devono vincere definitivamente il communismo. Questa attitudine è resa ancora più ferma dalle opinine assai diffusa che le condizioni in cui si trova la popolazione di Madrid sono disastrosa e che un altro inverno di privazioni e di stenti deimerà, con la tisi e la inanzione, giovan e donne.

Tuttavia la speranza di vittoria prossima è qui alquanto diminuita dopo gli avventimenti dell'Ebro. Non si dubita dell'esito finale, ma si è persuasi che esso domandi ancora grandi sforzi e mesi di combattimento." ASV: AES, Spagna: Fasc. 347 Pos. 938–440, 47r-48r.

38 "Indudablemente es erronea la idea de que pueden existir actos de venganza o tan siquiera otros que no se inspiren en los más elevados sentimentos de justicia. Bien a la vista está como se administra ésta en la España Nacional, en la que, llegando el caso, se aplicaré le Ley con espíritu de exacta realidad e inclinándose siempre, en la duda, a la benevolencia. [. . .] A la España roja solo le queda un camino; la rendición entregánndose a la generosidad del Generalísimo Franco. El Generalísimo estima en todo su valor la actitud del Santo Padre y la agradece de todo corazón." ASV: AES, Spagna: Fasc. 347 Pos. 938–440, 51r.

39 "Chiedere se il Santo Padre non avesse potuto intervenire come intermediario. Ho risposto che nessuno quanto la Santa Sede desiderava la fine del conflitto ma che la mediazione, a presecindere dal resto, no poteva esser pressa in considerazione dal momento che una della parti, cioè il Generale Franco, non ne voleva sapere." ASV: AES, Spagna: Fasc. 347 Pos. 938–440, 62r-v.

40 ASV: AES, Spagna: Fasc. 347 Pos. 938–440, 62v.

41 "El recrudecimiento extraordinario en la Campaña que el Gobierno de los Rojos de Barcelona lleva a cabo para tartar de dar la impresión al mundo y muy especial a la Santa Sede de un cambio radical en su politica de cruel persecusión a la Iglesia católica y sus Ministros que ha cubierto de sangre la tierra de España . . . Unas veces son los articulos publicados en periodicos poco escrupulosos, . . . ; se utilizan también las emisoras de radio, colaboradoras recientísimas de la Diplomacia, cuando no se pueden justificar los coloquios directos, y echan mano en suma de cuanto recursos están a su alcance, creyendo así poder dar al mundo una impression de orden y respeto a la Religión, cuando esta ha sido escarnecida siempre bajo su autoridad . . . " ASV: AES, Spagna: Fasc. 344 Pos. 935, 40r-40v.

42 ASV: AES, Spagna: Fasc. 344 Pos. 935, 40v.

43 ASV: AES, Spagna: Fasc. 344 Pos. 935, 42r.

44 "Creo de mi deber atraer la atención de Vuestra Eminencia Reverendisima sobre el carácter transcendental de esta gloriosa Victoria militar, cuyas

consecuencias se reflejarán, sin duda, eficazmente en el resultado de la guerra." ASV: AES, Spagna: Fasc. 344 Pos. 935, 45r-v.

45 "Giungono da varie parti nuove e reiterate insistenze perchè Santa Sede interponga mediazione conflitto spagnolo.

Già si è rispetto constare che Governo Nazionale non intende accettare mediazione alcuma.

Qualora tutavia si presentasse qualche possibilità in proposito, voglia V.E. tener presente che Santa Sede nel desiderio di ridonare sospirata pace cotesta diletta et tanto provata Nazione, sarebbe sempre disposta ad intervenire." ASV: AES, Spagna: Fasc. 347 Pos. 938–440, 68r.

46 "Por lo que a mi Gobierno respecta, en reiteradas ocasiones ha expresado esta Representación a la Secretaria de Estado su resolución firmisima de no admitir ningún intento de mediación ni armisticio con los Rojos. Me remito a las Notas enviadas y a las conversaciones en que he tenido al honor de exponer a Vuestra Eminencia Reverendisima el Estado de espíritu de la católica Nación española, que rotundamente rechaza toda componeda, con la que solo se serviria a los Rojos. Se alzarian contra ella las sombras del medio millon de innocentes víctimas inmoladas por los enemigos de Dios y de la Patria.

Seguimos y seguiremos hasta el fín con este mismo propósito irrevocable, por entender que la justicia no puede pactar con el crimen, ni la civilización católica, con la barbarie soviética. Seguiremos hasta el fín victorioso de la guerra, por tener la intima y justificadisima convicción de que tan solo el triunfo total de Franco asegurará en España esl respeto al Altar, a las conciencidas, a la persona humana, a la familia, a la Sociedad española y a la civilización católica." ASV: AES, Spagna: Fasc. 347 Pos. 938–440, 86r-v.

47 José M. Sánchez, *The Spanish Civil War as a Religious Tragedy* (Notre Dame, Indiana: University of Notre Dame Press, 1987), pp. 132–4.

48 "Ministro Esteri mi manifesta constargli che Governo Bacellona appoggiato da Potenze straniere si propone dirigersi Santo Padre perchè nel discorso occasione auguri natale tratta questione spagnola, suggerendo mediazione.

Ministro qualifica questo come nuova manovra del governo rossa per terntare salvataggio dinnanzi alla sconfitta; et . . . che mediazione è rigettata risolutamente dalla Spagna autentica e apporta . . . grave pregiudizio Governo nazionale deciso dare conflitto soluzione definitive e con questa dare al Paese orientazione sicura." ASV: AES, Spagna: Fasc. 347 Pos. 938–440, 89r.

49 "Il Generalissimo Franco in seguito alle voci corse al riguardo, ha fatto di propria iniziativa sapere anche in questi ultimi giorni, sia per mezzo della Nunziature sia per mezzo di questa Ambasciata, che non intende accogliere proposte di mediazione. Perciò Sua Santità non vede possibilità intervenire." ASV: AES, Spagna: Fasc. 347 Pos. 938–440, 94r.

50 "Voglia V.E.R. investigare e riferire colla massima sollecitudine se cotesto Governo accoglierebbe favorevolmente appello Santo Padre alle due parti belligeranti per breve trugua Natalizia, anche solo di ventiquattro o quar-

antotto ore, a somiglianza di quanto fece Benedetto XV primi anno guerra mondiale." ASV: AES, Spagna: Fasc. 347 Pos. 938–440, 98birs.

51 The role of the Vatican in international conflicts has long been an interest for historians. As Stewart A. Stehlin has suggested, the belligerents of WWI looked to the Vatican to support their cause, but Vatican calls for peace and mediation were frequently misinterpreted by the governments. After WWI, the Holy See saw itself as an international entity dealing with both religious and political concerns. The Spanish Rebels, however, appeared to reject the power of the Holy See to moderate such conflicts, presumably affecting its ability to act during future conflict, such as WWII. Stewart A. Stehlin, "The Emergence of a New Vatican Diplomacy during the Great War and Its Aftermath" in Peter C. Kent and John F. Pollard (eds.), *Papal Diplomacy in the Modern Age* (Westport, CT: Praeger, 1994), pp. 75–85.

Bibliography

Primary Sources/Archives
Archivio Segreto Vaticano (ASV), Vatican City
Affari Ecclesiastici Straordinari, Spagna: (ASV: AES, Spagna)

Fasc. 116–123 Pos. 784 Proclamazione della Repubblicha Spangnola.
Fasc. 133–135 Pos. 788 Incendi e saccheggi di chiese e conventi.
Fasc. 136–139 Pos. 789 Nuova Costituzione Repubblicana.
Fasc. 147–152 Pos. 791 Soppressione degli Ordini Religiosi.
Fasc. 155–166 Pos. 794 Azione Cattolica.
Fasc. 170 Pos. 799 Concordato.
Fasc. 183–187 Pos. 805 Leggi speciali su le Confessioni e Congregazioni Religiose .
Fasc. 192–193 Pos. 809 Matrimonio civile e divorzio.
Fasc. 200 Pos. 823 Laicizzazione dei cimiteri. Funerali civili. Cremazione.
Fasc. 208–210 Pos. 833 Enciclica "Dilectissima Nobis" sulla triste situazione della Chiesa in Spagna.
Fasc. 213 Pos. 835 Governo di Lerroux.
Fasc. 240–242 Pos. 856 Partecipazione dei cattolici al III governo Lerroux e conseguente Rivoluzione.
Fasc. 252 Pos. 876 Elezioni politiche.
Fasc. 253 Pos. 879 Nuovo Governo dopo le elezioni del 1936.
Fasc. 285–286 Pos. 895 Proteste della Santa Sede per gli eccidi della rivoluzione.
Fasc. 287–301 Pos. 896 L'atteggiamento dei Baschi nella guerra civile.
Fasc. 302–303 Pos. 899 La Francia chiede alla Santa Sede di unirsi al progetto franco-inglese di un passo presso la Germania, Portogallo, Italia e Russia per il non intervento in Spagna.
Fasc. 311 Pos. 904 Scambio di ostaggi fra nazionalisti e baschi.
Fasc. 328 Pos. 918 Rimpatrio volontari ed intervento Santa Sede.
Fasc. 331–335 Pos. 923 Governo di Valencia. Circa l'apertura delle chiese al culto pubblico e tendenza a riallacciare le relazioni diplomatiche. Assistenza religiosa per la zona rossa..
Fasc. 341 Pos. 929 Contro i bombardamenti aerei su città aperte.
Fasc. 344 Pos. 935 Nuovo Ambasciatore del Governo Nazionale (Burgos).
Fasc. 347 Pos. 940 Tentativi di mediazione nella guerra spagnola.
Fasc. 351 Pos. 948 Pratiche relative ai legionari italiani combattenti nella guerra civile spagnola.

Centro Documental de la Memoria Histórica, Salamanca, Spain

Periodicals on Microfilm
MF/R 1415: *Mujeres.*
MF/R 2263: *ERI.*
MF/R 4546: *DIC, Cruz y Raya, Tierra Vasca.*

Published Sources

Andrés-Gallego, José Antón M. Pazos. *Archivo Gomá: Documentos de la Guerra Civil—1936–1939, Volumes 1–13.* Madrid: Consejo Superior de Investigaciones Científicas, 2001.

British Documents on Foreign Affairs. London: Her Majesty's Royal Office, 1931–1939.

Carta Colectiva De Los Obispos Españoles a Los De Todo El Mundo Con Motivo De La Guerra Espanola, 1937.

Documents Diplomatiques Français. Paris: Imprimerie Nationale, 1931–1939.

Lateran Treaty, 1929.

Mayor, Andres (translator). *Ciano's Diary 1937–1938.* London: Methuen & Co. Ltd., 1952

Pagano, Sergio, Marcel Chappin, and Giovanni Coco. *I "fogli di udienza" del cardinale Eugenio Pacelli, Segretario di Stato, 1930.* Vatican City: Vatican Secret Archives, 2010.

Papers Relating to the Foreign Relations of the United States (1931–1939), Washington, D.C.: United States Government Printing Office.

Pope Pius XI, *Dilectissima Nobis,* 3 June 1933.

Secondary Sources

Published Books

Aguilar, Paloma. *Memory and Amnesia: The Role of the Spanish Civil War in the Transition to Democracy.* New York: Berghahn Books, 2002.

Albertí, J. *La Iglesia en Llamas: La Persecución Religiosa en España durante la Guerra Civil.* Barcelona: Ediciones Destino, S.A., 2008.

Alexander, Martin S. and Helen Graham (eds). *The French and Spanish Popular Fronts: Comparative Perspectives* Cambridge: Cambridge University Press, 2002.

Álvarez Bolado, Alfonso. *Para Ganar la Guerra, Para Ganar la Paz: Iglesia y Guerra Civil, 1936–1939.* Madrid: UPCo, 1995.

Álvarez Junco, José. *The Emergence of Mass Politics in Spain.* Brighton: Sussex Academic Press, 2002.

Álvarez Tardío, Manuel. *Anticlericalismo y libertad de conciencia: Política, religion en la Segunda República Española, 1931–1936.* Madrid: Centros de Estudios Políticos y Costitucionales, 2002.

Álvarez Tardío, Manuel and Fernando del Rey Reguillo (eds). *The Second Republic Revisited: From Democratic Hopes to Civil War (1931–1936).* Eastbourne: Sussex Academic Press, 2012.

Arasa, Daniel. *Católicos del bando rojo.* Barcelona: Styria de Ediciones y Publicaciones, S.L., 2009.

Arnal, Oscar L. *Ambivalent Alliance: The Catholic Church and the Action Française, 1899–1939*. Pittsburgh: University of Pittsburgh Press, 1985.

Blázquez, Feliciano. *La traición de los clérigos en la España de Franco*. Madrid: Editorial Trotta, S.A., 1991.

Botti, Alfonso. *Cielo y Dinero: El nacionalcatolicismo en España (1881–1975)*. Madrid: Alianza Editorial, 1992.

Bowen, Wayne and Alvarez, J. (eds). *A Military History of Modern Spain: From the Napoleonic Era to the International War on Terror*. Westport, CT: Praeger Security International, 2007.

Brenan, Gerald. *The Spanish Labyrinth: The Social and Political Background of the Spanish Civil War*. Cambridge: Cambridge University Press, 1943.

Buchanan, Tom. *Britain and the Spanish Civil War*. Cambridge: Cambridge University Press, 1997.

Buchanan, Tom. *The Impact of the Spanish Civil War on Britain: War, Loss, and Memory*. Eastbourne: Sussex Academic Press, 2007.

Bunk, Brian D. *Ghosts of Passion: Martyrdom, Gender, and the Origins of the Spanish Civil War*. Durham: Duke University Press, 2007.

Callahan, William J. *The Catholic Church in Spain, 1875–1998*. Washington, D.C., The Catholic University of America Press, 2001.

Cárcel Ortí, Vicente. *La gran persecución: España, 1931–1939*. Barcelona: Planeta, 2000.

Cárcel Ortí, Vincente. *Pio XI Entre la República Y Franco*. Madrid: Biblioteca de Autores Cristianos, 2008.

Casanova, Julián. *La Iglesia de Franco*. Barcelona: Crítica, 2005.

Casanova, Julián. *The Spanish Republic and Civil War*. New York: Cambridge University Press, 2010.

Ceci, Lucia. *Il papa non deve parlare*. Bari: Gius, Laterza, & Figli, 2010.

Colmeiro, José F. *Memoria histórica e identidad cultural: De la postguerra a la postmodernidad*. Barcelona: Anthropos, 2005.

Conway, Martin. *Catholic Politics in Europe, 1918–1945*. London: Routledge, 1997.

Coppa, Frank J. *Pope Pius IX: Crusader in a Secular Age*. Boston: Twayne Publishers, 1979.

Coppa, Frank J. (ed.). *Controversial Concordats*. Washington, D.C.: Catholic University of America Press, 1999.

Coppa, Frank J. *Encyclopedia of the Vatican and the Papacy*. Santa Barbara, CA: Greenwood Press, 1999.

Coppa, Frank J. *The Papacy, the Jews, and the Holocaust*. Washington, D.C.: Catholic University of American Press, 2008.

Coppa, Frank J. *The Policies and Politics of Pope Pius XII*. New York: Peter Lang, 2011.

Cornwell, John. *Hitler's Pope: The Secret History of Pope Pius XII*. New York: Penguin, 2008.

Corti, Paola and Alejandro Pizarróso Quintéro. *Giornali contro: "Il Legionario" e "Il Garibaldino": La propaganda degli italiani nella guerra di Spagna*. Alessandria: Edizioni dell'Orso, 1993.

Costa Pinto, António. *Salazar's Dictatorship and European Fascism: Problems of Interpretation*. Boulder: East European Monographs, 1995.
Coverdale, John F. *Italian Intervention in the Spanish Civil War*. Princeton: Princeton University Press, 1975.
Crussells, Magí. *La Guerra Civil española: Cine y propaganda*. Barcelona: A&M Grafic, S.L., 2000.
De la Cueva, Julio and Feliciano Montero (eds). *Izquierda Obrera y Religión en España (1900–1939)*. Alcalá de Henares: Universidad de Alcalá, 2012.
De la Cueva, Julio and Feliciano Montero (eds). *La Secularización Conflictiva: España (1898–1931)*. Madrid: Biblioteca Nueva, 2007.
De Meer Lecha-Marzo, Fernando. *La Constitución de la II República: Autonomías, Propiedad, Iglesia, Eseñanza*. Pamplona: EUNSA, 1978.
Duce, Alessandro. *La Santa Sede e la Questione Ebraica*. Roma: Edizione Studium: 2006.
Ellwood, Sheelagh. *Spanish Fascism in the Franco Era: Falange Española de los JONS, 1936–1976*. New York: St. Martin's Press, 1987.
Escuela Española de Historia y Arqueología de Roma. *Italia y la Guerra Civil Española*. Madrid: Centro de Estudios Historicos, 1986.
Esenwein, George Richard and Adrian Shubert. *Spain at War: The Spanish Civil War in Context, 1931–1939*. London: Longman, 1995.
Fattorini, Emma. *Hitler, Mussolini, and the Vatican*. Cambridge: Polity Press, 2011.
Fiorentino, Carlo M. *All'ombra di Pietro: La Chiesa cattolica e lo spionaggio fascista in Vaticano (1929–1939)*. Rome: Le Lettere, 1999.
Gallagher, Charles R., S.J. *Vatican Secret Diplomacy: Joseph P. Hurley and Pope Pius XII*. New Haven: Yale University Press, 2008.
Graham, Helen. *The Spanish Republic at War, 1936–1939*. Cambridge: Cambridge University Press, 2002.
Graham, Robert A., S.J. *The Vatican and Communism in World War II: What Really Happened?* San Francisco: Ignatius Press, 1996.
Grimaldos, Alfredo. *La Iglesia en España, 1977–2008*. Barcelona: Ediciones Península, 2008.
González Cuevas, Pedro Carlos. *Acción Española: Teología Política y Nacionalismo Autoritario en España, 1913–1936*. Madrid: Editorial Tecnos, S.A., 1998.
Harper, Glenn T. *German Economic Policy in Spain*. The Hague: Mouton & Co., 1967.
Hernández Figueiredo, José Ramón. *Destrucción del patrimonio en la II República (1931–1936): A la luz de los informes inéditos del Archivo Secreto Vaticano*. Madrid: Biblioteca de Autores Cristianos, 2009.
Holguín, Sandie. *Creating Spaniards: Cultural and National Identity in Republican Spain*. Madison: University of Wisconsin Press, 2002.
Hooper, John. *The New Spaniards*. Penguin: London, 1995.
Hopkins, James K. *Into the Heart of the Fire: The British and the Spanish Civil War*. Stanford: Stanford University Press, 1998.
Jackson, Gabriel. *The Spanish Republic and the Civil War, 1931–1939*. Princeton: Princeton University Press, 1965.

Kamen, Henry. *Empire: How Spain Became a World Power, 1492–1736.* New York: HarperCollins, 2003.

Keene, Judith. *Fighting for Franco: International Volunteers in Nationalist Spain During the Spanish Civil War, 1936–1939.* London: Leicester University Press, 2001.

Kent, Peter C. *The Pope and the Duce: The International Impact of the Lateran Agreements.* New York: St. Martin's Press, 1981.

Kent, Peter C. and John F. Pollard (eds). *Papal Diplomacy in the Modern Age.* Westport, CT: Praeger, 1994.

Kleine-Ahlbrandt, WM Laird. *The Policy of Simmering: A Study of British Foreign Policy During the Spanish Civil War.* Martinus Nijhoff: The Hague, 1962.

Kowalsky, Daniel. *La Unión Soviética y la Guerra Civil Española.* Barcelona: Crítica, 2003.

Lannon, Frances. *Privilege, Persecution, and Prophecy: The Catholic Church in Spain, 1875–1975.* Oxford: Clarendon Press, 1987.

Leitz, Christian and David Joseph Dunthorn (eds). *Spain in an International Context: 1936–1959.* London: Berghahn Books, 1999.

Lewis, Paul H. *Latin Fascist Elites: The Mussolini, Franco, and Salazar Regimes.* London: Praeger, 2002.

Little, Douglas. *"Malevolent Neutrality:" The United States, Great Britain, and the Origins of the Spanish Civil War.* Ithaca: Cornell University Press, 1985.

Lowe, Sid. *Catholicism, War, and the Foundation of Francoism: The Juventud De Acción Popular in Spain, 1931–1939.* Eastbourne: Sussex Academic Press, 2010.

Madridejos, Mateo. *Diccionario onomástico de la guerra civil.* Barcelona: Flor de Viento Ediciones, 2006.

Mangini, Shirley. *Memories of Resistance: Women's Voices from the Spanish Civil War.* New Haven: Yale University Press, 1995.

Mann, Michael. *Fascists.* Cambridge: Cambridge University Press, 2004.

Márquez, Carlos José. *Cómo se ha escrito la Guerra Civil española.* Madrid: Ediciones Lengua de Trapo, SL, 2006.

Marquina Barrio, Antonio. *La Diplomacia Vaticana y la España de Franco, 1936–1945.* Madrid: CSIC, 1983.

Mazower, Mark. *Dark Continent: Europe's Twentieth Century.* London: Penguin, 1998.

Moa, Pio. *Los Orígenes de la Guerra Civil Española 5ª edición.* Madrid: Ediciones Encuentro, 2009.

Moradiellos, Enrique. *1936: Los Mitos de la Guerra Civil.* Barcelona: Ediciones Península, 2004.

Moral Roncal, Antonio Manuel. *Diplomacia, humanitarismo y espionaje en la Guerra Civil española.* Madrid: Editorial Biblioteca Nueva, 2008.

Morodo, Raúl. *Los orígenes ideológicos del franquismo: Acción Española.* Madrid: Alianza Editorial, 1985.

Mugnaini, Marco (ed.). *Stato, Chiesa e Relazioni Internazionali.* Milano: FrancoAngeli, 2003.

Murphy, Francis J. *Communists and Catholics in France, 1936–1939: The Politics of the Outstretched Hand.* Gainesville: University of Florida Press, 1989.

Nash, Mary. *Defying Male Civilization: Women in the Spanish Civil War.* Denver: Arden Press, Inc., 1995.

Nichols, Peter. *The Politics of the Vatican.* New York: Praeger, 1968.

Passmore, Kevin. *Fascism: A Very Short Introduction.* Oxford: Oxford University Press, 2002.

Payne, Stanley. *The Collapse of the Spanish Republic, 1933–1936: Origins of the Civil War.* New Haven: Yale University Press, 2006.

Payne, Stanley. *Fascism in Spain, 1923–1977.* Madison: University of Wisconsin Press, 1999.

Payne, Stanley. *The Franco Regime, 1936–1975.* Madison: University of Wisconsin Press, 1987.

Payne, Stanley. *A History of Fascism, 1914–1945.* Madison: University of Wisconsin Pres, 1996.

Payne, Stanley. *Spain's First Democracy: The Second Republic, 1931–1936.* Madison: University of Wisconsin Press, 1993.

Pichon, Charles. Translated by Jean Misrahi. *The Vatican and Its Role on World Affairs.* Westport, CT: Greenwood Press Publishers, 1950.

Pike, David Wingate. *France Divided: The French and the Civil War in Spain.* Eastbourne: Sussex Academic Press, 2011.

Pollard, John F. *The Vatican and Italian Fascism, 1929–32.* Cambridge: Cambridge University Press, 1985.

Pollard, John F. *Money and the Rise of the Modern Papacy: Financing the Vatican, 1850–1950.* Cambridge: Cambridge University Press, 2005.

Preston, Paul. *The Coming of the Spanish Civil War: Reform, Reaction and Revolution in the Second Republic.* London: Routledge, 1978.

Preston, Paul. *Franco: A Biography.* London: Harper Collins Publishers, 1993.

Preston, Paul. *The Politics of Revenge: Fascism and the Military in Twentieth-Century Spain.* London: Routledge, 1995.

Preston, Paul (ed.). *Revolution and War in Spain, 1931–1939.* London: Routledge, 2002.

Preston, Paul. *The Spanish Civil War: Reaction, Reform, and Revenge: Revised and Expanded.* London: HarperCollins Press, 2006.

Preston, Paul. *The Spanish Holocaust: Inquisition and Extermination in Twentieth-Century Spain.* London: W.W. Norton & Company, 2012.

Preston, Paul and Ann L. Mackenzie (eds.). *The Republic Besieged: Civil War in Spain 1936–1939.* Edinburgh: Edinburgh University Press, 1996.

Prévotat, Jacques. *Les catholiques el l'Action française: Histoire d'une condamnation, 1889–1939.* Paris: Librairie Arthème Fayard, 2001.

Quiroga, Alejandro. *Making Spaniards: Primo de Rivera and the Nationalization of the Masses, 1923–1930.* New York: Palgrave Macmillan, 2007.

Quiroga, Alejandro and Miguel Ángel del Arco (eds.). *Right-wing Spain in the Civil War Era: Soldiers of God and Apostles of the Fatherland, 1914–1945.* London: Continuum International Publishing Group, 2012.

Raguer Suñer, Hilari M. *Gunpowder and Incense: The Catholic Church and the Spanish Civil War.* London: Routledge, 2007.

Redondo, Gonzalo, *Historia de la Iglesia en España 1931–1939*, 2 Volumes. Madrid: Ediciones Rialp, S.A., 1993.
Rhodes, Anthony. *The Vatican in the Age of the Dictators, 1922–1945*. New York: Holt, Rinehart and Winston, 1973.
Rittner, Carol and John K. Roth (eds.). *Pope Pius XII and the Holocaust*. London: Leicester University Press, 2002.
Ruíz Giménez, Joaquín. *Iglesia, Estado y Sociedad en España, 1930–1982*. Barcelona: Editorial Argos Vergara, S.A., 1984.
Salas, Nicolás. *La Otra Memoria Histórica*. Madrid: Almuzara, 2006.
Sanabria, Enrique A. *Republicanism and Anticlerical Nationalism in Spain*. New York: Palgrave Macmillan, 2009.
Sánchez, José M. *The Spanish Civil War as a Religious Tragedy*. Notre Dame, Indiana: University of Notre Dame Press, 1987.
Saz Campos, Ismael. *Fascismo y Franquismo*. Valencia: Universitat de València Press, 2004.
Shubert, Adrian. *A Social History of Modern Spain*. New York: Routledge, 1996.
Suárez, Federico. *Manual Azaña y La Guerra de 1936*. Madrid, Ediciones Rialp, S.A., 2000.
Suárez, Luis. *Franco y la Iglesia*. Madrid: Bibliotheca Homolegens, 2011.
Teeling, William. *Pope Pius XI and World Affairs*. New York: Frederick A. Stokes, 1937.
Thomas, Maria. *The Faith and the Fury: Popular Anticlerical Violence and Iconoclasm in Spain, 1931–1936*. Eastbourne: Sussex Academic Press, 2013.
Towson, Nigel. *The Crisis of Democracy in Spain: Centrist Politics Under the Second Republic, 1931–1936*. Eastbourne: Sussex Academic Press, 2000.
Tusell, Javier. *La crisis de los años treinta: República y Guerra Civil*. Madrid: Taurus Bolsillo, 2000.
Tusell, Javier (ed.). *Fascismo y Franquismo: Cara a Cara*. Madrid: Editorial Biblioteca Nueva, 2004.
Ventresca, Robert A. *Soldier of Christ: The Life of Pope Pius XII*. Cambridge: Harvard University Press, 2013.
Viñas, Ángel. *Guerra, Dinero, Dictadura*. Barcelona: Editorial Crítica, 1984.
Viñas, Ángel. *La Soledad de la República: El abandono de la democracias y el viraje Hacia la Unión Sovietica*. Barcelona: Crítica, 2006.
Viñas, Ángel (ed.). *Al Servicio del la República: Diplomáticos y Guerra Civil*. Madrid: Marcel Pons, Ediciones de Historia, 2010.
Whealey, Robert H. *Hitler and Spain: The Nazi Role in the Spanish Civil War*. Lexington: University of Kentucky Press, 1989.
Wolf, Hubert. *Pope and Devil*. Cambridge, MA: The Belknap Press, 2010.
Wolff, Richard J. and Jörg K. Hoensch, Eds. *Catholics, the State, and the European Radical Right, 1919–1945*. Boulder: Social Science Monographs, 1987.
Zavala, José María. *1939: La Cara Oculta de los Últimos Días de la Guerra Civil*. Barcelona: Random House Mondadori, S.A., 2009.
Zuccotti, Susan. *Under His Very Windows: The Vatican and the Holocaust in Italy*. New Haven: Yale University Press, 2000.

Published Articles

Aguilar, Paloma. "Collective Memory of the Spanish Civil War: The Case of Political Amnesty in the Spanish Transition to Democracy." *Democratization.* 4, 4 (1997): 88–109.

Albonico, Aldo. "Los Católicos Italianos y La Guerra de España." *Revista Española de Historia.* 38, 139 (1978): 373–404.

Alpert, Michael. "The Clash of Spanish Armies: Contrasting Ways of War in Spain." *War in History* 6, 3 (1999): 331–351.

Alpert, Michael. "The Popular Army of the Spanish Republic, 1936–39" in Wayne Bowen and José Álvarez (eds.). *A Military History of Modern Spain* (Westport: Praeger, 2007): 93–109.

Álvarez Chillida, Gonzalo. "Movimiento Liberatrio y Religión durante la Segunda República" in De la Cueva, Julio and Feliciano Montero (eds). *Izquierda Obrera y Religión en España (1900–1939)*, (Alcalá de Henares: Universidad de Alcalá, 2012): 99–128.

Álvarez Tardío, Manuel. "The CEDA: Threat or Opportunity" in Álvarez Tardío, Manuel and Fernando del Rey Reguillo (eds.). *The Second Republic Revisited: From Democratic Hopes to Civil War (1931–1936),* (Eastbourne: Sussex Academic Press, 2012): 58–79.

Arbeloa, Víctor Manuel. "El Partido Socialista y la Iglesia (1879–1935), a través de Pablo Iglesias." in De la Cueva, Julio and Feliciano Montero (eds). *Izquierda Obrera y Religión en España (1900–1939),* (Alcalá de Henares: Universidad de Alcalá, 2012): 49–70.

Arranz Notario, Luis. "Could the Second Republic have become a Democracy?" in Álvarez Tardío, Manuel and Fernando del Rey Reguillo (eds.). *The Second Republic Revisited: From Democratic Hopes to Civil War (1931–1936),* (Eastbourne: Sussex Academic Press, 2012): 20–39.

Askew, William C. "Italian Intervention in Spain: The Agreement of March 31, 1934 with the Spanish Monarchist Parties." *The Journal of Modern History* 24, 2 (1952): 181–183.

Aviv, Aviva and Isaac. "The Madrid Working Class, the Spanish Socialist Party, and the Collapse of the Second Republic." *Journal of Contemporary History* 16, 2 (1981): 229–250.

Bannister, Chris. "Antonio Primo de Rivera: Catholic Fascism" in Quiroga, Alejandro and Miguel Ángel del Arco (eds.). *Right-wing Spain in the Civil War Era: Soldiers of God and Apostles of the Fatherland, 1914–1945.* London: Continuum International Publishing Group (2012): 91–116.

Blatt, Joel. "Action Française and the Vatican" in *Encyclopedia of the Vatican and Papacy.*" Frank J. Coppa (ed.). Westport: Greenwood Press (1999): 3–5.

Blatt, "Ralliement" in *Encyclopedia of the Vatican and Papacy.*" Frank J. Coppa (ed.). Westport: Greenwood Press (1999): 350–1.

Brownfeld, Peter. "London's Policies towards British Volunteers for the International Brigades: An Attempt to Safeguard her Precarious Diplomacy." *International Journal of Iberian Studies* 15, 1 (2002): 14–29.

Buchanan, Tom. "Edge of Darkness: British 'Front-line' Diplomacy in the Spanish Civil War, 1936–1937." *Contemporary European History* 12, 3 (2003): 279–303.

Bunk, Brian, "'Your Comrades will not Forget:' Revolutionary Memory and the Breakdown of the Spanish Second Republic, 1934–1936." *History and Memory*, 14, 1–2 (2002): 65–92.

Cabrera, Miguel A. "Developments in Contemporary Spanish Historiography: From Social History to the New Cultural History." *Journal of Modern History* 77, 4 (2005): 988–1023.

Coppa, Frank. "Pope Pius XI's 'Encyclical' *Humani Generis Unitas* Against Racism and Anti-Semitism and the 'Silence' of Pope Pius XII." *Journal of Church and State* 40, 4 (1998): 775–795.

Coppa, Frank. "Between Anti-Judaism and Anti-Semitism, Pius XI's Response to Nazi Persecution of the Jews: Precursor to Pius XII's 'Silence'?" *Journal of Church and State* 47, 1 (2005): 63–89.

Coppa, Frank. "Pope Pius XII: From Diplomacy of Impartiality to the Silence of the Holocaust." *Journal of Church and State* 55, 2 (2012): 1–21.

De Busser, Cathlijne. "Church-state Relations in Spain: Variations on a National-Catholic Theme?" *GeoJournal* 67, 4 (2006): 283–294.

De la Cueva, Julio. "Religious Persecution, Anticlerical Tradition and Revolution: On Atrocities against the Clergy during the Spanish Civil War." *Journal of Contemporary History* 33, 3 (1998): 355–369.

De la Cueva Merino, Julio. "Socialistas y Religión en la Segunda República: De la Liga Nacional Laica al Inicio de la Guerra Civil" in De la Cueva, Julio and Feliciano Montero (eds). *Izquierda Obrera y Religión en España (1900–1939)* (Alcalá de Henares: Universidad de Alcalá, 2012): 71–98.

Duncan, Martha Grace. "Spanish Anarchism Refracted: Theme and Image in the Millenarian and Revisionist Literature." *Journal of Contemporary History* 23, 3 (1988): 323–346.

Esenwein, George. "Spanish Civil War: Franco's Nationalist Army" in Wayne Bowen and José Álvarez (eds.). *A Military History of Modern Spain* (Westport: Praeger, 2007): 68–92.

Fleming, Shannon E. "Spanish Morocco and the Alzamiento Nacional, 1936–1939: The Military, Economic and Political Mobilization of a Protectorate." *Journal of Contemporary History* 18, 1 (1983): 27–42.

Gallagher, M. D. "Leon Blum and the Spanish Civil War." *Journal of Contemporary History* 6, 3 (1971): 56–64.

García de las Heras González, Mariano. "La Revolución de Asturias, ¿Primer Acto de la Guerra Civil?" *Ab Initio: Revista digital para estudiantes de Historia* 1, 1 (2010): 169–194.

Goda, Norman J.W. "Franco's Bid for Empire: Spain, Germany, and the Western Mediterranean in World War II." *Mediterranean Historical Review* 13, 1–2 (1998): 168–194.

Gomez-Reino y Carnot, Enrique "La Libertad de Expresion en la Segunda República." *Revista de Derecho Político* 12 (1981–2): 159–187.

Guerrero Moreno, Rafael "La Prensa en la Segunda República: breve aproximación como contexto vital de don Diego Martínez Barrio." *Ámbitos: Revista andaluza de comunicación* 7–8 (2002): 327–337.

Hale, Frederick. "Fighting over the Fight in Spain: The Pro-Franco Campaign

of Bishop Peter Amigo of Southwick." *The Catholic Historical Review.* 91 (2005): 462–483.
Jackson, Peter. "French Strategy and the Spanish Civil War" in Christian Leitz and David J. Dunthorn (eds.). *Spain in an International Context* (New York: Berghahn Books, 1999): 55–79.
Kent, Peter C. "A Tale of Two Popes: Pius XI, Pius XII and the Rome-Berlin Axis." *Journal of Contemporary History* 23, 4 (1998): 589–608.
Kent, Peter C. "The Vatican and the Spanish Civil War." *European History Quarterly.* 16, 4 (1986): 441–64.
Ledesma, José Luis. "Enemigos Seculares: La Violencia Anticlerical (1936–1939)" in De la Cueva, Julio and Feliciano Montero (eds). *Izquierda Obrera y Religión en España (1900–1939)*, (Alcalá de Henares: Universidad de Alcalá, 2012): 219–244.
Ledesma, José Luis. "The Enemy par excellence: Anticlerical Violence in the Spanish Civil War (1936–39)." Salzburg, 9th Global Conference: Violence—Probing the Boundaries (2010).
Linz, Juan J. "Religion and Politics in Spain: From Conflict to Consensus above Cleavage." *Social Compass.* 27, 2–3 (1980): 255–277.
Little, Douglas. "Red Scare, 1936: Anti-Bolshevism and the Origins of British Non-Intervention in the Spanish Civil War." *Journal of Contemporary History* 23, 2 (1988): 291–311.
Macarro Vera, José Manuel. "The Socialists and Revolution" in Álvarez Tardío, Manuel and Fernando del Rey Reguillo (eds.). *The Second Republic Revisited: From Democratic Hopes to Civil War (1931–1936)*, (Eastbourne: Sussex Academic Press, 2012): 40–57.
Mackay, Angus. "Review: Narrative History and Spanish History." *The International Historical Review* 4 (1982): 421–431.
Maddox, Richard. "Revolutionary Anticlericalism and Hegemonic Processes in an Andalusian Town, August 1936." *American Ethnologist* 22, 11 (1995): 125–143.
Marquina Barrio, Antonio. "Planes Internacionales de Mediación durante la Guerra Civil." *UNISCI Discussion Papers* 11 (2006): 229–248.
Marquina Barrio, Antonio. "El Vaticano y el Estallido de la Guerra Civil: El Cardinal Gomá reparó el fracaso diplomático del Marqués de Magaz." *UNISCI Discussion Papers* 12 (2006): 229–244.
Martínez-Sánchez, Santiago. "Mons. Antoniutti el clero nacionalista vasca (Julio–Octubre de 1937)." *Sancho el Sabio: Revista de cultura e investigación vasca* 27 (2007): 39–78.
Mees, Ludger. "Clase, Religión y Nación. El Sindicalismo Nacionalista en el País Vasco hasta la Guerra Civil" in De la Cueva, Julio and Feliciano Montero (eds). *Izquierda Obrera y Religión en España (1900–1939)* (Alcalá de Henares: Universidad de Alcalá, 2012): 155–178.
Milkowski, Tadeusz. "The Spanish Church and the Vatican During the Spanish Civil War." *The Polish Foreign Affairs Digest* 3 (2004): 207–242.
Miralles, Ricardo. "The International Policy of the Second Republic During the Spanish Civil War." *Mediterranean Historical Review* 13, 1 (1998): 135–149.
Moradiellos, Enrique. "Francisco Franco: The Soldier Who Became Caudillo"

in Quiroga, Alejandro and Miguel Ángel del Arco (eds.). *Right-wing Spain in the Civil War Era: Soldiers of God and Apostles of the Fatherland, 1914–1945.* London: Continuum International Publishing Group (2012): 117–146.

O'Connell, James. "The Spanish Republic: Further Reflections on Its Anticlerical Policies." *The Catholic Historical Review* 57, 2 (July 1971): 275–289.

Payne, Stanley. "Spain: The Church, the Second Republic, and the Franco Regime" in Richard J. Wolff and Jörg K. Hoensch (eds.). *Catholics, the State, and the European Radical Right, 1919–1945* (Boulder: Social Science Monographs, 1987): 182–198.

Payne, Stanley. "Fascist Italy and Spain, 1922–1945." *Mediterranean Historical Review.* 13, 1 (June-Dec: 1998): 99–115.

Pizarroso Quintero, Alejandro. "Intervención extranjera y propaganda. La Propaganda Exterior de las dos Españas." *Historia y Communicación Social* 6 (2001): 63–96.

Preston, Paul. "Spain's October Revolution and the Rightists Grasp for Power." *Journal of Contemporary History* 10, 4 (1975): 555–578.

Ranzato, Gabriele. "The Republican Left and the Defense of Democracy, 1934–1936" in Álvarez Tardío, Manuel and Fernando del Rey Reguillo (eds.). *The Second Republic Revisited: From Democratic Hopes to Civil War (1931–1936),* (Eastbourne: Sussex Academic Press, 2012): 80–96.

Rodríguez Ballano, Elena. "Un socialista y una atalaya del SIDE en Berna" in Viñas, A. (ed.). *Al Servicio del la República: Diplomáticos y Guerra Civil* Madrid: Marcel Pons, Ediciones de Historia (2010): 177–206.

Sánchez, José M. "The Second Spanish Republic and the Holy See: 1931–1936." *The Catholic Historical Review,* 49, 1 (1963): 47–68.

Sánchez, José M. "The Popes and Nazi Germany: The View from Madrid." *Journal of Church and State* 38, 2 (1996): 365–376.

Saz, Ismael. "Fascism and Empire: Fascist Italy Against Republican Spain." *Mediterranean Historical Review.* 13, 1 (1998): 116–134.

Sotomayor Blázquez, Carmen T. "El moro traidor, el moro engañado: variantes del estereotipo en el Romancero republicano." Anaquel de Estudios Árabes" 16 (2005): 233–249.

Stone, Glyn. "Yvon Delbos and Anthony Eden: Anglo-French Cooperation, 1936–38" in Glyn Stone and Thomas G. Otte (eds). *Anglo-French Relations since the Later Eighteenth Century* (London: Routledge, 2009): 165–186.

Stehlin, Stewart A. "The Emergence of a New Vatican Diplomacy during the Great War and Its Aftermath, 1914–1929" in Peter C. Kent and John F. Pollard (eds.). *Papal Diplomacy in the Modern Age* (Westport, CT: Praeger, 1994): 76–95.

Suárez Cortina, Manuel. "Clases Populares, Republicanismo y Anticlericalismo en la España del Primer Tercio del Siglo XX" in De la Cueva, Julio and Feliciano Montero (eds). *Izquierda Obrera y Religión en España (1900–1939)* (Alcalá de Henares: Universidad de Alcalá, 2012): 19–48.

Sullivan, Brian R. "Fascist Italy's Military Involvement in the Spanish Civil War." *The Journal of Military History* 59 (1995): 697–727.

Townson, Nigel. "A Third Way? Centrist Politics under the Republic" in Álvarez

Tardío, Manuel and Fernando del Rey Reguillo (eds.). *The Second Republic Revisited: From Democratic Hopes to Civil War (1931–1936)*, (Eastbourne: Sussex Academic Press, 2012): 97–113.

Trybus, Karl J. "For the Republic or the Church: The Vatican's Reactions to the Development of Spain's Second Republic in 1931." *Bulletin for Spanish and Portuguese Historical Studies* 36, 1 (2011): 22–44.

Trybus, Karl J. "The Sad and Painful News from Spain: Vatican Relations with the Second Spanish Republic at the Start of the Spanish Civil War, 1936." *International Journal of Iberian Studies* 24, 2 (2012): 91–107.

Valaik, J. David. "American Catholics and the Second Spanish Republic, 1911–1936." *Journal of Church and State* 10 (1968): 13–28.

Veatch, Richard. "The League of Nations and the Spanish Civil War, 1936–9." *European History Quarterly* 20 (1990): 181–207.

Viñas, Ángel and Carlos Collado Seidel. "Franco's Request to the Third Reich for Military Assistance." *Contemporary European History* 11, 2 (2002): 191–210.

Warner, Geoffrey. "France and Non-Intervention in Spain, July–August 1936." *International Affairs* 38, 2 (1962): 203–220.

Whealey, Robert H. "Nazi Propagandist Joseph Goebbels Looks at the Spanish Civil War." *The Historian* 61, 2 (1999): 341–360.

Index

ABC, 22, *205n*
Aerial Bombardments, 5, 100, 128–9, 134, 168–76, *205n*
Aguirre, José Antonio (Basque Politician), 111, 113–14, 162
Alcalá-Zamora, Niceto, 19–20, 23, 32, 34, 37, 40, 53, 57–8, 60, 69, *198n*
Alfonso XII (King), 15
Alfonso XIII (King), 16–18, 147, *198n*
Aliosi Masella, Benedetto (Nuncio to Brazil), 136
Álvarez Tardío, Manuel, 19, 34, 53, 55, *193n, 202n, 205n*
Anarchism/Anarchists, 12, 15–16, 22, 54–6, 77, 80–1, 86, 88, 90, 93–4, 96–7, 99, 104, 106–8, 111–12, 114, 116–17, 150, 184, 188, *195n, 199n, 216n, 228n*
Andalucía, 16, *195n, 205n*
Anticlericalism, 1, 7, 10–13, 15, 18, 20–2, 24–6, 32–3, 35, 44–5, 49, 55–6, 60, 62, 71, 77–8, 80–1, 87–8, 90, 99, 107, 112, 117, 170, 188, 189, 191–2, *194n, 196n, 198n, 206n, 217n*
Anti-Semitism, 7
Antoniutti, Ildebrando (Chargé d'Affaires and Nuncio), 153, 166, 169, 171–3, 175
Army of Africa, 56, 66
Article 3 (Constitution), 29
Article 26 (Constitution), 25, 31–5, 37, 46, 56, 69, *202n*
Asturias, 50–1, 55–6, 62–8, 71, 74, 77, 89, 187
Atheism, 2, 20, 29–30, 37, 59, 78, 91, 94, 102, 113, 117–18, 141–2, 147–8, 152, 155, 158, 168, 183, 191
Au milieu des solicitudes, 28
Azaña, Manuel, 34, 40, 42–3, 47, 49–50, 57–61, 63–4, 67–8, 71–2, 75–9, *198n, 208n*

Barcelona, 1, 15–16, 21, 60–1, 63–4, 87–9, 128–9, 134, 141–2, 146, 168, 170–3, 175–9, 182–4, *196n, 204n*
Basque, 5, 8, 61–2, 70, 99, 105–118, 123, 128, 147, 149–68, 172, 183, 189–91, *198n, 200n, 205n, 214n, 225n, 226n, 227n, 228n, 238n*
Basque Country, *see* País Vasco
Benedict XV (Pope), 183
Benedict XVI (Pope), 1
Bernardini, Felipe (Nuncio to Switzerland), 102–4
Bieno Negro, 56
Bilbao, 114, 161, 163–4, 166
Blum, Léon (Popular Front President of France), 115, 121–4, 131
Boncour, Paul (French Minister of Foreign Affairs), 134
Bourbons, 10, 17, 147
Brazil, 136–7
Burgos, 3, 90, 99, 101, 105, 107–9, 113, 117, 127–30, 143–4, 148, 150–3, 157–61, 163–4, 166–9, 173–81, 183–4, 189–92, *193n, 238n*

Cádiz, 12, *205n*
Callahan, William, 6, 13–15, 33, 39, 48, 55, 80, 85, 150, *195n, 196n, 203n, 204n, 205n, 223n*
Calvo Sotelo, José, 51, 75
Cánovas del Castillo, Antonio, 15
Cárcel Ortí, Vicente, 6, *194n, 197n, 210n, 221n, 225n*
Carlist, 14, 105
Carta colectiva de los obispos españoles, 109
Cataluña, 16, 20–1, 51, 56, 58, 60–5, 71, 74, 77, 85, 87, 114, 134, 155, 168–70, 178–80, *220n, 240n*
Catholic Action, 33, 44
Catholic Church, 1–4, 6–8, 10–16, 18–19, 21–3, 25–7, 29–31, 35–43, 45–52,

57–65, 67–9, 71–3, 76–8, 80–3, 86, 88–9, 92, 95–6, 101, 103, 106, 108–9, 111–14, 116, 120, 124, 130, 133, 137, 139–40, 150–2, 156, 162–3, 169, 175–6, 179, 181, 183–92, *193n, 195n, 196n, 203n, 205n, 222n*

Ceci, Lucia, 7, 82–3, 92

CEDA (Confederación Española de Derechas Autónomas), 51, 53–58, 60, 62, 66, 68–71, 74, 76, 78, 187–8, *208n, 210n, 214n*

Cemeteries, 25, 35–6, 38–9, 49, *203n, 204n*

Cessation, 119, 125, 146, 149–50, 168, 170, 172, 182

Charles-Roux, François (French Ambassador to Holy See), 133, 135, 190

Christmas, 60, 145–6, 166, 182–3

Ciano, Galeazzo (Italian Foreign Minister), 138–9

Cicognani, Gaetano (Nuncio), 39, 141, 153, 175, 177–8, 182

Círculo Monárquico, 22, *198n*

Clericalism, 1, 7, 10–17, 24, 28, 31–2, 41, 49, 56, 77–8, 84, 88, 184, *194n*

Comité Espagnol pour la Paix Civile, 143–7, 182

Communism, 2, 12, 20, 22, 27, 30–1, 43, 51–2, 54–7, 60, 63, 67–71, 73–82, 84–6, 88, 94, 96–7, 99, 101–2, 104, 106–9, 111, 112–18, 120–4, 126, 128, 137–9, 141, 148, 150, 152, 155–6, 158, 161–4, 166, 171–3, 175–7, 181–4, 188, 191, *199n, 205n, 210n, 214n, 223n, 228n, 243n*

Companys, Lluis (Catalan Politician), 21, 60, *211n*

Concordat, 10, 13, 48, 54, 82

Concordat of 1851, 14, 48

Confederación Nacional del Trabajo (CNT), 55, 88, *195n, 200n, 228n*

Conservatism, 1, 3, 5–6, 10–13, 15, 17–18, 20, 23, 26–8, 32, 34, 40, 43, 50–7, 61, 65–6, 68–9, 75–7, 80–1, 83, 85–8, 91, 100, 102, 104, 110, 117, 123, 131, 150, 152, 156, 160, 170, 188, *198n, 200n, 205n, 214n, 230n, 240n*

Constitution (Second Republican), 19, 22, 24–35, 37, 40, 42, 44, 46, 48–50, 52, 56, 59, 61, 63, 69, 71–2, 91, 105, 152–3, 186–7, *208n*

Constitutional Convention of 1931, 19, 22, 25–6, 28–9, 33, 50, 187

Convents, 22, 27, 70–1, 87, 94, *220n*

Coppa, Frank, ix, 3, 7, 13, 58, 81–2

Cortes, 27, 35, 38, 53, 57–60, 69, 71, 74, 78, *200n*

Cremation, 36–8

Crusade, 2–3, 91, 106, 149, 152, 167–8, 181, 183, 188, 191

Cruz y Raya, 46

Daladier, Édouard (French Minister of War), 131

Dávila, Fidel (General), 107–8, 164

De Albornoz Liminiana, Álvaro (Justice Minister), 33, 42

De Irujo, Manuel (PNV Minister in Second Republic), 151

Delbos, Yvon (French Minister of Foreign Affairs), 131–3, *230n*

Del Castillo, José (Socialist Assault Guard Commander), 51, 75

Del Río e Vargas, Ruiz (Radical Socialists MP), 46

De Meer Lecha Marzo, Fernando, 32, *195n*

Desamortización, 13

De Valera, Éamon (Irish Prime Minister), 176

Dilectissima Nobis, 7, 25, 43, 46–7, 49, 52, 187, 190

Divini Redemptoris, 190

Divorce, 35–6, 45, 139, *203n*

Duca, Borgongini (Cardinal), 102

Duce, Alessandro, 7, 82–3

Eden, Anthony (British Foreign Secretary), 115, 125–6, 131, *230n*

Education, 1, 14, 27, 31–3, 35, 40–1, 43, 54, 77, *196n, 198n, 205n*

Elections of 1931, 17, 19, 26, 28, 50, 186, *196n*

Elections of 1933, 50–3, 55, 58–61, 187

Elections of 1936, 50–1, 68–76, 78, 124, 188

Ethiopia, 83, 92, *233n*

Excommunication, 149, 157–9, 191

Fabra Ribas, Antonio (PSOE Minister in Second Republic), 102–3, 117

Falange, 51, 107, 110, *216n, 223n*

Fascism, 4, 7, 10, 51, 55, 57, 67, 75, 82–3, 85–6, 90, 102, 105, 110–11, 114, 117,

Fabra Ribas, Antonio (PSOE Minister in Second Republic) *(continued)* 119–124, 128, 132, 137–41, 148, 154, 184, 190, 192, *210n, 216n, 222n, 223n, 224n*

Fattorini, Emma, 7, 82–3

Ferdinand VII (King), 11–12

First Spanish Republic, 14–15

Foreign Office (United Kingdom), 122, 125–6

France, 12, 17, 57, 65, 67, 85, 119, 121–5, 130–2, 134, 136–8, 141–2, 153, 163, 172, 174, 180, 190, *196n, 224n, 230n*

Francis I (Pope), 1

Franco, Francisco, 9, 36, 39, 56, 66, 68, 77, 84–6, 100, 102, 105–7, 112–13, 115–17, 119, 127, 129, 131, 134–5, 137–142, 144, 146–50, 152–3, 155–63, 165–79, 181–4, 186, 189–92, *203n, 209n, 225n*

Franquista, *see* Rebels

French Third Republic, 28, 131

Funerals, 35, 38–9, 41

Galicia, 21, 63, *197n, 198n, 200n, 210n, 211n, 214n*

Gasparri, Pietro (Vatican Secretary of State), 4, 82, 191

Gil Robles, José María (CEDA Leader), 51, 54, 56, 60, 66

Gomá y Tomás, Isidro (Archbishop), 70, 72–4, 76, 95, 106–9, 112–17, 119, 149, 156–67, *223n, 225n, 238n*

Gómez-Jordana Sousa, Francisco (Burgos Minister of Foreign Affairs), 177

Great Britain, 85, 119–25, 127, 130–1, 136, 138, 142, 153, 180, 190, *224n, 230n*

Guadalajara, 116

Guernica, 115–16, 123, 128, 163, *241n*

Hitler, Adolf (German *Führer*), 102, 115, 122, 133, 135, 140, 190

Holocaust, 6–7, 186

Holy See, viii, 1–5, 7–12, 14, 18–23, 25–9, 31, 33–9, 42–50, 57–64, 67–69, 71–2, 75–106, 108, 110–13, 115–21, 123, 125–63, 166–92, *195n, 206n, 218n, 245n*

Humani Generis Unitas, 7, 191

Ibárruri, Dolores (PCE), 74

Ilundaín, Eustaquio (Cardinal), 36, *223n*

Immortale Dei, 28

Insurgents, *see* Rebels

International Brigades, 126

Isabel (Queen), 13–14, 48

Italy, 4, 7, 10, 13, 67, 82–3, 85, 102, 104–5, 119–21, 124, 126, 130, 131–3, 137–42, 144, 149, 154, 184, 189–91, *224n, 230n*

Jackson, Gabriel, 27, 56, *200n*

Japan, 139

Jesuits, 22, 31–4, 41–2, 44–5, 65, 96, 139

Jeunesse Ouvrière Chrétienne (JOC), 143, 145, 147, 182

Juventud de Acción Popular (JAP), 74

La Civiltà Cattolica, 30–1, 46

Lannon, Frances, 6, 16, 32, 48, 84, 87, 105, 153, *196n*

Largo Caballero, Francisco (PSOE and UGT Leader), 55, 69, 74, 77, *198n, 228n*

Last Rights, 36

Lateran Accords, 4, 10, 82–3, 85, 119, 125, 128, 130, 139, 154, 179, 183–4, 189, 192, *218n*

Law of Confessions and Religious Congregations, 25, 41–49, 52, 54, 73, 77, *205n*

Law of Cultivation Contracts, 61

Law of Defense of the Republic, 40–1, 92, 94, *205n*

League of Nations, 67, 102–3, 105, 122–3, 156

Leche, John (British Minister at Barcelona), 129–30, *230n*

Leo XIII (Pope), 28

Lerroux, Alejandro (Radical Party Leader), 18–21, 23, 33–4, 51, 53–62, 65, 67–8, 77–8, *197n, 198n, 211n*

L'Esprit International, 31

Liberalism, 3, 6, 10–15, 17–19, 33, 42, 48–9, 52, 54, 57–8, 121, 150–1, 186, *193n, 195n, 197n, 198n, 200n, 205n, 214n*

London, 103, 105, 120–2, 126–7, 131–2, 175

L'Osservatore Romano, 46, 90, 176

Luftwaffe, 115, 124, 164

Macià, Francesc (Catalan Leader), 21, 60, 145

Magaz, Antonio (Marquis), 107

Maglione, Luigi (Nuncio), 132–3, 170

Malaga, 161, 189, *199n, 205n*
Manchuria (Manchukuo), 139
Maritain, Jacques (Catholic Theologian), 144
Marriage, 1, 25, 35–6, 44, 49, *203n*
Marxism, 70, 111, 154, 158, 177–8
Masons, 20, 37, 59, 85, 109, 143, *198n, 211n*
Massigli, Rene (Political Director of the Ministry of French Foreign Affairs), 134
Maura, Miguel (Interior Minister), 23, *198n*
McNicholas, John (Bishop of Cincinnati), 47
Media, 31, 33, 113, 115–16, 175–6, 179–80
Mediation, 5, 8, 10, 71, 104, 112, 119–21, 128–9, 135–8, 140, 142–4, 146–9, 151–3, 155–9, 163, 169–70, 177–84, 190–1, *197n*
Mendizábal, Alfredo (Spanish Committee for Civil Peace), 143, 173
Mexico, 85, 136, 156
Militias, 22–3, 55, 63, 74–5, 77, 80–1, 85–9, 92–7, 100–2, 104–5, 117, 125, 137, 163, 188, *221n, 223n, 228n*
Mit Brennender Sorge, 83, 190
Mola, Emilio (General), 84, 115, 162–4
Monarchism, 12, 17, 22, 52–3, 106, *199n, 200n, 205n, 214n, 226n*
Monks, 13, 22, 86, 170
Moreno Zuleta, Francisco (Count), 154
Motta, Giuseppe (Swiss Conservative Politician), 104
Múgica, Mateo (Bishop), 95, 106–9, 112, 118, 189, *226n*
Mussolini, Benito (Italian *Duce*), 83, 102, 122, 138–40, *233n*

Nationalists, *see* Rebels
Nazi Germany, 7, 10, 67, 76, 82–3, 85, 117, 119, 121–2, 124, 132–3, 137, 167–8, 190, *221n, 224n, 230n*
Neutrality, 4, 85–6, 92, 97–8, 114, 119–20, 125, 128, 131, 138, 140, 142–3, 147, 174–5, *218n*
Non Abbiamo Bisogno, 190
Non-Intervention, 85, 103, 119–26, 129–33, 135–8, 142, 174, 190, *224n*
Nuns, 15, 70, 86–7, 94–5, 126, 188
Nunziatura, 84, 94, 101, 153, 182

October Revolution, *see* Asturias

Office of Extraordinary Affairs (AES, Vatican), 27–8, 43, 109–11, 168, 179
Olaechea, Marcelino (Bishop), 91, 106
Osborne, Francis D'Arcy (British Minister to the Holy See), 125–6, *229n*

Pact of San Sebastian, 19
Pacelli, Eugenio (Vatican Secretary of State), 3–4, 6–7, 17, 19, 21–3, 30, 33–4, 36, 38, 41, 46, 48, 58–9, 61, 70, 72, 76–7, 81–4, 86, 105, 107–8, 112–13, 117, 126, 132–5, 140–1, 145, 148–9, 152–6, 159, 161–6, 170, 172–3, 176–7, 180–2, 184, 186–92, *194n, 227n*
País Vasco, 5, 8, 21, 56, 61–2, 70–1, 77, 85–6, 99, 105–18, 123, 126, 128, 147, 149–51, 153–68, 172, 183–4, 189–91, *205n, 225n, 228n, 238n*
Partido Obrero de Unificación Marxista (POUM), 88, *214n*
Partido Popular (PP), 1
Partido Socialista Obrero Español (PSOE), 88, 102
Payne, Stanley, 5, 40, 53, *194n, 197n, 199n, 200n, 216n*
Pius IX (Pope), 13–14
Pius XI (Pope), viii, 3–4, 6–7, 10, 34, 43, 46, 52, 58, 76, 81–4, 105, 108, 117, 129, 148–9, 152–3, 164–5, 184, 186–7, 189–92, *193n, 194n*
Pius XII (Pope), *see* Pacelli
Pizzardo, Giuseppe (Cardinal), 46, 126, 169
Plá y Deniel, Enrique (Bishop), 80, 120
Popular Front, 7, 50–2, 57, 68–74, 76–9, 84, 89, 92, 108–12, 114, 116–17, 120–2, 124–5, 131, 159, 161, 188–9, *210n, 214n, 216n, 230n*
Portugal, 13, 85, 131, 137–8
Preston, Paul, 4, 54, 56, 66, 85–7, 96, 106, 120–1, *218n, 223n, 234n, 235n, 240n*
Priests, 12, 22, 39, 41, 54, 65–7, 73, 86, 90–2, 96, 101, 106–7, 109, 114, 116, 126, 134, 150, 163–4, 166, 170, 189, *203n, 205n, 225n*
Primo de Rivera, Miguel (Dictator), 11, 16–17, 21
Prisoners, 5, 74, 101, 129, 143–4, 162, 166–7

Quod apostolici muneris, 28

Radical Party, 7, 18, 20, 29, 34, 50–1, 53–4, 56–60, 62, 68, 72, 187, *198n, 211n*
Radical Socialists, 12, 10–20, 32–4, 46–7, 51–2, 54–5, 59, *197n, 198n, 200n, 202n, 211n*
Raguer, Hilari, 6, 28, 85, 111
Rebels, 2–6, 8–9, 40, 56, 66–7, 80–1, 84–7, 91–4, 96–7, 99–104, 106–12, 114–21, 123–31, 133, 135–6, 138–44, 146–56, 158–70, 172–185, 188–92, *193n, 223n, 235n, 245n*
Redondo, Gonzalo, 6, 17, 20, 81, 86, *198n, 219n, 220n, 223n*
Regionalism, 21, 51, 58, 60–5, 68, 77, 106, 109–11, 116, 150, 169, 189, *210n*
Reichskonkordat, 10, 82
Religious Organizations, 23, 29, 94
Repression, 5, 6, 9, 66, 68, 77, 88, 106, 115, 149, 152–3, 165, 167, 183–4, 188, 190
Republicans, 2–9, 11–12, 14–15, 17–26, 28–30, 32–38, 40–3, 45–7, 49, 52–7, 60, 62–3, 65, 68–9, 71–4, 78, 80–1, 85–97, 100, 102–7, 112, 115, 117–21, 123–5, 128–9, 131, 136–40, 142–4, 146–8, 150–7, 161, 163–4, 166, 169, 171–4, 176–80, 182–3, 186–8, 192, *197n, 198n, 199n, 200n, 206n, 208n, 209n, 211n, 214n, 217n, 221n, 223n, 226n, 234n, 238n, 240n, 241n*
Revenge, 29, 118, 128, 169, 174, 177–9, 190
Rio Tinto, 122
Robinson, Paschal (Nuncio to Ireland), 176–7
Rocha, José (Minister of State and War), 67, *211n*

Salamanca, 115, 159, 172
Sánchez, José, 6, 18, 28, 56, 112, 181, *195n*
Sanjuro, José (General), 84
Secret Vatican Archives (Archivio Segreto Vaticano, ASV), viii, 3–5, 7, 8, 20, 26–7, 37, 60, 78, 83, 130, 138, 151, 168
Second Spanish Republic, ix, 2–3, 4–8, 10–12, 14–15, 17–19, 22–3, 25, 27–8, 30, 32, 34–5, 43, 47–52, 59–61, 67–8, 77–9, 81, 86–7, 92–3, 95, 105, 108, 122, 138, 151, 186, 192, *193n, 195n, 203n, 210n, 225n*
Secularization, 1–2, 11, 15, 25, 38–9, 47, 58–9, 150, *203n, 204n, 208n*

Segura y Sáenz, Pedro (Cardinal), 18, 27–8, 95, 120, *225n*
Sericano, Silvio (Nuncio), 94–6, 100–1, *221n*
Sevilla, 54, 96–7, 172, *205n, 211n*
Socialists, 1, 12, 15–6, 19–20, 26, 28, 30–4, 46–7, 51–5, 57, 59, 61, 63, 74–5, 80–1, 88, 102–3, 106, 108, 110–11, 122, 150, 188, *196n, 197n, 200n, 202n, 205n, 206n, 208n, 211n, 214n*
Society of Jesus, *see* Jesuits
Spanish-American War, 16
Spanish Catholic Hierarchy, 3–5, 18, 28–30, 38, 41, 48, 62, 70, 80, 86, 91–2, 98–100, 106, 118–19, 150, 152, 156, *210n*
Spanish Civil War, 2–9, 17, 23, 39–40, 49, 52, 56–7, 69, 71, 75–6, 79–82, 85–6, 91, 93–5, 97, 99, 102–7, 109, 111, 113–128, 130–1, 133–42, 144, 146–7, 149–55, 159, 165–8, 174–6, 180–4, 186, 188–92, *193n, 198n, 234n*
Spanish Communist Party (PCE), 76, 124

Tedeschini, Federico (Nuncio), 3, 18–23, 27, 29–30, 33–4, 36–9, 42–3, 46, 48, 59–62, 64–72, 74–5, 77–8, 86–7, 153, *197n*
Tragic Week, 15, *196n*
Truce, 119–20, 125, 145, 147, 154, 168, 175, 182–3, 189, 191

Unión General de Trabajadores (UGT), 16, 55, 69
Union of Soviet Socialist Republics, 20, 30, 79, 82, 85, 101, 104–5, 109, 124, 130, 138
United Kingdom, *see* Great Britain
United States of America, 59, 85, 140–1
Uprising (Alzamiento), 2–3, 7, 9, 36, 50, 56, 67, 76–7, 84–5, 87–8, 89, 94, 98, 109–11, 120, 122–3, 125, 150, 152–3, 188–9, *203n, 217n*
Uruguay, 136–7

Valencia, 21, 73, 85, 104, 116, 137, 155–6, 168–9, *199n, 214n, 230n*
Valeri, Valerio (Nuncio to France), 134–5, 163, 173, 179, 182
Vatican, 1–5, 7–8, 10–11, 13–14, 17–23, 25–6, 28–30, 32–6, 39, 41, 46, 49–52, 54, 59–60, 62–3, 71, 74, 76–8, 80–2, 84–92, 94, 97–100, 102–6, 108, 110,

112–13, 116–21, 124–63, 165, 167–9, 171–6, 178–92, *218n, 245n*
Vatican Diplomacy, ix, x, 6, 8–9, 11, 23, 99, 120
Vatican Hierarchy, 1, 4, 11–12, 18, 20, 22–3, 26, 30, 32–3, 36–8, 50–2, 60, 68–70, 73, 79–81, 83, 92, 95–7, 99–100, 102, 108, 113, 117, 119–20, 126, 131–3, 140, 142, 148, 152–3, 162, 169, 171, 180, 184, *208n, 223n*
Vidal i Barraquer, Francesc (Cardinal), 58–9, 62–4, 68, 76, 153, *210n*

Wolf, Hubert, 7, 82–4
World War II, 7, 121, 186, *233n*